American History I
Primary Source Documents

CUSTOM EDITION

Learning Solutions

New York Boston San Francisco
London Toronto Sydney Tokyo Singapore Madrid
Mexico City Munich Paris Cape Town Hong Kong Montreal

Pearson Learning Solutions, 501 Boylston Street, Suite 900, Boston, MA 02116
A Pearson Education Company
www.pearsoned.com

Printed in the United States of America

11 12 13 14 15 V092 16 15 14

000200010270606582

SB/CM

ISBN 10: 0-558-85588-1
ISBN 13: 978-0-558-85588-8

Contents

PART ONE
MEETING OF THREE CULTURES

1-1 Marco Polo Recounts His Travels Through Asia (1324)

Marco Polo's recollections of his travels through Asia planted seeds of curiosity, wanderlust, and want in the minds of Europeans within a century after his death in 1324. Known at the time as *The Description of the World* or *The Travels of Marco Polo*, his account of the wealth of Cathay (China) and the exotic customs of the Orient made his book a bestseller. Although criticized by some as fiction, his narrative nevertheless captured readers through the centuries and served as the foremost description of the world outside Europe available at the time.

> **Source:** Marco Polo, *Voyages and Travels of Marco Polo* (New York: The F. M. Lupton Publishing Company, [n.d.]).

Ten miles off Cambalu is a certain great river named Pulisangan, emptying itself into the ocean, by which many ships with much merchandise ascend; and in that place there is a very fair bridge, all of serpentine stone, curiously wrought, containing three hundred paces in length, and eight in breadth, so broad that ten men may ride abreast; on each side it is secured with a wall of marble, and pillars set in a row, and in the height of this ascent is a great and high pillar, at the feet whereof is a great lion, and on the top another, and so quite through the bridge: one pace and a half distance are pillars with lions on the tops, and a fair wall with wrought marble work betwixt, to keep men from falling. Having passed over the river and bridge, and proceeding thirty miles westward (in which palaces are continually seen, with vineyards and fertile fields), you come to the city Gouza, both fair and great, having many monasteries of idols. Cloths of gold and silk are made there, and the purest and finest cambrics or lawns; and many common inns for strangers or travellers are found in that city. The citizens are artificers and merchants. A mile without this city the way parteth, one leading west, the other south-east; that to the west leadeth through the province of Cathay, but the other, towards the country of Mangi, from the city of Gouza to the kingdom of Tainfu.

You ride ten days through Cathay, always finding many fair cities, well furnished with vineyards and tilled fields, from whence wine is carried to Cathay, where there is none; there are many mulberry-trees for silkworms, the people civil, and cities very numerous and populous. Tainfu is the name of the kingdom, and of the chief city, which is great and fair, hath much trade, with store of ammunition, fit for the Khan's armies. The wine about this city serveth the whole province. Seven days further westward is a pleasant country beautified with many castles and cities, in which also there is great trade in different merchandise carried on. After which you come to a city very great, named Pianfu, in which there is vast abundance of silk and much trade. Westward from Pianfu stands a very pleasant castle, named Thaigin, anciently built by a king called Dor; in it is a spacious palace, wherein is a fine hall, in which are painted all the famous kings which have reigned there, and it is a fair spectacle. Of this king Dor, they say he was potent, and was attended only by young damsels, of which he had many in his court. These also, when he had a mind to take his pleasure, carried him in a small light chariot through the castle, which was so fortified by art and nature, that the governor thereof feared none, no, not Umcan his lord, against whom he rebelled.

But seven men, professing fidelity and service to Dor, took him at a disadvantage in hunting, and brought him prisoner to Presbyter John, or Umcan, who put him on vile cloths, and appointed him to keep his cattle, and set over him a strong guard, till two years were ended: after which he commanded him to be brought before him, and being dressed in princely apparel, he giving him his pardon, after a sharp admonition, sent him well attended to the re-possession of his kingdom. About twenty miles beyond the castle Thaigin is the river Caramaran, which, by reason of the exceeding breadth and depth thereof, hath no bridge over it in all the space from thence till it floweth to the ocean. On the shore thereof are many cities and castles built, wherein great trade is carried on. This country abounds with ginger, silk, and fowl, especially pheasants, so that three of them are bought for a Venetian groat. There grow reeds in vast plenty, so thick that some are a foot, and others a foot and a half in compass, which are applied to many uses. Passing this river, after two days' journey, is the famous city called Carianfu, where many cloths of gold and silk are made. Here grow ginger, galingale spike, and many spices. The people are idolaters.

Proceeding seven days' journey westward, many cities and towns, lovely fields and gardens, are found, and everywhere mulberries for silkworms. As for the people, they are mostly idolaters; but there are also Christians, Turks, Nestorians, and some Saracens. There is a vast abundance here of wild beasts and fowl. If you proceed seven days' journey farther, you shall come to a certain great city named Quensanfu, which is the chief city of the kingdom, in which have reigned many famous kings; and at this day the son of the Great Khan, called Mangalu, hath the command thereof. That country yields great plenty of silk, cloth of gold, and all other things necessary for furnishing an army, and for the preservation of man's life. The inhabitants worship idols, and there are some Christians, Turks, and Saracens. Five miles without this city standeth the palace of Mangalu, seated in a plain, where are many springs, rivulets, and places of game. There is a high wall encompassing a park of five miles, where are all sorts of wild beasts and fowls. In the midst is an excellent palace, having many halls and chambers, great and fair, all painted with gold and azure, and numberless statues adorning it. The king, with his courtiers, delights himself in hunting the wild beasts, and taking of fowl, and following his father's examples in justice and equity, is much beloved of his people.

Proceeding three days' journey westward from the said palace, through a very beautiful plain, where many cities and castles are, which abound with silk merchandise and manufactures, you come to a country where in the mountains and valleys are frequent habitations, and many villages of the province of Chunchian. The inhabitants as to religion are idolaters; and as to employment, husbandmen. Also in that country they hunt lions, bears, stags, roebucks, deer, and wolves. Ths plain is two days' journey over, and the country is about twenty days' journey westward, well inhabited, being finely diversified into mountains, valleys, and woods. After these twenty days towards the west, there lies a province called Achbaluch Mangi, that is, the white city, on the borders of Mangi, which is well peopled. This province, for two days' journey, hath a plain, in which are an infinite number of villages: beyond these lie mountains, valleys, and wood, all well inhabited. It hath plenty of wild beasts, and of those creatures that yield musk. In this province ginger grows in great plenty, as also corn and rice.

After twenty days' journey through those hills is a plain, and a province in the confines of Mangi, named Sindinfu. The chief city hath the same name, and is very great, and exceeding rich, being twenty miles in circuit. It hath had many rich and mighty kings; but an old king dying, left three sons successors in the kingdom, who divided the city into three parts, compassing every part with their proper walls; all which, notwithstanding, were contained within the former wall; but the Great Khan subjected nevertheless that city and kingdom. Through this city run many rivers, and many places round about, some half a mile over, some two hundred paces, very deep; on them are many bridges of stone, very fair, eight paces broad, set on both sides with marble pillars, which bear up a timber frame that covers the bridge, each bridge having streets and shops thereupon. When the rivers have passed through the city they become one great river, called Quian, which runs one hundred days' journey hence to the ocean. Near these rivers are many cities and castles, and on them innumerable ships for merchandise. Proceeding four days' journey farther, through a very fine plain, many cities, castles, and villages are found, in which five lawns extend in beautiful order. There are also many wild beasts there. Beyond the plain, which we have now mentioned, is the wide province of Thibet, which the Great Khan vanquished and wasted; for in it lie many cities destroyed and castles overthrown, by the space of twenty days' journey; and because it is become a wilderness, wanting inhabitants, wild beasts and lions are increased excessively, and it is requisite therefore that travellers carry victuals with them. Very large cane grows in this country, ten paces in length, and three palms in thickness, and as much from knot to knot. When travellers therefore will rest at night secure from beasts, they take great bundles of the greener reeds, and putting fire under, kindle them, which makes such a crackling, and so great a noise, that it may be heard two miles off; which terrible sound the wild beasts hearing, flee away; but it has sometimes happened that horses and other beasts, which merchants use for their journey, hearing this noise and cracking, have grown also much afraid, and betaking themselves to flight have escaped from their masters; and therefore wiser travellers binding their feet together detain them in their proper places.

1. What aspects of Marco Polo's description of the Orient might early readers have found alluring? What might have given them pause?
2. Skeptics question the authenticity of Marco Polo's account, citing his omission of such things as the Great Wall, tea, and calligraphy. How important is the veracity of the narrative to our overall assessment of its value to history?

1-2 The Columbian Exchange (1590)

Coined by historian Alfred W Crosby, Jr., the phrase "Columbian exchange" refers to the global redistribution of plants, animals, and diseases that occurred in the sixteenth century following the initial contacts between European colonizers and the indigenous people of the Americas. In his scientific and historical work, *Natural and Moral History of the Indians (1590),* Father Jose de Acosta described for the curious Spanish crown the agricultural exotica of the New World as well as the Spanish attempts to introduce new plants to the Americas.

Source: Jose de Acosta, Historian natural y moral de las Indias (I590)
http://www.sc.edu/library/pubserv/reserve/scardaville/hist420/doc7.htm and
http://www.sc.edu/library/pubserv/reserve/scardaville/hist420/doc8.htm

[This document has been previously edited by DR. MICHAEL C. SCARDAVILLE, Associate Professor of History and Director of the Latin American Studies Prog ram at the University of South Carolina, Columbia, SC]

Turning to plants, I shall speak first of those which are more peculiar to the Indies and afterwards of those which are common both to those lands and to Europe. And because plants were created principally for the maintenance of man, and man sustains himself above all on bread, I should speak first of their bread. . . . The Indians have their own words to signify bread, which in Peru is called *tanta* and in other parts is given other names. But the quality and substance of the bread the Indians use is very different from ours, for they have no kind of wheat, barley, millet, panic grass, or any grain such as is used in Europe to make bread. Instead they have other kinds of grains and roots, among which maize, called Indian wheat in Castile and Turkey grain in Italy, holds the first place.

And just as wheat is the grain most commonly used by man in the regions of the Old World, which are Europe, Asia, and Africa, so in the New World the most widely used grain is maize, which is found in almost all the kingdoms of the West Indies; in Peru, New Spain, the New Kingdom of Granada, Guatemala, Chile, and in all the *Tierra Firme*. In the Windward Isles, which are Cuba, Hispaniola, Jamaica, Puerto Rico, it does not seem to have been used in earlier times; to this day they prefer to use yucca and cassava, of which more later. I do not think that maize is at all inferior to our wheat in strength and nourishment; but it is stouter and hotter and engenders more blood, so that if people who are not accustomed to it eat it in excess they swell up and get the itch.

Maize grows on canes or reeds; each one bears one or two ears, to which the grains are fastened, and though the grains are big they hold a large number of them, and some contain seven hundred grains. The seeds are planted one by one. Maize likes a hot and humid soil. It grows in many parts of the Indies in great abundance; a yield of three hundred *fanegas* from a sowing is not uncommon. There are various kinds of maize, as of wheat; one is large and nourishing; another, called *moroche*, is small and dry. The leaves of the maize and the green cane are a choice fodder for their beasts of burden, and when dry are also used as straw. The grain gives more nourishment to horses than barley, and therefore it is customary in those countries to water their horses before giving them maize to eat, for if they drank after feeding they would swell up and have gripes, as they do when they eat wheat.

Maize is the Indian bread, and they commonly eat it boiled in the grain, hot, when it is called *mote*. . .; sometimes they eat it toasted. There is a large and round maize, like that of the Lucanas, which the Spaniards eat as a delicacy; it has better flavor than toasted chickpeas. There is another and more pleasing way of preparing it, which consists in grinding the maize and making the flour into pancakes, which are put on the fire and are later placed on the table and eaten piping hot; in some places they call them *arepas*. . . .

Maize is used by the Indians to make not only their bread but also their wine; from it they make beverages which produce drunkenness more quickly than wine made of grapes. They make this maize wine in various ways, calling it *azua* in Peru and more generally throughout the Indies *chicha*. The strongest sort is made like beer, steeping the grains of maize until they begin to break, after which they boil the juice in a certain way, which makes it so strong that a few drinks will produce intoxication. In Peru, where it is called *sora*, its use is forbidden by law because of the terrific drinking it occasions. But the law is little observed, for they use it anyway, and stay up whole days and nights, dancing and drinking. . . .

The cacao tree is most esteemed in Mexico and coca is favored in Peru; both trees are surrounded with considerable superstition. Cacao is a bean smaller and fattier than the almond, and when roasted has not a bad flavor. It is so much esteemed by the Indians, and even by the Spaniards, that it is the object of one of the richest and largest lines of trade of New Spain; since it is a dry fruit, and one that keeps a long time without spoiling, they send whole ships loaded with it from the province of Guatemala. Last year an English corsair burned in the port of Guatulco, in New Spain, more than one hundred thousand *cargas* of cacao. They also use it as money, for five cacao beans will buy one thing, thirty another, and one hundred still another, and no objections are made to its use. They also use it as alms to give to the poor.

The chief use of this cacao is to make a drink that they call chocolate, which they greatly cherish in that country. But those who have not formed a taste for it dislike it, for it has a froth at the top and an effervescence like that formed in wine by dregs, so that one must really have great faith in it to tolerate it. In fine, it is the favorite drink of Indians and Spaniards alike, and they regale visitors to their country with it; the Spanish women of that land are particularly fond of the dark chocolate. They prepare it in various ways: hot, cold, and lukewarm. They usually put spices and much chili in it; they also make a paste of it, and they say that it is good for the chest and the stomach, and also for colds. Be that as it may, those who have not formed a taste for it do not like it.

The tree on which this fruit grows is of middling size and well-made, with a beautiful top; it is so delicate that to protect it from the burning rays of the sun they plant near it another large tree, which serves only to shade it; this is called the mother of the cacao. There are cacao plantations where it is raised as are the vine and the olive in Spain. The province of Guatemala is where they carry on the greatest commerce in this fruit.

The cacao does not grow in Peru; instead they have the coca, which is surrounded with even greater superstition and really seems fabulous. In Potosí alone the commerce in coca amounts to more than 5,000,000 pesos, with a consumption of from 90 to 100,000 hampers, and in the year 1583 it was 100,000. . . . This coca that they so greatly cherish is a little green leaf which grows upon shrubs about one estado high; it grows in very warm and humid lands and produces this leaf, which they call *trasmitas*, every four months. Being a very delicate plant, it requires a great deal of attention during cultivation and even more after it has been picked. They pack it with great care in long, narrow hampers and load it on the sheep of that country, which carry this merchandise in droves, bearing one, two, and three thousand hampers. It is commonly brought from the Andes, from valleys of insufferable heat, where it rains the greater part of the year, and it costs the Indians much labor and takes many lives, for they must leave their highlands and cold climates in order to cultivate it and carry it away. Hence there have been great disputes among lawyers and wise men about whether the coca plantations should be done away with or no—but there they still are.

The Indians prize it beyond measure, and in the time of the Inca kings plebeians were forbidden to use coca without the permission of the Inca or his governor. Their custom is to hold it in their mouths, chewing and sucking it; they do not swallow it; they say that it gives them great strength and is a great comfort to them. Many serious men say that this is pure superstition and imagination. To tell the truth, I do not think so; I believe that it really does lend strength and endurance to the Indians, for one sees effects that cannot be attributed to imagination, such as their ability to journey two whole days on a handful of coca, eating nothing else, and similar feats. . . . All would be well, except that its cultivation and commerce endanger and occupy so many people. . . .

The maguey is the tree of wonders, to which the newly-come Spaniards, or *chapetones* (as they call them in the Indies), attribute miracles, saying that it yields water and wine, oil and vinegar, honey, syrup, thread, needles, and a thousand other things. The Indians of New Spain value it greatly, and they commonly have one or several of these trees near their homes to supply their needs. It grows in the fields, and there they cultivate it. Its leaves are wide and thick, with strong, sharp points which they use as fastening pins or sewing needles; they also draw a certain fiber or thread from the leaves.

They cut through the thick trunk when it is tender; there is a large cavity inside, where the sap rises from the roots; it is a liquor which they drink like water, since it is fresh and sweet. When this liquor is boiled it turns into a kind of wine, and if it is left to sour it becomes vinegar. But when boiled for a longer time it becomes like honey, and cooked half as long it turns into a healthful syrup of good flavor, superior in my judgment to syrup made of grapes. Thus they boil different substances from this sap, which they obtain in great quantity, for at a certain season they extract several azumbres a day.

The Indies have been better repaid in the matter of plants than in any other kind of merchandise; for those few that have been carried from the Indies into Spain do badly there, whereas the many that have come over from Spain prosper in their new homes. I do not know whether to attribute this to the excellence of the plants that go from here or to the bounty of the soil over there. Nearly every good thing grown in Spain is found there; in some regions they do better than in others. They include wheat, barley, garden produce and greens and vegetables of all kinds, such as lettuce, cabbage, radishes, onions, garlic, parsley, turnips, carrots, eggplants, endive, salt-wort, spinach, chickpeas, beans, and lentils —in short, whatever grows well here, for those who have gone to the Indies have been careful to take with them seeds of every description. . . .

The trees that have fared best there are the orange, lemon, citron, and others of that sort. In some parts there are already whole forests and groves of orange trees. Marveling at this, I asked on a certain island who had planted so many orange trees in the fields. To which they replied that it might have happened that some oranges fell to the ground and rotted, whereupon the seeds germinated, and, some being borne by the waters to different parts, gave rise to these dense groves. This seemed a likely reason. I said before that orange trees have generally done well in the Indies, for nowhere have I found a place where oranges were not to be found; this is because everywhere in the Indies the soil is hot and humid, which is what this tree most needs. It does not grow in the highlands; oranges are transported there from the valleys or the coast. The orange preserve which is made in the islands is the best I have ever seen, here or there.

Peaches and apricots also have done well, although the latter have fared better in New Spain. . . . Apples and pears are grown, but in moderate yields; plums give sparingly; figs are abundant, chiefly in Peru. Quinces are found everywhere, and in New Spain they are so plentiful that we received fifty choice ones for half a real. Pomegranates are found in abundance, but they are all sweet, for the people do not like the sharp variety. The melons are very good in some regions, as in *Tierra Firme* and Peru. Cherries, both wild and cultivated, have not so far prospered in the Indies. . . . In conclusion, I find that hardly any of the finer fruits is lacking in those parts. As for nuts, they have no acorns or chestnuts, nor, as far as I know, have any been grown over there until now. Almonds grow there, but sparingly. Almonds, walnuts, and filberts are shipped there from Spain for the tables of epicures.

By profitable plants I mean those plants which not only yield fruit but bring money to their owners. The most important of these is the vine, which gives wine, vinegar, grapes, raisins, verjuice, and syrup—but the wine is the chief concern. Wine and grapes are not products of the islands or of *Tierra Firme*; in New Spain there are vines which bear grapes but do not yield wine. The reason must be that the grapes do not ripen completely because of the rains which come in July and August and hinder their ripening; they are good only for eating. Wine is shipped from Spain and the Canary Islands to all parts of the Indies, except Peru and Chile, where they have vineyards and make very good wine. This industry is expanding continually, not only because of the goodness of the soil, but because they have a better knowledge of winemaking.

The vineyards of Peru are commonly found in warm valleys where they have water channels; they are watered by hand, because rain never falls in the coastal plains, and the rains in the mountains do not come at the proper time. . . . The vineyards have increased so far that because of them the tithes of the churches are now five and six times what they were twenty years ago. The valleys most fertile in vines are Victor, near Arequipa; Yca, hard by Lima; and Caracaro, close to Chuquiavo. The wine that is made there is shipped to Potosi and Cuzco and various other parts, and it is sold in great quantities, because since it is produced so abundantly it sells at five or six ducats the jug, or *arroba*, whereas Spanish wine (which always arrives with the fleets) sells for ten and twelve. . . . The wine trade is no small affair, but does not exceed the limits of the province.

The silk which is made in New Spain goes to other provinces—to Peru, for example. There was no silk industry before the Spaniards came; the mulberry trees were brought from Spain, and they grow well, especially in the province called Misteca, where they raise silkworms and make good taffetas; they do not yet make damasks, satins, or velvets, however.

The sugar industry is even wider in scope, for the sugar not only is consumed in the Indies but is shipped in quantity to Spain. Sugar cane grows remarkably well in various parts of the Indies. In the islands, in Mexico, in Peru, and elsewhere they have built sugar mills that do a large business. I was told that the Nasca [Peru] sugar mill earned more than thirty thousand pesos a year. The mill at Chicama, near Trujillo [Peru], was also a big enterprise, and those of New Spain are no smaller, for the consumption of sugar and preserves in the Indies is simply fantastic. From the island of Santo Domingo, in the fleet in which I came, they brought eight hundred and ninety-eight chests and boxes of sugar. I happened to see the sugar loaded at the port of Puerto Rico, and it seemed to me that each box must contain eight arrobas. The sugar industry is the principal business of those islands—such a taste have men developed for sweets!

Olives and olive trees are also found in the Indies, in Mexico, and in Peru, but up to now they have not set up any mills to make olive oil. Actually, it is not made at all, for they prefer to eat the olives, seasoning them well. They find it unprofitable to make olive oil, and so all their oil comes from Spain.

1. According to Father Acosta, what was the most widely used grain in the New World? What were some of its uses?
2. What is cacao? Where was it found and what were its various uses?
3. Father Acosta notes that the Spanish had some success in transplanting Old World plants to the Americas. What were some of the more successful transplantations?

PART TWO
COLONIZING THE NEW WORLD

2-1 John White, The Lost Colony (1590)

John White (English explorer, artist, first governor of Raleigh's colony at Roanoke Island, 1545–1606) left the colony at Roanoke Island in early fall, 1587, to obtain supplies for the struggling colony. Unable to return to Roanoke until 1590 (due to difficulties with both the French and Spanish), he found that little remained of his colony. Here is the account of his return voyage to Raleigh's colony at Roanoke Island (now Manteo, North Carolina).

> **Source:** "The Fifth Voyage of John White," in Henry S. Burrage, ed., *Early English and French Voyages, Chiefly from Hakluyt, Original Narratives of Early American History* (New York: Charles Scribner's Sons, 1906).

To the Worshipful and my very friend Master Richard Hakluyt, much happinesse in the Lord.

SIR, as well for the satisfying of your earnest request, as the performance of my promise made unto you at my last being with you in England, I have sent you (although in a homely stile, especially for the contentation of a delicate eare) the true discourse of my last voyage into the West Indies, and partes of America called Virginia, taken in hand about the end of Februarie, in the yeare of our redemption 590. And what events happened unto us in this our journey, you shall plainely perceive by the sequele of my discourse. There were at the time aforesaid three ships absolutely determined to goe for the West Indies, at the speciall charges of M. John Wattes of London Marchant. But when they were fully furnished, and in readinesse to make their departure, a generall stay was commanded of all ships thorowout England. Which so soone as I heard, I presently (as I thought it most requisite) acquainted Sir Walter Ralegh therewith, desiring him that as I had sundry times afore bene chargeable and troublesome unto him, for the supplies and reliefes of the planters in Virginia: so likewise, that by his endevour it would please him at that instant to procure license for those three ships to proceede on with their determined voyage, that thereby the people in Virginia (if it were Gods pleasure) might speedily be comforted and relieved without further charges unto him. Whereupon he by his good meanes obtained license of the Queenes Majestie, and order to be taken, that the owner of the 3 ships should be bound unto Sir Walter Ralegh or his assignes, in 3000 pounds, that those 3 ships in consideration of their releasement should take in, and transport a convenient number of passengers, with their furnitures and necessaries to be landed in Virginia. Neverthelesse that order was not observed, neither was the bond taken according to the intention aforesaid. But rather in contempt of the aforesaid order, I was by the owner and Commanders of the ships denied to have any passengers, or any thing els transported in any of the said ships, saving only my selfe and my chest; no not so much as a boy to attend upon me, although I made great sute, and earnest intreatie aswell to the chiefe Commanders, as to the owner of the said ships. Which crosse and unkind dealing, although it very much discontented me, notwithstanding the scarsity of time was such, that I could have no opportunity to go unto Sir Walter Ralegh with complaint: for the ships being then all in readinesse to goe to the Sea, would have bene departed before I could have made my returne. Thus both Governors, Masters, and sailers, regarding very smally the good of their countreymen in Virginia; determined nothing lesse then to touch at those places, but wholly disposed themselves to seeke after purchase and spoiles, spending so much time therein, that sommer was spent before we arrived at Virginia. And when we were come thither, the season was so unfit, and weather so foule, that we were constrained of force to forsake that coast, having not seene any of our planters, with losse of one of our ship-boates, and 7 of our chiefest men: and also with losse of 3 of our ankers and cables, and most of our caskes with fresh water left on shore, not possible to be had aboord. Which evils and unfortunate events (as wel to their owne losse as to the hinderance of the planters in Virginia) had not chanced, if the order set downe by Sir Walter Ralegh had bene observed, or if my dayly and continuall. petitions for the performance of the same might have taken any place. Thus may you plainely perceive the successe of my fift and last voiage to Virginia, which was no lesse unfortunately ended then frowardly begun, and as lucklesse to many, as sinister to my selfe. But I would to God it had bene as prosperous to all) as noysome to the planters; and as joyfull to me, as discomfortable to them. Yet seeing it is not my first crossed voyage, I remaine contented. And wanting my wishes, I leave off from prosecuting that whereunto I would to God my wealth were answerable to my will. Thus committing the reliefe of my discomfortable company the planters in Virginia, to the merciful help of the Almighty, whom I most humbly beseech to helpe and comfort them, according to his most holy will and their good desire, I take my leave: from my house at Newtowne in Kyhnore the 4 of February, 1593.
Your most welwishing friend,
John White

The fift voyage of M. John White into the West Indies and parts of America called Virginia, in the yeere 1590.

The 20 of March the three shippes the Hopewell, the John Evangelist, and the little John, put to sea from Plymmouth with two small Shallops.

The 25 at midnight both our Shallops were sunke being towed at the ships stearnes by the Boatswaines negligence.

On the 30 we saw a head us that part of the coast of Barbary, lying East of Cape Cantyn, and the Bay of Asaphi[1]

The next day we came to the Ile of Mogador,[2] where rode, at our passing by, a Pinnesse of London called the Mooneshine.

Aprill

On the first of Aprill we ankored in Santa Cruz rode;[3] where we found two great shippes of London lading in Sugar, of whom we had 2 shipboats to supply the losse of our Shallops.

On the 2 we set sayle from the rode of Santa Cruz, for the Canaries.

On Saturday the 4 we saw Alegranza, the East Ile of the Canaries.

On Sunday the 5 of April we gave chase to a double flyboat, the which we also the same day fought with, and tooke her, with losse of three of their men slaine, and one hurt.

On Munday the 6 we saw Grand Canarie, and the next day we landed and tooke in fresh water on the Southside thereof.

On the 9 we departed from Grand Canary, and framed our course for Dominica.[4]

The last of Aprill we saw Dominica, and the same night we came to an anker on the Southside thereof.

May

The first of May in the morning many of the Salvages came aboord our ships in their Canowes, and did traffique with us; we also the same day landed and entered their Towne from whence we returned the same day aboord without any resistance of the Salvages; or any offence done to them.

The 2 of May our Admirall and our Pinnesse departed from Dominica leaving the John our Viceadmirall playing off and on about Dominica, hoping to take some Spaniard outwardes bound to the Indies; the same night we had sight of three smal Ilands called Los Santos,[5] leaving Guadalupe and them on our starboord.

The 3 we had sight of S. Christophers Iland, bearing Northeast and by East off us.

On the 4 we sayled by the Virgines, which are many broken Ilands, lying at the East ende of S. Johns Iland: and the same day towards evening we landed upon one of them called Blanca,[6] where we killed an incredible number of foules: here we stayed but three houres, and from thence stood into the shore Northwest, and having brought this Iland Southeast off us, we put towards night thorow an opening or swatch, called The passage,[7] lying betweene the Virgines, and the East end of S. John: here the Pinnesse left us, and sayled on the South side of S. John.

The 5 and 6 the Admirall sayled along the North side of S. John, so neere the shore that the Spaniards discerned us to be men of warre; and therefore made fires along the coast as we sailed by, for so their custome is, when they see any men of warre on their coasts.

The 7 we landed on the Northwest end of S. John, where we watered in a good river called Yaguana, [8] and the same night following we tooke a Frigate of tenne Tunne comming from Gwathanelo[9] laden with hides and ginger. In this place Pedro a Mollato, who knewe all our state, ranne from us to the Spaniards.

On the 9 we departed from Yaguana.

The 13 we landed on an Iland called Mona,[10] whereon were 10 or 12 houses inhabited of the Spaniards; these we burned and tooke from them a Pinnesse, which they had drawen a ground and sunke, and carried all her sayles, mastes, and rudders into the woods, because we should not take them away; we also chased the Spaniards over all the Iland; but they hid them in eaves, hollow rockes, and bushes, so that we could not find them.

1. On the African coast, about a latitude of 32_¼.
2. A short distance farther down the African coast.
3. The most southerly seaport of Morocco, now Agadeer or Agadir.
4. The course across the Atlantic was that of the voyage of 1587.
5. Northwest of Guadeloupe.
6. Probably Culebra, or Passage Island, one of the Virgin Islands off the east coast of Porto Rico.
7. Passing throught the Passage, the vessels proceeded along the northerly side of Porto Rico. The pinnace skirted the southern shores of the island.
8. Probably the Yagüez.
9. Guatemala.
10. A small island in the Mona Passage.

On the 14 we departed from Mona, and the next day after wee came to an Iland called Saona,[11] about 5 leagues distant from Mona, lying on the Southside of Hispaniola neere the East end: betweene these two Ilands we lay off and on 4 or 5 dayes, hoping to take some of the Domingo fleete doubling this Iland, as a neerer way to Spaine then by Cape Tyburon,[12] or by Cape S. Anthony.[13]

On Thursday being the 19 our Viceadmirall, from whom we departed at Dominica, came to us at Saona, with whom we left a Spanish Frigate, and appointed him to lie off and on other five daies betweene Saona and Mona to the ende aforesaid; then we departed from them at Saona for Cape Tyburon. Here I was enformed that our men of the Viceadmirall, at their departure from Dominica brought away two young Salvages, which were the chiefe Casiques sonnes of that Countrey and part of Dominica, but they shortly after ran away from them at Santa Cruz Iland,[14] where the Viceadmirall landed to take in ballast.

On the 21 the Admirall came to the Cape Tyburon, where we found the John Evangelist our Pinnesse staying for us: here we tooke in two Spaniards almost starved on the shore, who made a fire to our ships as we passed by. Those places for an 100 miles in length are nothing els but a desolate and meere wildernesse, without any habitation of people, and full of wilde Bulles and Bores, and great Serpents.

The 22 our Pinnesse came also to an anker in Aligato Bay at cape Tyburon. Here we understood of M. Lane, [15] Captaine of the Pinnesse; how he was set upon with one of the kings Gallies belonging to Santo Domingo, which was manned with 400 men, who after he had fought with him 3 or 4 houres, gave over the fight and forsooke him, without any great hurt done on eyther part.

The 26 the John our Vizadmirall came to us to cape Tyburon and the Frigat which we left with him at Saona. This was the appointed place where we should attend for the meeting with the Santo Domingo Fleete.

On Whitsunday Even at Cape Tyburon, one of our boyes ranne away from us, and at tenne dayes end returned to our ships almost starved for want of food. In sundry places about this part of Cape Tyburon we found the bones and carkases of divers men, who had perished (as wee thought) by famine in those woods, being either straglead from their company, or landed there by some men of warre.

June

On the 14 of June we tooke a smal Spanish frigat which fell amongst us so suddenly, as he doubled the point at the Bay of Cape Tyburon, where we road, so that he could not escape us. This frigat came from Santo Domingo, and had but three men in her, the one was an expert Pilot, the other a Mountainer, and the thirde a Vintener, who escaped all out of prison at Santo Domingo, purposing to fly to Yaguana which is a towne in the West parts of Hispaniola where many fugitive Spaniards are gathered together.

The 17 being Wednesday Captaine Lane was sent to Yaguana with his Pinnesse and a Frigat to take a shippe, which was there taking in fraight, as we understood by the old Pylot, whom we had taken three dayes before.

The 24 the Frigat returned from Captaine Lane at Yaguana, and brought us word to cape Tyburon, that Captaine Lane had taken the shippe, with many passengers and Negroes in the same; which proved not so rich a prize as we hoped for, for that a Frenchman of warre had taken and spoyled her before we came. Neverthelesse her loading was thought worth 1000 or 1300 pounds, being hides, ginger, Cannafistula, Copperpannes, and Casavi.

July

The second of July Edward Spicer whom we left in England came to us at cape Tyburon, accompanied with a small Pinnesse, whereof one M. Harps was Captaine. And the same day we had sight of a fleete of 14 saile all of Santo Domingo, to whom we presently gave chase, but they upon the first sight of us fled, and separating themselves scattered here and there: Wherefore we were forced to divide our selves and so made after them untill 12 of the clocke at night. But then by reason of the darkenesse we lost sight of ech other, yet in the end the Admirall and the Moonelight happened to be together the same night at the fetching up of the Vizadmirall of the Spanish fleete, against whom the next morning we fought and tooke him,[16] with losse of one of our men and two hurt, and of theirs 4 slaine and 6 hurt. But what was become of our Viceadmirall, our Pinnesse, and Prize, and two Frigates, in all this time, we were ignorant.

11. An island off the southeast end of Santo Domingo.
12. Cape Tiburon, the western extremity of Hayti.
13. Cape Antonio, the western extremity of Cuba.
14. The largest of the Virgin Islands.
15. William Lane, not Ralph, according to an entry in the margin.
16. The fight, we are informed by the margin, took place in sight of Navassa, an island at the southwest entrance of the Windward Passage.

The 3 of July we spent about rifling, romaging, and fitting the Prize to be sayled with us.

The 6 of July we saw Jamayca the which we left on our larboord, keeping Cuba in sight on our starboord.

Upon the 8 of July we saw the Iland of Pinos,[17] which lieth on the Southside of Cuba nigh unto the West end or Cape called Cape S. Anthony. And the same day we gave chase to a Frigat, but at night we lost sight of her, partly by the slow sayling of our Admirall, and lacke of the Moonelight our Pinnesse, whom Captaine Cooke had sent to the Cape the day before.

On the 11 we came to Cape S. Anthony, where we found our consort the Moonelight and her Pinnesse abiding for our comming, of whom we understood that the day before there passed by them 22 saile, some of them of the burden of 300 and some 400.tunnes loaden with the Kings treasure from the maine, bound for Havana: from this 11 of July untill 22 we were much becalmed: and the winde being very scarse, and the weather exceeding boat, we were much pestered with the Spaniards we bad taken: wherefore we were driven to land all the Spaniards saving three, but the place where we landed them was of their owne choise on the Southside of Cuba neere unto the Organes and Rio de Puercos.

The 23 we had sight of the Cape of Florida, and the broken Ilands thereof called the Martires.[18] The 25 being S. James day in the morning, we fell in with the Matanqas,[19] a head-land 8 leagues towards the East of Havana, where we purposed to take fresh water in, and make our abode two or three dayes.

On Sunday the 26 of July plying too and fro betweene the Matan as and Havana, we were espied of three small Pinnasses of S. John de Ullua bound for Havana, which were exceedingly richly loaden. These 3 Pinnasses came very boldly up unto us, and so continued untill they came within musket shot of us. And we supposed them to be Captaine Harps Pinnesse, and two small Frigats taken by Captaine Harpe: wherefore we shewed our flag. But they presently upon the sight of it turned about and made all the saile they could from us toward the shore, and kept themselves in so shallow water, that we were not able to follow them, and therefore gave them over with expence of shot and pouder two no purpose. But if we had not so rashly set out our flagge, we might have taken them all three, for they would not have knowen us before they had beene in our hands. This chase brought us so far to leeward as Havana: wherfore not finding any of our consorts at the Matan as, we put over againe to the cape of Florida, and from thence thorow the chanel of Bahama.

On the 28 the Cape of Florida bare West of us.

The 30 we lost sight of the coast of Florida, and stood to Sea for to gaine the helpe of the current[20] which runneth much swifter a farre off then in sight of the coast. For from the Cape to Virginia all along the shore are none but eddie currents, setting to the South and Southwest.

The 31 our three ships were clearely disbocked.,[21] the great prize, the Admirall, and the Mooneshine, but our prize being thus disbocked departed from us without taking leave of our Admirall or consort, and sayled directly for England.

August

On the first of August the winde scanted, and from thence forward we had very fowl weather with much raine, thundering, and great spouts, which fell round about us nigh unto our ships.

The 3 we stoode againe in for the shore, and at midday we tooke the height of the same. The height of that place we found to be 34 degrees of latitude. Towards night we were within three leagues of the Low sandie Ilands West of Wokokon. But the weather continued so exceeding foule, that we could not come to an anker nye the coast: wherefore we stood off againe to Sea untill Monday the 9 of August.

On munday the storme ceased, and we had very great likelihood of faire weather: therefore we stood in againe for the shore: and came to an anker at 11 fadome in 35 degrees of latitude, within a mile of the shore, where we went on land on the narrow sandy Island, being one of the Landes West of Wokokon: in this Iland we tooke in some fresh water and caught great store of fish in the shallow water. Betweene the maine (as we supposed) and that Iland it was but a mile over and three or foure foote deepe in most places.

On the 12 in the morning we departed from thence toward night we came to an anker at the Northeast end of the Iland of Croatoan, by reason of a breach which we perceived to lie out two or three leagues into the Sea: here we road all that night.

The 13 in the morning before we wayed our ankers, our boates were sent to sound over this breach: our ships riding on the side thereof at 5 fadome; and a ships length from us we found but 4 and a quarter, and then deeping and shallowing for the space of two miles, so that sometimes we found 5 fadome, and by and by 7, and within two casts with the

---

17. Isle of Pines.
18. The Florida Keys.
19. Matanzas.
20. The Gulf Stream.
21. Meaning, apparently, "had got out into the open sea."

lead 9, and then 8, next cast 5, and then 6, and then 4, and then 9 againe, and deeper; but 3 fadome was the last, 2 leagues off from the shore. This breach is in 35. degr. and a halfe, and lyeth at the very Northeast point of Croatoan, whereas goeth a fret out of the maine Sea into the inner waters, which part the Ilandes and the maine land.

The 15 of August towards Evening we came to an anker at Hatorask, in 36 degr. and one third, in five fadom water, three leagues from the shore. At our first comming to anker on this shore we saw a great smoke rise in the Ile Roanoak neere the place where I left our Colony in the yeere 1587, which smoake put us in good hope that some of the Colony were there expecting my returne out of England.

The 16 and next morning our 2 boates went a shore, and Captaine Cooke, and Cap. Spicer, and their company with me, with intent to passe to the place at Roanoak where our countreymen were left. At our putting from the ship we commanded our Master gunner to make readie 2 Minions and a Falkon well loden, and to shoot them off with reasonable space betweene every shot, to the ende that their reportes might bee heard to the place where wee hoped to finde some of our people. This was accordingly performed, and our twoe boats put off unto the shore, in the Admirals boat we sounded all the way and found from our shippe untill we came within a mile of the shore nine, eight, and seven fadome: but before we were halfe way betweene our ships and the shore we saw another great smoke to the Southwest of Kindrikers mountes: we therefore thought good to goe to that second smoke first: but it was much further from the harbour where we landed, then we supposed it to be, so that we were very sore tired before wee came to the smoke. But that which grieved us more was that when we came to the smoke, we found no man nor signe that any had bene there lately, nor yet any fresh water in all this waye to drinke. Being thus wearied with this journey we returned to the harbour where we left our boates, who in our absence had brought their caske a shore for fresh water, so we deferred our going to Roanoak untill the next morning, and caused some of those saylers to digge in those sandie hills for fresh water whereof we found very sufficient. That night wee returned aboord with our boates and our whole company in safety.

The next morning being the 17 of August, our boates and company were prepared againe to goe up to Roanoak, but Captaine Spicer had then sent his boat ashore for fresh water, by meanes whereof it was ten of the clocke afternoone before we put from our ships which were then come to an anker within two miles of the shore. The Admirals boat was halfeway toward the shore, when Captaine Spicer put off from his ship. The Admirals boat first passed the breach, but not without some danger of sinking, for we had a sea brake into our boat which filled us halfe full of water, but by the will of God and carefull styrage of Captaine Cooke we came safe ashore, saving onely that our furniture, victuals, match and powder were much wet and spoyled. For at this time the winde blue at Northeast and direct into the harbour so great a gale, that the Sea brake extremely on the barre, and the tide went very forcibly at the entrance. By that time our Admirals boat was balled ashore, and most of our things taken out to dry, Captaine Spicer came to the entrance of the breach with his mast standing up, and was halfe passed over, but by the rash and undiscreet styrage of Ralph Skinner his Masters mate, a very dangerous Sea brake into their boate and overset them quite, the men kept the boat some in it, and some hanging on it, but the next sea set the boat on ground, where it beat so, that some of them were forced to let goe their hold, hoping to wade ashore: but the Sea still beat them downe, so that they could neither stand nor swimme, and the boat twise or thrise was turned the keele upward, whereon Captaine Spicer and Skinner hung untill they sunke, and were seene no more. But foure that could swimme a litle kept themselves in deeper water and were saved by Captaine Cookes meanes, who so soone as he saw their oversetting, stripped himselfe, and foure other that could swimme very well, and with all haste possible rowed unto them, and saved foure. There were 11 in all and 7 of the chiefest were drowned, whose names were Edward Spicer, Ralph Skinner, Edward Kelly, Thomas Bevis, Hance the Surgion, Edward Kelborne, Robert Coleman. This mischance did so much discomfort the saylers, that they were all of one mind not to goe any further to seeke the planters. But in the end by the commandement and perswasion of me and Captaine Cooke, they prepared the boates: and seeing the Captaine and me so resolute, they seemed much more willing. Our boates and all things fitted againe, we put off from Hatorask, being the number of 19 persons in both boates: but before we could get to the place where our planters were left, it was so exceeding darke, that we overshot the place a quarter of a mile: there we espied towards the North ende of the Island the light of a great fire thorow the woods, to which we presently rowed: when wee came right over against it, we let fall our Grapnel neere the shore and sounded with a trumpet a Call, and afterwardes many familiar English tunes of Songs, and called to them friendly; but we had no answere, we therefore landed at day-breake, and comming to the fire, we found the grasse and sundry rotten trees burning about the place. From hence we went thorow the woods to that part of the Iland directly over against Dasamongwepeuk, and from thence we returned by the water side, round about the North point of the Iland, untill we came to the place where I left our Colony in the yeere 1586. In all this way we saw in the sand the print of the Salvages feet of 2 or 3 sorts troaden the night, and as we entred up the sandy banke upon a tree, in the very browe thereof were curiously carved these faire Romane letters C R O: which letters presently we knew to signifie the place, where I should find the planters seated, according to a secret token agreed upon betweene them and me at my last departure from them, which was, that in any wayes they should not faile to write or carve on the trees or posts of the dores the name of the place where they should be seated; for at my comming away they were prepared to remove from Roanoak 50 miles into the maine. Therefore at my departure from them in An. 1587 I willed them, that if they should happen to be distressed in any of those places, that then they should carve over the letters or name, a Crosse + in this forme, but we found no such signe of distresse.. And having well considered of this, we passed toward the place where they were left in sundry houses, but we found the houses taken downe, and the place very strongly enclosed with a high palisado of great trees, with cortynes[22] and flankers very Fortlike, and one of the chiefe trees or postes at the right side of the entrance had the barke taken off, and 5 foote from the ground in fayre Capitall letters was graven CROATOAN without any crosse or signe of distresse; this done, we entred into the palisado, where we found many barres of iron) two pigges of Lead, foure yron fowlers, Iron sacker-shotte, [23] and such like heavie thinges, throwen here and there, almost overgrowen with grasse and weedes. From thence wee went along by the water side, towards the poynt of the Creeke to see if we could find any of their botes or Pinnisse, but we could perceive no signe of them, nor any of the last Falkons and small Ordinance which were left with them, at my departure from them. At our returne from the Creeke, some of our Saylers meeting us, told us that they had found where divers chests had bene hidden, and long sithence digged up againe and broken up, and much of the goods in them spoyled and scattered about, but nothing left, of such things as the Savages knew any use of, undefaced. Presently Captaine Cooke and I went to the place, which was in the ende of an olde trench, made two yeeres past by Captaine Amadas: wheere wee found five Chests, that had bene carefully hidden of the Planters, and of the same chests three were my owne, and about the place many of my things spoyled and broken, and my bookes torne from the covers, the frames of some of my pictures and Mappes rotten and spoyled with rayne, and my armour almost eaten through with rust; this could bee no other but the deede of the Savages our enemies at Dasamongwepeuk, who had watched the departure of our men to Croatoan; and assoone as they were departed digged up every place where they suspected any thing to be buried: but although it much grieved me to see such spoyle of my goods, yet on the other side I greatly joyed that I had safely found a certaine token of their safe being at Croatoan, which is the place where Manteo, was borne, and the Savages of the Iland our friends.[24]

When we had scene in this place so much as we could, We returned to our Boates, and departed from the shoare towards our shippes, with as much speede as we could: For the weather beganne to overcast, and very likely that a foule and stormie night would ensue. Therefore the same Livening with much danger and labour, we got our selves aboard, by which time the winde and seas were so greatly risen, that wee doubted our Cables and Anchors would scarcely holde untill Morning: wherefore the Captaine caused the Boate to be manned by five lusty men, who could swimme all well, and sent them to the little Iland on the right hand of the Harbour, to bring aboard sixe of our men, who had filled our caske with fresh water: the Boate the same night returned aboard with our men, but all our Caske ready filled they left behinde, unpossible to bee had aboard without danger of casting away both men and Boates: for this night prooved very stormie and foule.

The next Morning it was agreed by the Captaine and my selfe, with the Master and others, to wey anchor, and goe for the place at Croatoan, where our planters were: for that then the winde was good for that place, and also to leave that Caske with fresh water on shoare in the Iland untill our returne. So then they brought the cable to the Capston, but when the anchor was almost apecke, the Cable broke, by meanes whereof we lost another Anchor, wherewith we drove so fast into the shoare, that wee were forced to let fall a third Anchor: which came so fast home that the Shippe was almost aground by Kenricks mounts: so that we were forced to let slippe the Cable ende for ende. And if it had not chanced that wee had fallen into a chanell of deeper water, closer by the shoare then wee accompted of, wee could never have gone cleare of the poynt that lyeth to the Southwardes of Kenricks mounts. Being thus cleare of some dangers, and gotten into deeper waters, but not without some losse: for wee had but one Cable and Anchor left us of foure, and the weather grew to be fouler and fouler; our victuals scarse, and our caske and fresh water lost: it was therefore determined that we should goe for Saint John or some other Iland to the Southward for fresh water. And it was further purposed, that if wee could any wayes supply our wants of victuals and other necessaries, either at Hispaniola, Sant John, or Trynidad, that then we should continue in the Indies all the Winter following, with hope to make 2. rich voyages of one, and at our returne to visit our countreymen at Virginia. The captaine and the whole company in the Admirall (with my earnest petitions) thereunto agreed, so that it rested onely to knowe what the Master of the Moone-light our consort would doe herein. But when we demanded them if they would accompany us in that new determination, they alledged that their weake and leake Shippe was not able to continue it; wherefore the same night we parted, leaving the Moone-light to goe directly for England, and the Admirall set his course for Trynidad, which course we kept two dayes.

---

22. Curtains.
23. Shot for sakers, or large cannon.
24. On the theory, not generally held, that the colony was not wholly destroyed, and that descendants of some of its members are still to be found in North Carolina, see Weeks, "The Lost Colony of Roanoke: Its Fate and Survival," in *Papers of the American Historical Association*, v. 107.

On the 28 the winde changed, and it was sette on foule weather every way: but this storme brought the winde West and Northwest, and blewe so forcibly, that wee were able to beare no sayle, but our fore-course halfe mast high, where-with wee ranne upon the winde perforce, the due course for England, for that wee were driven to change our first determination for Trynidad, and stoode for the Ilands of A ores, where wee purposed to take in fresh water, and also there hoped to meete with some English men of warre about those Ilands, at whose hands wee might obtaine some supply of our wants. And thus continuing our course for the A ores, sometimes with calmes, and sometimes with very scarce windes, on the fifteenth of September the winde came South Southeast, and blew so exceedingly, that wee were forced to lye atry[25] all that day. At this time by account we judged our selves to be about twentie leagues to the West of Cuervo and Flores, but about night the Btorme ceased, and fayre weather ensued.

On Thursday the seventeenth wee saw Cuervo and Flores, but we could not come to anker that night, by reason the winde shifted. The next Morning being the eighteenth, standing in againe with Cuervo, we escryed a sayle a head us, to whom we gave chase: but when wee came neere him, wee knew him to be a Spanyard, and hoped to make sure purchase of him: but we understood at our speaking with him, that he was a prize, and of the Domingo fleete already taken by the John our consort, in the Indies. We learned also of this prize, that our Viceadmirall and Pinnesse had fought with the rest of the Domingo fleete, and had forced them with their Admirall to flee unto Jamaica under the Fort for succour, and some of them ran themselves aground, whereof one of them they brought away, and tooke out of some others so much as the time would permit. And further wee understood of them, that in their returne from Jamaica about the Organes neere Cape Saint Anthony, our Viceadmirall mette with two Shippes of the mayne land, come from Mexico, bound for Havana, with whom he fought: in which fight our Viceadmirals Lieutenant was slaine, and the Captaines right arrne strooken off, with foure other of his men slaine, and sixteene hurt. But in the ende he entred, and tooke one of the Spanish shippes, which was so sore shot by us under water, that before they could take out her treasure she sunke; so that we lost thirteene Pipes of silver which sunke with her, besides much other rich marchandize. And in the meane time the other Spanish shippe being pearced with nine shotte under water, got away; whom our Viceadmirall intended to pursue: but some of their men in the toppe made certaine rockes, which they saw above water neere the shoare, to be Gallies of Havana and Cartagena, comming from Havana to rescue the two Ships; Wherefore they gave over their chase, and went for England. After this intelligence was given us by this our prize, he departed from us, and went for England.

On Saturday the 19. of September we came to an Ancre neere a small village on the North side of Flores, where we found ryding 5. English men of warre, of whom we understood that our Viceadmirall And Prize were gone thence for England. One of these five was the Moonelight our consort, who upon the first sight of our comming into Flores, Bet sayle and went for England, not taking any leave of us.

On Sunday the 20. the Mary Rose, Admirall of the Queenes fleete, wherein was Generall Sir John Hawkins, stood in with Flores, and divers other of the Queenes ships, namely the Hope, the Nonpareilia, the Rainebow, the Swift-sure, the Foresight, with many other good merchants ships of warre, as the Edward Bonaventure, the Marchant Royal, the Amitie, the Eagle, the Dainty of sir John Hawkins, and many other good ships and pinnesses, all attending to meete with the king of Spaines fleete, comming from Terra firma of the West Indies.

The 22. of September we went aboard the Raynebow, and towards night we spake with the Swift-sure, and gave him 3. pieces. The captaines desired our company; wherefore we willingly attended on them: who at this time with 10. other ships stood for Faial. But the Generall with the rest of the Fleete were separated from us, making two fleetes, for the surer meeting with the Spanish fleete.

On Wednesday the 23. we saw Gratiosa,[26] where the Admiral and the test of the Queenes fleete were come together. The Admirall put forth a flag of counsel, in which was determined that the whole fleete should go for the mayne, and spred themselves on the coasts of Spaine and Portugal, so farre as conveniently they might, for the suer meeting of the Spanish fleete in those parts.

The 26. we came to Faial, where the Admiral with some other of the fleete ankred, other some plyed up and downe betweene that and the Pico untill midnight, at which time the Anthony shot off a piece and weyed, shewing his light: after whom the whole fleete stood to the East, the winde at Northeast by East.

On Sunday the 27. towards Evening wee tooke our leave of the Admirall and the whole fleete, who stood to the East. But our shippe accompanied with a Flyboate stoode in again with S. George, where we purposed to take in more fresh water, and some other fresh victuals.

On Wednesday the 30. of September, seeing the winde hang so Northerly, that wee could not atteine the Iland of S. George, we gave over our purpose to water there, and the next day framed our due course for England.

---

25. Heave to.
26. Of the Azores group; so also are Fayal, Pico, São Jorge, and São Miguel, mentioned in the following paragraphs.

October

The 2. of October in the Morning we saw S. Michaels Iland on our Starre board quarter.

      The 23. at 10. of the clocke afore noone, we saw Ushant in Britaigne.[27]

      On Saturday the 24. we came in safetie, God be thanked, to an anker at Plymmouth.

1. What kinds of delays does the author experience as he attempts to get his return voyage to Virginia underway?
2. Identify and explain what seems to be the policy of John White's ships regarding foreign ships and trade vessels.
3. What are the presumed signs of the colony that John White and his fellow journeymen follow in hopes of finding the inhabitants of Roanoke? What are their experiences as they attempt to locate the colony?
4. What events seem to have prevented or delayed a more extensive search for the Roanoke colonists?

---

27. The most western of the islands of Brittany.

2-2 An Act Concerning Servants and Slaves

The transition from indentured servitude to chattel slavery in Virginia brought new legal and social questions to the forefront. What legal rights did indentured servants have? Were their limits to the rights of slave owners? What was to be done about runaways? Even questions regarding race relations needed to be addressed. The following statutes passed by the Virginia colonial legislature addressed these issues and attempted, for the time being at least, to establish a status quo for servants and slaves.

> **Source:** William Waller Hening, *The Statutes at Large; Being a Collection of all the Laws of Virginia, from the First Session of the Legislature in the Year 1619,* (New York: R & W & G. Bartow, 1823). Vol. I.
> http://www.law.du.edu/russell/lh/alh/docs/virginiaslaverystatutes.html

I. *Be it enacted, by the governor, council, and burgesses, of this present general assembly, and it is hereby enacted, by the authority of the same,* That all servants brought into this country without indenture, if the said servants be Christians, and of Christian parentage, and above nineteen years of age, shall serve but five years; and if under nineteen years of age, 'till they shall become twenty-four years of age, and no longer.

II. *Provided always,* That every such servant be carried to the country court, within six months after his or her arrival into this colony, to have his or her age adjudged by the court, otherwise shall be a servant no longer than the accustomary five years, although much under the age of nineteen years; and the age of such servant being adjudged by the court, within the limitation aforesaid, shall be entered upon the records of the said court, and be accounted, deemed, and taken, for the true age of the said servant, in relation to the time of service aforesaid.

III. *And also be it enacted, by the authority aforesaid, and it is herby enacted,* That when any servant sold for the custom, shall pretend to have indentures, the master or owner of such servant, for discovery of the truth thereof, may bring the said servant before a justice of the peace; and if the said servant cannot produce the indenture then, but shall still pretend to have one, the said justice shall assign two months time for the doing thereof, in which time, if the said servant shall not produce his or her indenture, it shall be taken for granted that there never was one, and shall be a bar to his or her claim of making use of one afterwards, or taking any advantage by one.

IV. *And also be it enacted, by the authority aforesaid, and it is hereby enacted,* That all servants imported and brought into this country, by sea or land, who were not Christians in their native country, (except Turks and Moors in amity with her majesty, and others that can make due proof of their being free in England, or any other Christian country, before they were shipped, in order to transportation hither) shall be accounted and be slaves, and as such be here bought and sold notwithstanding a conversion to Christianity afterwards.

V. *And be it enacted, by the authority aforesaid, and it is hereby enacted,* That if any person or persons shall hereafter import into this colony, and here sell as a slave, any person or persons that shall have been a freeman in any Christian country, island, or plantation, such importer and seller as aforesaid, shall forfeit and pay, to the party from whom the said freeman shall recover his freedom, double the sum for which the said freeman was sold. To be recovered, in any court of record within this colony, according to the course of the common law, wherein the defendant shall not be admitted to plead in bar, any act or statute for limitation of actions.

VI. *Provided always,* That a slave's being in England, shall not be sufficient to discharge him of his slavery, without other proof of his being manumitted there.

VII. *And also be it enacted, by the authority aforesaid, and it is hereby enacted,* That all masters and owners of servants, shall find and provide for their servants, wholesome and competent diet, clothing, and lodging, by the discretion of the county court; and shall not, at any time, give immoderate correction; neither shall, at any time, whip a Christian white servant naked, without an order from a justice of the peace: And if any, notwithstanding this act, shall presume to whip a Christian white servant naked, without such order, the person so offending, shall forfeit and pay for the same, forty shillings sterling, to the party injured: To be recovered, with costs, upon petition, without the formal process of an action, as in and by this act is provided for servants complaints to be heard; provided complaint be made within six months after such whipping.

VIII. *And also be it enacted, by the authority aforesaid, and it is herby enacted,* That all servants, (not being slaves,) whether imported, or become servants of their own accord here, or bound by any court or church-wardens, shall have their complaints received by a justice of the peace, who, if he find cause, shall bind the master over to answer the complaint at court; and it shall be there determined: And all complaints of servants, shall and may, by virtue hereof, be received at any time, upon petition, in the court of the county wherein they reside, without the formal process of an action; and also full power and authority is hereby given to the said court, by their discretion, (having first summoned the masters or owners to justify themselves, if they think fit,) to adjudge, order, and appoint what shall be necessary, as to diet, lodging, clothing, and correction: 1 And if any master or owner shall not thereupon comply with the said court's order, the said court is hereby authorised and empowered, upon a second just complaint, to order such servant to be immediately sold at an outcry, by the sheriff, and after charges deducted, the remainder of what the said servant shall be sold for, to be paid and satisfied to such owner.

IX. *Provided always, and be it enacted,* That if such servant be so sick or lame, or otherwise rendered so incapable, that he or she cannot be sold for such a value, at least, as shall satisfy the fees, and other incident charges accrued, the said court shall then order the church-wardens of the parish to take care of and provide for the said servant, until such servant's time, due by law to the said master, or owner, shall be expired, or until such servant, shall be so recovered, as to be sold for defraying the said fees and charges: And further, the said court, from time to time, shall order the charges of keeping the said servant, to be levied upon the goods and chattels of the master or owner of the said servant, by distress.

X. *And be it also enacted,* That all servants, whether, by importation, indenture, or hire here, as well feme coverts, as others, shall, in like manner, as is provided, upon complaints of misusage, have their petitions received in court, for their wages and freedom, without the formal process of an action; and proceedings, and judgment, shall, in like manner, also, be had thereupon.

XI. And for a further Christian care and usage of all Christian servants, *Be it also enacted, by the authority aforesaid, and it is hereby enacted,* That no negros, mulattos, or Indians, although Christians, or Jews, Moors, Mahometans, or other infidels, shall, at any time, purchase any Christian servant, nor any other, except of their own complexion, or such as are declared slaves by this act: And if any negro, mulatto, or Indian, Jew, Moor, Mahometan, or other infidel, or such as are declared slaves by this act, shall, notwithstanding, purchase any Christian white servant, the said servant shall, *ipso facto,* become free and acquit from any service then due, and shall be so held, deemed, and taken: And if any person, having such Christian servant, shall intermarry with any such negro, mulatto, or Indian, Jew, Moor, Mahometan, or other infidel, every Christian white servant of every such person so intermarrying, shall, *ipso facto,* become free and acquit from any service then due to such master or mistress so intermarrying, as aforesaid.

XII. *And also be it enacted, by the authority aforesaid, and it is hereby enacted,* That no master or owner of any servant shall during the time of such servant's servitude, make any bargain with his or her said servant for further service, or other matter or thing relating to liberty, or personal profit, unless the same be made in the presence, and with the approbation, of the court of that county where the master or owner resides: And if any servants shall, at any time bring in goods or money, or during the time of their service, by gift, or any other lawful ways or means, come to have any goods or money, they shall enjoy the propriety thereof, and have the sole use and benefit thereof to themselves. And if any servant shall happen to fall sick or lame, during the time of service, so that he or she becomes of little or no use to his or her master or owner, but rather a charge, the said master or owner shall not put away the said servant, but shall maintain him or her, during the whole time he or she was before obliged to serve, by indenture, custom or order of court: And if any master or owner, shall put away any such sick or lame servant, upon pretence of freedom, and that servant shall become chargeable to the parish, the said master or owner shall forfeit and pay ten pounds current money of Virginia, to the church-wardens of the parish where such offence shall be committed, for the use of the said parish: To be recovered by action of debt, in any court of record in this her majesty's colony and dominion, in which no essoin, protection, or wager of law, shall be allowed.

XIII. And whereas there has been a good and laudable custom of allowing servants corn and cloaths for their present support, upon their freedom; but nothing in that nature ever made certain, *Be it also enacted, by the authority aforesaid, and it is hereby enacted,* That there shall be paid and allowed to every imported servant, not having yearly wages, at the time of service ended, by the master or owner of such servant, viz: To every male servant, ten bushels of indian corn, thirty shillings in money, or the value thereof, in goods, and one well fixed musket or fuzee, of the value of twenty shillings, at least: and to every woman servant, fifteen bushels of indian corn, and forty shillings in money, or the value thereof, in goods: Which, upon refusal, shall be ordered, with costs, upon petition to the county court, in manner as is herein before directed, for servants complaints to be heard.

XIV. *And also be it enacted, by the authority aforesaid, and it is hereby enacted,* That all servants shall faithfully and obediently, all the whole time of their service, do all their masters or owners just and lawful commands. And if any servant shall resist the master, or mistress, or overseer, or offer violence to any of them, the said servant shall, for every such offence, be adjudged to serve his or her said master or owner, one whole year after the time, by indenture, custom, or former order of court, shall be expired.

XV. *And also be it enacted, by the authority aforesaid, and it is hereby enacted,* That no person whatsoever shall buy, sell, or receive of, to, or from, any servant, or slave, any coin or commodity whatsoever, without the leave, licence, or consent of the master or owner of the said servant, or slave: And if any person shall, contrary hereunto, without the leave or licence aforesaid, deal with any servant, or slave, he or she so offending, shall be imprisoned one calendar month, without bail or main-prize; and then, also continue in prison, until he or she shall find good security, in the sum of ten pounds current money of Virginia, for the good behaviour for one year following; wherein, a second offence shall be a breach of the bond and moreover shall forfeit and pay four times the value of the things so bought, sold, or received, to the master or owner of such servant, or slave: To be recovered, with costs, by action upon the case, in any court of record in this her majesty's colony and dominion, wherein no essoin protection, or wager of law, or other than one imparlance, shall be allowed.

XVI. *Provided always, and be it enacted,* That when any person or persons convict for dealing with a servant, or slave, contrary to this act, shall not immediately give good and sufficient security for his or her good behaviour, as afore-said: then, in such case, the court shall order thirty-nine lashes, well laid on, upon the bare back of such offender, at the common whipping-post of the county, and the said offender to be thence discharged of giving such bond and security.

XVII. *And also be it enacted, by the authority aforesaid, and it is hereby enacted, and declared,* That in all cases of penal laws, whereby persons free are punishable by fine, servants shall be punished by whipping, after the rate of twenty lashes for every five hundred pounds of tobacco, or fifty shillings current money, unless the servant so culpable, can and will procure some person or persons to pay the fine; in which case, the said servant shall be adjudged to serve such benefactor, after the time by indenture, custom, or order of court, to his or her then present master or owner, shall be expired, after the rate of one month and a half for every hundred pounds of tobacco; any thing in this act contained, to the contrary, in any-wise, notwithstanding.

XVIII. And if any women servant shall be delivered of a bastard child within the time of her service aforesaid, *Be it enacted, by the authority aforesaid, and it is hereby enacted,* That in recompense of the loss and trouble occasioned her master or mistress thereby, she shall for every such offence, serve her said master or owner one whole year after her time by indenture, custom, and former order of court, shall be expired; or pay her said master or owner, one thousand pounds of tobacco; and the reputed father, if free, shall give security to the church-wardens of the parish where that child shall be, to maintain the child, and keep the parish indemnified; or be compelled thereto by order of the county court, upon the said church-wardens complaint: But if a servant, he shall make satisfaction of the parish, for keeping the said child, after his time by indenture, custom, or order of court, to his then present master or owner, shall be expired; or be compelled thereto, by order of the county court, upon complaint of the church wardens of the said parish, for the time being. And if any woman servant shall be got with child by her master, neither the said master, nor his executors, administrators, nor assigns, shall have any claim of service against her, for or by reason of such child; but she shall, when her time due to her said master, by indenture, custom or order of court, shall be expired, be sold by the church-wardens, for the time being, of the parish wherein such child shall be born, for one year, or pay one thousand pounds of tobacco; and the said one thou-sand pounds of tobacco, or whatever she shall be sold for, shall be emploied, by the vestry, to the use of the said parish. And if any woman servant shall have a bastard child by a negro, or mulatto, over and above the years service due to her master or owner, she shall immediately, upon the expiration of her time to her then present master or owner, pay down to the church-wardens of the parish wherein such child shall be born, for the use of the said parish fifteen pounds current money of Virginia, or be by them sold for five years to the use aforesaid: And if a free Christian white woman shall have such bastard child, by a negro, or mulatto, for every such offence, she shall, within one month after her delivery of such bastard child, pay to the church-wardens for the time being, of the parish wherein such child shall be born, for the use of the said parish fifteen pounds current money of Virginia, or be by them sold for five years to the use aforesaid: And in both the said cases, the church-wardens shall bind the said child to be a servant, until it shall be of thirty one years of age.

XIX. And for a further prevention of that abominable mixture and spurious issue, which hereafter may increase in this her majesty's colony and dominion, as well by English, and other white men and women intermarrying with negros or mulattos, as by their unlawful coition with them, *Be it enacted, by the authority aforesaid, and it is hereby enacted,* That whatsoever English, or other white man or woman, being free, shall intermarry with a negro or mulatto man or woman, bond or free, shall, by judgment of the county court, be committed to prison, and there remain, during the space of six months, without bail or mainprize; and shall forfeit and pay ten pounds current money of Virginia, to the use of the parish, as aforesaid.

XX. *And be it further enacted,* That no minister of the church of England, or other minister, or person whatso-ever, within this colony and dominion, shall hereafter wittingly presume to marry a white man with a negro or mulatto woman; or to marry a white woman with a negro or mulatto man, upon pain of forfeiting and paying, for every such mar-riage the sum of ten thousand pounds of tobacco; one half to our sovereign lady the Queen, her heirs and successors, for and towards the support of the government, and the contingent charges thereof; and the other half to the informer; To be recovered, with costs, by action of debt, bill, plaint, or information, in any court of record within this her majesty's colony and dominion, wherein no essoin, protection, or wager of law, shall be allowed.

XXI. And because poor people may not be destitute of emploiment, upon suspicion of being servants, and ser-vants also kept from running away, *Be it enacted, by the authority aforesaid, and it is hereby enacted,* That every servant, when his or her time of service shall be expired, shall repair to the court of the county where he or she served the last of his or her time, and there, upon sufficient testimony, have his or her freedom entered; and a certificate thereof from the clerk of the said court, shall be sufficient to authorise any person to entertain or hire such servant, without any danger of this law. And if it shall at any time happen, that such certificate is won out, or lost, the said clerk shall grant a new one, and therein also recite the accident happened to the old one. And whoever shall hire such servant, shall take his or her certificate, and keep it, 'till the contracted time shall be expired. And if any person whatsoever, shall harbour or entertain any servant by importation, or by contract, or indenture made here, not having such certificate, he or she so offending, shall pay to the master or owner of such servant, sixty pounds of tobacco for every natural day he or she shall so harbour or entertain such runaway: To be recovered, with costs, by action of debt, in any court of record within this her majesty's colony and dominion, wherein no essoin, protection, or wager of law, shall be allowed. And also, if any runaway shall make use of a forged certificate, or after the same shall be delivered to any master or mistress, upon being hired, shall steal the same away, and thereby procure entertainment, the person entertaining such servant, upon such forged or stolen certificate, shall not be culpable by this law: But the said runaway, besides making reparation for the loss of time, and charges in recovery, and other penalties by this law directed, shall, for making use of such forged or stolen certificate, or for such theft aforesaid, stand two hours in the pillory, upon a court day: And the person forging such certificate, shall forfeit and pay ten pounds current money; one half thereof to be to her majesty, her heirs and successors, for and towards the support of this government, and the contingent charges thereof, and the other half to the master or owner of such servant, if he or she will inform or sue for the same, otherwise to the informer: To be recovered, with costs, by action of debt, bill, plaint or information, in any court of record in this her majesty's colony and dominion, wherein no essoin, protection, or wager of law, shall be allowed. And if any person or persons convict of forging such certificate, shall not immediately pay the said ten pounds, and costs, or give security to do the same within six months, he or she so convict, shall receive, on his or her bare back, thirty-nine lashes, well laid on, at the common whipping post of the county; and shall be thence discharged of paying the said ten pounds, and costs, and either of them.

    XXII. *Provided,* That when any master or mistress shall happen to hire a runaway, upon a forged certificate, and a servant deny that he delivered any such certificate, the *Onus Probandi* shall lie upon the person hiring, who upon failure therein, shall be liable to the fines and penalties, for entertaining runaway servants, without certificate.

    XXIII. And for encouragement of all persons to take up runaways, *Be it enacted, by the authority aforesaid, and it is hereby enacted,* That for the taking up of every servant, or slave, if ten miles, or above, from the house or quarter where such servant, or slave was kept, there shall be allowed by the public, as a reward to the taker-up, two hundred pounds of tobacco; and if above five miles, and under ten, one hundred pounds of tobacco: Which said several rewards of two hundred, and one hundred pounds of tobacco, shall also be paid in the county where such taker-up shall reside, and shall be again levied by the public upon the master or owner of such runaway, for reimbursement of the same to the public. And for the greater certainty in paying the said rewards and reimbursement of the public, every justice of the peace before whom such runaway shall be brought, upon the taking up, shall mention the proper-name and sur-name of the taker-up, and the county of his or her residence, together with the time and place of taking up the said runaway; and shall also mention the name of the said runaway, and the proper-name and sur-name of the master or owner of such runaway, and the county of his or her residence, together with the distance of miles, in the said justice's judgment, from the place of taking up the said runaway, to the house or quarter where such runaway was kept.

    XXIV. *Provided,* That when any negro, or other runaway, that doth not speak English, and cannot, or through obstinacy will not, declare the name of his or her masters or owner, that then it shall be sufficient for the said justice to certify the same, instead of the name of such runaway, and the proper name and sur-name of his or her master or owner, and the county of his or her residence and distance of miles, as aforesaid; and in such case, shall, by his warrant, order the said runaway to be conveyed to the public gaol, of this country, there to be continued prisoner until the master or owner shall be known; who, upon paying the charges of the imprisonment, or give caution to the prison-keeper for the same, together with the reward of two hundred or one hundred pounds of tobacco, as the case shall be, shall have the said runaway restored.

    XXV. And further, the said justice of the peace, when such runaway shall be brought before him, shall, by his warrant commit the said runaway to the next constable, and therein also order him to give the said runaway so many lashes as the said justice shall think fit, not exceeding the number of thirty-nine; and then to be conveyed from constable to constable, until the said runaway shall be carried home, or to the country gaol, as aforesaid, every constable through whose hands the said runaway shall pass, giving a receipt at the delivery; and every constable failing to execute such warrant according to the tenor thereof, or refusing to give such receipt, shall forfeit and pay two hundred pounds of tobacco to the church-wardens of the parish wherein such failure shall be, for the use of the poor of the said parish: To be recovered, with costs, by action of debt, in any court of record in this her majesty's colony and dominion, wherein no essoin, protection or wager of law, shall be allowed. And such corporal punishment shall not deprive the master or owner of such runaway of the other satisfaction here in this act appointed to be made upon such servant's running away.

    XXVI. *Provided always, and be it further enacted,* That when any servant or slave, in his or her running away, shall have crossed the great bay of Chesapeak, and shall be brought before a justice of the peace, the said justice shall, instead of committing such runaway to the constable, commit him or her to the sheriff, who is hereby required to receive every such runaway, according to such warrant, and to cause him, her, or them, to be transported again across the bay, and delivered to a constable there; and shall have, for all his trouble and charge herein, for every such servant or slave, five hundred pounds of tobacco, paid by the public; which shall be reimbursed again by the master or owner of such runaway, as aforesaid, in manner aforesaid.

XXVII. *Provided also,* That when any runaway servant that shall have crossed the said bay, shall get up into the country, in any county distant from the bay, that then, in such case, the said runaway shall be committed to a constable, to be conveyed from constable to constable, until he shall be brought to a sheriff of some county adjoining to the said bay of Chesapeak, which sheriff is also hereby required, upon such warrant, to receive such runaway, under the rules and conditions aforesaid; and cause him or her to be conveyed as aforesaid; and shall have the reward, as aforesaid.

XXVIII. And for the better preventing of delays in returning of such runaways, *Be it enacted,* That if any sheriff, under sheriff, or other officer of, or belonging to the sheriffs, shall cause or suffer any such runaway (so committed for passage over the bay) to work, the said sheriff, to whom such runaway shall be so committed, shall forfeit and pay to the master or owner, of every such servant or slave, so put to work, one thousand pounds of tobacco; To be recovered, with costs, by action of debt, bill, plaint, or information, in any court of record within this her majesty's colony and dominion, wherein no essoin, protection, or wager of law, shall be allowed.

XXIX. *And be it enacted, by the authority aforesaid, and it is hereby enacted,* That if any constable, or sheriff, into whose hands a runaway servant or slave shall be committed, by virtue of this act, shall suffer such runaway to escape, the said constable or sheriff shall be liable to the action of the party grieved, for recovery of his damages, at the common law with costs.

XXX. *And also be it enacted, by the authority aforesaid, and it is hereby enacted,* That every runaway servant, upon whose account, either of the rewards aforementioned shall be paid, for taking up, shall for every hundred pounds of tobacco so paid by the master or owner, serve his or her said master or owner, after his or her time by indenture, custom, or former order of court, shall be expired, one calendar month and an half, and moreover, shall serve double the time such servant shall be absent in such running away; and shall also make reparation, by service, to the said master or owner, for all necessary disbursements and charges, in pursuit and recovery of the said runaway; to be adjudged and allowed in the county court, after the rate of one year for eight hundred pounds of tobacco, and so proportionally for a greater or lesser quantity.

XXXI. *Provided,* That the masters or owners of such runaways, shall carry them to court the next court held for the said county, after the recovery of such runaway, otherwise it shall be in the breast of the court to consider the occasion of delay, and to hear, or refuse the claim, according to their discretion, without appeal, for the refusal.

XXXII. *And also be it enacted, by the authority aforesaid, and it is hereby enacted,* That no master, mistress, or overseer of a family, shall knowingly permit any slave, not belonging to him or her, to be and remain upon his or her plantation, above four hours at any one time, without the leave of such slave's master, mistress, or overseer, on penalty of one hundred and fifty pounds of tobacco to the informer; cognizable by a justice of the peace of the county wherein such offence shall be committed.

XXXIII. *Provided also,* That if any runaway servant, adjudged to serve for the charges of his or her pursuit and recovery, shall, at the time, he or she is so adjudged, repay and satisfy, or give good security before the court, for repaiment and satisfaction of the same, to his or her master or owner, within six months after, such master or owner shall be obliged to accept thereof, in lieu of the service given and allowed for such charges and disbursements.

XXXIV. And if any slave resist his master, or owner, or other person, by his or her order, correcting such slave, and shall happen to be killed in such correction, it shall not be accounted felony; but the master, owner, and every such other person so giving correction, shall be free and acquit of all punishment and accusation for the same, as if such accident had never happened: And also, if any negro, mulatto, or Indian, bond or free, shall at any time, lift his or her hand, in opposition against any Christian, not being negro, mulatto, or Indian, he or she so offending, shall, for every such offence, proved by the oath of the party, receive on his or her bare back, thirty lashes, well laid on; cognizable by a justice of the peace for that county wherein such offence shall be committed.

XXXV. *And also be it enacted, by the authority aforesaid, and it is hereby enacted,* That no slave go armed with gun, sword, club, staff, or other weapon, nor go from off the plantation and seat of land where such slave shall be appointed to live, without a certificate of leave in writing, for so doing, from his or her master, mistress, or overseer: And if any slave shall be found offending herein, it shall be lawful for any person or persons to apprehend and deliver such slave to the next constable or head-borough, who is hereby enjoined and required, without further order or warrant, to give such slave twenty lashes on his or her bare back, well laid on, and so send him or her home: And all horses, cattle, and hogs, now belonging, or that hereafter shall belong to any slave, or of any slaves mark in this her majesty's colony and dominion, shall be seised and sold by the church-wardens of the parish, wherein such horses, cattle, or hogs shall be, and the profit thereof applied to the use of the poor of the said parish: And also, if any damage shall be hereafter committed by any slave living at a quarter where there is no Christian overseer, the master or owner of such slave shall be liable to action for the trespass and damage, as if the same had been done by him or herself.

XXXVI. *And also it is hereby enacted and declared,* That baptism of slaves doth not exempt them from bondage; and that all children shall be bond or free, according to the condition of their mothers, and the particular directions of this act.

18

XXXVII. And whereas, many times, slaves run away and lie out, hid and lurking in swamps, woods, and other obscure places, killing hogs, and committing other injuries to the inhabitants of this her majesty's colony and dominion, *Be it therefore enacted, by the authority aforesaid, and it is hereby enacted,* That in all such cases, upon intelligence given of any slaves lying out, as aforesaid, any two justices (*Quorum unus*) of the peace of the county wherein such slave is supposed to lurk or do mischief, shall be and are empowered and required to issue proclamation against all such slaves, reciting their names, and owners names, if they are known, and thereby requiring them, and every of them, forthwith to surrender themselves; and also empowering the sheriff of the said county, to take such power with him, as he shall think fit and necessary, for the effectual apprehending such out-lying slave or slaves, and go in search of them: Which proclamation shall be published on a Sabbath day, at the door of every church and chapel, in the said county, by the parish clerk, or reader, of the church, immediately after divine worship: And in case any slave, against whom proclamation hath been thus issued, and once published at any church or chapel, as aforesaid, stay out, and do not immediately return home, it shall be lawful for any person or persons whatsoever, to kill and destroy such slaves by such ways and means as he, she, or they shall think fit, without accusation or impeachment of any crime for the same: And if any slave, that hath run away and lain out as aforesaid, shall be apprehended by the sheriff, or any other person, upon the application of the owner of the said slave, it shall and may be lawful for the county court, to order such punishment to the said slave, either by dismembering, or any other way, not touching his life, as they in their discretion shall think fit, for the reclaiming any such incorrigible slave, and terrifying others from the like practices.

XXXVIII. *Provided always, and it is further enacted,* That for every slave killed, in pursuance of this act, or put to death by law, the master or owner of such slave shall be paid by the public:

XXXIX. And to the end, the true value of every slave killed, or put to death, as aforesaid, may be the better known; and by that means, the assembly the better enabled to make a suitable allowance thereupon, *Be it enacted,* That upon application of the master or owner of any such slave, to the court appointed for proof of public claims, the said court shall value the slave in money, and the clerk of the court shall return a certificate thereof to the assembly, with the rest of the public claims.

1. It is easy to examine laws such as these and see the many ways in which servants and slaves were denied legal rights and social status in colonial Virginia. See if you can discern, however, the ways that these same statutes limit the power of slave owners and masters of indentured servants.
2. How did runaways pose particularly difficult legal problems for Virginia colonists? How did these statutes solve the dilemmas?

2-3 The trial of Anne Hutchinson (1638)

Anne Hutchinson, the articulate and resolute wife of a prominent New England merchant, was placed on trial before the General Court in 1637 for challenging the authority of the ministry and promoting individualism—provocative issues in Puritan society. During the first two days of examination she defended her position well, frustrating the best efforts of Governor Winthrop and others to convict her. Finally, her claim of direct divine inspiration brought her a conviction on the grounds of blasphemy. She was banished from the colony in 1638.

Source: *The American Colonist's Library, Primary Source Documents Pertaining to Early American History,* http://personal.pitnet.net/primarysources/hutchinson.html

MR. [JOHN] WINTHROP, GOVERNOR: Mrs Hutchinson, you are called here as one of those that have troubled the peace of the commonwealth and the churches here; you are known to be a woman that hath had a great share in the promoting and divulging of those opinions that are the cause of this trouble, and to be nearly joined not only in affinity and affection with some of those the court had taken notice of and passed censure upon, but you have spoken divers things, as we have been informed, very prejudicial to the honour of the churches and ministers thereof, and you have maintained a meeting and an assembly in your house that hath been condemned by the general assembly as a thing not tolerable nor comely in the sight of God nor fitting for your sex, and notwithstanding that was cried down you have continued the same. Therefore we have thought good to send for you to understand how things are, that if you be in an erroneous way we may reduce you that so you may become a profitable member here among us. Otherwise if you be obstinate in your course that then the court may take such course that you may trouble us no further. Therefore I would intreat you to express whether you do assent and hold in practice to those opinions and factions that have been handled in court already, that is to say, whether you do not justify Mr. Wheelwright's sermon and the petition.

MRS. HUTCHINSON: I am called here to answer before you but I hear no things laid to my charge.

GOV.: I have told you some already and more I can tell you.

MRS. H.: Name one, Sir.

GOV.: Have I not named some already?

MRS. H.: What have I said or done?

GOV.: Why for your doings, this you did harbor and countenance those that are parties in this faction that you have heard of.

MRS. H.: That's matter of conscience, Sir.

GOV.: Your conscience you must keep, or it must be kept for you.

MRS. H.: Must not I then entertain the saints because I must keep my conscience.

GOV.: Say that one brother should commit felony or treason and come to his brother's house, if he knows him guilty and conceals him he is guilty of the same. It is his conscience to entertain him, but if his conscience comes into act in giving countenance and entertainment to him that hath broken the law he is guilty too. So if you do countenance those that are transgressors of the law you are in the same fact.

MRS. H.: What law do they transgress?

GOV.: The law of God and of the state.

MRS. H.: In what particular?

GOV.: Why in this among the rest, whereas the Lord doth say honour thy father and thy mother.

MRS. H.: Ey Sir in the Lord.

GOV.: This honour you have broke in giving countenance to them.

MRS. H.: In entertaining those did I entertain them against any act (for there is the thing) or what God has appointed?

GOV.: You knew that Mr. Wheelwright did preach this sermon and those that countenance him in this do break a law.

MRS. H.: What law have I broken?

GOV.: Why the fifth commandment.

MRS. H.: I deny that for he [Mr. Wheelwright] saith in the Lord.

GOV.: You have joined with them in the faction.

MRS. H.: In what faction have I joined with them?

GOV.: In presenting the petition.

MRS. H.: Suppose I had set my hand to the petition. What then?

GOV.: You saw that case tried before.

MRS. H.: But I had not my hand to [not signed] the petition.

GOV.: You have councelled them.

MRS. H.: Wherein?

GOV.: Why in entertaining them.

MRS. H.: What breach of law is that, Sir?

GOV.: Why dishonouring the commonwealth.

MRS. H.: But put the case, Sir, that I do fear the Lord and my parents. May not I entertain them that fear the Lord because my parents will not give me leave?

GOV.: If they be the fathers of the commonwealth, and they of another religion, if you entertain them then you dishonour your parents and are justly punishable.

MRS. H.: If I entertain them, as they have dishonoured their parents I do.

GOV.: No but you by countenancing them above others put honor upon them.

MRS. H.: I may put honor upon them as the children of God and as they do honor the Lord.

GOV.: We do not mean to discourse with those of your sex but only this: you so adhere unto them and do endeavor to set forward this faction and so you do dishonour us.

MRS. H.: I do acknowledge no such thing. Neither do I think that I ever put any dishonour upon you.

GOV.: Why do you keep such a meeting at your house as you do every week upon a set day?

MRS. H.: It is lawful for me to do so, as it is all your practices, and can you find a warrant for yourself and condemn me for the same thing? The ground of my taking it up was, when I first came to this land because I did not go to such meetings as those were, it was presently reported that I did not allow of such meetings but held them unlawful and therefore in that regard they said I was proud and did despise all ordinances. Upon that a friend came unto me and told me of it and I to prevent such aspersions took it up, but it was in practice before I came. Therefore I was not the first.

GOV.: . . . By what warrant do you continue such a course?

MRS. H.: I conceive there lies a clear rule in Titus that the elder women should instruct the younger and then I must have a time wherein I must do it.

GOV.: All this I grant you, I grant you a time for it, but what is this to the purpose that you Mrs. Hutchinson must call a company together from their callings to come to be taught of you?. . .

MRS. H.: If you look upon the rule in Titus it is a rule to me. If you convince me that it is no rule I shall yield.

GOV.: You know that there is no rule that crosses another, but this rule crosses that in the Corinthians. But you must take it in this sense that elder women must instruct the younger about their business and to love their husbands and not to make them to clash.. . .

MRS. H.: Will it please you to answer me this and to give me a rule for then I will willingly submit to any truth. If any come to my house to be instructed in the ways of God what rule have I to put them away? . . . . Do you think it not lawful for me to teach women and why do you call me to teach the court?

GOV.: We do not call you to teach the court but to lay open yourself. . . .

[They continue to argue over what rule she had broken]

GOV.: Your course is not to be suffered for. Besides that we find such a course as this to be greatly prejudicial to the state. Besides the occasion that it is to seduce many honest persons that are called to those meetings and your opinions and your opinions being known to be different from the word of God may seduce many simple souls that resort unto you. Besides that the occasion which hath come of late hath come from none but such as have frequented your meetings, so that now they are flown off from magistrates and ministers and since they have come to you. And besides that it will not well stand with the commonwealth that families should be neglected for so many neighbors and dames and so much time spent. We see no rule of God for this. We see not that any should have authority to set up any other exercises besides what authority hath already set up and so what hurt comes of this you will be guilty of and we for suffering you.

MRS. H.: Sir, I do not believe that to be so.

GOV.: Well, we see how it is. We must therefore put it away from you or restrain you from maintaining this course.

Mrs H. If you have a rule for it from God's word you may.

GOV.: We are your judges, and not you ours and we must compel you to it.

MRS. H.: If it please you by authority to put it down I will freely let you for I am subject to your authority.. . .

DEPUTY GOVERNOR, THOMAS DUDLEY: I would go a little higher with Mrs. Hutchinson. About three years ago we were all in peace. Mrs Hutchinson, from that time she came hath made a disturbance, and some that came over with her in the ship did inform me what she was as soon as she was landed. I being then in place dealt with the pastor and teacher of Boston and desired them to enquire of her, and then I was satisfied that she held nothing different from us. But within half a year after, she had vented divers of her strange opinions and had made parties in the country, and at length it comes that Mr. Cotton and Mr. Vane were of her judgment, but Mr. Cotton had cleared himself that he was not of that mind. But now it appears by this woman's meeting that Mrs. Hutchinson hath so forestalled the minds of many by their resort to her meeting that now she hath a potent party in the country. Now if all these things have endangered us as from that foundation and if she in particular hath disparaged all our ministers in the land that they have preached a covenant of works, and only Mr. Cotton a covenant of grace, why this is not to be suffered, and therefore being driven to the foundation and it being found that Mrs. Hutchinson is she that hath depraved all the ministers and hath been the cause of what is fallen out, why we must take away the foundation and the building will fall.

Mrs. H.: I pray, Sir, prove it that I said they preached nothing but a covenant of works.

Dep. Gov.: Nothing but a covenant of works. Why a Jesuit may preach truth sometimes.

Mrs. H.: Did I ever say they preached a covenant of works then?

Dep. Gov.: If they do not preach a covenant of grace clearly, then they preach a covenant of works.

Mrs. H.: No, Sir. One may preach a covenant of grace more clearly than another, so I said.. . . .

Dep. Gov.: When they do preach a covenant of works do they preach truth?

Mrs. H.: Yes, Sir. But when they preach a covenant of works for salvation, that is not truth.

Dep. Gov.: I do but ask you this: when the ministers do preach a covenant of works do they preach a way of salvation?

Mrs. H.: I did not come hither to answer questions of that sort.

Dep. Gov.: Because you will deny the thing.

Mrs. H.: Ey, but that is to be proved first.

Dep. Gov.: I will make it plain that you did say that the ministers did preach a covenant of works.

Mrs. H.: I deny that.

Dep. Gov.: And that you said they were not able ministers of the New Testament, but Mr. Cotton only.

Mrs. H.: If ever I spake that I proved it by God's word.

Court: Very well, very well.

Mrs. H.: If one shall come unto me in private, and desire me seriously to tell them what I thought of such an one, I must either speak false or true in my answer.

Dep. Gov.: Likewise I will prove this that you said the gospel in the letter and words holds forth nothing but a covenant of works and that all that do not hold as you do are in a covenant of works.

Mrs. H.: I deny this for if I should so say I should speak against my own judgment. . . .

Mr. Hugh Peters: That which concerns us to speak unto, as yet we are sparing in, unless the court command us to speak, then we shall answer to Mrs. Hutchinson notwithstanding our brethren are very unwilling to answer.

[The Governor says to do so. Six ministers then testify to the particular charges and that she was "not only difficult in her opinions, but also of an intemperate spirit"]

Mr Hugh Peters: . . . . [I asked her] What difference do you conceive to be between your teacher and us?. . . Briefly, she told me there was a wide and broad difference. . . . He preaches the covenant of grace and you the covenant of works, and that you are not able ministers of the New Testament and know no more than the apostles did before the resurrection of Christ. I did then put it to her, What do you conceive of such a brother? She answered he had not the seal of the spirit.

Mrs. H.: If our pastor would shew his writings you should see what I said, and that many things are not so as is reported.

Mr. Wilson: . . . what is written [here now] I will avouch.

Mr. Weld: [agrees that Peters related Hutchinson's words accurately]

Mr. Phillips: [agrees that Peters related Hutchinson's words accurately and added] Then I asked her of myself (being she spake rashly of them all) because she never heard me at all. She likewise said that we were not able ministers of the New Testament and her reason was because we were not sealed.

Mr. Simmes: Agrees that Peters related Hutchinson's words accurately

Mr. Shephard: Also to Same.

Mr. Eliot: [agrees that Peters related Hutchinson's words accurately]

Dep. Gov.: I called these witnesses and you deny them. You see they have proved this and you deny this, but it is clear. You say they preached a covenant of works and that they were not able ministers of the New Testament; now there are two other things that you did affirm which were that the scriptures in the letter of them held forth nothing but a covenant of works and likewise that those that were under a covenant of works cannot be saved.

Mrs. H.: Prove that I said so.

Gov.: Did you say so?

Mrs. H.: No, Sir, it is your conclusion.

Dep. Gov.: What do I do charging of you if you deny what is so fully proved?

Gov.: Here are six undeniable ministers who say it is true and yet you deny that you did say that they preach a covenant of works and that they were not able ministers of the gospel, and it appears plainly that you have spoken it, and whereas you say that it was drawn from you in a way of friendship, you did profess then that it was out of conscience that you spake.. . .

MRS. H.: . . . . They thought that I did conceive there was a difference between them and Mr. Cotton. . . . I might say they might preach a covenant of works as did the apostles, but to preach a covenant of works and to be under a covenant of works is another business.

DEP. GOV.: There have been six witnesses to prove this and yet you deny it. [and then he mentions a seventh, Mr. Nathaniel Ward]

MRS. H.: I acknowledge using the words of the apostle to the Corinthians unto him, [Mr. Ward] that they that were ministers of the letter and not the spirit did preach a covenant of works.

GOV.: Mrs. Hutchinson, the court you see hath laboured to bring you to acknowledge the error of your way that so you might be reduced, the time grows late, we shall therefore give you a little more time to consider of it and therefore desire that you attend the court again in the morning. [The next morning]

GOV.: We proceeded . . . as far as we could . . . There were divers things laid to her charge: her ordinary meetings about religious exercises, her speeches in derogation of the ministers among us, and the weakening of the hands and hearts of the people towards them. Here was sufficient proof made of that which she was accused of, in that point concerning the ministers and their ministry, as that they did preach a covenant of works when others did preach a covenant of grace, and that they were not able ministers of the New Testament, and that they had not the seal of the spirit, and this was spoken not as was pretended out of private conference, but out of conscience and warrant from scripture alleged the fear of man is a snare and seeing God had given her a calling to it she would freely speak. Some other speeches she used, as that the letter of the scripture held forth a covenant of works, and this is offered to be proved by probable grounds.. . .

Controversy—should the witnesses should be recalled and made swear an oath, as Mrs. Hutchinson desired, is resolved against doing so

GOV.: I see no necessity of an oath in this thing seeing it is true and the substance of the matter confirmed by divers, yet that all may be satisfied, if the elders will take an oath they shall have it given them.. . .

MRS. H.: After that they have taken an oath I will make good what I say.

GOV.: Let us state the case, and then we may know what to do. That which is laid to Mrs. Hutchinson charge is that, that she hath traduced the magistrates and ministers of this jurisdiction, that she hath said the ministers preached a covenant of works and Mr. Cotton a covenant of grace, and that they were not able ministers of the gospel, and she excuses it that she made it a private conference and with a promise of secrecy, &c. Now this is charged upon her, and they therefore sent for her seeing she made it her table talk, and then she said the fear of man was a snare and therefore she would not be affeared of them.. . .

DEP. GOV.: Let her witnesses be called.

GOV.: Who be they?

MRS. H.: Mr. Leveret and our teacher and Mr. Coggeshall.

GOV.: Mr. Coggeshall was not present.

Mr. Coggeshall: Yes, but I was. Only I desired to be silent till I should be called.

GOV.: Will you, Mr. Coggeshall, say that she did not say so?

MR. COGGESHALL: Yes, I dare say that she did not say all that which they lay against her.

MR. PETERS: How dare you look into the court to say such a word?

MR. COGGESHALL: Mr. Peters takes upon him to forbid me. I shall be silent.

MR. STOUGHTON [ASSISTANT OF THE COURT]: Ey, but she intended this that they say.

GOV.: Well, Mr. Leveret, what were the words? I pray, speak.

MR. LEVERET: To my best remembrance when the elders did send for her, Mr. Peters did with much vehemency and intreaty urge her to tell what difference there was between Mr. Cotton and them, and upon his urging of her she said "The fear of man is a snare, but they that trust upon the Lord shall be safe." And being asked wherein the difference was, she answered that they did not preach a covenant of grace so clearly as Mr. Cotton did, and she gave this reason of it: because that as the apostles were for a time without the spirit so until they had received the witness of the spirit they could not preach a covenant of grace so clearly.

GOV.: Don't you remember that she said they were not able ministers of the New Testament?

MRS. H.: Mr. Weld and I had an hour's discourse at the window and then I spake that, if I spake it.. . .

GOV.: Mr Cotton, the court desires that you declare what you do remember of the conference which was at the time and is now in question.

MR. COTTON: I did not think I should be called to bear witness in this cause and therefore did not labor to call to remembrance what was done; but the greatest passage that took impression upon me was to this purpose. The elders spake that they had heard that she had spoken some condemning words of their ministry, and among other things they did first pray her to answer wherein she thought their ministry did differ from mine. How the comparison sprang I am ignorant, but sorry I was that any comparison should be between me and my brethren and uncomfortable it was. She told them to this purpose that they did not hold forth a covenant of grace as I did. But wherein did we differ? Why she said that they did not hold forth the seal of the spirit as he doth. Where is the difference there? Say they, why saith she, speaking to one or other of them, I know not to whom. You preach of the seal of the spirit upon a work and he upon free grace without a work or without respect to a work; he preaches the seal of the spirit upon free grace and you upon a work. I told her I was very sorry that she put comparisons between my ministry and theirs, for she had said more than I could myself, and rather I had that she had put us in fellowship with them and not have made that discrepancy. She said, she found the difference.. . .

        This was the sum of the difference, nor did it seem to be so ill taken as it is and our brethren did say also that they would not so easily believe reports as they had done and withal mentioned that they would speak no more of it, some of them did; and afterwards some of them did say they were less satisfied than before. And I must say that I did not find her saying that they were under a covenant of works, nor that she said they did preach a covenant of works.

[more back and forth between Rev. John Cotton, trying to defend Mrs. Hutchinson, and Mr. Peters, about exactly what Mrs. Hutchinson said]

MRS. H.: If you please to give me leave I shall give you the ground of what I know to be true. Being much troubled to see the falseness of the constitution of the Church of England, I had like to have turned Separatist. Whereupon I kept a day of solemn humiliation and pondering of the thing; this scripture was brought unto me—he that denies Jesus Christ to be come in the flesh is antichrist. This I considered of and in considering found that the papists did not deny him to be come in the flesh, nor we did not deny him—who then was antichrist? Was the Turk antichrist only? The Lord knows that I could not open scripture; he must by his prophetical office open it unto me. So after that being unsatisfied in the thing, the Lord was pleased to bring this scripture out of the Hebrews. he that denies the testament denies the testator, and in this did open unto me and give me to see that those which did not teach the new covenant had the spirit of antichrist, and upon this he did discover the ministry unto me; and ever since, I bless the Lord, he hath let me see which was the clear ministry and which the wrong. Since that time I confess I have been more choice and he hath left me to distinguish between the voice of my beloved and the voice of Moses, the voice of John the Baptist and the voice of antichrist, for all those voices are spoken of in scripture. Now if you do condemn me for speaking what in my conscience I know to be truth I must commit myself unto the Lord.

MR. NOWEL [ASSISTANT TO THE COURT]: How do you know that was the spirit?

MRS. H.: How did Abraham know that it was God that bid him offer his son, being a breach of the sixth commandment?

DEP. GOV.: By an immediate voice.

MRS. H.: So to me by an immediate revelation.

DEP. GOV.: How! an immediate revelation.

MRS. H.: By the voice of his own spirit to my soul. I will give you another scripture, Jer[emiah] 46: 27–28—out of which the Lord showed me what he would do for me and the rest of his servants. But after he was pleased to reveal himself to me I did presently, like Abraham, run to Hagar. And after that he did let me see the atheism of my own heart, for which I begged of the Lord that it might not remain in my heart, and being thus, he did show me this (a twelvemonth after) which I told you of before.. . . Therefore, I desire you to look to it, for you see this scripture fulfilled this day and therefore I desire you as you tender the Lord and the church and commonwealth to consider and look what you do. You have power over my body but the Lord Jesus hath power over my body and soul; and assure yourselves thus much, you do as much as in you lies to put the Lord Jesus Christ from you, and if you go on in this course you begin, you will bring a curse upon you and your posterity, and the mouth of the Lord hath spoken it.

DEP. GOV.: What is the scripture she brings?

MR. STOUGHTON [ASSISTANT TO THE COURT]: Behold I turn away from you.

MRS. H.: But now having seen him which is invisible I fear not what man can do unto me.

GOV.: Daniel was delivered by miracle; do you think to be deliver'd so too?

MRS. H.: I do here speak it before the court. I look that the Lord kshould deliver me by his providence.. . . [because God had said to her] though I should meet with affliction, yet I am the same God that delivered Daniel out of the lion's den, I will also deliver thee.

MR. HARLAKENDEN [ASSISTANT TO THE COURT]: I may read scripture and the most glorious hypocrite may read them and yet go down to hell.

MRS. H.: It may be so.. . .

GOV.: I am persuaded that the revelation she brings forth is delusion.

[The trial text here reads:] All the court but some two or three ministers cry out, we all believe it—we all believe it. [Mrs. Hutchinson was found guilty]

Gov.: The court hath already declared themselves satisfied concerning the things you hear, and concerning the trouble-someness of her spirit and the danger of her course amongst us, which is not to be suffered. Therefore if it be the mind of the court that Mrs. Hutchinson for these things that appear before us is unfit for our society, and if it be the mind of the court that she shall be banished out of our liberties and imprisoned till she be sent away, let them hold up their hands.

[All but three did so]

Gov.: Mrs. Hutchinson, the sentence of the court you hear is that you are banished from out of our jurisdiction as being a woman not fit for our society, and are to be imprisoned till the court shall send you away.

Mrs. H.: I desire to know wherefore I am banished?

Gov.: Say no more. The court knows wherefore and is satisfied.

1. How was Anne Hutchinson able to frustrate the best efforts of the court to find her guilty during the early stages of the trial?
2. Aggravating the situation at the General Court was the fact that the authority of the ministry was being challenged by a woman. How do you think other women of similar status in New England society viewed Anne Hutchinson? Was she inspirational or foolish?

2-4   The Examination and confession of Ann Foster at Salem Village (1692)

The Salem witchcraft trials have become one of the most infamous periods in American History and the language and nature of the trials have provided a context for many subsequent events. In this selection, the "testimony" of Ann Foster demonstrates the basis for the accusations and the hysteria and illuminates the mindsets of the accusers and, to a degree, the accused.

After a while Ann ffoster conffesed that the devil apered to her in the shape of a bird at several Times, such a bird as she neuer saw the like before; & that she had had this gift (viz. of striking ye afflicted downe with her eye euer since) & being askt why she thought yt bird was the diuill she answered because he came white & vanished away black & yt the diuill told her yt she should haue this gift & yt she must beliue him & told her she should haue prosperity & she said yt he had apeared to her three times & was always as a bird, and the last time was about half a year since, & sat upon a table had two legs & great eyes & yt it was the second time of his apearance that he promised her prosperity & yt it was Carriers wife about three weeks agoe yt came & perswaded her to hurt these people.

16 July 1692. Ann ffoster Examined confessed yt it was Goody Carrier yt made her a witch yt she came to her in person about Six yeares agoe & told her it she would not be a witch ye diuill should tare her in peices & carry her away at which time she promised to Serve the diuill yt she had bewitched a hog of John Loujoys to death & that she had hurt some persons in Salem Villige, yt goody Carier came to her & would have her bewitch two children of Andrew Allins & that she had then two popets made & stuck pins in them to bewitch ye said children by which one of them dyed ye other very sick, that she was at the meeting of the witches at Salem Vilige, yt Goody Carier came & told her of the meeting and would haue her goe, so they got upon Sticks & went said Jorny & being there did see Mr. Buroughs ye minister who spake to them all, & this was about two months agoe that there was then twenty five persons meet together, that she tyed a knot in a Rage & threw it into the fire to hurt Tim. Swan & that she did hurt the rest yt complayned of her by Squesing popets like them & so almost choked them.

18 July 1692. Ann ffoster Examined confessed yt ye deuil in shape of a man apeared to her wth Goody carier about six yeare since when they made her a witch & that she promised to serve the diuill two years, upon which the diuill promised her prosperity and many things but neuer performed it, that she & martha Carier did both ride on a stick or pole when they went to the witch meeting at Salem Village & that the stick broak: as they were caried in the aire aboue the tops of the trees, & they fell but she did hang fast about the neck of Goody Carier & ware presently at the vilage, that she was then much hurt of her Leg, she further saith that she heard some of the witches say there was three hundred & fiue in the whole Country & that they would ruin that place ye Vilige, also said there was present at that meetting two men besides Mr. Burroughs ye minister & one of them had gray haire, she saith yt she formerly frequented the publique metting to worship god. but the diuill had such power ouer her yt she could not profit there & yt was her undoeing: she saith yt about three or foure yeares agoe Martha Carier told her she would bewitch James Hobbs child to death & the child dyed in twenty four hours.

21 July 92. Ann ffoster Examined Owned her former conffesion being read to her and further conffessed that the discourse amongst ye witches at ye meeting at Salem village was that they would afflict there to set up the Diuills Kingdome. This confesion is true as witness my hand.

Ann ffoster Signed & Owned the aboue Examination & Conffesion before me

Salem 10th September 1692. John Higginson, Just Peace.

1. According to Ann Foster's testimony, in what ways was a witch thought to bring harm to other people?
2. How might a testimony such as Ann Foster's seem to make sense in light of actual events occurring in Salem village?

2-5 James Oglethorpe: The Stono Rebellion (1739)

The Stono Rebellion was the largest uprising of enslaved Africans to take place during the colonial period. On the morning of September 9, 1739, about twenty slaves in Saint Paul's Parish, South Carolina, broke into a small store and took guns, powder, and shot. When the owners of the store suddenly arrived, they were killed and their heads were left on the porch. From here, the slaves, led by Jemmy, tried to make their way to Saint Augustine, where the Spanish government had promised them freedom. On their way, they recruited others to join them, while at the same time killing any whites who crossed their path. That evening, they were overtaken and defeated by the colony's militia. James Oglethorpe, as governor of Georgia, was concerned about this incident, and described itÑas well as the measures he thought would prevent a recurrence of such an uprising.

Source: Allen Chandler, ed., *The Colonial Records of the State of Georgia*, vol. 22 (Atlanta: Chas. P. Byrd Press, 1913), pp. 232–236.

Sometime since there was a Proclamation published at Augustine, in which the King of Spain (then at Peace with Great Britain) promised Protection and Freedom to all Negroes Slaves that would resort thither. Certain Negroes belonging to Captain Davis escaped to Augustine, and were received there. They were demanded by General Oglethorpe who sent Lieutenant Demere to Augustine, and the Governour assured the General of his sincere Friendship, but at the same time showed his Orders from the Court of Spain, by which he was to receive all Run away Negroes. Of this other Negroes having notice, as it is believed, from the Spanish Emissaries, four or five who were Cattel-Hunters, and knew the Woods, some of whom belonged to Captain Macpherson, ran away with His Horses, wounded his Son and killed another Man. These marched f [sic] for Georgia, and were pursued, but the Rangers being then newly reduced [sic] the Countrey people could not overtake them, though they were discovered by the Saltzburghers, as they passed by Ebenezer. They reached Augustine, one only being killed and another wounded by the Indians in their flight. They were received there with great honours, one of them had a Commission given to him, and a Coat faced with Velvet. Amongst the Negroe Salves there are a people brought from the Kingdom of Angola in Africa, many of these speak Portugueze [which Language is as near Spanish as Scotch is to English,] by reason that the Portugueze have considerable Settlement, and the Jesuits have a Mission and School in that Kingdom and many Thousands of the Negroes there profess the Roman Catholic Religion. Several Spaniards upon diverse Pretences have for some time past been strolling about Carolina, two of them, who will give no account of themselves have been taken up and committed to Jayl in Georgia. The good reception of the Negroes at Augustine was spread about, Several attempted to escape to the Spaniards, & were taken, one of them was hanged at Charles Town. In the latter end of July last Don Pedro, Colonel of the Spanish Horse, went in a Launch to Charles Town under pretence of a message to General Oglethorpe and the Lieutenant Governour.

On the 9th day of September last being Sunday which is the day the Planters allow them to work for themselves, Some Angola Negroes assembled, to the number of Twenty; and one who was called Jemmy was their Captain, they suprized a Warehouse belonging to Mr. Hutchenson at a place called Stonehow [sicÑ]; they there killed Mr. Robert Bathurst, and Mr. Gibbs, plundered the House and took a pretty many small Arms and Powder, which were there for Sale. Next they plundered and burnt Mr. Godfrey's house, and killed him, his Daughter and Son. They then turned back and marched Southward along Pons Pons, which is the Road through Georgia to Augustine, they passed Mr. Wallace's Taxern towards day break, and said they would not hurt him, for he was a good Man and kind to his Slaves, but they broke open and plundered Mr. Lemy's House, and killed him, his wife and Child. They marched on towards Mr. Rose's resolving to kill him; but he was saved by a Negroe, who having hid him went out and pacified the others. Several Negroes joyned them, they calling out Liberty, marched on with Colours displayed, and two Drums beating, pursuing all the white people they met with, and killing Man Woman and Child when they could come up to them. Collonel Bull Lieutenant Governour of South Carolina, who was then riding along the Road, discovered them, was pursued, and with much difficulty escaped & raised the Countrey. They burnt Colonel Hext's house and killed his Overseer and his Wife. They then burnt Mr. Sprye's house, then Mr. Sacheverell's, and then Mr. Nash's house, all lying upon the Pons Pons Road, and killed all the white People they found in them. Mr. Bullock got off, but they burnt his House, by this time many of them were drunk with the Rum they had take in the Houses. They increased every minute by new Negroes coming to them, so that they were above Sixty, some say a hundred, on which they halted in a field, and set to dancing, Singing and beating Drums, to draw more Negroes to them, thinking they were now victorious over the whole Province, having marched ten miles & burnt all before them without Opposition, but the Militia being raised, the Planters with great briskness pursued them and when they came up, dismounting; charged them on foot. The Negroes were soon routed, though they behaved boldly several being killed on the Spot, many ran back to their Plantations thinking they had not been missed, but they were there taken and [sic] Shot, Such as were taken in the field also, were after being examined, shot on the Spot, And this is to be said to the honour of the Carolina Planters, that not with standing the Provocation they had received from so many Murders, they did not torture one Negroe, but only put them to an easy death. All the proved to be forced & were not concerned in the Murders & Burnings were pardoned, And this sudden Courage in the field, & the Humanity afterwards hath had so good an Effect that there hath been no farther Attempt, and the very Spirit of Revolt seems over. About 30 escaped from the fight, of which ten marched about 30 miles Southward, and being overtaken by the Planters on horseback, fought stoutly for some time and were all killed on the Spot. The rest are yet untaken. In the whole action about 40 Negroes and 20 whites were killed. The Lieutenant Governour sent an account of this to General Oglethorpe, who met the advices on his return form the Indian Nation He immediately ordered a Troop of Rangers to be ranged, to patrole through Georgia, placed some Men in the Garrison at Palichocolas, which was before abandoned, and near which the Negroes formerly passed, being the only place where Horses can come to swim over the River Savannah for near 100 miles, ordered out the Indians in pursuit, and a Detachment of the Garrison at Port Royal to assist the Planters on any Occasion, and published a Proclamation ordering all the Constables &c. of Georgia to pursue and seize all Negroes, with a Reward for any that should be taken. It is hoped these measures will prevent any Negroes from getting down to the Spaniards.

1. Summarize the extent and size of the Stono Rebellion. How much of a threat did the group represent to whites? What kind of threat did the rebellion pose to the preservation of slavery in the southern states?
2. Discuss the nature of the acts of "courage" and "humanity" that are credited for putting down the rebellion.
3. What international political and religious factors may have played a role in the establishment of Augustine as a safe haven for slaves?

PART THREE
MATURING COLONIAL SOCIETY

3-1 Navigation Act of September 13, 1660

In an effort to enforce mercantilism and produce "a favorable balance of trade with the colonies," Parliament passed a series of Navigation Acts. The first Navigation Act (1651) was aimed primarily at the Dutch and excluded nearly all foreign shipping from the English and colonial trade. Widely ignored, this first attempt at regulating colonial trade was followed by additional Navigation Acts beginning with the one excerpted here—all providing a convenient justification for mercantilism.

Source: http://www.founding.com/library/lbody.cfm?id=83&parent=17

For the increase of shipping and encouragement of the navigation of this nation wherein, under the good providence and protection of God, the wealth, safety, and strength of this kingdom is so much concerned; (2) be it enacted by the king's most excellent Majesty, and by the Lords and Commons in this present Parliament assembled, and by the authority thereof, that from and after the first day of December, one thousand six hundred and sixty, and from thence forward, no goods or commodities whatsoever shall be imported into or exported out of any lands, islands, plantations, or territories to his Majesty belonging or in his possession, or which may hereafter belong unto or be in the possession of his Majesty, his heirs, and successors, in Asia, Africa, or America, in any other ship or ships, vessel or vessels whatsoever, but in such ships or vessels as do truly and without fraud belong only to the people of England or Ireland, dominion of Wales or town of Berwick upon Tweed, or are of the built of and belonging to any the said lands, islands, plantations, or territories, as the proprietors and right owners thereof, and whereof the master and three fourths of the mariners at least are English; (3) under the penalty of the forfeiture and loss of all the goods and commodities which shall be imported into or exported out of any the aforesaid places in any other ship or vessel, as also of the ship or vessel, with all its guns, furniture, tackle, ammunition, and apparel; one third part thereof to his Majesty, his heirs and successors; one third part to the governor of such land, plantation, island, or territory where such default shall be committed, in case the said ship or goods be there seized, or otherwise that third part also to his Majesty, his heirs and successors; and the other third part to him or them who shall seize, inform, or sue for the same in any court of record, by bill, information, plaint, or other action, wherein no essoin, protection, or wager of law shall be allowed; (4) and all admirals and other commanders at sea of any the ships of war or other ship having commission from his Majesty or from his heirs or successors, are hereby authorized and strictly required to seize and bring in as prize all such ships or vessels as shall have offended contrary hereunto, and deliver them to the court of admiralty, there to be proceeded against; and in case of condensation, one moiety of such forfeitures shall be to the use of such admirals or commanders and their companies, to be divided and proportioned amongst them according to the rules and orders of the sea in case of ships taken prize; and the other moiety to the use of his Majesty, his heirs and successors.

II. And be it enacted, that no alien or person not born within the allegiance of our sovereign lord the king, his heirs and successors, or naturalized, or made a free denizen, shall from and after the first day of February, which will be in the year of our Lord one thousand six hundred sixty-one, exercise the trade or occupation of a merchant or factor in any the said places; (2) upon pain of the forfeiture and loss of all his goods and chattels, or which are in his possession; one third to his Majesty, his heirs and successors; one third to the governor of the plantation where such person shall so offend; and the other third to him or them that shall inform or sue for the same in any of his Majesty's courts in the plantation where such offence shall be committed; (3) and all governors of the said lands, islands, plantations, or territories, and every of them, are hereby strictly required and commanded, and all who hereafter shall be made governors of any such islands, plantations, or territories, by his Majesty, his heirs or successors, shall before their entrance into their government take a solemn oath to do their utmost, that every the afore-mentioned clauses, and all the matters and things therein contained, shall be punctually and *bona fide* observed according to the true intent and meaning thereof; (4) and upon complaint and proof made before his Majesty, his heirs or successors, or such as shall be by him or them thereunto authorized and appointed, that any the said governors have been willingly and wittingly negligent in doing their duty accordingly, that the said governor so offending shall be removed from his government.

III. And it is further enacted by the authority aforesaid, that no goods or commodities whatsoever, of the growth, production or manufacture of Africa, Asia, or America, or of any part thereof, or which are described or laid down in the usual maps or cards of those places, be imported into England, Ireland, or Wales, islands of Guernsey and Jersey, or town of Berwick upon Tweed, in any other ship or ships, vessel or vessels whatsoever, but in such as do truly and without fraud belong only to the people of England or Ireland, dominion of Wales, or town of Berwick upon Tweed, or of the lands, islands, plantations or territories in Asia, Africa, or America, to his Majesty belonging, as the proprietors and right owners thereof, and whereof the master, and three fourths at least of the mariners are English; (2) under the penalty of the forfeiture of all such goods and commodities, and of the ship or vessel in which they were imported, with all her guns, tackle, furniture, ammunition, and apparel; one moiety to his Majesty, his heirs and successors; and the other moiety to him or them who shall seize, inform or sue for the same in any court of record, by bill, information, plaint or other action wherein no essoin, protection or wager of law shall be allowed.

XVIII. And it is further enacted by the authority aforesaid, that from and after the first day of April, which shall be in the year of our Lord one thousand six hundred sixty-one, no sugars, tobacco, cotton-wool, indigoes, ginger, rustic, or other dyeing wood, of the growth, production, or manufacture of any English plantations in America, Asia, or Africa, shall be shipped, carried, conveyed, or transported from any of the said English plantations to any land, island, territory, dominion, port, or place whatsoever, other than to such other English plantations as do belong to his Majesty, his heirs and successors, or to the kingdom of England or Ireland, or principality of Wales, or town of Berwick upon Tweed, there to be laid on shore; (2) under the penalty of the forfeiture of the said goods, or the full value thereof, as also of the ship, with all her guns, tackle, apparel, ammunition, and furniture; the one moiety to the king's Majesty, his heirs and successors, and the other moiety to him or them that shall seize, inform, or sue for the same in any court of record, by bill, plaint, or information, wherein no ession, protection, or wager of law shall be allowed.

XIX. And be it further enacted by the authority aforesaid, that for every ship or vessel, which from and after the five and twentieth day of December in the year of our Lord one thousand six hundred and sixty shall set sail out of or from England, Ireland, Wales, or town of Berwick upon Tweed, for any English plantation in America, Asia, or Africa, sufficient bond shall be given with one surety to the chief officers of the custom-house and such port of place from whence the said ship shall set sail, to the value of one thousand pounds, if the ship be of less burden that one hundred tons; and of the sum of two thousand pounds, if the ship shall be of greater burden; that in case the said ship or vessel shall load any of the said commodities at any of the said English plantations, that the same commodities shall be by the said ship brought to some port of England, Ireland, Wales, or to the port or town of Berwick upon Tweed, and shall there unload and put on shore the same, the danger of the seas only expected; (2) and for all ships coming from any other port or place to any of the aforesaid plantations, who by this act are permitted to trade there, that the governor of such English plantations shall before the said ship or vessel be permitted to load on board any of the said commodities, take bond in manner and to the value aforesaid, for each respective ship or vessel, that such ship or vessel shall carry all the aforesaid goods that shall be laden on board in the said ship to some other of his Majesty's English plantations, or to England, Ireland, Wales, or town of Berwick upon Tweed; (3) and that every ship or vessel which shall load or take on board any of the aforesaid goods, until such bond given to the said governor, or certificate produced from the officers of any custom-house of England, Ireland, Wales, or of the town of Berwick, that such bonds have been there duly given, shall be forfeited with all her guns, tackle, apparel, and furniture, to be employed and recovered in manner as aforesaid; and the said governors and every of them shall twice in every year after the first day of January one thousand six hundred and sixty, return true copies of all such bonds by him so taken, to the chief officers of the custom in London.

1. The Navigation Act of 1651 required that all goods imported into England or the colonies had to arrive on English ships and the majority of the crew on board those ships must be English. How does the Navigation Act of 1660 make this regulation more limiting?
2. How do you think Parliament could enforce an act such as this—especially the provisions found in Section XVIII (the "enumerated" goods)?

3-2 Nathaniel Bacon's Challenge to William Berkeley and the Governor's Response (1676)

William Berkeley faced many challenges during his almost thirty years in power as Governor of Virginia—not the least of which was discontent over depressed tobacco prices, rising taxes, and the Indian presence in the backcountry. These issues came to a head in July 1676 when Nathaniel Bacon defied the governor's authority and led a band of frontier vigilantes against all the local Indians and even the governor himself. What followed was a brief conflict called Bacon's Rebellion that left many people dead, Jamestown in ruins, and the power of the governor and his councilors confirmed.

Source: A Hypertext on American History From the Colonial Period Until Modern Times
http://odur.let.rug.nl/~usa/D/1651-1700/bacon_rebel/bacon_i.htm
http://odur.let.rug.nl/~usa/D/1651-1700/bacon_rebel/berke.htm

The Declaracion of the People.

1. For haveing upon specious pretences of publiqe works raised greate unjust taxes upon the Comonality for the advancement of private favorites and other sinister ends, but noe visible effects in any measure adequate, For not haveing dureing this long time of his Gouvernement in any measure advanced this hopefull Colony either by fortificacons Townes or Trade.
2. For haveing abused and rendred contemptable the Magistrates of Justice, by advanceing to places of Judicature, scandalous and Ignorant favorites.
3. For haveing wronged his Majesties prerogative and interest, by assumeing Monopoly of the Beaver trade, and for haveing in that unjust gaine betrayed and sold his Majesties Country and the lives of his loyall subjects, to the barbarous heathen.
4. For haveing, protected, favoured, and Imboldned the Indians against his Majesties loyall subjects, never contriveing, requireing, or appointing any due or proper meanes of sattisfaction for theire many Invasions, robberies, and murthers comitted upon us.
5. For haveing when the Army of English, was just upon the track of those Indians, who now in all places burne, spoyle, murther and when we might with ease have destroyed them: who then were in open hostillity, for then haveing expressly countermanded, and sent back our Army, by passing his word for the peaceable demeanour of the said Indians, who imediately prosecuted theire evill intentions, comitting horred murthers and robberies in all places, being protected by the said engagement and word past of him the said Sir William Berkeley, haveing ruined and laid desolate a greate part of his Majesties Country, and have now drawne themselves into such obscure and remote places, and are by theire success soe imboldned and confirmed, by theire confederacy soe strengthned that the cryes of blood are in all places, and the terror, and constimation of the people soe greate, are now become, not onely a difficult, but a very formidable enimy, who might att first with ease have beene destroyed.
6. And lately when upon the loud outcryes of blood the Assembly had with all care raised and framed an Army for the preventing of further mischeife and safeguard of this his Majesties Colony.
7. For haveing with onely the privacy of some few favorites, without acquainting the people, onely by the alteracon of a figure, forged a Comission, by we know not what hand, not onely without, but even against the consent of the people, for the raiseing and effecting civill warr and destruction, which being happily and without blood shed prevented, for haveing the second time attempted the same, thereby calling downe our forces from the defence of the fronteeres and most weekely exposed places.
8. For the prevencon of civill mischeife and ruin amongst ourselves, whilst the barbarous enimy in all places did invade, murther and spoyle us, his majesties most faithfull subjects.

Of this and the aforesaid Articles we accuse Sir William Berkeley as guilty of each and every one of the same, and as one who hath traiterously attempted, violated and Injured his Majesties interest here, by a loss of a greate part of this his Colony and many of his faithfull loyall subjects, by him betrayed and in a barbarous and shamefull manner exposed to the Incursions and murther of the heathen, And we doe further declare these the ensueing persons in this list, to have beene his wicked and pernicious councellours Confederates, aiders, and assisters against the Comonality in these our Civill comotions.

Sir Henry Chichley	William Claiburne Junior
Lieut. Coll. Christopher	Thomas Hawkins
Wormeley	William Sherwood

Phillip Ludwell   John Page Clerke
Robert Beverley   John Cluffe Clerke
Richard Lee   John West
Thomas Ballard   Hubert Farrell
William Cole   Thomas Reade
Richard Whitacre   Matthew Kempe
Nicholas Spencer
Joseph Bridger

And we doe further demand that the said Sir William Berkeley with all the persons in this list be forthwith delivered up or surrender themselves within fower days after the notice hereof, Or otherwise we declare as followeth.

That in whatsoever place, howse, or ship, any of the said persons shall reside, be hidd, or protected, we declaire the owners, Masters or Inhabitants of the said places, to be confederates and trayters to the people and the estates of them is alsoe of all the aforesaid persons to be confiscated, and this we the Comons of Virginia doe declare, desiering a firme union amongst our selves that we may joyntly and with one accord defend our selves against the common Enimy, and lett not the faults of the guilty be the reproach of the inocent, or the faults or crimes of the oppressours devide and separate us who have suffered by theire oppressions.

These are therefore in his majesties name to command you forthwith to seize the persons above mentioned as Trayters to the King and Country and them to bring to Midle plantacon, and there to secure them untill further order, and in case of opposition, if you want any further assistance you are forthwith to demand itt in the name of the people in all the Counties of Virginia.

Nathaniel Bacon
Generall by Consent of the people.

The declaration and Remonstrance of Sir William Berkeley his most sacred Majesties Governor and Captain Generall of Virginia

Sheweth That about the yeare 1660 Coll. Mathews the then Governor dyed and then in consideration of the service I had don the Country, in defending them from, and destroying great numbers of the Indians, without the loss of three men, in all the time that warr lasted, and in contemplation of the equall and uncorrupt Justice I had distributed to all men, Not onely the Assembly but the unanimous votes of all the Country, concurred to make me Governor in a time, when if the Rebells in England had prevailed, I had certainly dyed for accepting itt, 'twas Gentlemen an unfortunate Love, shewed to me, for to shew myselfe grateftill for this, I was willing to accept of this Governement againe, when by my gracious Kings favour I might have had other places much more proffitable, and lesse toylesome then this hath beene. Since that time that I returned into the Country, I call the great God Judge of all things in heaven and earth to wittness, that I doe not know of any thing relateive to this Country wherein I have acted unjustly, corruptly, or negligently in distributeing equall Justice to all men, and takeing all possible care to preserve their proprietys, and defend the from their barbarous enimies.

But for all this, perhapps I have erred in things I know not of, if I have I am soe conscious of humane frailty, and my owne defects, that I will not onely acknowledge them, but repent of, and amend them, and not like the Rebell Bacon persist in an error, onely because I have comitted itt, and tells me in diverse of his Letters that itt is not for his honnor to confess a fault, but I am of opinion that itt is onely for divells to be incorrigable, and men of principles like the worst of divells, and these he hath, if truth be reported to me, of diverse of his expressions of Atheisme, tending to take away all Religion and Laws.

And now I will state the Question betwixt me as a Governor and Mr. Bacon, and say that if any enimies should invade England, any Councellor Justice of peace or other inferiour officer, might raise what forces they could to protect his Majesties subjects, But I say againe, if after the Kings knowledge of this invasion, any the greatest peere of England, should raise forces against the kings prohibition this would be now, and ever was in all ages and Nations accompted treason. Nay I will goe further, that though this peere was truly zealous for the preservation of his King, and subjects, and had better and greater abibitys then all the rest of his fellow subjects, doe his King and Country service, yett if the King (though by false information) should suspect the contrary, itt were treason in this Noble peere to proceed after the King's prohibition, and for the truth of this I appeale to all the laws of England, and the Laws and constitutions of all other Nations in the world, And yett further itt is declared by this Parliament that the takeing up Armes for the King and Parliament is treason, for the event shewed that what ever the pretence was to seduce ignorant and well affected people, yett the end was ruinous both to King and people, as this will be if not prevented, I doe therefore againe declar that Bacon proceedeing against all Laws of all Nations modern and ancient, is Rebell to his sacred Majesty and this Country, nor will I insist upon the sweareing of men to live and dye togeather, which is treason by the very words of the Law.

Now my friends I have lived 34 yeares amongst you, as uncorrupt and dilligent as ever Governor was, Bacon is a man of two yeares amongst you, his person and qualities unknowne to most of you, and to all men else, by any vertuous action that ever I heard of, And that very action which he boasts of, was sickly and fooleishly, and as I am informed treacherously carried to the dishonnor of the English Nation, yett in itt, he lost more men then I did in three yeares Warr, and by the grace of God will putt myselfe to the same daingers and troubles againe when I have brought Bacon to acknowledge the Laws are above him, and I doubt not but by God's assistance to have better success then Bacon hath had, the reason of my hopes are, that I will take Councell of wiser men then my selfe, but Mr. Bacon hath none about but the lowest of the people.

Yett I must further enlarge, that I cannot without your helpe, doe any thinge in this but dye in defence of my King, his laws, and subjects, which I will cheerefully doe, though alone I doe itt, and considering my poore fortunes, I can not leave my poore Wife and friends a better legacy then by dyeing for my King and you: for his sacred Majesty will easeily distinguish betweene Mr. Bacons actions and myne, and Kinges have long Armes, either to reward or punish.

Now after all this, if Mr. Bacon can shew one precedens or example where such actings in any Nation what ever, was approved of, I will mediate with the King and you for a pardon, and excuce for him, but I can shew him an hundred examples where brave and great men have beene putt to death for gaineing Victorys against the Comand of their Superiors.

Lastly my most assured friends I would have preserved those Indians that I knew were howerly att our mercy, to have beene our spyes and intelligence, to finde out our bloody enimies, but as soone as I had the least intelligence that they alsoe were trecherous enimies, I gave out Commissions to distroy them all as the Commissions themselves will speake itt.

To conclude, I have don what was possible both to friend and enimy, have granted Mr. Bacon three pardons, which he hath scornefully rejected, suppoaseing himselfe stronger to subvert then I and you to maineteyne the Laws, by which onely and Gods assisting grace and mercy, all men mwt hope for peace and safety. I will add noe more though much more is still remaineing to Justifie me and condenme Mr. Bacon, but to desier that this declaration may be read in every County Court in the Country, and that a Court be presently called to doe itt, before the Assembly meet, That your approbation or dissattisfaction of this declaration may be knowne to all the Country, and the Kings Councell to whose most revered Judgments itt is submitted, Given the xxixth day of May, a happy day in the xxv"ith yeare of his most sacred Majesties Reigne, Charles the second, who God grant long and prosperously to Reigne, and lett all his good subjects say Amen.

Sir William Berkeley
Governor

1. What, in general, are Nathaniel Bacon's complaints against Governor Berkeley? Who do you think would be most likely to join up with Bacon? Who would be least likely to do so?
2. How does William Berkeley present his case against Bacon? How do his views on relations with the Indians differ from Bacon's?

3-3   Edward Randolph Describes King Philip's War (1685)

Edward Randolph was sent by King James II to investigate colonial infringements of the Navigation Acts as well as other seemingly unpopular laws passed by Parliament. He was also asked to describe the overall state of affairs in New England. Here is the section from Randolph's 1685 account that addresses the war between the colonists and the Indians led by Metacom (or Metacomet, called King Philip by the English).

Source: *The American Colonist's Library, A Treasury of Primary Documents*
http://www.swarthmore.edu/SocSci/bdorsey/docs/45-ran.html

[Some spelling has been modernized.]

Eighth Enquiry. What hath been the original cause of the present war with the natives. What are the advantages or disadvantages arising thereby and will probably be the End?

Various are the reports and conjectures of the causes of the present Indian war. Some impute it to an imprudent zeal in the magistrates of Boston to Christianize those heathen before they were civilized and injoyning them the strict observation of their lawes, which, to a people so rude and licentious, hath proved even intolerable, and that the more, for that while the magistrates, for their profit, put the lawes severely in execution against the Indians, the people, on the other side, for lucre and gain, entice and provoke the Indians to the breach thereof, especially to drunkenness, to which those people are so generally addicted that they will strip themselves to their skin to have their fill of rum and brandy, the Massachusets having made a law that every Indian drunk should pay 10s. or be whipped, according to the discretion of the magistrate. Many of these poor people willingly offered their backs to the lash to save their money; whereupon, the magistrates finding much trouble and no profit to arise to the government by whipping, did change that punishment into 10 days worke for such as could not or would not pay the fine of 10s. which did highly incense the Indians.

Some believe there have been vagrant and jesuiticall priests, who have made it their businesses for some yeares past, to go from Sachim to Sachim, to exasperate the Indians against the English and to bring them into a confederacy, and that they were promised supplies from France and other parts to extirpate the English nation out of the continent of America. Others impute the cause to some injuries offered to the Sachim Philip; for he being possessed of a tract of land called Mount Hope, a very fertile, pleasant and rich soyle, some English had a mind to dispossesse him thereof, who never wanting one pretence or other to attain their end, complained of injuries done by Philip and his Indians to their stock and cattle, whereupon Philip was often summoned before the magistrate, sometimes imprisoned, and never released but upon parting with a considerable part of his land.

But the government of the Massachusets (to give it in their own words) do declare these are the great evills for which God hath given the heathen commission to rise against the: The wofull breach of the 5th commandment, in contempt of their authority, which is a sin highly provoking to the Lord: For men wearing long hair and perewigs made of women's hair; for women wearing borders of hair and for cutting, curling and laying out the hair, and disguising themselves by following strange fashions in their apparell: For profaneness in the people not frequenting their meetings, and others going away before the blessing be pronounced: For suffering the Quakers to live amongst them and to set up their threshholds by Gods thresholds, contrary to their old lawes and resolutions.

With many such reasons, but whatever be the cause, the English have contributed much to their misfortunes, for they first taught the Indians the use of armes, and admitted them to be present at all their musters and trainings, and shewed them how to handle, mend and fix their muskets, and have been furnished with all sorts of armes by permission of the government, so that the Indians are become excellent firemen. And at Natick there was a gathered church of praying Indians, who were exercised as trained bands, under officers of their owne; these have been the most barbarous and cruel enemies to the English of any others. Capt. Tom, their leader, being lately taken and hanged at Boston, with one other of their chiefs.

That notwithstanding the ancient law of the country, made in the year 1633, that no person should sell any armes or ammunition to any Indian upon penalty of £10 for every gun, £5 for a pound of powder, and 40s. for a pound of shot, yet the government of the Massachusets in the year 1657, upon designe to monopolize the whole Indian trade did publish and declare that the trade of furrs and peltry with the Indians in their jurisdiction did solely and properly belong to their commonwealth and not to every indifferent person, and did enact that no person should trade with the Indians for any sort of peltry, except such as were authorized by that court, under the penalty of £100 for every offence, giving liberty to all such as should have licence from them to sell, unto any Indian, guns, swords, powder and shot, paying to the treasurer 3d. for each gun and for each dozen of swords; 6d. for a pound of powder and for every ten pounds of shot, by which means the Indians have been abundantly furnished with great store of armes and ammunition to the utter ruin and undoing of many families in the neighbouring colonies to enrich some few of their relations and church members.

No advantage but many disadvantages have arisen to the English by the war, for about 600 men have been slain, and 12 captains, most of them brave and stout persons and of loyal principles, whilest the church members had liberty to stay at home and not hazard their persons in the wildernesse.

The losse to the English in the severall colonies, in their habitations and stock, is reckoned to amount to £150,000 there having been about 1200 houses burned, 8000 head of cattle, great and small, killed, and many thousand bushels of wheat, peas and other grain burned (of which the Massachusets colony hath not been damnifyed one third part, the great losse falling upon New Plymouth and Connecticot colonies) and upward of 3000 Indians men women and children destroyed, who if well managed would have been very serviceable to the English, which makes all manner of labour dear.

The war at present is near an end. In Plymouth colony the Indians surrender themselves to Gov. Winslow, upon mercy, and bring in all their armes, are wholly at his disposall, except life and transportation; but for all such as have been notoriously cruell to women and children, so soon as discovered they are to be executed in the sight of their fellow Indians.

The government of Boston have concluded a peace... .

1. According to Randolph, why are the colonists at least somewhat responsible for the instigation of hostilities between themselves and King Philip?
2. How would you characterize Randolph's description of King Philip and his followers? Where does Randolph's portrait of King Philip fit into one stereotypic seventeenth century image of the American Indian as a "noble savage"?

3-4   Excerpt from Cotton Mather's "Memorable Providences, Relating to Witchcrafts and Possessions" (1689)

In 1689, Cotton Mather, minister of the Old North Church in Boston, published an account of supposed witchcraft that occurred the previous year involving an Irish washerwoman named Glover. Mather's publication, entitled "Memorable Providences, Relating to Witchcrafts and Possessions," included a description of the signs of witchcraft. Owing in part to the minister's status and reputation, his commentary was widely circulated and discussed throughout Puritan New England. Samuel Parris, the Salem minister in whose house the events of 1692 were initiated, owned a copy.

Source: *Famous American Trials: Salem Witchcraft Trials, 1692*
http://www.law.umkc.edu/faculty/projects/ftrials/salem/ASA_MATH.HTM

[Some spelling has been modernized.]

Section I. There dwells at this time, in the south part of Boston, a sober and pious man, whose Name is John Goodwin, whose Trade is that of a Mason, and whose Wife (to which a Good Report gives a share with him in all the Characters of Vertue) has made him the Father of six (now living) Children. Of these Children, all but the Eldest, who works with his Father at his Calling, and the Youngest, who lives yet upon the Breast of its mother, have laboured under the direful effects of a (no less palpable than) stupendous Witchcraft. Indeed that exempted Son had also, as was thought, some lighter touches of it, in unaccountable stabbs and pains now and then upon him; as indeed every person in the Family at some time or other had, except the godly Father, and the sucking Infant, who never felt any impressions of it. But these Four Children mentioned, were handled in so sad and strange a manner, as has given matter of Discourse and Wonder to all the Contrary, and of History not unworthy to be considered by more than all the serious or the curious Readers in this New-English World.

Sect. II. The four Children (whereof the Eldest was about Thirteen, and the youngest was perhaps about a third part so many years of age) had enjoyed a Religious Education, and answered it with a very towardly Ingenuity. They had an observable Affection unto Divine and Sacred things; and those of them that were capable of it, seem'd to have such a Resentment, of their eternal Concernments as is not altogether usual. Their Parents also kept them to a continual Employment, which did more than deliver them from the Temptations of Idleness (and as young as they were, they took a delight in it) it may be as much as they should have done. In a word, Such was the whole Temper and Carriage of the Children, that there cannot easily be any thing more unreasonable, than to imagine that a Design to Dissemble could cause them to fall into any of their odd Fits; though there should not have happened, as there did, a thousand Things, wherein it was perfectly impossible for any Dissimulation of theirs to produce what scores of spectators were amazed at.

Sect. III. About Midsummer, in the year 1688, the Eldest of these Children, who is a Daughter, saw cause to examine their Washerwoman, upon their missing of some Linnen which twas fear'd she had stollen from them; and of what use this linnen might bee to serve the Witchcraft intended, the Theef's Tempter knows! This Laundress was the Daughter of an ignorant and a scandalous old Woman in the Neighbourhood; whose miserable Husband before he died, had sometimes complained of her, that she was undoubtedly a Witch, and that whenever his Head was laid, she would quickly arrive unto the punishments due to such an one. This Woman in her daughters Defence bestow'd very bad Language upon the Girl that put her to the Question; immediately upon which, the poor child became variously indisposed in her health, an visited with strange Fits, beyond those that attend an Epilepsy or a Catalepsy, or those that they call The Diseases of Astonishment.

Sect. IV. It was not long before one of her Sisters, and two of her Brothers, were seized, in order one after another with Affects like those that molested her. Within a few weeks, they were all four tortured every where in a manner s very grievous, that it would have broke an heart of stone to have seen their Agonies. Skilful Physicians were consulted for their Help, and particularly our worthy and prudent Friend Dr. Thomas Oakes, who found Himself so affronted by the Dist'empers of the children, that he concluded nothing but an hellish Witchcraft could be the Original of these Maladies. And that which yet more confirmed such Apprehension was, That for one good while, the children were tormented just in the same part of their bodies all at the same time together; and tho they saw and heard not one another's complaints, tho likewise their pains and sprains were swift like Lightening, yet when (suppose) the Neck, or the Hand, or the Back of one was Rack't, so it was at that instant with t'other too.

Sect. V. The variety of their tortures increased continually; and tho about Nine or Ten at Night they always had a Release from their miseries, and ate and slept all night for the most part indifferently well, yet in the day time they were handled with so many sorts of Ails, that it would require of us almost as much time to Relate them all, as it did of them to Endure them. Sometimes they would be Deaf, sometimes Dumb, and sometimes Blind, and often, all this at once. One while their Tongues would be drawn down their Throats; another-while they would be pull'd out upon their Chins, to a prodigious length. They would have their Mouths opened unto such a Wideness, that their Jaws went out of joint; and anon they would clap together again with a Force like that of a strong Spring-Lock. The same would happen to their Shoulder-Blades, and their Elbows, and Hand-wrists, and several of their joints. They would at times lie in a benummed condition and be drawn together as those that are ty'd Neck and Heels; and presently be stretched out, yea, drawn Backwards, to such a degree that it was fear'd the very skin of their Bellies would have crack'd. They would make most pitteous out-cries, that they were cut with Knives, and struck with Blows that they could not bear. Their Necks would be broken, so that their Neck-bone would seem dissolved unto them that felt after it; and yet on the sudden, it would become, again so stiff that there was no stirring of their Heads; yea, their Heads would be twisted almost round; and if main Force at any time obstructed a dangerous motion which they seem'd to be upon, they would roar exceedingly. Thus they lay some weeks most pittiful Spectacles; and this while as a further Demonstration of Witchcraft in these horrid Effects, when I went to Prayer by one of them, that was very desireous to hear what I said, the Child utterly lost her Hearing till our Prayer was over.

Sect. VI. It was a Religious Family that these Afflictions happened unto; and none but a Religious Contrivance to obtain Releef, would have been welcome to them. Many superstitious proposals were made unto them, by persons that were I know not who, nor what, with Arguments fetch't from I know not how much Necessity and Experience; but the distressed Parents rejected all such counsils, with a gracious Resolution, to oppose Devils with no other weapons but Prayers and Tears, unto Him that has the Chaining of them; and to try first whether Graces were not the best things to encounter Witchcrafts with. Accordingly they requested the four Ministers of Boston, with the Minister of Charlestown, to keep a Day of Prayer at their thus haunted house; which they did in the Company of some devout people there. Immediately upon this Day, the youngest of the four children was delivered, and never felt any trouble as afore. But there was yet a greater Effect of these our Applications unto our God!

Sect. VII. The Report of the Calamities of the Family for which we were thus concerned arrived now unto the ears of the Magistrates, who presently and prudently apply'd themselves, with a just vigour, to enquire into the story. The Father of the Children complained of his Neighbour, the suspected ill woman, whose name was Glover; and she being sent for by the Justices, gave such a wretched Account of her self, that they saw cause to commit her unto the Gaolers Custody. Goodwin had no proof that could have done her any Hurt; but the Hag had not power to deny her interest in the Enchantment of the Children; and I when she was asked, Whether she believed there was a God? her Answer was too blasphemous and horrible for any Pen of mine to mention. An Experiment was made, Whether she could recite the Lords Prayer; and it was found, that tho clause after clause was most carefully repeated unto her, yet when she said it after them that prompted her, she could not Possibly avoid making Nonsense of it, with some ridiculous Depravations. This Experiment I had the curiosity since to see made upon two more, and it had the same Event. Upon Commitment of this extraordinary Woman, all the Children had some present ease,; until one (related unto her) accidentally meeting one or two of them, entertained them with her Blessing, that is, Railing; upon which Three of them fell ill again, as they were before.

Sect. VIII. It was not long before the Witch thus in the Trap, was brought upon her Trial; at which, thro'the Efficacy of a Charm, I suppose, used upon her, by one or some of her Cruel the Court could receive Answers from her in one but the Irish, which was her Native Language; although she under-stood the English very well, and had accustomed her whole Family to none but that Language in her former Conversation; and therefore the Communication between the Bench and the Bar, was now cheefly convey'd by two honest and faithful men that were interpreters. It was long before she could with any direct Answers plead unto her Indictment and; when she did plead, it was with Confession rather than Denial of her Guilt. Order was given to search the old woman's house, from whence there were brought into the Court, several small Images, or Puppets, or Babies, made of Raggs, and stufft with Goat's hair, and other such Ingredients. When these were produced, the vile Woman acknowledged, that her way to torment the Objects of her malice, was by wetting of her Finger with her Spittle, and streaking of those little Images. The abused Children were then present, and the Woman still kept stooping and shrinking as one that was almost pressed to Death with a mighty Weight upon her. But one of the Images being brought unto her, immediately she started up after an odd manner, and took it into her hand; but she had no sooner taken it, than one of the Children fell into sad Fits, before the whole Assembly. This the Judges bad their just Apprehensions at; and carefully causing the Repetition of the Experiment, found again the same event of it. They asked her, Whether she had any to stand by her: She replied, She had; and looking very pertly in the Air, she added, No, He's gone. And she then confessed, that she had One, who was her Prince, with whom she maintained, I know not what Communion.

For which cause, the night after, she was heard expostulating with a Devil, for his thus deserting her; telling him that Because he had served her so basely and falsely, she had confessed all. However to make all clear, The Court appointed five or six Physicians one evening to examine her very strictly, whether she were not craz'd in her Intellectuals, and had not procured to her self by Folly and Madness the Reputation of a Witch. Diverse hours did they spend with her; and in all that while no Discourse came from her, but what was pertinent and agreeable: particularly, when they asked her, What she thought would become of her soul? she reply'd "You ask me, a very solemn Question, and I cannot well tell what to say to it." She own'd her self a Roman Catholick; and could recite her Pater Noster in Latin very readily; but there was one Clause or two alwaies too hard for her, whereof she said, "She could not repeat it, if she might have all the world." In the up-shot, the Doctors returned her Compos Mentis; and Sentence of Death was pass'd upon her.

1. What had this washerwoman done to put her under suspicion of witchcraft? What do you think might be a more tangible underlying reason for Mather's ill feeling toward her?
2. What was the experiment (trap) that "proved" Glover was a witch?

3-5 The Closing of the Frontier (1763)

The conclusion of the French and Indian War earned Britain only a short-term respite as problems regarding their newly-won western lands erupted soon thereafter. Colonial expansion beyond the Allegheny-Appalachian mountains led to clashes between white settlers and the Indian inhabitants on whose land they were encroaching. Parliament sought to keep the peace when it issued the Proclamation of 1763 prohibiting surveying and settlement west of the mountain range.

> **Source:** The Solon Law Archive
> http://www. solon.org/Constitutions/Canada/English/PreConfederation/rp_1763. html
> also in Henry Steele Commager, ed., *Documents of American History* (New York: Appleton-Century-Crofts, 1949), 47–50.

October 7, 1763
BY THE KING. A PROCLAMATION

Whereas We have taken into Our Royal Consideration the extensive and valuable Acquisitions in America, secured to our Crown by the late Definitive Treaty of Peace, concluded at Paris the 10th Day of February last; and being desirous that all Our loving Subjects, as well of our Kingdom as of our Colonies in America, may avail themselves with all convenient Speed, of the great Benefits and Advantages which must accrue therefrom to their Commerce, Manufactures, and Navigation, We have thought fit, with the Advice of our Privy Council, to issue this our Royal Proclamation, hereby to publish and declare to all our loving Subjects, that we have, with the Advice of our Said Privy Council, granted our Letters Patent, under our Great Seal of Great Britain, to erect, within the Countries and Islands ceded and confirmed to Us by the said Treaty, Four distinct and separate Governments, styled and called by the names of Quebec, East Florida, West Florida and Grenada, and limited and bounded as follows, viz.

First—The Government of Quebec bounded on the Labrador Coast by the River St. John, and from thence by a Line drawn from the Head of that River through the Lake St. John, to the South end of the Lake Nipissim; from whence the said Line, crossing the River St. Lawrence, and the Lake Champlain, in 45 Degrees of North Latitude, passes along the High Lands which divide the Rivers that empty themselves into the said River St. Lawrence from those which fall into the Sea; and also along the North Coast of the Baye des Chaleurs, and the Coast of the Gulph of St. Lawrence to Cape Rosieres, and from thence crossing the Mouth of the River St. Lawrence by the West End of the Island of Anticosti, terminates at the aforesaid River of St. John.

Secondly—The Government of East Florida, bounded to the Westward by the Gulph of Mexico and the Apalachicola River; to the Northward by a Line drawn from that part of the said River where the Chatahouchee and Flint Rivers meet, to the source of St. Mary's River, and by the course of the said River to the Atlantic Ocean; and to the Eastward and Southward by the Atlantic Ocean and the Gulph of Florida, including all Islands within Six Leagues of the Sea Coast.

Thirdly—The Government of West Florida, bounded to the Southward by the Gulph of Mexico, including all Islands within Six Leagues of the Coast, from the River Apalachicola to Lake Pontchartrain; to the Westward by the said Lake, the Lake Maurepas, and the River Mississippi; to the Northward by a Line drawn due East from that part of the River Mississippi which lies in 31 Degrees North Latitude, to the River Apalachicola or Chatahouchee; and to the Eastward by the said River.

Fourthly—The Government of Grenada, comprehending the Island of that name, together with the Grenadines, and the Islands of Dominico, St. Vincent's and Tobago. And to the end that the open and free Fishery of our Subjects may be extended to and carried on upon the Coast of Labrador, and the adjacent Islands. We have thought fit, with the advice of our said Privy Council to put all that Coast, from the River St. John's to Hudson's Streights, together with the Islands of Anticosti and Madelaine, and all other smaller Islands lying upon the said Coast, under the care and Inspection of our Governor of Newfoundland.

We have also, with the advice of our Privy Council, thought fit to annex the Islands of St. John's and Cape Breton, or Isle Royale, with the lesser Islands adjacent thereto, to our Government of Nova Scotia.

We have also, with the advice of our Privy Council aforesaid, annexed to our Province of Georgia all the Lands lying between the Rivers Alatamaha and St. Mary's.

And whereas it will greatly contribute to the speedy settling of our said new Governments, that our loving Subjects should be informed of our Paternal care, for the security of the Liberties and Properties of those who are and shall become Inhabitants thereof, We have thought fit to publish and declare, by this Our Proclamation, that We have, in the Letters Patent under our Great Seal of Great Britain, by which the said Governments are constituted, given express Power and Direction to our Governors of our Said Colonies respectively, that so soon as the state and circumstances of the said Colonies will admit thereof, they shall, with the Advice and Consent of the Members of our Council, summon and call General Assemblies within the said Governments respectively, in such Manner and Form as is used and directed in those Colonies and Provinces in America which are under our immediate Government: And We have also given Power to the said Governors, with the consent of our Said Councils, and the Representatives of the People so to be summoned as aforesaid, to make, constitute, and ordain Laws, Statutes, and Ordinances for the Public Peace, Welfare, and good Government of our said Colonies, and of the People and Inhabitants thereof, as near as may be agreeable to the Laws of England, and under such Regulations and Restrictions as are used in other Colonies; and in the mean Time, and until such Assemblies can be called as aforesaid, all Persons Inhabiting in or resorting to our Said Colonies may confide in our Royal Protection for the Enjoyment of the Benefit of the Laws of our Realm of England; for which Purpose We have given Power under our Great Seal to the Governors of our said Colonies respectively to erect and constitute, with the Advice of our said Councils respectively, Courts of Judicature and public Justice within our Said Colonies for hearing and determining all Causes, as well Criminal as Civil, according to Law and Equity, and as near as may be agreeable to the Laws of England, with Liberty to all Persons who may think themselves aggrieved by the Sentences of such Courts, in all Civil Cases. to appeal, under the usual Limitations and Restrictions, to Us in our Privy Council.

We have also thought fit, with the advice of our Privy Council as aforesaid, to give unto the Governors and Councils of our said Three new Colonies, upon the Continent full Power and Authority to settle and agree with the Inhabitants of our said new Colonies or with any other Persons who shall resort thereto, for such Lands, Tenements and Hereditaments, as are now or hereafter shall be in our Power to dispose of; and them to grant to any such Person or Persons upon such Terms, and under such moderate Quit-Rents, Services and Acknowledgments, as have been appointed and settled in our other Colonies, and under such other Conditions as shall appear to us to be necessary and expedient for the Advantage of the Grantees, and the Improvement and settlement of our said Colonies.

And Whereas, We are desirous, upon all occasions, to testify our Royal Sense and Approbation of the Conduct and bravery of the Officers and Soldiers of our Armies, and to reward the same, We do hereby command and impower our Governors of our said Three new Colonies, and all other our Governors of our several Provinces on the Continent of North America, to grant without Fee or Reward, to such reduced Officers as have served in North America during the late War, and to such Private Soldiers as have been or shall be disbanded in America, and are actually residing there, and shall personally apply for the same, the following Quantities of Lands, subject, at the Expiration of Ten Years, to the same Quit-Rents as other Lands are subject to in the Province within which they are granted, as also subject to the same Conditions of Cultivation and Improvement; viz.

To every Person having the Rank of a Field Officer—5,000 Acres.
To every Captain—3,000 Acres.
To every Subaltern or Staff Officer,—2,000 Acres.
To every Non-Commission Officer,—200 Acres.
To every Private Man—50 Acres.

We do likewise authorize and require the Governors and Commanders in Chief of all our said Colonies upon the Continent of North America to grant the like Quantities of Land, and upon the same conditions, to such reduced Officers of our Navy of like Rank as served on board our Ships of War in North America at the times of the Reduction of Louisbourg and Quebec in the late War, and who shall personally apply to our respective Governors for such Grants.

And whereas it is just and reasonable, and essential to our Interest, and the Security of our Colonies, that the several Nations or Tribes of Indians with whom We are connected, and who live under our Protection, should not be molested or disturbed in the Possession of such Parts of Our Dominions and Territories as, not having been ceded to or purchased by Us, are reserved to them, or any of them, as their Hunting Grounds. We do therefore, with the Advice of our Privy Council, declare it to be our Royal Will and Pleasure, that no Governor or Commander in Chief in any of our Colonies of Quebec, East Florida, or West Florida, do presume, upon any Pretence whatever, to grant Warrants of Survey, or pass any Patents for Lands beyond the Bounds of their respective Governments, as described in their Commissions: as also that no Governor or Commander in Chief in any of our other Colonies or Plantations in America do presume for the present, and until our further Pleasure be known, to grant Warrants of Survey, or pass Patents for any Lands beyond the Heads or Sources of any of the Rivers which fall into the Atlantic Ocean from the West and North West, or upon any Lands whatever, which, not having been ceded to or purchased by Us as aforesaid, are reserved to the said Indians, or any of them. And We do further declare it to be Our Royal Will and Pleasure, for the present as aforesaid, to reserve under our Sovereignty, Protection, and Dominion, for the use of the said Indians, all the Lands and Territories not included within the Limits of Our said Three new Governments, or within the Limits of the Territory granted to the Hudson's Bay Company, as also all the Lands and Territories lying to the Westward of the Sources of the Rivers which fall into the Sea from the West and North West as aforesaid.

And We do hereby strictly forbid, on Pain of our Displeasure, all our loving Subjects from making any Purchases or Settlements whatever, or taking Possession of any of the Lands above reserved, without our especial leave and Licence for that Purpose first obtained.

And, We do further strictly enjoin and require all Persons whatever who have either wilfully or inadvertently seated themselves upon any Lands within the Countries above described, or upon any other Lands which, not having been ceded to or purchased by Us, are, still reserved to the said Indians as aforesaid, forthwith to remove themselves from such Settlements.

And whereas great Frauds and Abuses have been committed in purchasing Lands of the Indians, to the great Prejudice of our Interests, and to the great Dissatisfaction of the said Indians: In order, therefore, to prevent such Irregularities for the future, and to the end that the Indians may be convinced of our Justice and determined Resolution to remove all reasonable Cause of Discontent, We do, with the Advice of our Privy Council strictly enjoin and require, that no private Person do presume to make any purchase from the said Indians of any Lands reserved to the said Indians, within those parts of our Colonies where, We have thought proper to allow Settlement: but that. if at any Time any of the Said Indians should be inclined to dispose of the said Lands, the same shall be Purchased only for Us, in our Name, at some public Meeting or Assembly of the said Indians, to be held for that Purpose by the Governor or Commander in Chief of our Colony respectively within which they shall lie: and in case they shall lie within the limits of any Proprietary Government, they shall be purchased only for the Use and in the name of such Proprietaries, conformable to such Directions and Instructions as We or they shall think proper to give for that Purpose: And we do, by the Advice of our Privy Council, declare and enjoin, that the Trade with the said Indians shall be free and open to all our Subjects whatever, provided that every Person who may incline to Trade with the said Indians do take out a Licence for carrying on such Trade from the Governor or Commander in Chief of any of our Colonies respectively where such Person shall reside. and also give Security to observe such Regulations as We shall at any Time think fit. by ourselves or by our Commissaries to be appointed for this Purpose, to direct and appoint for the Benefit of the said Trade.

And we do hereby authorize, enjoin, and require the Governors and Commanders in Chief of all our Colonies respectively, as well those under Our immediate Government as those under the Government and Direction of Proprietaries, to grant such Licences without Fee or Reward, taking especial Care to insert therein a Condition, that such Licence shall be void, and the Security forfeited in case the Person to whom the same is granted shall refuse or neglect to observe such Regulations as We shall think proper to prescribe as aforesaid.

And we do further expressly conjoin and require all Officers whatever, as well Military as those Employed in the Management and Direction of Indian Affairs, within the Territories reserved as aforesaid for the use of the said Indians, to seize and apprehend all Persons whatever, who standing charged with Treason, Misprisions of Treason, Murders, or other Felonies or Misdemeanors, shall fly from Justice and take Refuge in the said Territory, and to send them under a proper guard to the Colony where the Crime was committed of which they, stand accused, in order to take their Trial for the same.

Given at our Court at St. James's the 7th Day of October 1763, in the Third Year of our Reign.

GOD SAVE THE KING

1. What "type" of person would be most likely to venture forth across the Appalachians into the frontier? What could have been so appealing about these new lands recently wrested from French control?
2. Why were the colonists so troubled by the Proclamation of 1763? After all, how could the British possibly enforce the measure?

3-6 Alexander Falconbridge, The African Slave Trade (1788)

Taken from "An Account of the Slave Trade on the Coast of Africa", this selection is a vivid description of the "middle passage". Alexander Falconbridge, who was a surgeon on several slave ships, was well positioned to describe the horrors of the journey and his account became influential among English abolitionists. Later Falconbridge was named the Governor of a colony of freed slaves in Sierra Leone, Africa.

As soon as the wretched Africans, purchased at the fairs, fall into the hands of the black traders, they experience an earnest of those dreadful sufferings which they are doomed in future to undergo. And there is not the least room to doubt, but that even before they can reach the fairs, great numbers perish from cruel usage, want of food, travelling through inhospitable deserts, etc. They are brought from the places where they are purchased to Bonny, etc. in canoes; at the bottom of which they lie, having their hands tied with a kind of willow twigs, and a strict watch is kept over them. Their usage in other respects, during the time of passage, which generally lasts several days, is equally cruel. Their allowance of food is so scanty, that it is barely sufficient to support nature. They are, besides, much exposed to the violent rains which frequently fall here, being covered only with mats that afford but a slight defense; and as there is usually water at the bottom of the canoes, from their leaking, they are scarcely every dry.

Nor do these unhappying beings, after they become the property of the Europeans (from whom as a more civilized people, more humanity might naturally be expected), find their situation in the least amended. Their treatment is no less rigorous. The men Negroes, on being brought aboard the ship, are immediately fastened together, two and two, by hand-cuffs on their wrists, and irons riveted on their legs. They are then sent down between the decks, and placed in an apartment partitioned off for that purpose. The women likewise are placed in a separate room, on the same deck, but without being ironed. And an adjoining room, on the same deck is besides appointed for the boys. Thus are they placed in different apartments.

But at the same time, they are frequently stowed so close, as to admit of no other posture than lying on their sides. Neither will the height between decks, unless directly under the grating, permit them the indulgence of an erect posture; especially where there are platforms, which is generally the case. These platforms are a kind of shelf, about eight or nine feet in breadth, extending from the side of the ship towards the centre. They are placed nearly midway between the decks, at the distance of two or three feet from each deck. Upon these the Negroes are stowed in the same manner as they are on the deck underneath.

. . . About eight o'clock in the morning the Negroes are generally brought upon deck. Their irons being examined, a long chain, which is locked to a ring-bolt, fixed in the deck, is run through the rings of the shackles of the men, and then locked to another ring-bolt, fixed also in the deck. By this means fifty or sixty, and sometimes more, are fastened to one chain, in order to prevent them from rising, or endeavoring to escape. If the weather proves favorable, they are permitted to remain in that situation till four or five in the afternoon, when they are disengaged from the chain, and sent down.

. . . Upon the Negroes refusing to take sustenance, I have seen coals of fire, glowing hot, put on a shovel, and placed so near their lips, as to scorch and burn them. And this has been accompanied with threats, of forcing them to swallow the coals, if they any longer persisted in refusing to eat. These means have generally had the desired effect. I have also been credibly informed that a certain captain in the slave trade poured melted lead on such of the Negroes as obstinately refused their food.

Exercise being deemed necessary for the preservation of their health, they are sometimes obligated to dance, when the weather will permit their coming on deck. If they go about it reluctantly, or do not move with agility, they are flogged; a person standing by them all the time with at cat-o'-nine-tails in his hand for that purpose. Their music, upon these occasions, consists of a drum, sometimes with only one head; and when that is worn out, they do not scruple to make use of the bottom of one of the tubs before described. The poor wretches are frequently compelled to sing also; but when they do so, their songs are generally, as may naturally be expected, melancholy lamentations of their exile from their native country.

. . . On board some ships, the common sailors are allowed to have intercourse with such of the black women whose consent they can procure. And some of them have been known to take the inconstancy of their paramours so much to heart, as to leap overboard and drown themselves. The officers are permitted to indulge their passions among them at pleasure, and sometimes are guilty of such brutal excesses as disgrace human nature.

The hardships and inconveniences suffered by the Negroes during the passage are scarcely to be enumerated or conceived. They are far more violently affected by the seasickness than the Europeans. It frequently terminates in death, especially among the women. But the exclusion of the fresh air is among the most intolerable. For the purpose of admitting this needful refreshment, most of the ships in the slave trade are provided, between the decks, with five or six air-ports on each side of the ship, of about six inches in length, and four in breadth; in addition to which, some few ships, but not one in twenty, have what they denominate wind-sails. But whenever the sea is rough and the rain heavy, it becomes necessary to shut these, and every other conveyance by which the air is admitted. The fresh air being thus excluded, the Negroes' rooms very soon grow intolerably hot. The confined air, rendered noxious by the effluvia exhaled from their bodies, and by being repeatedly breathed, soon produces fevers and fluxes, which generally carries off great numbers of them.

. . . One morning, upon examining the place allotted for the sick Negroes, I perceived that one of them, who was so emaciated as scarcely to be able to walk, was missing, and was convinced that he must have gone overboard in the night, probably to put a more expeditious period to his sufferings. And, to conclude on this subject, I could not help being sensibly affected, on a former voyage, at observing with what apparent eagerness a black woman seized some dirt from off an African yam, and put it into her mouth, seeming to rejoice at the opportunity of possessing some of her native earth.

From these instances I think it may have been clearly deduced that the unhappy Africans are not bereft of the finer feelings, but have a strong attachment to their native country, together with a just sense of the value of liberty. And the situation of the miserable beings above described, more forcibly urges the necessity of abolishing a trade which is the source of such evils, than the most eloquent harangue, or persuasive arguments could do.

1. What conditions are the slaves subjected to by the black traders?
2. Describe the living conditions on board the European ships.
3. Identify the cruelties reported to be inflicted upon the slaves by the European sailors.

3-7 Olaudah Equiano, The Middle Passage (1788)

This account of the "middle passage" comes from one of the first writings by an ex-slave and the originator of the slave narrative. Equiano was born in Nigeria and was kidnapped into slavery at the age of eleven. After a time in the West Indies, he was sold to a Virginia planter before becoming the slave of a merchant. Years later he was able to buy his freedom and at the age of 44, he wrote "The Interesting Narrative of the Life of Olaudah Equiano, or Gustavus Vassa, The African. Written by Himself". Equiano became an abolitionist and made the expedition to settle the colony of ex-slaves at Sierra Leone.

. . . The first object which saluted my eyes when I arrived on the coast was the sea, and a slave ship, which was then riding at anchor, and waiting for its cargo. These filled me with astonishment, which was soon converted into terror when I was carried on board. I was immediately handled and tossed up to see if I were sound by some of the crew; and I was now persuaded that I had gotten into a world of bad spirits, and that they were going to kill me. Their complexions too differing so much from ours, their long hair, and the language they spoke, (which was very different from any I had ever heard) united to confirm me in this belief. Indeed such were the horrors of my views and fears at the moment, that, if ten thousand worlds had been my own, I would have freely parted with them all to have exchanged my condition with that of the meanest slave in my own country. When I looked round the ship too and saw a large furnace of copper boiling, and a multitude of black people of every description chained together, every one of their countenances expressing dejection and sorrow, I no longer doubted of my fate; and, quite overpowered with horror and anguish, I fell motionless on the deck and fainted. When I recovered a little I found some black people about me, who I believe were some of those who brought me on board, and had been receiving their pay; they talked to me in order to cheer me, but all in vain. I asked them if we were not to be eaten by those white men with horrible looks, red faces, and loose hair. They told me I was not; and one of the crew brought me a small portion of spirituous liquor in a wine glass; but, being afraid of him, I would not take it out of his hand. One of the blacks therefore took it from him and gave it to me, and I took a little down my palate, which, instead of reviving me, as they thought it would, threw me into the greatest consternation at the strange feeling it produced, having never tasted any such liquor before. Soon after this the blacks who brought me on board went off, and left me abandoned to despair. I now saw myself deprived of all chance or returning to my native country or even the least glimpse of hope of gaining the shore, which I now considered as friendly; and I even wished for my former slavery in preference to my present situation, which was filled with horrors of every kind, still heightened by my ignorance of what I was to undergo. I was not long suffered to indulge my grief; I was soon put down under the decks, and there I received such a salutation in my nostrils as I had never experienced in my life: so that, with the loathsomeness of the stench, and crying together, I became so sick and low that I was not able to eat, nor had I the least desire to taste anything. I now wished for the last friend, death, to relieve me; but soon, to my grief, two of the white men offered me eatables; and, on my refusing to eat, one of them held me fast by the hands, and laid me across I think the windlass, and tied my feet, while the other flogged me severely. I had never experienced anything of this kind before; and although, not being used to the water, I naturally feared that element the first time I saw it, yet nevertheless, could I have got over the nettings, I would have jumped over the side, but I could not; and, besides, the crew used to watch us very closely who were not chained down to the decks, lest we should leap into the water: and I have seen some of these poor African prisoners most severely cut for attempting to do so, and hourly whipped for not eating. This indeed was often the case with myself. In a little time after, amongst the poor chained men, I found some of my own nation, which in a small degree gave ease to my mind. I inquired of these what was to be done with us; they gave me to understand we were to be carried to these white people's country to work for them. I then was a little revived, and thought, if it were no worse than working, my situation was not so desperate: but still I feared I should be put to death, the white people looked and acted, as I thought, in so savage a manner; for I had never seen among any people such instances of brutal cruellty; and this not only shewn towards us blacks, but also to some of the whites themselves. One white man in particular I saw when we were permitted to be on deck, flogged so unmercifully with a large rope near the foremast, that he died in consequence of it; and they tossed him over the side as they would have done a brute. This made me fear these people the more; and I expected nothing less than to be treated in the same manner. I could not help expressing my fears and apprehensions to some of my countrymen: I asked them if these people had no country, but lived in this hollow place (the ship): they told me they did not, but came from a distant one. "Then," said I, "how comes it in all our country we never heard of them?" They told me because they lived so very far off. I then asked where were their women? had they any like themselves? "and why," said I, "do we not see them?" they answered, because they were left behind. . . .

The stench of the hold while we were on the coast was so intolerably loathsome, that it was dangerous to remain there for any time, and some of us had been permitted to stay on the deck for the fresh air; but now that the whole ship's cargo were confined together, it became absolutely pestilential. The closeness of the place, and the heat of the climate, added to the number in the ship, which was so crowded that each had scarcely room to turn himself, almost suffocated us. This produced copious perspirations, so that the air soon became unfit for respiration, from a variety of loathsome smells,

46

and brought on a sickness among the slaves, of which many died, thus falling victims to the improvident avarice, as I may call it, of their purchasers. This wretched situation was again aggravated by the galling of the chains, now become insupportable; and the filth of the necessary tubs, into which the children often fell, and were almost suffocated. The shrieks of the women, and the groans of the dying, rendered the whole a scene of horror almost inconceivable. Happily perhaps for myself I was soon reduced so low here that it was thought necessary to keep me almost always on deck; and from my extreme youth I was not put in fetters. In this situation I expected every hour to share the fate of my companions, some of whom were almost daily brought upon deck at the point of death, which I began to hope would soon put an end to my miseries. Often did I think many of the inhabitants of the deep much more happy than myself. I envied them the freedom they enjoyed, and as often wished I could change my condition for theirs. Every circumstance I met with served only to render my state more painful, and heighten my apprehensions, and my opinion of the cruelty of the whites. One day they had taken a number of fishes; and when they had killed and satisfied themselves with as many as they thought fit, to our astonishment who were on the deck, rather than give any of them to us to eat as we expected, they tossed the remaining fish into the sea again, although we begged and prayed for some as well as we could, but in vain; and some of my countrymen, being pressed by hunger, took an opportunity, when they thought no one saw them, of trying to get a little privately; but they were discovered, and the attempt procured them some very severe floggings. . . .

. . . I and some few more slaves, that were not saleable amongst the rest, from very much fretting, were shipped off in a sloop for North America. . . . While I was in this plantation [in Virginia] the gentleman, to whom I suppose the estate belonged, being unwell, I was one day sent for to his dwelling house to fan him; when I came into the room where he was I was very much affrighted at some things I saw, and the more so as I had seen a black woman slave as I came through the house, who was cooking the dinner, and the poor creature was cruelly loaded with various kinds of iron machines; she had one particularly on her head, which locked her mouth so fast that she could scarcely speak; and could not eat nor drink. I was much astonished and shocked at this contrivance, which I afterwards learned was called the iron muzzle . . .

1. Note the author's beliefs regarding the intent and character of his captors on board the ship. In what terms does he describe his captors? What does he assume is their purpose in capturing him?
2. How does he view the prospect of work once they reach their destination?
3. Identify and analyze the author's conclusions about the civilization of his captors based on their behavior.

PART FOUR
PRELUDE TO REVOLUTION

4-1 Benjamin Franklin, Testimony Against the Stamp Act (1766)

In 1765 Parliament passed the first internal tax on the colonists, known as the Stamp Act. Benjamin Franklin was a colonial agent in London at the time and, as colonial opposition to the act grew, found himself representing these views to the British government. In his testimony from Parliament he describes the role of taxes in Pennsylvania and the economic relationship between the colonies and the mother country.

Q. What is your name, and place of abode?

A. Franklin, of Philadelphia.

Q. Do the Americans pay any considerable taxes among themselves?

A. Certainly many, and very heavy taxes.

Q. What are the present taxes in Pennsylvania, laid by the laws of the colony?

A. There are taxes on all estates, real and personal; a poll tax; a tax on all offices, professions, trades, and businesses, according to their profits; an excise on all wine, rum, and other spirit; and a duty of ten pounds per head on all Negroes imported, with some other duties.

Q. For what purposes are those taxes laid?

A. For the support of the civil and military establishments of the country, and to discharge the heavy debt contracted in the last [Seven Years'] war. . . .

Q. Are not all the people very able to pay those taxes?

A. No. The frontier counties, all along the continent, have been frequently ravaged by the enemy and greatly impoverished, are able to pay very little tax. . . .

Q. Are not the colonies, from their circumstances, very able to pay the stamp duty?

A. In my opinion there is not gold and silver enough in the colonies to pay the stamp duty for one year.

Q. Don't you know that the money arising from the stamps was all to be laid out in America?

A. I know it is appropriated by the act to the American service; but it will be spent in the conquered colonies, where the soldiers are, not in the colonies that pay it. . . .

Q. Do you think it right that America should be protected by this country and pay no part of the expense?

A. That is not the case. The colonies raised, clothed, and paid, during the last war, near 25,000 men, and spent many millions.

Q. Where you not reimbursed by Parliament?

A. We were only reimbursed what, in your opinion, we had advanced beyond our proportion, or beyond what might reasonably be expected from us; and it was a very small part of what we spent. Pennsylvania, in particular, disbursed about 500,000 pounds, and the reimbursements, in the whole, did not exceed 60,000 pounds. . . .

Q. Do you think the people of America would submit to pay the stamp duty, if it was moderated?

A. No, never, unless compelled by force of arms. . . .

Q. What was the temper of America towards Great Britain before the year 1763?

A. The best in the world. They submitted willingly to the government of the Crown, and paid, in all their courts, obedience to acts of Parliament. . . .

Q. What is your opinion of a future tax, imposed on the same principle with that of the Stamp Act? How would the Americans receive it?

A. Just as they do this. They would not pay it.

Q. Have not you heard of the resolutions of this House, and of the House of Lords, asserting the right of Parliament relating to America, including a power to tax the people there?

A. Yes, I have heard of such resolutions.

Q. What will be the opinion of the Americans on those resolutions?

A. They will think them unconstitutional and unjust.

Q. Was it an opinion in America before 1763 that the Parliament had no right to lay taxes and duties there?

A. I never heard any objection to the right of laying duties to regulate commerce; but a right to lay internal taxes was never supposed to be in Parliament, as we are not represented there. . . .

Q. Did the Americans ever dispute the controlling power of Parliament to regulate the commerce?

A. No.

Q. Can anything less than a military force carry the Stamp Act into execution?

A. I do not see how a military force can be applied to that purpose.

Q. Why may it not?

A. Suppose a military force sent into America; they will find nobody in arms; what are they then to do? They cannot force a man to take stamps who chooses to do without them. They will not find a rebellion; they may indeed make one.

Q. If the act is not repealed, what do you think will be the consequences?

A. A total loss of the respect and affection the people of America bear to this country, and of all the commerce that depends on that respect and affection.

Q. How can the commerce be affected?

A. You will find that, if the act is not repealed, they will take very little of your manufactures in a short time.

Q. Is it in their power to do without them?

A. I think they may very well do without them.

Q. Is it their interest not to take them?

A. The goods they take from Britain are either necessaries, mere conveniences, or superfluities. The first, as cloth, etc., with a little industry they can make at home; the second they can do without till they are able to provide them among themselves; and the last, which are mere articles of fashion, purchased and consumed because the fashion in a respected country; but will now be detested and rejected. The people have already struck off, by general agreement, the use of all goods fashionable in mourning. . . .

Q. If the Stamp Act should be repealed, would it induce the assemblies of America to acknowledge the right of Parliament to tax them, and would they erase their resolutions [against the Stamp Act]?

A. No, never.

Q. Is there no means of obliging them to erase those resolutions?

A. None that I know of; they will never do it, unless compelled by force of arms.

Q. Is there a power on earth that can force them to erase them?

A. No power, how great soever, can force men to change their opinions. . . .

Q. What used to be the pride of the Americans?

A. To indulge in the fashions and manufactures of Great Britain.

Q. What is now their pride?

A. To wear their old clothes over again, till they can make new ones.

1. According to Franklin, how had Americian sentiment toward England changed between 1763 and the time of this testimony? What factors led to this change?
2. What kind of a rebellion does Franklin suggest may occur if taxes on goods manufactured in England continues?
3. What does Franklin mean by saying that the pride of America is wearing their old clothes over again, till they can make new ones"? What does this day about American attitudes toward England?

4-2 The Boston "Massacre" or Victims of Circumstance? (1770)

The tragic event labeled as a "massacre" for generations to come grew in part out of the escalating tensions in Boston between the city's discontented inhabitants and the embodiment of the Crown's authority—British soldiers—dubbed "lobster backs" by their detractors. John Adams, who later defended the indicted soldiers in court, said his clients had been provoked by a "motley rabble of saucy boys, negroes and mulattoes, Irish teagues and outlandish Jack tars." Responsibility for the events that occurred in front of the Customs House on March 5, 1770, undoubtedly lay on both sides, but it was hardly a massacre—no matter how one looks at it.

> **Source:** *The American Colonist's Library: Primary Source Documents Pertaining to Early American History*
> http://personal.pitnet.net/primarysources/boston.html
> http://www.ukans.edu/carrie/docs/texts/preston.html

BOSTON GAZETTE AND COUNTRY JOURNAL, MARCH 12, 1770.

On the evening of Monday, being the fifth current, several soldiers of the 29th Regiment were seen parading the streets with their drawn cutlasses and bayonets, abusing and wounding numbers of the inhabitants. A few minutes after nine o'clock four youths, named Edward Archbald, William Merchant, Francis Archbald, and John Leech, jun., came down Cornhill together, and separating at Doctor Loring's corner, the two former were passing the narrow alley leading to Murray's barrack in which was a soldier brandishing a broad sword of an uncommon size against the walls, out of which he struck fire plentifully. A person of mean countenance armed with a large cudgel bore him company. Edward Archbald admonished Mr. Merchant to take care of the sword, on which the soldier turned round and struck Archbald on the arm, then pushed at Merchant and pierced through his clothes inside the arm close to the armpit and grazed the skin. Merchant then struck the soldier with a short stick he had; and the other person ran to the barrack and brought with him two soldiers, one armed with a pair of tongs, the other with a shovel. He with the tongs pursued Archbald back through the alley, collared and laid him over the head with the tongs. The noise brought people together; and John Hicks, a young lad, coming up, knocked the soldier down but let him get up again; and more lads gathering, drove them back to the barrack where the boys stood some time as it were to keep them in. In less than a minute ten or twelve of them came out with drawn cutlasses, clubs, and bayonets and set upon the unarmed boys and young folk who stood them a little while but, finding the inequality of their equipment, dispersed. On hearing the noise, one Samuel Atwood came up to see what was the matter; and entering the alley from dock square, heard the latter part of the combat; and when the boys had dispersed he met the ten or twelve soldiers aforesaid rushing down the alley towards the square and asked them if they intended to murder people? They answered Yes, by G-d, root and branch! With that one of them struck Mr. Atwood with a club which was repeated by another; and being unarmed, he turned to go off and received a wound on the left shoulder which reached the bone and gave him much pain. Retreating a few steps, Mr. Atwood met two officers and said, gentlemen, what is the matter? They answered, you'll see by and by. Immediately after, those heroes appeared in the square, asking where were the boogers? where were the cowards? But notwithstanding their fierceness to naked men, one of them advanced towards a youth who had a split of a raw stave in his hand and said, damn them, here is one of them. But the young man seeing a person near him with a drawn sword and good cane ready to support him, held up his stave in defiance; and they quietly passed by him up the little alley by Mr. Silsby's to King Street where they attacked single and unarmed persons till they raised much clamour, and then turned down Cornhill Street, insulting all they met in like manner and pursuing some to their very doors. Thirty or forty persons, mostly lads, being by this means gathered in King Street, Capt. Preston with a party of men with charged bayonets, came from the main guard to the commissioner's house, the soldiers pushing their bayonets, crying, make way! They took place by the custom house and, continuing to push to drive the people off, pricked some in several places, on which they were clamorous and, it is said, threw snow balls. On this, the Captain commanded them to fire; and more snow balls coming, he again said, damn you, fire, be the consequence what it will! One soldier then fired, and a townsman with a cudgel struck him over the hands with such force that he dropped his firelock; and, rushing forward, aimed a blow at the Captain's head which grazed his hat and fell pretty heavy upon his arm. However, the soldiers continued the fire successively till seven or eight or, as some say, eleven guns were discharged.

CAPTAIN THOMAS PRESTON'S ACCOUNT OF THE BOSTON MASSACRE

It is [a] matter of too great notoriety to need any proofs that the arrival of his Majesty's troops in Boston was extremely obnoxious to its inhabitants. They have ever used all means in their power to weaken the regiments, and to bring them into contempt by promoting and aiding desertions, and with impunity, even where there has been the clearest evidence of the fact, and by grossly and falsely propagating untruths concerning them. On the arrival of the 64th and 65th their ardour seemingly began to abate; it being too expensive to buy off so many, and attempts of that kind rendered too dangerous from the numbers.

One of their justices, most thoroughly acquainted with the people and their intentions, on the trial of a man of the 14th Regiment, openly and publicly in the hearing of great numbers of people and from the seat of justice, declared "that the soldiers must now take care of themselves, nor trust too much to their arms, for they were but a handful; that the inhabitants carried weapons concealed under their clothes, and would destroy them in a moment, if they pleased". This, considering the malicious temper of the people, was an alarming circumstance to the soldiery. Since which several disputes have happened between the townspeople and the soldiers of both regiments, the former being encouraged thereto by the countenance of even some of the magistrates, and by the protection of all the party against government. In general such disputes have been kept too secret from the officers. On the 2d instant two of the 29th going through one Gray's ropewalk, the rope-makers insultingly asked them if they would empty a vault. This unfortunately had the desired effect by provoking the soldiers, and from words they went to blows. Both parties suffered in this afftay, and finally the soldiers retired to their quarters. The officers, on the first knowledge of this transaction, took every precaution in their power to prevent any ill consequence. Notwithstanding which, single quarrels could not be prevented, the inhabitants constantly provoking and abusing the soldiery. The insolence as well as utter hatred of the inhabitants to the troops increased daily, insomuch that Monday and Tuesday, the 5th and 6th instant, were privately agreed on for a general engagement, in consequence of which several of the militia came from the country armed to join their friends, menacing to destroy any who should oppose them. This plan has since been discovered.

On Monday night about 8 o'clock two soldiers were attacked and beat. But the party of the townspeople in order to carry matters to the utmost length, broke into two meeting houses and rang the alarm bells, which I supposed was for fire as usual, but was soon undeceived. About 9 some of the guard came to and informed me the town inhabitants were assembling to attack the troops, and that the bells were ringing as the signal for that purpose and not for fire, and the beacon intended to be fired to bring in the distant people of the country. This, as I was captain of the day, occasioned my repairing immediately to the main guard. In my way there I saw the people in great commotion, and heard them use the most cruel and horrid threats against the troops. In a few minutes after I reached the guard, about 100 people passed it and went towards the custom house where the king's money is lodged. They immediately surrounded the sentry posted there, and with clubs and other weapons threatened to execute their vengeance on him. I was soon informed by a townsman their intention was to carry off the soldier from his post and probably murder him. On which I desired him to return for further intelligence, and he soon came back and assured me he heard the mobb declare they would murder him. This I feared might be a prelude to their plundering the king's chest. I immediately sent a noncommissioned officer and 12 men to protect both the sentry and the king's money, and very soon followed myself to prevent, if possible, all disorder, fearing lest the officer and soldiers, by the insults and provocations of the rioters, should be thrown off their guard and commit some rash act. They soon rushed through the people, and by charging their bayonets in half-circles, kept them at a little distance. Nay, so far was I from intending the death of any person that I suffered the troops to go to the spot where the unhappy affair took place without any loading in their pieces; nor did I ever give orders for loading them. This remiss conduct in me perhaps merits censure; yet it is evidence, resulting from the nature of things, which is the best and surest that can be offered, that my intention was not to act offensively, but the contrary part, and that not without compulsion. The mob still increased and were more outrageous, striking their clubs or bludgeons one against another, and calling out, come on you rascals, you bloody backs, you lobster scoundrels, fire if you dare, G-d damn you, fire and be damned, we know you dare not, and much more such language was used. At this time I was between the soldiers and the mob, parlaying with, and endeavouring all in my power to persuade them to retire peaceably, but to no purpose. They advanced to the points of the bayonets, struck some of them and even the muzzles of the pieces, and seemed to be endeavouring to close with the soldiers. On which some well behaved persons asked me if the guns were charged. I replied yes. They then asked me if I intended to order the men to fire. I answered no, by no means, observing to them that I was advanced before the muzzles of the men's pieces, and must fall a sacrifice if they fired; that the soldiers were upon the half cock and charged bayonets, and my giving the word fire under those circumstances would prove me to be no officer. While I was thus speaking, one of the soldiers having received a severe blow with a stick, stepped a little on one side and instantly fired, on which turning to and asking him why he fired without orders, I was struck with a club on my arm, which for some time deprived me of the use of it, which blow had it been placed on my head, most probably would have destroyed me.

On this a general attack was made on the men by a great number of heavy clubs and snowballs being thrown at them, by which all our lives were in imminent danger, some persons at the same time from behind calling out, damn your bloods—why don't you fire. Instantly three or four of the soldiers fired, one after another, and directly after three more in the same confusion and hurry. The mob then ran away, except three unhappy men who instantly expired, in which number was Mr. Gray at whose rope-walk the prior quarrels took place; one more is since dead, three others are dangerously, and four slightly wounded. The whole of this melancholy affair was transacted in almost 20 minutes. On my asking the soldiers why they fired without orders, they said they heard the word fire and supposed it came from me. This might be the case

51

as many of the mob called out fire, fire, but I assured the men that I gave no such order; that my words were, don't fire, stop your firing. In short, it was scarcely possible for the soldiers to know who said fire, or don't fire, or stop your firing. On the people's assembling again to take away the dead bodies, the soldiers supposing them coming to attack them, were making ready to fire again, which I prevented by striking up their firelocks with my hand. Immediately after a townsman came and told me that 4 or 5000 people were assembled in the next street, and had sworn to take my life with every man's with me. On which I judged it unsafe to remain there any longer, and therefore sent the party and sentry to the main guard, where the street is narrow and short, there telling them off into street firings, divided and planted them at each end of the street to secure their rear, momently expecting an attack, as there was a constant cry of the inhabitants to arms, to arms, turn out with your guns; and the town drums beating to arms, I ordered my drums to beat to arms, and being soon after joined by the different companies of the 29th regiment, I formed them as the guard into street firings. The 14th regiment also got under arms but remained at their barracks. I immediately sent a sergeant with a party to Colonel Dalrymple, the commanding officer, to acquaint him with every particular. Several officers going to join their regiment were knocked down by the mob, one very much wounded and his sword taken from him. The lieutenant-governor and Colonel Carr soon after met at the head of the 29th regiment and agreed that the regiment should retire to their barracks, and the people to their houses, but I kept the picket to strengthen the guard. It was with great difficulty that the lieutenant-governor prevailed on the people to be quiet and retire. At last they all went off, excepting about a hundred.

A Council was immediately called, on the breaking up of which three justices met and issued a warrant to apprehend me and eight soldiers. On hearing of this procedure I instantly went to the sheriff and surrendered myself, though for the space of 4 hours I had it in my power to have made my escape, which I most undoubtedly should have attempted and could easily executed, had I been the least conscious of any guilt. On the examination before the justices, two witnesses swore that I gave the men orders to fire. The one testified he was within two feet of me; the other that I swore at the men for not firing at the first word. Others swore they heard me use the word "fire," but whether do or do not fire, they could not say; others that they heard the word fire, but could not say if it came from me. The next day they got 5 or 6 more to swear I gave the word to fire. So bitter and inveterate are many of the malcontents here that they are industriously using every method to fish out evidence to prove it was a concerted scheme to murder the inhabitants. Others are infusing the utmost malice and revenge into the minds of the people who are to be my jurors by false publications, votes of towns, and all other artifices. That so from a settled rancour against the officers and troops in general, the suddenness of my trial after the affair while the people's minds are all greatly inflamed, I am, though perfectly innocent, under most unhappy circumstances, having nothing in reason to expect but the loss of life in a very ignominous manner, without the interposition of his Majesty's royal goodness.

1. Although each is rather self-serving, which account of the Boston "Massacre" is more believable? Why?
2. Why do you think the occurrence on March 5, 1770, was (and still is) referred to as the "Boston Massacre?"

4-3   John Andrews to William Barrell, Letter Regarding the Boston Tea Party (1773)

In an attempt to support the badly mismanaged British East India Company, Parliament authorized the company to send its tea directly to its own agents in the American colonies, bypassing the usual middlemen. In this way, the company's agents could undersell American retailers and even smugglers, giving the British East India Company a virtual monopoly on teaÑthe most popular beverage in colonial AmericaÑin the colonies. This Parliamentary interference in American commerce was unacceptable to many, especially in Boston, where the memory of the "massacre" was still fresh. On November 27, 1773, three ship-loads of tea arrived in Boston, but were not allowed to unload their cargo. Two nights later, Bostonians held a meeting, and decided to send the tea back to EnglandÑwithout paying the tax (three pence per pound) on it. Governor Hutchinson of Massachusetts responded by saying that the ships could certainly leave, but not without paying the tax on the cargo to the colony (this was a very important source of revenue for the colony). Two weeks later, on the night of December 16, a group of colonists, rather thinly disguised as Mohawk Indians, boarded the ships and dumped the tea into Boston Harbor.

Source: *Proceedings of the Massachusetts Historical Society,* 1st series, vol. 8 (Boston: Massachusetts Historical Society, 1864–1865), pp. 324–326.

December 18th.

However precarious our situation may be, yet *such* is the present calm composure of the people that a stranger would hardly think that ten thousand pounds sterling of the East India Company's *tea* was destroy'd the night, or rather evening before last, yet its a serious truth; and if your's, together with ye other Southern provinces, should rest satisfied with *their* quota being stor'd, poor Boston will feel the whole weight of ministerial vengeance. However, its the opinion of most. people that we stand an equal chance now, whether troops are sent in consequence of it or not; whereas, had it been stor'd, we should inevitably have had 'em, to enforce the sale of it.

The affair was transacted with the greatest regularity and despatch. Mr. Rotch finding he exposed himself not only to the loss of his ship but for ye value of the tea in case he sent her back with it, *without a clearance from the custom house,* as ye Admiral kept a ship in readiness to make a seizure of it whenever it should sail under *those circumstances;* therefore declin'd complying with his former promises, and absolutely declar'd his vessel should not carry it, without a *proper* clearance could be procur'd or he to be indemnified for the value of her: Ñwhen a general muster was assembled, from this and all ye neighbouring towns, to the number of five or six thousand, at 10 o'clock Thursday morning in the Old South Meeting house, where they pass'd a *unanimous* vote that the *Tea* should go out of the *harbour* that afternoon, and sent a committee with Mr. Rotch to ye. Custom house to *demand* a clearance, which the collector told 'em was not in his power to give, without the duties being first paid. They then sent Mr. Rotch to Milton, to ask a pass from ye Governor, who sent for answer, that "consistent with the rules of government and his duty to the King he could not grant one without they produc'd a previous clearance from the office." ÑBy the time he return'd with this message the candles were light in [the] house, and upon reading it, such prodigious shouts were made, that induc'd me, while drinking -tea at home, to go out and know the cause of it. The house was so crouded I could get no farther than ye porch, when I found the mod-erator was just declaring the meeting to be *dissolv'd,* which caused another general shout, out doors and in, and three cheers. What with that, and the consequent noise of breaking up the meeting, you'd thought that the inhabitants of the infernal regions had broke loose. For my part, I went contentedly home and finish'd my tea, but was soon inform'd what was going forward: but still not crediting it without ocular demonstration, I went and was *satisfied.* They muster'd I'm told, upon Fort Hill, to the number of about two hundred, and procceded, two by two, to Griffin's wharf, where Hall, Bruce, and Coffin lay, each with 114 chests of the *ill fated* article on board; the two former with *only* that article, but ye latter arriv'd at ye wharf only ye day before, was freighted with a large quantity of other goods, which they took the *greatest* care not to injure in the least, and before *nine* o'clock in ye evening, every chest from on board the three vessels was knock'd to pieces and flung over ye sides.

They say the actors were *Indians* from *Narragansett.* Whether they were or not, to a transient observer they appear'd as such, being cloath'd in Blankets with the heads muffled, and copper color'd countenances, being, each arm'd with a hatchet or axe, and pair pistols, nor was their dialect different from what I conceive these geniusses to *speak,* as their jargon was unintelligible to all but themselves. Not the least insult was offer'd to any person, save one Captain Conner, a letter of horses in this place, not many years since remov'd from *dear Ireland,* who had ript up the lining of his coat and waistcoat under the arms, and watch-ing, his opportunity had nearly fill'd them with tea, but being detected, was handled pretty roughly. They not only stripp'd him of his cloaths, but gave him a coat of mud, with a severe bruising into the bargain; and nothing but their utter aversion to make any disturbance pre-vented his being tar'd and feather'd.

Should not have troubled you with this, by this Post, hadn't I thought you would be glad of a more particular account of so *impor-tant a transaction,* than you could have obtain'd by common report; and if it affords my brother but a *temporary* amusement, I shall be more than repaid for the trouble of writing it. . ..

Sunday Evening. [December 19th.]

I give you joy of your easy riddance of *the banefull herb;* being just inform'd by ye arrival of the post, that it's gone from whence it came. You may bless your stars that you have not a HÑn and board of Commissioners resident with you. Ñ I forgot to acquaint you last evening that *Loring,* in a brig belonging to *Clark,* one of ye consignees, is on sbore at ye back of Cape Cod, drove thither by a storm last Fryday week, who has the last quota of Tea for this place, being 58 chests, which compleats the 400. Ñ Am inform'd some *Indians* were met on ye road to Plimouth, which is almost fifty miles this side of Cape Cod. Its unlucky that Loring has ye lamps on board for illuminating our streets. Am sorry if they are lost, as we shall be depriv'd of their benefit this winter in consequence of it.

1. As an observer of the Tea Party, what are John Andrews' most notable observations regarding the event? What are his impressions of the participants and their actions?
2. How has Boston set an example for the nation, as suggested in the opening of the letter dated December 18? What may be the consequences of these.

PART FIVE
THE AMERICAN REVOLUTION

5-1 A Freelance Writer Urges His Readers To Use Common Sense (1776)

In January 1776, Thomas Paine, a Philadelphia journalist and essayist, published a pamphlet entitled *Common Sense*. While other political tracts advocated protest against Parliament, Paine's political pamphlet placed the blame for colonial suffering directly on George III. Moreover, Paine urged his readers to abandon the king and declare independence. *Common Sense* became the equivalent of a best-seller, with over 150,000 copies in circulation during the first three months of its publication, and was no doubt an influence upon Thomas Jefferson when he drafted the Declaration of Independence.

> **Source:** *A Hypertext on American History From the Colonial Period Until Modern Times*
> http://odur.let.rug.nl/~usa/D/1776-1800/paine/CM/sense03.htm

MANKIND being originally equals in the order of creation, the equality could only be destroyed by some subsequent circumstance; the distinctions of rich, and poor, may in a great measure be accounted for, and that without having recourse to the harsh, ill-sounding names of oppression and avarice. Oppression is often the consequence, but seldom or never the means of riches; and though avarice will preserve a man from being necessitously poor, it generally makes him too timorous to be wealthy.

But there is another and greater distinction for which no truly natural or religious reason can be assigned, and that is, the distinction of men into KINGS and SUBJECTS. Male and female are the distinctions of nature, good and bad the distinctions of heaven; but how a race of men came into the world so exalted above the rest, and distinguished like some new species, is worth enquiring into, and whether they are the means of happiness or of misery to mankind.

In the early ages of the world, according to the scripture chronology, there were no kings; the consequence of which was there were no wars; it is the pride of kings which throw mankind into confusion. Holland without a king hath enjoyed more peace for this last century than any of the monarchial governments in Europe. Antiquity favors the same remark; for the quiet and rural lives of the first patriarchs hath a happy something in them, which vanishes away when we come to the history of Jewish royalty.

Government by kings was first introduced into the world by the Heathens, from whom the children of Israel copied the custom. It was the most prosperous invention the Devil ever set on foot for the promotion of idolatry. The Heathens paid divine honors to their deceased kings, and the Christian world hath improved on the plan by doing the same to their living ones. How impious is the title of sacred majesty applied to a worm, who in the midst of his splendor is crumbling into dust.

As the exalting one man so greatly above the rest cannot be justified on the equal rights of nature, so neither can it be defended on the authority of scripture; for the will of the Almighty, as declared by Gideon and the prophet Samuel, expressly disapproves of government by kings. All anti-monarchial parts of scripture have been very smoothly glossed over in monarchial governments, but they undoubtedly merit the attention of countries which have their governments yet to form. 'Render unto Caesar the things which are Caesar's' is the scriptural doctrine of courts, yet it is no support of monarchial government, for the Jews at that time were without a king, and in a state of vassalage to the Romans.

Near three thousand years passed away from the Mosaic account of the creation, till the Jews under a national delusion requested a king. Till then their form of government (except in extraordinary cases, where the Almighty interposed) was a kind of republic administered by a judge and the elders of the tribes. Kings they had none, and it was held sinful to acknowledge any being under that title but the Lords of Hosts. And when a man seriously reflects on the idolatrous homage which is paid to the persons of Kings, he need not wonder, that the Almighty, ever jealous of his honor, should disapprove of a form of government which so impiously invades the prerogative of heaven.

Monarchy is ranked in scripture as one of the sins of the Jews, for which a curse in reserve is denounced against them. The history of that transaction is worth attending to. The children of Israel being oppressed by the Midianites, Gideon marched against them with a small army, and victory, thro' the divine interposition, decided in his favor. The Jews elate with success, and attributing it to the generalship of Gideon, proposed making him a king, saying, Rule thou over us, thou and thy son and thy son's son. Here was temptation in its fullest extent; not a kingdom only, but an hereditary one, but Gideon in the piety of his soul replied, I will not rule over you, neither shall my son rule over you, THE LORD SHALL RULE OVER YOU. Words need not be more explicit; Gideon doth not decline the honor but denieth their right to give it; neither doth he compliment them with invented declarations of his thanks, but in the positive stile of a prophet charges them with disaffection to their proper sovereign, the King of Heaven.

About one hundred and thirty years after this, they fell again into the same error. The hankering which the Jews had for the idolatrous customs of the Heathens, is something exceedingly unaccountable; but so it was, that laying hold of the misconduct of Samuel's two sons, who were entrusted with some secular concerns, they came in an abrupt and clamorous manner to Samuel, saying, Behold thou art old and thy sons walk not in thy ways, now make us a king to judge us like all the other nations. And here we cannot but observe that their motives were bad, viz. that they might be like unto other nations, i. e. the

Heathens, whereas their true glory laid in being as much unlike them as possible. But the thing displeased Samuel when they said, give us a king to judge us; and Samuel prayed unto the Lord, and the Lord said unto Samuel, Hearken unto the voice of the people in all that they say unto thee, for they have not rejected thee, but they have rejected me, THE I SHOULD NOT REIGN OVER THEM. According to all the works which have done since the day; wherewith they brought them up out of Egypt, even unto this day; wherewith they have forsaken me and served other Gods; so do they also unto thee. Now therefore hearken unto their voice, howbeit, protest solemnly unto them and show them the manner of the king that shall reign over them, i. e. not of any particular king, but the general manner of the kings of the earth, whom Israel was so eagerly copying after. And notwithstanding the great distance of time and difference of manners, the character is still in fashion, And Samuel told all the words of the Lord unto the people, that asked of him a king. And he said, This shall be the manner of the king that shall reign over you; he will take your sons and appoint them for himself for his chariots, and to be his horsemen, and some shall run before his chariots (this description agrees with the present mode of impressing men) and he will appoint him captains over thousands and captains over fifties, and will set them to ear his ground and to read his harvest, and to make his instruments of war, and instruments of his chariots; and he will take your daughters to be confectioneries and to be cooks and to be bakers (this describes the expense and luxury as well as the oppression of kings) and he will take your fields and your olive yards, even the best of them, and give them to his servants; and he will take the tenth of your seed, and of your vineyards, and give them to his officers and to his servants (by which we see that bribery, corruption, and favoritism are the standing vices of kings) and he will take the tenth of your men servants, and your maid servants, and your goodliest young men and your asses, and put them to his work; and he will take the tenth of your sheep, and ye shall be his servants, and ye shall cry out in that day because of your king which ye shall have chosen, AND THE LORD WILL NOT HEAR YOU IN THAT DAY. This accounts for the continuation of monarchy; neither do the characters of the few good kings which have lived since, either sanctify the title, or blot out the sinfulness of the origin; the high encomium given of David takes no notice of him officially as a king, but only as a man after God's own heart. Nevertheless the People refused to obey the voice of Samuel, and they said. Nay, but we will have a king over us, that we may be like all the nations, and that our king may judge us, and go out before us and fight our battles. Samuel continued to reason with them, but to no purpose; he set before them their ingratitude, but all would not avail; and seeing them fully bent on their folly, he cried out, I will call unto the Lord, and he shall sent thunder and rain (which then was a punishment, being the time of wheat harvest) that ye may perceive and see that your wickedness is great which ye have done in the sight of the Lord, IN ASKING YOU A KING. So Samuel called unto the Lord, and the Lord sent thunder and rain that day, and all the people greatly feared the Lord and Samuel And all the people said unto Samuel, Pray for thy servants unto the Lord thy God that we die not, for WE HAVE ADDED UNTO OUR SINS THIS EVIL, TO ASK A KING. These portions of scripture are direct and positive. They admit of no equivocal construction. That the Almighty hath here entered his protest against monarchial government is true, or the scripture is false. And a man hath good reason to believe that there is as much of king-craft, as priest-craft in withholding the scripture from the public in Popish countries. For monarchy in every instance is the Popery of government.

To the evil of monarchy we have added that of hereditary succession; and as the first is a degradation and lessening of ourselves, so the second, claimed as a matter of right, is an insult and an imposition on posterity. For all men being originally equals, no one by birth could have a right to set up his own family in perpetual preference to all others for ever, and though himself might deserve some decent degree of honors of his contemporaries, yet his descendants might be far too unworthy to inherit them. One of the strongest natural proofs of the folly of hereditary right in kings, is, that nature disapproves it, otherwise she would not so frequently turn it into ridicule by giving mankind an ass for a lion.

Secondly, as no man at first could possess any other public honors than were bestowed upon him, so the givers of those honors could have no power to give away the right of posterity, and though they might say 'We choose you for our head,' they could not, without manifest injustice to their children, say 'that your children and your children's children shall reign over ours for ever.' Because such an unwise, unjust, unnatural compact might (perhaps) in the next succession put them under the government of a rogue or a fool. Most wise men, in their private sentiments, have ever treated hereditary right with contempt; yet it is one of those evils, which when once established is not easily removed; many submit from fear, others from superstition, and the more powerful part shares with the king the plunder of the rest.

This is supposing the present race of kings in the world to have had an honorable origin; whereas it is more than probable, that could we take off the dark covering of antiquity, and trace them to their first rise, that we should find the first of them nothing better than the principal ruffian of some restless gang, whose savage manners of preeminence in subtlety obtained him the title of chief among plunderers; and who by increasing in power, and extending his depredations, overawed the quiet and defenseless to purchase their safety by frequent contributions. Yet his electors could have no idea of giving hereditary right to his descendants, because such a perpetual exclusion of themselves was incompatible with the free and unrestrained principles they professed to live by. Wherefore, hereditary succession in the early ages of monarchy could not take place as a matter of claim, but as something casual or complemental; but as few or no records were extant in those days, and traditionary history stuffed with fables, it was very easy, after the lapse of a few generations, to trump up some superstitious tale, conveniently timed, Mahomet like, to cram hereditary right down the throats of the vulgar. Perhaps the disorders which threatened, or seemed to threaten on the decease of a leader and the choice of a new one (for elections among ruffians could not be very orderly) induced many at first to favor hereditary pretensions; by which means it happened, as it hath happened since, that what at first was submitted to as a convenience, was afterwards claimed as a right.

England, since the conquest, hath known some few good monarchs, but groaned beneath a much larger number of bad ones, yet no man in his senses can say that their claim under William the Conqueror is a very honorable one. A French bastard landing with an armed banditti, and establishing himself king of England against the consent of the natives, is in plain terms a very paltry rascally original. It certainly hath no divinity in it. However, it is needless to spend much time in exposing the folly of hereditary right, if there are any so weak as to believe it, let them promiscuously worship the ass and lion, and welcome. I shall neither copy their humility, nor disturb their devotion.

Yet I should be glad to ask how they suppose kings came at first? The question admits but of three answers, viz. either by lot, by election, or by usurpation. If the first king was taken by lot, it establishes a precedent for the next, which excludes hereditary succession. Saul was by lot yet the succession was not hereditary, neither does it appear from that transaction there was any intention it ever should. If the first king of any country was by election, that likewise establishes a precedent for the next; for to say, that the right of all future generations is taken away, by the act of the first electors, in their choice not only of a king, but of a family of kings for ever, hath no parallel in or out of scripture but the doctrine of original sin, which supposes the free will of all men lost in Adam; and from such comparison, and it will admit of no other, hereditary succession can derive no glory. For as in Adam all sinned, and as in the first electors all men obeyed; as in the one all mankind were subjected to Satan, and in the other to Sovereignty; as our innocence was lost in the first, and our authority in the last; and as both disable us from reassuming some former state and privilege, it unanswerably follows that original sin and hereditary succession are parallels. Dishonorable rank! Inglorious connection! Yet the most subtle sophist cannot produce a juster simile.

As to usurpation, no man will be so hardy as to defend it; and that William the Conqueror was an usurper is a fact not to be contradicted. The plain truth is, that the antiquity of English monarchy will not bear looking into.

But it is not so much the absurdity as the evil of hereditary succession which concerns mankind. Did it ensure a race of good and wise men it would have the seal of divine authority, but as it opens a door to the foolish, the wicked; and the improper, it hath in it the nature of oppression. Men who look upon themselves born to reign, and others to obey, soon grow insolent; selected from the rest of mankind their minds are early poisoned by importance; and the world they act in differs so materially from the world at large, that they have but little opportunity of knowing its true interests, and when they succeed to the government are frequently the most ignorant and unfit of any throughout the dominions.

Another evil which attends hereditary succession is, that the throne is subject to be possessed by a minor at any age; all which time the regency, acting under the cover of a king, have every opportunity and inducement to betray their trust. The same national misfortune happens, when a king worn out with age and infirmity, enters the last stage of human weakness. In both these cases the public becomes a prey to every miscreant, who can tamper successfully with the follies either of age or infancy.

The most plausible plea, which hath ever been offered in favor of hereditary succession, is, that it preserves a nation from civil wars; and were this true, it would be weighty; whereas, it is the most barefaced falsity ever imposed upon mankind. The whole history of England disowns the fact. Thirty kings and two minors have reigned in that distracted kingdom since the conquest, in which time there have been (including the Revolution) no less than eight civil wars and nineteen rebellions. Wherefore instead of making for peace, it makes against it, and destroys the very foundation it seems to stand on.

The contest for monarchy and succession, between the houses of York and Lancaster, laid England in a scene of blood for many years. Twelve pitched battles, besides skirmishes and sieges, were fought between Henry and Edward. Twice was Henry prisoner to Edward, who in his turn was prisoner to Henry. And so uncertain is the fate of war and the temper of a nation, when nothing but personal matters are the ground of a quarrel, that Henry was taken in triumph from a prison to a palace, and Edward obliged to fly from a palace to a foreign land; yet, as sudden transitions of temper are seldom lasting, Henry in his turn was driven from the throne, and Edward recalled to succeed him. The parliament always following the strongest side.

This contest began in the reign of Henry the Sixth, and was not entirely extinguished till Henry the Seventh, in whom the families were united. Including a period of 67 years, viz. from 1422 to 1489.

In short, monarchy and succession have laid (not this or that kingdom only) but the world in blood and ashes. 'Tis a form of government which the word of God bears testimony against, and blood will attend it.

If we inquire into the business of a king, we shall find that in some countries they have none; and after sauntering away their lives without pleasure to themselves or advantage to the nation, withdraw from the scene, and leave their successors to tread the same idle round. In absolute monarchies the whole weight of business civil and military, lies on the king; the children of Israel in their request for a king, urged this plea 'that he may judge us, and go out before us and fight our battles.' But in countries where he is neither a judge nor a general, as in England, a man would be puzzled to know what is his business.

The nearer any government approaches to a republic the less business there is for a king. It is somewhat difficult to find a proper name for the government of England. Sir William Meredith calls it a republic; but in its present state it is unworthy of the name, because the corrupt influence If the crown, by having all the places in its disposal, hath so effectually swallowed up the power, and eaten out the virtue of the house of commons (the republican part in the constitution) that the government of England is nearly as monarchical as that of France or Spain. Men fall out with names without understanding them. For it is the republican and not the monarchical part of the constitution of England which Englishmen glory in, viz. the liberty of choosing an house of commons from out of their own body and it is easy to see that when the republican virtue fails, slavery ensues. My is the constitution of England sickly, but because monarchy hath poisoned the republic, the crown hath engrossed the commons?

In England a king hath little more to do than to make war and give away places; which in plain terms, is to impoverish the nation and set it together by the ears. A pretty business indeed for a man to be allowed eight hundred thousand sterling a year for, and worshipped into the bargain! Of more worth is one honest man to society, and in the sight of God, than all the crowned ruffians that ever lived.

1. What, according to Paine, are the arguments against a monarchy? How does he use history to support his conclusions?
2. Discuss the elements from this excerpt of *Common Sense* that were most likely to be influential in Jefferson's drafting of the Declaration of Independence.

5-2 Abigail Adams and John Adams Letters: Abigail Adams Letter to Mercy Otis Warren

These letters are written between Abigail Adams and her husband John, the future president, then a member of the Continental Congress in Pennsylvania. Many women were active in the Revolutionary War-from supporting the war effort by raising money to billeting soldiers-and Abigail Adams's letter is an example of how involvement in the Revolution raised questions about what freedom for all would mean. Abigail Adams's letter to her husband is followed by one to their friend, the historian, poet, and playwright, Mercy Otis Warren.

From *The Adams Family Correspondence*, eds. L. H. Butterfield et al. (Cambridge: Belknap Press of Harvard University Press, 1963), vol. I, 29-31.

[Abigail Adams to John Adams, March 31, 1776]

I long to hear that you have declared an independancy [sic]-and by the way in the new Code of Laws which I suppose it will be necessary for you to make I would desire you would Remember
the Ladies, and be more generous and favourable to them than your ancestors. Do not put such unlimited power into the hands of the Husbands. Remember all men would be tyrants if they could. If
perticuliar care and attention is not paid to the Ladies we are determined to foment a Rebelion, and will not hold ourselves bound by any Laws in which we have no voice, or Representation.

That your Sex are Naturally Tyrannical is a Truth so thoroughly established as to admit of no dispute, but such of you as wish to be happy willingly give up the harsh title of Master for the more tender and endearing one of Friend. Why then, not put it out of the power of the vicious and the Lawless to use us with cruelty and indignity with impunity. Men of Sense in all Ages abhor those customs which treat us only as the vassals of your Sex. Regard us then as Beings placed by providence under your protection and in immitation of the Supreem Being make use of that power only for our happiness.

[John Adams to Abigail Adams, April 14, 1776]

As to Declarations of Independency, be patient. Read our Privateering Laws, and our Commercial Laws. What signifies a Word.

As to your extraordinary Code of Laws, I cannot but laugh. We have been told that our Struggle has loosened the bands of Government every where. That Children and Apprentices were disobedient-that schools and Colledges were grown turbulent -that Indians slighted their Guardians and Negroes grew insolent to their Masters. But your Letter was the first Intimation that another

Tribe more numerous and powerfull than all the rest were grown discontented.-This is rather too coarse a Compliment but you are so saucy, I wont blot it out.

Depend upon it, We know better than to repeal our Masculine systems. Altho they are in full Force, you know they are little more than Theory. We dare not exert our Power in its full Latitude. We are obliged to go fair, and softly, and in Practice you know We are the subjects. We have only the Name of Masters, and rather than give up this, which would compleatly subject Us to the Despotism of the Peticoat, I hope General Washington, and all our brave Heroes would fight....

[Abigail Adams to Mercy Otis Warren]

Braintree April 27 1776
He is very saucy to me in return for a List of Female Grievances which I transmitted to him. I think I will get you to join me in a petition to Congress. I thought it was very probable our wise Statesmen would erect a New Government and form a new code of Laws. I ventured to speak a word on behalf of our Sex, who are rather hardly dealte with by the Laws of England which gives such unlimited power to the Husband to use his wife Ill.

I requested that our Legislators would consider our case and as all Men of Delicacy and Sentiment are adverse to Exercising the power they possess, yet as there is a natural propensity in Human Nature to domination, I thought the most generous plan was to put it out of the power of the Arbitrary and tyranick to injure us with impunity by Establishing some Laws in favour upon just and Liberal principals.

I believe I even threatened fomenting a Rebellion in case we were not considered and assured him we would not hold ourselves bound by any Laws in which we had neither a voice nor representation.

In return he tells me he cannot but Laugh at my extraordinary Code of Laws. That he had heard their Struggle had loosened the bands of Government, that children and apprentices were disobedient,

that Schools and Colleges had grown turbulent, that Indians slighted their Guardians, and Negroes grew insolent to their Masters. But my Letter was the first intimation that another Tribe more numerous and powerful than all the rest were grown discontented. This is rather too coarse a complement, he adds, but that I am so saucy he wont blot it out.

So I have helped the Sex abundantly, but I will tell him I have only been making trial of the Disinterestedness of his Virtue, and when weigh'd in the balance have found it wanting.

It would be bad policy to grant us greater power say they since under all the disadvantages we Labour we have the ascendency over their Hearts.

And charm by accepting, by submitting sway.

[Abigail Adams to John Adams, May 7, 1776]

I can not say that I think you very generous to the Ladies, for whilst you are proclaiming peace and good will to men, Emancipating all Nations, you insist upon retaining an absolute power over Wives. But you must remember that Arbitrary power is like most other things which are very hard, very liable to be broken [2] and notwithstanding all your wise Laws and Maxims we have it in our

power not only to free our selves but to subdue our Masters, and without violence throw both your natural and legal authority at our feet [2]

"Charm by accepting, by submitting sway

Yet have our Humour most when we obey."

1. What is Abigail Adams' opinion of men in power and what is her request to John Adams as they declare independence?
2. How does John Adams respond to her concerns? In light of Abigail Adams' letter to Mercy Otis Warren, does this response seem to satisfy Abigail Adams? What does the second letter to John Adams suggest?

5-3 Joseph Warren, "Account of the Battle of Lexington" (1775)

An early and vocal American revolutionary, Joseph Warren was a doctor with a promising career when he was politicized by the Stamp Act and other British measures. He became a close friend and ally of Samuel Adams, wrote many articles against British "tyranny", and served on the Committee of Correspondence before being commissioned in the Massachusetts force. Warren was present at Lexington where his example was an inspiration to his men. He was killed early in the war becoming the first colonial officer to die in combat.

Source: Hezekiah Niles, ed., *Principles and Acts of the Revolution* (Baltimore: W.O. Niles, 1822), 434–435.

MASSACHUSETTS.
IN PROVINCIAL CONGRESS
Watertown, April 26, 1775
TO THE INHABITANTS OF GREAT BRITAIN.

Friends and fellow subjects,

Hostilities are at length commenced in this colony, by the troops under command of general Gage; and it being of the greatest importance, that an early, true, and authentic account of this inhuman proceeding should be know to you, the congress of this colony have transmitted the same, and for want of a session of the hon. continental congress, think it proper to address you on this alarming occasion.

By the clearest depositions, relative to this transaction, it will appear, *that,* on the night preceding the 19th of April, instant, a body of the king's troops, under command of colonel Smith, were secretly landed at Cambridge, with an apparent design to take or destroy the military and other stores, provided for the defence of this colony, and deposited at Concord; that some inhabitants of the colony, on the night aforesaid whilst travelling peaceable on the road between Boston and Concord, were seized and greatly abused by armed men, who appeared to be officers of general Gage's army; that the town of Lexington, by these means, was alarmed, and a company of the inhabitants mustered on the occasion; that the regular troops, on their way to Concord, marched into the said town of Lexington, and the said company, on their approach, began to disperse; that notwithstanding this, the regulars rushed on with great violence, and first began hostilities, by firing on the said Lexington company, whereby, they killed eight, and wounded several others; that the regulars continued their fire until those of the said company, who were neither killed nor wounded, had made their escape; that colonel Smith, with the detachment, then marched to Concord, where a number of provincials were again fired on by the troops, two of them killed and several wounded, before any of the provincials fired on them; and that these hostile measures of the troops produced an engagement that lasted through the day, in which many of he provincials, and more of the regular troops, were killed and wounded.

To give a particular account of the ravages of the troops, as they retreated from Concord to Charles Town, would be very difficult, if not impracticable; let it suffice to say, that a great number of the houses on the road were plundered, and rendered unfit for use; several were burnt; women in child-bed were driven by the soldiery naked into the streets; old men, peaceably in their houses, were shot dead, and such scenes exhibited, as would disgrace the annals of he most uncivilized nations.

These, brethren, are marks of ministerial vengeance against this colony, for refusing, with her sister colonies, a submission to slavery; but they have not yet detached us from our royal sovereign we profess to be his loyal and dutiful subjects; and so hardly dealt with as we have been, are still ready, with our lives and fortunes, to defend his person, family, crown and dignity; nevertheless, to the persecution and tyranny of his cruel ministry, we will not tamely submit; appealing to Heaven for the justice of our cause, "we determine to die, or be free."

We cannot think that the honor, wisdom, and valor of Britons, will suffer them to be longer inactive spectators of *measures,* in which they themselves are so deeply interested; measures pursued in opposition to the solemn protests of many noble lords, and expressed sense of conspicuous commons, whose knowledge and virtue have long characterized them as some of the greatest men in the nation; *measures,* executing, contrary to the interest, petitions, and resolves of many large, respectable counties, cities, and boroughs, in Great Britain; *measures* highly incompatible with justice, but still pursued with a specious pretence of easing he nation of its burthens; *measures* which, if successful, must end in the ruin and slavery of Britain, as well as the persecuted American colonies.

We sincerely hope, that the Great Sovereign of the Universe, who hath so often appeared for the English nation, will support you in every rational and manly exertion with these colonies, for saving it form ruin, and that, in a constitutional connection with our mother country, we shall soon be altogether a free and happy people.

Signed by order,
JOS. WARREN, president

1. Who are the primary aggressors according to this account? Describe some of the actions detailed in this account as evidence of this aggression.
2. What appeal is made to the people of Britain by the author of this letter? What is the goal of this document?

5-4 Rights of Women in an Independent Republic

Abigail and John Adams had one of the most extraordinary partnerships of their (or any other) time. Two powerful minds are revealed in their correspondence, and the influence of Abigail Adams on her husband is revealed in these letters. Arguably, the most important questions raised by the move for independence was who should share in the newly posited freedoms. These letters illuminate this struggle that continues to this day.

Abigail Adams to John Adams, Braintree, 31 March 1776

I long to hear that you have declared an independancy-and by the way in the new Code of Laws which I suppose it will be necessary for you to make I desire you would Remember the Ladies, and be more generous and favourable to them than your ancestors. Do not put such umlimited power into the hands of the Husbands. Remember all Men would be tyrants if they could. If perticuliar care and attention is not paid to the Laidies we are determined to foment a Rebelion, and will not hold ourselves bound by any Laws in which we have no voice, or Representation.

That your Sex are Naturally Tyrannical is a Truth so thoroughly established as to admit of no dispute, but such of you as wish to be happy willingly give up the harsh title of Master for the more tender and endearing one of Friend. Why then, not put it out of the power of the vicious and the Lawless to use us with cruelty and indignity with impunity. Men of Sense in all Ages abhor those customs which treat us only as the vassals of your Sex. Regard us then as Beings placed by providence under your protection and in immitation of the Supreem Being make use of that power only for our happiness.

John Adams to Abigail Adams, Philadelphia, 14 April 1776

As to Declarations of Independency, be patient. Read our Privateering Laws, and our Commercial Laws. What signifies a Word.

As to your extraordinary Code of Laws, I cannot but laugh. We have been told that our Struggle has loosened the bands of Government every where. That Children and Apprentices were disobedient-that schools and Colledges were grown turbulent-that Indians slighted their Guardians and Negroes grew insolent to their Masters. But your Letter was the first Intimation that another Tribe more numerous and powerful than all the rest were grown discontented.-This is rather too coarse a Compliment but you are so saucy, I wont blot it out.

Depend upon it, We know better than to repeal our Masculine systems. Altho they are in full Force, you know they are little more than Theory. We dare not exert our Power in its full Latitude. We are obliged to go fair, and softly, and in Practice you know We are the subjects. We have only the Name of Masters, and rather than give up this, which would compleatly subject Us to the Despotism of the Peticoat, I hope General Washington, and all our brave Heroes would fight. I am sure every good Politician would plot, as long as he would against Despotism, Empire, Monarchy, Aristocracy, Oligarchy, or Ochlocracy.-A fine Story indeed. I begin to think the Ministry as deep as they are wicked. After stirring up Tories, Landjobbers, Trimmers, Bigots, Canadians, Indians, Negrows, Hanoverians, Hessians, Russians, Irish Roman Catholicks, Scotch Renegadoes, at last they have stimulated the [illegible in original] to demand new Priviledges and threaten to rebell.

John Adams to John Sullivan, Philadelphia, 26 May 1776

It is certain in Theory, that the only moral Foundation of Government is the Consent of the People. But to what an Extent Shall We carry this Principle? Shall We Say, that every Individual of the Community, old and young, male and female, as well as rich and poor, must consent, expressly to every Act of Legislation? No, you will Say. This is impossible. How then does the Right arise in the Majority to govern the Minority, against their Will? Whence arises the Right of the Men to govern Women, without their Consent? Whence the Right of the old to bind the Young, without theirs.

But let us first Suppose, that the whole Community of every Age, Rank, Sex, and Condition, has a Right to vote. This Community, is assembled-a Motion is made and carried by a Majority of one Voice. The Minority will not agree to this. Whence arises the Right of the Majority to govern, and the Obligation of the Minority to obey? from Necessity, you will Say, because there can be no other Rule, But why exclude Women? You will Say, because their Delicacy renders them unfit for Practice and Experience, in the great Business of Life, and the hardy Enterprizes of War, as well as the arduous Cares of State. Besides, their attention is So much engaged with the necessary Nurture of their Children, that Nature has made them fittest for domestic Cares. And Children have not Judgment or Will of their own. True. But will not these Reasons apply to others? Is it not equally true, that Men in general in every Society, who are wholly destitute of Property, and also too little acquainted with public Affairs to form a Right Judgment, and too dependent upon other Men to have a Will of their own? If this is a Fact, if you give to every Man, who has no Property, a Vote, will you not make a fine encouraging Provision for Corruption by your fundamental Law? Such is the Frailty of the human Heart, that very few

Men, who have no Property, have any Judgment of their own. They talk and vote as they are directed by Some Man of Property, who has attached their Minds to his Interest.

Upon my Word, sir, I have long thought an Army, a Piece of Clock Work and to be governed only by Principles and Maxims, as fixed as any in Mechanicks, and by all that I have read in the History of Mankind, and in Authors, who have Speculated upon Society and Government, I am much inclined to think, a Government must manage a Society in the Same manner; and that this is Machinery too.

Harrington has Shewn that Power always follows property. This I believe to be as infallible a Maxim, in Politics, as, that Action and Reaction are equal, as in Mechanicks. Nay I believe We may advance one Step farther and affirm that the Ballance of Power in a Society, accompanies the Ballance of Property in Land. The only possible Way then of preserving the Ballance of Power on the side of equal Liberty and public Virtue, is to make the Acquisition of Land easy to every Member of Society: to make a Division of the Land into Small Quantities, So that the Multitude may be possessed of landed Estates. If the Multitude is possessed of the Ballance of real Estate, the Multitude will have the Ballance of Power, and in that Case the Multitude will take Care of the Liberty, Virtue, and Interest of the Multitude in all Acts of Government.

I believe these Principles have been felt, if not understood in the Massachusetts Bay, from the Beginning: And therefore I Should think that Wisdom and Policy would dictate in these Times, to be very cautious of making Alterations. Our people have never been very rigid in Scrutinizing into the Qualifications of Voters, and I presume they will not now begin to be so. But I would not advise them to make any alteration in the Laws, at present, respecting the Qualifications of Voters.

Your Idea, that those Laws, which affect the Lives and personal Liberty of all, or which inflict corporal Punishment, affect those, who are not qualified to vote, as well as those who are, is just. But, So they do Women, as well as Men, Children as well as Adults. What Reason Should there be, for excluding a Man of Twenty years, Eleven Months and twenty-seven days old, from a Vote when you admit one, who is twenty one? The Reason is, you must fix Some Period in Life, when the Understanding and Will of Men in general is fit to be trusted by the Public. Will not the Same Reason justify the State in fixing upon Some certain Quantity of Property, as a Qualification.

The Same Reasoning, which will induce you to admit all Men, who have no Property, to vote, with those who have, for those Laws, which affect the Person will prove that you ought to admit Women and Children: for generally Speaking, Women and Children, have as good Judgment, and as independent Minds as those Men who are wholly destitute of Property: these last being to all Intents and Purposes as much dependent upon others, who will please to feed, cloath, and employ them, as Women are upon their Husbands, or Children on their Parents.

As to your Idea, or proportioning the Votes of Men in Money Matters, to the Property they hold, it is utterly impracticable. There is no possible Way of Ascertaining, at any one Time, how much every Man in a Community, is worth; and if there was, So fluctuating is Trade and Property, that this State of it, would change in half an Hour. The Property of the whole Community, is Shifting every Hour, and no Record can be kept of the Changes.

Society can be governed only by general Rules. Government cannot accommodate itself to every particular Case, as it happens, nor to the Circumstances of particular Persons. It must establish general, comprehensive Regulations for Cases and Persons. The only Question is, which general Rule, will accommodate most Cases and most Persons.

Depend upon it, sir, it is dangerous to open So fruitfull a Source of Controversy and Altercation, as would be opened by attempting to alter the Qualifications of Voters. There will be no End of it. New Claims will arise. Women will demand a Vote. Lads from 12 to 21 will think their Rights not enough attended to, and every Man, who has not a Farthing, will demand an equal Voice with any other in all Acts of State. It tends to confound and destroy all Distinctions, and prostrate all Ranks, to one common Levell. I am &c.

1. Examine and summarize the reasons given by John Adams for excluding women and men without property from voting?
2. Identify and explain John Adams' reasoning and plan for ensuring that the multitude of people possess the balance of power.
3. What reasoning does John Adams use to argue against allowing all men, regardless of personal property, to vote? Overall what are his opinions regarding any change in voter qualifications?

PART SIX
FORGING A CONSTITUTION

6-1 Shay's Rebellion: Letters of Generals William Shepard and Benjamin Lincoln to Governor James Bowdoin of Massachusetts (1787)

Shay's Rebellion was a reaction to the poor economic times following the Revolutionary War and before the Constitutional Convention. Led by former Revolutionary Army Captain Daniel Shays, the rebellion protested high property taxes, poll taxes and unstable currency. Shay's Rebellion was put down militarily but its impact was great as it became one of the precipitating causes of the constitutional convention and the creation of a stronger central government.

[General Shepard to Governor Bowdoin]

Springfield
January 26, 1787

The unhappy time is come in which we have been obliged to shed blood. Shays, who was at the head of about twelve hundred men, marched yesterday afternoon about four o'clock, towards the public buildings in battle array. He marched his men in an open column by platoons. I sent several times by one of my aides, and two other gentlemen, Captains Buffington and Woodbridge, to him to know what he was after, or what he wanted. His reply was, he wanted barracks, and barracks he would have and stores. The answer returned was he must purchase them dear, if he had them.

He still proceeded on his march until he approached within two hundred and fifty yards of the arsenal. He then made a halt. I immediately sent Major Lyman, one of my aides, and Capt. Buffington to inform him not to march his troops any nearer the arsenal on his peril, as I was stationed here by order of your Excellency and the Secretary at War, for the defence of the public property; in case he did I should surely fire on him and his men. A Mr. Wheeler, who appeared to be one of Shays' aides, met Mr. Lyman, after he had delivered my orders in the most peremptory manner, and made answer, that was all he wanted. Mr. Lyman returned with his answer.

Shays immediately put his troops in motion, and marched on rapidly near one hundred yards. I then ordered Major Stephens, who commanded the artillery, to fire upon them. He accordingly did. The two first shots he endeavored to overshoot them, in hopes they would have taken warning without firing among them, but it had no effect on them. Major Stephens then directed his shot through the center of his column. The fourth or fifth shot put their whole column into the utmost confusion. Shays made an attempt to display the column, but in vain. We had one howitz which was loaded with grapeshot, which when fired, gave them great uneasiness.

Had I been disposed to destroy them, I might have charged upon their rear and flanks with my infantry and the two field pieces, and could have killed the greater part of his whole army within twenty-five minutes. There was not a single musket fired on either side. I found three men dead on the spot, and one wounded, who is since dead. One of our artillery men by inattention was badly wounded. Three muskets were taken up with the dead, which were all deeply loaded.

I have received no reinforcement yet, and expect to be attacked this day by their whole force combined.

[General Lincoln to Governor Bowdoin]

Head Quarters, Springfield
January 28th, 1787

We arrived here yesterday about noon with one regiment from Suffolk, one from Essex, one from Middlesex, and one from Worcester, with three companies of artillery, a corps of horse, and a volunteer corps under the command of Colonel Baldwin; the other company of artillery with the other regiment from Middlesex and another from Worcester which were as a cover to our stores arrived about eight o'clock in the evening. On my arrival, I found that Shays had taken a post at a little village six miles north of this, with the whole force under his immediate command, and that Day had taken post in West Springfield, and that he had fixed a guard at the ferry house on the west side of the river, and that he had a guard at the bridge over Agawam river. By this disposition all communication from the north and west in the usual paths was cut off.

From a consideration of this insult on Government, that by an early move we should instantly convince the insurgents of its ability and determination speedily to disperse them; that we wanted the houses occupied by these men to cover our own troops; that General Patterson was on his march to join us, which to obstruct was an object with them; that a successful movement would give spirits to the troops; that it would be so was reduced to as great a certainty, as can be had in operations of this kind; from these considerations, Sir, with many others, I was induced to order the troops under arms at three o'clock in the afternoon, although the most of them had been so from one in the morning.

We moved about half after three, and crossed the river upon the ice, with the four regiments; four pieces of artillery; the light horse, and the troops of this division, under General Shepard moved up the river on the ice, with an intention to fall in between Shays who was on the east side of the river, and Day on the west, and to prevent a junction as well as to cut off Day's retreat. We supposed that we should hereby encircle him with a force so superior that he would not dare to fire upon us which would effectually prevent bloodshed, as our troops were enjoined in the most positive manner not to fire without orders. The moment we showed ourselves upon the river the guard at the ferry house turned out and left the pass open to us. They made a little show of force for a minute or two near the meeting house, and then retired in the utmost confusion and disorder. Our horse met them at the west end of the village, but the insurgents found means by crossing the fields and taking to the woods to escape them; some were taken who are aggravatedly guilty, but not the most so.

The next news we had of them, was by an express from Northampton, that part of them arrived in the south end of their town about eleven o'clock. Shays also in a very precipitate manner left his post a[t] Chickabee, and some time in the night passed through South Hadley, on his way to Amherst.

As soon as our men are refreshed this morning, we shall move northward, leaving General Shepard here as a cover to the magazines; perhaps we may overtake Shays and his party, we shall do it, unless they disperse. If they disperse, I shall cover the troops in some convenient place, and carry on our operations in a very different way.

1. What actions does General Shepard seem to have taken to avert and then minimize the loss of life in putting down the rebellion?
2. Analyze the response of the participants in Shay's rebellion to the advances of the armed forces.

6-2 Divergent Reactions to Shay's Rebellion

In 1786, western Massachusetts erupted in violence as disgruntled farmers led by Revolutionary War veteran Daniel Shays sought relief from burdensome taxes and mounting debt. In 1787, the "Shaysites," numbering over 1200, marched on the federal arsenal at Springfield only to be turned back by local militia. General Benjamin Lincoln arrived on the scene with reinforcements and soon put the rebellion to an end. While armed protests such as this raised concerns about the power of the Confederation government and the possibility of anarchy, not all of the leaders of the new republic were in agreement over the seriousness of the situation.

> **Source:** *Archiving Early America, Historic Documents From 18th Century America*
> http://www.earlyamerica.com/review/summer/letter.html
> The George Washington Papers at the Library of Congress, 1741–1799. *The Writings of George Washington from the Original Manuscript Sources, 1745–1799.* John C. Fitzpatrick, Editor.—vol. 29
> http://lcweb2.loc.gov/cgi-bin/query/r?ammem/mgw:@field(DOCID+@lit(gw290127
> http://lcweb2.loc.gov/cgi-bin/query/r?ammem/mgw:@field(DOCID+@lit(gw290129

THOMAS JEFFERSON TO JAMES MADISON

Paris, January 30th, 1787
Dear Sir,

My last to you was of the 16th of December; since which, I have received yours of November 25 and December 4, which afforded me, as your letters always do, a treat on matters public, individual, and economical. I am impatient to learn your sentiments on the late troubles in the Eastern states. So far as I have yet seen, they do not appear to threaten serious consequences. Those states have suffered by the stoppage of the channels of their commerce, which have not yet found other issues. This must render money scarce and make the people uneasy. This uneasiness has produced acts absolutely unjustifiable; but I hope they will provoke no severities from their governments. A consciousness of those in power that their administration of the public affairs has been honest may, perhaps, produce too great a degree of indignation; and those characters, wherein fear predominates over hope, may apprehend too much from these instances of irregularity. They may conclude too hastily that nature has formed man insusceptible of any other government than that of force, a conclusion not founded in truth or experience.

Societies exist under three forms, sufficiently distinguishable: (1) without government, as among our Indians; (2) under governments, wherein the will of everyone has a just influence, as is the case in England, in a slight degree, and in our states, in a great one; (3) under governments of force, as is the case in all other monarchies, and in most of the other republics.

To have an idea of the curse of existence under these last, they must be seen. It is a government of wolves over sheep. It is a problem, not clear in my mind, that the first condition is not the best. But I believe it to be inconsistent with any great degree of population. The second state has a great deal of good in it. The mass of mankind under that enjoys a precious degree of liberty and happiness. It has its evils, too, the principal of which is the turbulence to which it is subject. But weigh this against the oppressions of monarchy, and it becomes nothing. Malo periculosam libertatem quam quietam servitutem. Even this evil is productive of good. It prevents the degeneracy of government and nourishes a general attention to the public affairs.

I hold it that a little rebellion now and then is a good thing, and as necessary in the political world as storms in the physical. Unsuccessful rebellions, indeed, generally establish the encroachments on the rights of the people which have produced them. An observation of this truth should render honest republican governors so mild in their punishment of rebellions as not to discourage them too much. It is a medicine necessary for the sound health of government. . . .

Yours affectionately,
Th. Jefferson

GEORGE WASHINGTON TO BENJAMIN LINCOLN, FEBRUARY 24, 1787

Mount Vernon, February 24, 1787.

Sir: I have received your letter of the 24th. Ulto. and receipt for Messrs. Josiah Watson and Co. bill of Exchange which was enclosed. I am much obliged to you for the account of the political situation of your State which you gave me, and am very happy to find by later advices that matters are likely soon to terminate entirely in favour of Government by the total suppression of the insurgents, and it adds much to the satisfaction which these accounts give that it may be effected with so little bloodshed, I hope some good will come out of so much evil, by giving energy and respectability to the Government. General Lincoln's situation must have been very painful to be obliged to march against those men whom he had heretofore looked upon as his fellow Citizens and some of whom had perhaps been his companions in the field, but as they had by their repeated outrages forfeited all right to Citizenship, his duty and patriotism must have got the better of every other consideration and led him with alacrity to support the Government. I am, etc.

GEORGE WASHINGTON TO HENRY KNOX, FEBRUARY 25, 1787

Mount Vernon, February 25, 1787.

Accept, my dear General Knox my affectionate thanks for your obliging favors of the 29th, 30th, and 31st. of Jany. and 1st. 8th. and 12th. of the present month. They were indeed, exceedingly satisfactory, and relieving to my mind which had been filled with great and anxious uneasiness for the issue of General Lincoln's operations, and the dignity of Government. On prospect of the happy termination of this insurrection I sincerely congratulate you; hoping that good may result from the cloud of evils which threatned, not only the hemisphere of Massachusetts but by spreading its baneful influence, the tranquility of the Union. Surely Shays must be either a weak man, the dupe of some characters who are yet behind the curtain, or has been deceived by his followers. Or which may be more likely, he did not conceive that there was energy enough in the Government to bring matters to the crisis to which they have been pushed. It is to be hoped the General Court of that State concurred in the report of the Committee, that a rebellion did actually exist. This would be decisive, and the most likely means of putting the finishing stroke to the business.

We have nothing new in this quarter except the dissentions which prevailed in, and occasioned the adjournment of, the Assembly of Maryland; that an appeal might be made to the people for their sentiments on the conduct of their representative in the Senate and Delegates respecting a paper omission; which was warmly advocated by the latter and opposed by the former, and which may be productive of great, and perhaps dangerous divisions. Our Affairs, generally, seem really, to be approaching to some awful crisis. God only knows what the result will be. It shall be my part to hope for the best; as to see this Country happy whilst I am gliding down the stream of life in tranquil retirement is so much the wish of my Soul, that nothing on this side Elysium can be placed in competition with it. I hope the postponement of your journey to this State does not amount to a relinquishment of it, and that it is unnecessary to assure you of the sincere pleasure I should have at seeing you under this roof. Mrs. Washington unites with me in every good wish for Mrs. Knox yourself and family. With sentiments of the warmest friendship etc.

PS. I had wrote this letter and was on the point of sending it with others to the Post Office when your favor of the 15th. instt. was handed to me. The spirit and decision of the Court is very pleasing and I hope will be attended with happy consequences.

1. What does Thomas Jefferson mean when he says "a little rebellion now and then is a good thing?" Do you think he was being a little too complacent?
2. What do you think explains the divergent opinions of Jefferson and Washington concerning Shays's rebellion?

6-3 Patrick Henry Speaks Against Ratification of the Constitution (1788)

Patrick Henry, the noted Virginia delegate to the Constitutional Convention, opposed a federal form of government in the United States. Here, at a debate during the convention, Henry discusses his objections to the new form of government.

Source: Jonathan Elliot, ed., *The Debates in the Several State Conventions on the Adoption of the Federal Constitution* 2nd ed., 5 vols. (Philadelphia: J. B. Lippincott Company, 1907).

Mr. Chairman, the public mind, as well as my own, is extremely uneasy at the proposed change of government. Give me leave to form one of the number of those who wish to be thoroughly acquainted with the reasons of this perilous and uneasy situation, and why we are brought hither to decide on this great national question. I consider myself as the servant of the people of this commonwealth, as a sentinel over their rights, liberty, and happiness. I represent their feelings when I say that they are exceedingly uneasy at being brought from that state of full security, which they enjoyed, to the present delusive appearance of things. A year ago, the minds of our citizens were at perfect repose. Before the meeting of the late federal Convention at Philadelphia, a general peace and a universal tranquillity prevailed in this country; but, since that period, they are exceedingly uneasy and disquieted. When I wished for an appointment to this Convention, my mind was extremely agitated for the situation of public affairs. I conceived the republic to be in extreme danger. If our situation be thus uneasy, whence has arisen this fearful jeopardy? It arises from this fatal system; it arises from a proposal to change our governmentÑa proposal that goes to the utter annihilation of the most solemn engagements of the statesÑa proposal of establishing nine states into a confederacy, to the eventual exclusion of four states. It goes to the annihilation of those solemn treaties we have formed with foreign nations.

The present circumstances of FranceÑthe good offices rendered us by that kingdomÑrequire our most faithful and most punctual adherence to our treaty with her. We are in alliance with the Spaniards, the Dutch, the Prussians; those treaties bound us as thirteen states confederated together. Yet here is a proposal to sever that confederacy. Is it possible that we shall abandon all our treaties and national engagements?Ñand for what? I expected to hear the reasons for an event so unexpected to my mind and many others. Was our civil polity, or public justice, endangered or sapped? Was the real existence of the country threatened, or was this preceded by a mournful progression of events? This proposal of altering our federal government is of a most alarming nature! Make the best of this new governmentÑsay it is composed by any thing but inspirationÑyou ought to be extremely cautious, watchful, jealous of your liberty; for, instead of securing your rights, you may lose them forever. If a wrong step be now made, the republic may be lost forever. If this new government will not come up to the expectation of the people, and they shall be disappointed, their liberty will be lost, and tyranny must and will arise. I repeat it again, and I beg gentlemen to consider, that a wrong step, made now, will plunge us into misery, and our republic will be lost. It will be necessary for this Convention to have a faithful historical detail of the facts that preceded the session of the federal Convention, and the reasons that actuated its members in proposing an entire alteration of government, and to demonstrate the dangers that awaited us. If they were of such awful magnitude as to warrant a proposal so extremely perilous as this, I must assert, that this Convention has an absolute right to a thorough discovery of every circumstance relative to this great event. And here I would make this inquiry of those worthy characters who composed a part of the late federal Convention. I am sure they were fully impressed with the necessity of forming a great consolidated government, instead of a confederation. That this is a consolidated government is demonstrably clear; and the danger of such a government is, to my mind, very striking I have the highest veneration for those gentlemen; but, sir, give me leave to demand, What right had they to say, *We, the people?* My political curiosity, exclusive of my anxious solicitude for the public welfare, leads me to ask, Who authorized them to speak the language of, *We, the people,* instead of, *We, the states?* States are the characteristics and the soul of a confederation. If the states be not the agents of this compact, it must be one great, consolidated, national government, of the people of all the states. . .. It is not mere curiosity that actuates me: I wish to hear the real, actual, existing danger, which should lead us to take those steps, so dangerous in my conception.

Disorders have arisen in other parts of America; but here, sir, no dangers, no insurrection or tumult have happened; every thing has been calm and tranquil. But, notwithstanding this, we are wandering on the great ocean of human affairs. . . . The federal Convention ought to have amended the old system; for this purpose they were solely delegated; the object of their mission extended to no other consideration. You must, therefore, forgive the solicitation of one unworthy member to know what danger could have arisen under the present Confederation, and what are the causes of this proposal to change our government. . . .

. . .Under the same despised government, we commanded the respect of all Europe: wherefore are we now reckoned otherwise? The American spirit has fled from hence: it has gone to regions where it has never been expected; it has gone to the people of France, in search of a splendid governmentÑa strong, energetic government. Shall we imitate the example of those nations who have gone from a simple to a splendid government? Are those nations more worthy of our imitation? What can make an adequate satisfaction to them for the loss they have suffered in attaining such a governmentÑfor the loss of their liberty? If we admit this consolidated government, it will be because we like a great, splendid one. Some way or other we must be a great and mighty empire; we must have an army, and a navy, and a number of things. When the American spirit was in its youth, the language of America was different: liberty, sir, was then the primary object. We are descended from a people whose government was founded on liberty: our glorious forefathers of Great Britain made liberty the foundation of every thing. That country is become a great, mighty, and splendid nation; not because their government is strong and energetic, but, sir, because liberty is its direct end and foundation. We drew the spirit of liberty from our British ancestors: by that spirit we have triumphed over every difficulty. But now, sir, the American spirit, assisted by the ropes and chains of consolidation, is about to convert this country into a powerful and mighty empire. If you make the citizens of this country agree to become the subjects of one great consolidated empire of America, your government will not have sufficient energy to keep them together. Such a government is incompatible with the genius of republicanism. There will be no checks, no real balances, in this government. What can avail your specious, imaginary balances, your rope-dancing, chain-rattling, ridiculous ideal checks and contrivances? But, sir, we are not feared by foreigners; we do not make nations tremble. Would this constitute happiness, or secure liberty? I trust, sir, our political hemisphere will ever direct their operations to the security of those objects. . ..

. . .With respect to that part of the proposal which says that every power not granted remains with the people, it must be previous to adoption, or it will involve this country in inevitable destruction. To talk of it as a thing subsequent, not as one of your unalienable rights, is leaving it to the casual opinion of the Congress who shall take up the consideration of that matter. They will not reason with you about the effect of this Constitution. They will not take the opinion of this committee concerning its operation. They will construe it as they please. If you place it subsequently, let me ask the consequences. Among ten thousand implied powers which they may assume, they may, if we be engaged in war, liberate every one of your slaves if they please. And this must and will be done by men, a majority of whom have not a common interest with you. They will, therefore, have no feeling of your interests. It has been repeatedly said here, that the great object of a national government was national defence. That power which is said to be intended for security and safety may be rendered detestable and oppressive. If they give power to the general government to provide for the general defence, the means must be commensurate to the end. All the means in the possession of the people must be given to the government which is intrusted with the public defence. In this state there are two hundred and thirty-six thousand blacks, and there are many in several other states. But there are few or none in the Northern States; and yet, if the Northern States shall be of opinion that our slaves are numberless, they may call forth every national resource. May Congress not say, that every black man must fight? Did we not see a little of this last war? We were not so hard pushed as to make emancipation general; but acts of Assembly passed that every slave who would go to the army should be free. Another thing will contribute to bring this event about. Slavery is detested. We feel its fatal effectsÑwe deplore it with all the pity of humanity. Let all these considerations, at some future period, press with full force on the minds of Congress. Let that urbanity, which I trust will distinguish America, and the necessity of national defence,Ñlet all these things operate on their minds; they will search that paper, and see if they have power of manumission. And have they not, sir? Have they not power to provide for the general defence and welfare? May they not think that these call for the abolition of slavery? May they not pronounce all slaves free, and will they not be warranted by that power? This is no ambiguous implication or logical deduction. The paper speaks to the point: they have the power in clear, unequivocal terms, and will clearly and certainly exercise it. As much as I deplore slavery, I see that prudence forbids its abolition. I deny that the general government ought to set them free, because a decided majority of the states have not the ties of sympathy and fellow-feeling for those whose interest would be affected by their emancipation. The majority of Congress is to the north, and the slaves are to the south.

In this situation, I see a great deal of the property of the people of Virginia in jeopardy, and their peace and tranquillity gone. I repeat it again, that it would rejoice my very soul that every one of my fellow-beings was emancipated. As we ought with gratitude to admire that decree of Heaven which has numbered us among the free, we ought to lament and deplore the necessity of holding our fellowmen in bondage. But is it practicable, by any human means, to liberate them without producing the most dreadful and ruinous consequences? We ought to possess them in the manner we inherited them from our ancestors, as their manumission is incompatible with the felicity of our country. But we ought to soften, as much as possible, the rigor of their unhappy fate. I know that, in a variety of particular instances, the legislature, listening to complaints, have admitted their emancipation. Let me not dwell on this subject. I will only add that this, as well as every other property of the people of Virginia, is in jeopardy, and put in the hands of those who have no similarity of situation with us. This is a local matter, and I can see no propriety in subjecting it to Congress.

1. To what events does Patrick Henry attribute the disruption of peace and tranquility formerly prevalent in the country?
2. How is a consolidated government a threat to the original spirit of America according to Henry?
3. Explain how the issue of slavery plays a part in Henry's reasoning in this piece? What are Patrick Henry's beliefs regarding the right of Congress to emancipate slaves? Identify the conflict between state rights and national authority as it relates to slavery.

PART SEVEN
THE FEDERALIST ERA

7-1 James Madison Defends the Constitution (1788)

The Constitutional debates between Federalists and Anti-Federalists were often heated. Here, James Madison responds to Patrick Henry's concerns about the power of the federal government to directly tax the people.

Source: Jonathan Elliot, ed., *The Debates in the Several State Conventions on the Adoption of the Federal Constitution.* 2nd ed., 5 vols. (Philadelphia: J. B. Lippincott Company, 1907).

Comparisons have been made between the friends of this Constitution and those who oppose it: although I disapprove of such comparisons, I trust that in point of truth, honor, candor, and rectitude of motives, the friends of this system, here and in other states, are not inferior to its opponents. But professions of attachment to the public good, and comparisons of parties, ought not to govern or influence us now. We ought, sir, to examine the Constitution on its own merits solely: we are to inquire whether it will promote the public happiness: its aptitude to produce this desirable object ought to be the exclusive subject of our present researches. In this pursuit, we ought not to address our arguments to the feelings and passions, but to those understandings and judgments which were selected by the people of this country, to decide this great question by a calm and rational investigation. I hope that gentlemen, in displaying their abilities on this occasion, instead of giving opinions and making assertions, will condescend to prove and demonstrate, by a fair and regular discussion. . ... I must take the liberty to make some observations on what was said by another gentleman (Mr. Henry) He told us that this Constitution ought to be rejected because it endangered the public liberty, in his opinion, in many instances. Give me leave to make one answer to that observation: Let the dangers which this system is supposed to be replete with be clearly pointed out: if any dangerous and unnecessary powers be given to the general legislature, let them be plainly demonstrated, and let us not rest satisfied with general assertions of danger, without examination. If powers be necessary, apparent danger is not a sufficient reason against conceding them. . ...

. . . I must confess I have not been able to find his usual consistency in the gentleman's argument on this occasion. He informs us that the people of the country are at perfect repose,Ñthat is, every man enjoys the fruits of his labor peaceably and securely, and that every thing is in perfect tranquillity and safety. I wish sincerely, sir, this were true. If this be their happy situation, why has every state acknowledged the contrary? Why were deputies from all the states sent to the general Convention? Why have complaints of national and individual distresses been echoed and reechoed throughout the continent? Why has our general government been so shamefully disgraced, and our Constitution violated? Wherefore have laws been made to authorize a change, and wherefore are we now assembled here? A federal government is formed for the protection of its individual members. Ours has attacked itself with impunity. Its authority has been disobeyed and despised. I think I perceive a glaring inconsistency in another of his arguments. He complains of this Constitution, because it requires the consent of at least three fourths of the states to introduce amendments which shall be necessary for the happiness of the people. The assent of so many he urges as too great an obstacle to the admission of salutary amendments, which, he strongly insists, ought to be at the will of a bare majority. We hear this argument, at the very moment we are called upon to assign reasons for proposing a constitution which puts it in the power of nine states to abolish the present inadequate, unsafe, and pernicious Confederation! In the first case, he asserts that a majority ought to have the power of altering the government, when found to be inadequate to the security of public happiness. In the last case, he affirms that even three fourths of the community have not a right to alter a government which experience has proved to be subversive of national felicity! nay, that the most necessary and urgent alterations cannot be made without the absolute unanimity of all the states! Does not the thirteenth article of the Confederation expressly require that no alteration shall be made without the unanimous consent of all the states? Could any thing in theory be more perniciously improvident and injudicious than this submission of the will of the majority to the most trifling minority? Have not experience and practice actually manifested this theoretical inconvenience to be extremely impolite? Let me mention one fact, which I conceive must carry conviction to the mind of any one: the smallest state in the Union has obstructed every attempt to reform the government; that little member has repeatedly disobeyed and counteracted the general authority; nay, has even supplied the enemies of its country with provisions. Twelve states had agreed to certain improvements which were proposed, being thought absolutely necessary to preserve the existence of the general government; but as these improvements, though really indispensable, could not, by the Confederation, be introduced into it without the consent of every state, the refractory dissent of that little state prevented their adoption. The inconveniences resulting from this requisition, of unanimous concurrence in alterations in the Confederation, must be known to every member in this Convention; it is therefore needless to remind them of them. Is it not self-evident that a trifling minority ought not to bind the majority? Would not foreign influence be exerted with facility over a small minority? Would the honorable gentleman agree to continue the most radical defects in the old system, because the petty state of Rhode Island would not agree to remove them? . . ..

Give me leave to say something of the nature of the government, and to show that it is safe and just to vest it with the power of taxation. There are a number of opinions; but the principal question is, whether it be a federal or consolidated government. In order to judge properly of the question before us, we must consider it minutely in its principal parts. I conceive myself that it is of a mixed nature; it is in a manner unprecedented; we cannot find one express example in the experience of the world. It stands by itself. In some respects it is a government of a federal nature; in others, it is of a consolidated nature. Even if we attend to the manner in which the Constitution is investigated, ratified, and made the act of the people of America, I can say, notwithstanding what the honorable gentleman has alleged, that this government is not completely consolidated, nor is it entirely federal. Who are parties to it? The peopleÑbut not the people as composing one great body; but the people as composing thirteen sovereignties. Were it, as the gentleman asserts, a consolidated government, the assent of a majority of the people would be sufficient for its establishment; and, as a majority have adopted it already, the remaining states would be bound by the act of the majority, even if they unanimously reprobated it. Were it such a government as is suggested, it would be now binding on the people of this state, without having had the privilege of deliberating upon it. But, sir, no state is bound by it, as it is, without its own consent. Should all the states adopt it, it will be then a government established by the thirteen states of America, not through the intervention of the legislatures, but by the people at large. In this particular respect, the distinction between the existing and proposed governments is very material. The existing system has been derived from the dependent derivative authority of the legislatures of the states; whereas this is derived from the superior power of the people. If we look at the manner in which alterations are to be made in it, the same idea is, in some degree, attended to. By the new system, a majority of the states cannot introduce amendments; nor are all the states required for that purpose; three fourths of them must concur in alterations; in this there is a departure from the federal idea. The members to the national House of Representatives are to be chosen by the people at large, in proportion to the numbers in the respective districts. When we come to the Senate, its members are elected by the states in their equal and political capacity. But had the government been completely consolidated, the Senate would have been chosen by the people in their individual capacity, in the same manner as the members of the other house. Thus it is of a complicated nature; and this complication, I trust, will be found to exclude the evils of absolute consolidation, as well as of a mere confederacy. If Virginia was separated from all the states, her power and authority would extend to all cases: in like manner, were all powers vested in the general government, it would be a consolidated government; but the powers of the federal government are enumerated; it can only operate in certain cases; it has legislative powers on defined and limited objects, beyond which it cannot extend its jurisdiction.

But the honorable member has satirized, with peculiar acrimony, the powers given to the general government by this Constitution. I conceive that the first question on this subject is, whether these powers be necessary; if they be, we are reduced to the dilemma of either submitting to the inconvenience or losing the Union. Let us consider the most important of these reprobated powers; that of direct taxation is most generally objected to. With respect to the exigencies of government, there is no question but the most easy mode of providing for them will be adopted. When, therefore, direct taxes are not necessary, they will not be recurred to. It can be of little advantage to those in power to raise money in a manner oppressive to the people. To consult the conveniences of the people will cost them nothing, and in many respects will be advantageous to them. Direct taxes will only be recurred to for great purposes. What has brought on other nations those immense debts, under the pressure of which many of them labor? Not the expenses of their governments, but war. If this country should be engaged in war,Ñand I conceive we ought to provide for the possibility of such a case,Ñhow would it be carried on? By the usual means provided from year to year? As our imports will be necessary for the expenses of government and other common exigencies, how are we to carry on the means of defence? How is it possible a war could be supported without money or credit? And would it be possible for a government to have credit without having the power of raising money? No; it would be impossible for any government, in such a case, to defend itself. Then, I say, sir, that it is necessary to establish funds for extraordinary exigencies, and to give this power to the general government; for the utter inutility of previous requisitions on the states is too well known. . . .. This must be obvious to every member here; I think, therefore, that it is necessary, for the preservation of the Union, that this power shall be given to the general government.

But it is urged that its consolidated nature, joined to the power of direct taxation, will give it a tendency to destroy all subordinate authority; that its increasing influence will speedily enable it to absorb the state governments. I cannot think this will be the case. If the general government were wholly independent of the governments of the particular states, then, indeed, usurpation might be expected to the fullest extent. But, sir, on whom does this general government depend? It derives its authority from these governments, and from the same sources from which their authority is derived. The members of the federal government are taken from the same men from whom those of the state legislatures are taken. If we consider the mode in which the federal representatives will be chosen, we shall be convinced that the general will never destroy the individual governments; . . .

1. What are Madison's disagreements with Patrick Henry regarding the general welfare of America and the laws concerning the number of states' votes needed to make alterations to the Constitution?
2. What is Madison's argument for the right of government to tax the people?

7-2 Alexander Hamilton, Final Version of "An Opinion on the Constitutionality of an Act to Establish a Bank" (1791)

An important document in the history of constitutional interpretation, this document sought to avoid a veto by President Washington of Alexander Hamilton's National Bank. In the early years of the Republic, finances were in great disarray and Hamilton, who had been Washington's aide de camp, a chief writer of the Federalist Papers, and was now the nation's first Secretary of the Treasury, sought to stabilize this condition with a national bank. Madison and others were violently opposed and Washington himself was poised to veto the measure. Hamilton's defense of the Bank became a classic statement of the implied powers of the Constitution.

The Secretary of the Treasury having perused with attention the papers containing the opinions of the Secretary of State and Attorney General [Edmund Randolph and Thomas Jefferson] concerning the constitutionality of the bill for establishing a National Bank proceeds according to the order of the President [George Washington] to submit the reasons which have induced him to entertain a different opinion.

It will naturally have been anticipated that, in performing this task he would feel uncommon solicitude. Personal considerations alone arising from the reflection that the measure originated with him would be sufficient to produce it: The sense which he has manifested of the great importance of such an institution to the successful administration of the department under his particular care; and an expectation of serious ill consequences to result from a failure of the measure, do not permit him to be without anxiety on public accounts. But the chief solicitude arises from a firm persuasion, that principles of construction like those espoused by the Secretary of State and the Attorney General would be fatal to the just & indispensible authority of the United States.

In entering upon the argument it ought to be premised, that the objections of the Secretary of State and Attorney General are founded on a general denial of the authority of the United States to erect corporations. The latter indeed expressly admits, that if there be any thing in the bill which is not warranted by the constitution, it is the clause of incorporation.

Now it appears to the Secretary of the Treasury, that this *general principle* is *inherent* in the very *definition of Government* and *essential* to every step of the progress to be made by that of the United States; namely-that every power vested in a Government is in its nature *sovereign*, and includes by *force* of the *term*, a right to employ all the *means* requisite, and fairly *applicable* to the attainment of the *ends* of such power; and which are not precluded by restrictions & exceptions specified in the constitution; or not immoral, or not contrary to the essential ends of political society.

This principle in its application to Government in general would be admitted as an axiom. And it will be incumbent upon those, who may incline to deny it, to *prove* a distinction; and to shew that a rule which in the general system of things is essential to the preservation of the social order is inapplicable to the United States.

The circumstances that the powers of sovereignty are in this country divided between the National and State Governments, does not afford the distinction required. It does not follow from this, that each of the *portions* of powers delegated to the one or to the other is not sovereign *with regard to its proper objects*. It will only *follow* from it, that each has sovereign power as to *certain things*, and not as to *other things*. To deny that the Government of the United States has sovereign power as to its declared purposes & trusts, because its power does not extend to all cases, would be equally to deny, that the State Governments have sovereign power in any case; because their power does not extend to every case. The tenth section of the first article of the constitution exhibits a long list of very important things which they may not do. And thus the United States would furnish the singular spectacle of a *political society* without *sovereignty*, or of a people *governed* without *government*.

If it would be necessary to bring proof to a proposition so clear as that which affirms that the powers of the federal government, *as to its objects*, are sovereign, there is a clause of its constitution which would be decisive. It is that which declares, that the constitution and the laws of the United States made in pursuance of it, and all treaties made or which shall be made under their authority shall be the supreme law of the land. The power which can create the *Supreme law* of the land, in any case, is doubtless sovereign *as to such case*.

This general & indisputable principle puts at once an end to the *abstract* question-Whether the United States have power to *erect a corporation*? that is to say, to give a *legal* or *artificial capacity* to one or more persons, distinct from the natural. For it is unquestionably incident to *sovereign power* to erect corporations, and consequently to *that* of the United Strates, in *relation to the objects* intrusted to the management of the government. The difference is this-where the authority of the government is general, it can create corporations in *all cases*; where it is confined to certain branches of legislation, it can create corporations only in those cases.

Here then as far as concerns the reasonings of the Secretary of State & the Attorney General, the affirmative of the constitutionality of the bill might be permitted to rest. It will occur to the President that the principle here advanced has been untouched by either of them. . . .

It is not denied, that there are *implied*, as well as *express* powers, and that the former are as effectually delegated as the latter. And for the sake of accuracy it shall be mentioned, that there is another class of powers, which may be properly denominated *resulting* powers. It will not be doubted that if the United States should make a conquest of any of the territories of its neighbours, they would possess sovereign jurisdiction over the conquered territory. This would rather be a result from the whole mass of the powers of the government & from the nature of political society, than a consequence of either of the powers specially enumerated.

But be this as it may, it furnishes a striking illustration of the general doctrine contended for it. It shews an extensive case, in which a power of erecting corporations is either implied in, or would result from some or all of the powers, vested in the National Government. The jurisdiction acquired over such conquered territory would certainly be competent to every species of legislation.

To return-It is conceded, that implied powers are to be considered as delegated equally with express ones.

Then it follows, that as a power of erecting a corporation may as well be *implied* as any other thing; it may as well be employed as an *instrument* or *mean* of carrying into execution any of the specified powers, as any other instrument or mean whatever. The only question must be, in this as in every other case, whether the mean to be employed, or in this instance the corporation to be erected, has a natural relation to any of the acknowledged objects or lawful ends of the government. Thus a corporation may not be erected by congress, for superintending the police of the city of Philadelphia because they are not authorised to *regulate* the *police* of that city; but one may be erected in relation to the collection of the taxes, or to the trade with foreign countries, or to the trade between the States, or with the Indian Tribes, because it is the province of the federal government to regulate those objects & because it is incident to a general *sovereign* or *legislative power* to *regulate* a thing, to employ all the means which relate to its regulation to the *best* & *greatest advantage*.

A strange fallacy seems to have crept into the manner of thinking & reasoning upon the subject. Imagination appears to have been unusually busy concerning it. An incorporation seems to have been regarded as some great, independent, substantive thing-as a political end of peculiar magnitude & moment; whereas it is truly to be considered as a *quality, capacity*, or *mean* to an end. Thus a mercantile company is formed with a certain capital for the purpose of carrying on a particular branch of business. Here the business to be prosecuted is the *end*; the association in order to form the requisite capital is the primary mean. Suppose that an incorporation were added to this; it would only be to add a new *quality* to that association; to give it an artificial capacity by which it would be enabled to prosecute the business with more safety & convenience.

That the importance of the power of incorporaton has been exaggerated, leading to erroneous conclusions, will further appear from tracing it to its origin. The roman law is the source of it, according to which a *voluntary* association of individuals at *any time* or *for any purpose* was capable of producing it. In England, whence our notions of it are immediately borrowed, it forms a part of the executive authority, & the exercise of it has been often *delegated* by that authority. Whence therefore the ground of the supposition, that it lies beyond the reach of all those very important portions of sovereign power, legislative as well as executive, which belong to the government of the United States?

To this mode of reasoning respecting the right of employing all the means requisite to the execution of the specified powers of the Government, it is objected that none but *necessary* & proper means are to be employed, & the Secretary of State [Jefferson] maintains, that no means are to be considered as *necessary*, but those without which the grant of the power would be *nugatory*. Nay so far does he go in his restrictive interpretation of the word, as even to make the case of *necessity* which shall warrant the constitutional exercise of the power to depend on *casual & temporary* circumstances, an idea which alone refutes the construction. The *expediency* of exercising a particular power, at a particular time, must indeed depend on *circumstance* but the constitutional right of exercising it must be uniform & invariable-the same to day, as to morrow.

All the arguments therefore against the constitutionality of the bill derived from the accidental existence of certain State-banks: institutions which *happen* to exist to day, & for ought that concerns the government of the United States, may disappear to morrow, must not only be rejected as fallacious, but must be viewed as demonstrative, that there is a *radical* source of error in the reasoning.

It is essential to the being of the National government, that so erroneous a conception of the meaning of the word *necessary*, should be exploded.

It is certain, that neither the grammatical, or popular sense of the term requires that construction. According to both, *necessary* often means no more *than needful, requisite, incidental, useful,* or *conducive* to. It is a common mode of expression to say, that it is *necessary* for a government or a person to do this or that thing, when nothing more is intended or understood, than that the interests of the government or person require, or will be promoted, by the doing of this or that thing. The imagination can be at no loss for exemplifications of the use of the word in this sense.

And it is the true one in which it is to be understood as used in the constitution. The whole turn of the clause containing it, indicates that it was the intent of the convention, by that clause to give a liberal latitude to the exercise of the specified powers. The expressions have peculiar comprehensiveness. They are-"to make *all laws,* necessary & proper for *carrying into execution* the foregoing powers & all *other powers* vested by the constituion in the *government* of the United States, or in any *department* or *officer* thereof." To understand the word as the Secretary of State does, would be to depart from its obvious & popular sense, and to give it a *restrictive* operation; an idea never before entertained. It would be to give it the same force as if the word *absolutely* or *indispensibly* had been prefixed to it.

Such a construction would beget endless uncertainty & embarassment. The cases must be palpable & extreme in which it could be pronounced with certainty, that a measure was absolutely necessary, or one without which the exercise of a given power would be nugatory. There are few measures of any government, which would stand so severe a test. To insist upon it, would be to make the criterion of the exercise of any implied power a *case of extreme necessity*; which is rather a rule to justify the overleaping of the bounds of constitutional authority, than to govern the ordinary exercise of it.

It may be truly said of every government, as well as of that of the United States, that it has only a right, to pass such laws as are necessary & proper to accomplish the objects intrusted to it. For no government has a right to do *merely what it pleases*. Hence by a process of reasoning similar to that of the Secretary of State, it might be proved, that neither of the State governments has a right to incorporate a bank. It might be shewn, that all the public business of the State, could be performed without a bank, and inferring thence that it was unnecessary it might be argued that it could not be done, because it is against the rule which has been just mentioned. A like mode of reasoning would prove, that there was no power to incorporate the Inhabitants of a town, with a few to a more perfect police: For it is certain, that an incorporation may be dispensed with, though it is better to have one. It is to be remembered, that there is no *express* power in any State constitution to erect corporations.

The *degree* in which a measure is necessary, can never be a test of the *legal* right to adopt it. That must ever be a matter of opinion; and can only be a test of expediency. The *relation* between the *measure* and the *end*, between the *nature* of *the mean* employed towards the execution of a power and the object of that power, must be the criterion of constitutionality not the more or less of *necessity* or *utility*. . . .

This restrictive interpretation of the word *necessary* is also contrary to this sound maxim of construction namely, that the powers contained in a constitution of government, especially those which concern the general administration of the affairs of a country, its finances, trade, defence & ought to be construed liberally, in advancement of the public good. This rule does not depend on the particular form of a government or on the particular demarkation of the boundaries of its powers, but on the nature and objects of government itself. The means by which national exigencies are to be provided for, national inconveniences obviated, national prosperity promoted, are of such infinite variety, extent and complexity, that there must, of necessity, be great latitude of discretion in the selection & application of those means. Hence consequently, the necessity & propriety of exercising the authorities intrusted to a government on principles of liberal construction. . . .

The truth is that difficulties on this point are inherent in the nature of the federal constitution. They result inevitably from a division of the legislative power. The consequence of this division is, that there will be cases clearly within the power of the National Government; others clearly without its power; and a third class, which will leave room for controversy & difference of opinion, & concerning which a reasonable latitude of judgment must be allowed.

But the doctrine which is contended for is not chargeable with the consequence imputed to it. It does not affirm that the National government is sovereign in all respects, but that it is sovereign to a certain extent: that is, to the extent of the objects of its specified powers.

It leaves therefore a criterion of what is constitutional, and of what is not so. This criterion is the *end* to which the measure relates as a *mean*. If the end be clearly comprehended within any of the specified powers, & if the measure have an obvious relation to that end, and is not forbidden by any particular provision of the constitution-it may safely be deemed to come within the compass of the national authority. There is also this further criterion which may materially assist the decision. Does the proposed measure abridge a preexisting right of any State, or of any individual? If it does not, there is a strong presumption in favour of its constitutionality; & slighter relations to any declared object of the constitution may be permitted to turn the scale. . . .

A hope is entertained, that it has by this time been made to appear, to the satisfaction of the President, that a bank has a natural relation to the power of collecting taxes; to that of borrowing money; to that of regulating trade; to that of providing for the common defence: and that as the bill under consideration contemplates the government in the light of a joint proprietor of the stock of the bank, it brings the case within the provision of the clause of the constitution which immediately respects the property of the United States.

1. Identify and Summarize Hamilton's opinion regarding the establishment of a National Bank
2. How does his consideration of what is "necessary" in government affect his reasoning?

7-3   Questions Concerning the Constitutionality of the Naional Bank

On December 14, 1780, Secretary of the Treasury Alexander Hamilton presented to Congress his plan for the establishment of a national bank-an institution necessary he believed, to ensure a stable currency and the proper allocation of capital for development. Unsure of the constitutionality of Hamilton's proposal, President Washington sought the opinion of Thomas Jefferson (as well as Hamilton and Attorney General Edmund Randolph). Jefferson's argument against the bank was based upon his belief in the limited powers and strict construction of the Constitution. Washington, however, ultimately sided with Hamilton's doctrine of implied powers and his assertion of broad federal authority.

> **Source:** The Avalon Project at the Yale Law School
> http://www.yale.edu/lawweb/avalon/jeffop1.htm

OPINION ON THE CONSTITUTIONALITY OF A NATIONAL BANK

February 15, 1791

The bill for establishing a National Bank undertakes among other things:

1. The subscribers into a corporation.
2. To enable them in their corporate capacities to receive grants of land; and so far is against the laws of Mortmain.
3. To make alien subscribers capable of holding lands; and so far is against the laws of Alienage.
4. To transmit these lands, on the death of a proprietor, to a certain line of successors; and so far changes the course of Descents.
5. To put the lands out of the reach of forfeiture or escheat; and so far is against the laws of Forfeiture and Escheat.
6. To transmit personal chattels to successors in a certain line; and so far is against the laws of Distribution.
7. To give them the sole and exclusive right of banking under the national authority; and so far is against the laws of Mono   poly.
8. To communicate to them a power to make laws paramount to the laws of the States: for so they must be construed, to protect the institution from the control of the State legislatures; and so, probably, they will be construed.

I consider the foundation of the Constitution as laid on this ground: That "all powers not delegated to the United States, by the Constitution, nor prohibited by it to the States, are reserved to the States or to the people." [Xth amendment.] To take a single step beyond the boundaries thus specially drawn around the powers of Congress, is to take possession of a boundless field of power, no longer susceptible of any definition. The incorporation of a bank, and the powers assumed by this bill, have not, in my opinion, been delegated to the United States, by the Constitution.

I. They are not among the powers specially enumerated: for these are: 1st A power to lay taxes for the purpose of paying the debts of the United States; but no debt is paid by this bill, nor any tax laid. Were it a bill to raise money, its origination in the Senate would condemn it by the Constitution.

2d. "To borrow money." But this bill neither borrows money nor ensures the borrowing it. The proprietors of the bank will be just as free as any other money holders, to lend or not to lend their money to the public. The operation proposed in the bill, first, to lend them two millions, and then to borrow them back again, cannot change the nature of the latter act, which will still be a payment, and not a loan, call it by what name you please.

3. To "regulate commerce with foreign nations, and among the States, and with the Indian tribes." To erect a bank, and to regulate commerce, are very different acts. He who erects a bank, creates a subject of commerce in its bills; so does he who makes a bushel of wheat, or digs a dollar out of the mines; yet neither of these persons regulates commerce thereby. To make a thing which may be bought and sold, is not to prescribe regulations for buying and selling. Besides, if this was an exercise of the power of regulating commerce, it would be void, as extending as much to the internal commerce of every State, as to its external. For the power given to Congress by the Constitution does not extend to the internal regulation of the commerce of a State, (that is to say of the commerce between citizen and citizen,) which remain exclusively with its own legislature; but to its external commerce only, that is to say, its commerce with another State, or with foreign nations, or with the Indian tribes. Accordingly the bill does not propose the measure as a regulation of trade, but as "productive of considerable advantages to trade." Still less are these powers covered by any other of the special enumerations.

II. Nor are they within either of the general phrases, which are the two following: —

1. To lay taxes to provide for the general welfare of the United States, that is to say, "to lay taxes for the purpose of providing for the general welfare." For the laying of taxes is the power, and the general welfare the purpose for which the power is to be exercised. They are not to lay taxes ad libitum for any purpose they please; but only to pay the debts or provide for the welfare of the Union. In like manner, they are not to do anything they please to provide for the general welfare, but only to lay taxes for that purpose. To consider the latter phrase, not as describing the purpose of the first, but as giving a distinct and independent power to do any act they please, which might be for the good of the Union, would render all the preceding and subsequent enumerations of power completely useless.

It would reduce the whole instrument to a single phrase, that of instituting a Congress with power to do whatever would be for the good of the United States; and, as they would be the sole judges of the good or evil, it would be also a power to do whatever evil they please.

It is an established rule of construction where a phrase will bear either of two meanings, to give it that which will allow some meaning to the other parts of the instrument, and not that which would render all the others useless. Certainly no such universal power was meant to be given them. It was intended to lace them up straitly within the enumerated powers, and those without which, as means, these powers could not be carried into effect. It is known that the very power now proposed as a means was rejected as an end by the Convention which formed the Constitution. A proposition was made to them to authorize Congress to open canals, and an amendatory one to empower them to incorporate. But the whole was rejected, and one of the reasons for rejection urged in debate was, that then they would have a power to erect a bank, which would render the great cities, where there were prejudices and jealousies on the subject, adverse to the reception of the Constitution.

2. The second general phrase is, "to make all laws necessary and proper for carrying into execution the enumerated powers." But they can all be carried into execution without a bank. A bank therefore is not necessary, and consequently not authorized by this phrase.

It has been urged that a bank will give great facility or convenience in the collection of taxes. Suppose this were true: yet the Constitution allows only the means which are "necessary," not those which are merely "convenient" for effecting the enumerated powers. If such a latitude of construction be allowed to this phrase as to give any non-enumerated power, it will go to every one, for there is not one which ingenuity may not torture into a convenience in some instance or other, to some one of so long a list of enumerated powers. It would swallow up all the delegated powers, and reduce the whole to one power, as before observed. Therefore it was that the Constitution restrained them to the necessary means, that is to say, to those means without which the grant of power would be nugatory.

But let us examine this convenience and see what it is. The report on this subject, page 3, states the only general convenience to be, the preventing the transportation and re-transportation of money between the States and the treasury, (for I pass over the increase of circulating medium, ascribed to it as a want, and which, according to my ideas of paper money, is clearly a demerit.) Every State will have to pay a sum of tax money into the treasury; and the treasury will have to pay, in every State, a part of the interest on the public debt, and salaries to the officers of government resident in that State. In most of the States there will still be a surplus of tax money to come up to the seat of government for the officers residing there. The payments of interest and salary in each State may be made by treasury orders on the State collector. This will take up the greater part of the money he has collected in his State, and consequently prevent the great mass of it from being drawn out of the State. If there be a balance of commerce in favor of that State against the one in which the government resides, the surplus of taxes will be remitted by the bills of exchange drawn for that commercial balance. And so it must be if there was a bank. But if there be no balance of commerce, either direct or circuitous, all the banks in the world could not bring up the surplus of taxes but in the form of money. Treasury orders then, and bills of exchange may prevent the displacement of the main mass of the money collected, without the aid of any bank; and where these fail, it cannot be prevented even with that aid.

Perhaps, indeed, bank bills may be a more convenient vehicle than treasury orders. But a little difference in the degree of convenience, cannot constitute the necessity which the constitution makes the ground for assuming any non-enumerated power.

Besides; the existing banks will, without a doubt, enter into arrangements for lending their agency, and the more favorable, as there will be a competition among them for it; whereas the bill delivers us up bound to the national bank, who are free to refuse all arrangement, but on their own terms, and the public not free, on such refusal, to employ any other bank. That of Philadelphia, I believe, now does this business, by their post-notes, which, by an arrangement with the treasury, are paid by any State collector to whom they are presented. This expedient alone suffices to prevent the existence of that necessity which may justify the assumption of a non-enumerated power as a means for carrying into effect an enumerated one. The thing may be done, and has been done, and well done, without this assumption; therefore, it does not stand on that degree of necessity which can honestly justify it.

It may be said that a bank whose bills would have a currency all over the States, would be more convenient than one whose currency is limited to a single State. So it would be still more convenient that there should be a bank, whose bills should have a currency all over the world. But it does not follow from this superior conveniency, that there exists anywhere a power to establish such a bank; or that the world may not go on very well without it.

Can it be thought that the Constitution intended that for a shade or two of convenience, more or less, Congress should be authorised to break down the most ancient and fundamental laws of the several States; such as those against Mortmain, the laws of Alienage, the rules of descent, the acts of distribution, the laws of escheat and forfeiture, the laws of monopoly? Nothing but a necessity invincible by any other means, can justify such a prostitution of laws, which constitute the pillars of our whole system of jurisprudence. Will Congress be too straight-laced to carry the constitution into honest effect, unless they may pass over the foundation-laws of the State government for the slightest convenience of theirs?

The negative of the President is the shield provided by the constitution to protect against the invasions of the legislature: 1. The right of the Executive. 2. Of the Judiciary. 3. Of the States and State legislatures. The present is the case of a right remaining exclusively with the States, and consequently one of those intended by the Constitution to be placed under its protection.

It must be added, however, that unless the President's mind on a view of everything which is urged for and against this bill, is tolerably clear that it is unauthorised by the Constitution; if the pro and the con hang so even as to balance his judgment, a just respect for the wisdom of the legislature would naturally decide the balance in favor of their opinion. It is chiefly for cases where they are clearly misled by error, ambition, or interest, that the Constitution has placed a check in the negative of the President.

1. According to Jefferson, how might Hamilton's national bank violate the yet to be ratified Tenth Amendment?
2. It can be argued that Jefferson's objections to Hamilton's plan extend beyond the issue of its constitutionality. Discuss the ways in which the national bank could support Hamilton in building up his own political power?

7-4 Opposing Visions for the New Nation (1791)

As Secretary of the Treasury during the Washington Administration, Alexander Hamilton released on December 5, 1791, what in essence way the capstone of his comprehensive economic program—the "Report on Manufactures." His plan included the establishment of a program of protective tariffs and the use of government revenue to support new industries. The result, he believed, would be the development of an industrial economy in the United States. Secretary of State Thomas Jefferson, on the other hand, espoused the virtues of the yeoman farmer. Twelve years Hamilton's senior, Jefferson wrote in his *Notes on Virginia* that "Those that labor in the earth are the chosen people of God. . . ." The opposing ideologies of these two men still resonate today.

> **Source:** *The Works of Alexander Hamilton*, ed. H. C. Lodge (New York: G. P. Putnam's Sons, 1904).
> http://www.multied.com/documents/Manufactures.html
> The Avalon Project at the Yale Law School
> http://www.yale.edu/lawweb/avalon/jevifram.htm

REPORT ON MANUFACTURES (1791)

The expediency of encouraging manufactures in the United States . . . appears at this time to be pretty generally admitted. The embarrassments which have obstructed the progress of our external trade, have led to serious reflections on the necessity of enlarging the sphere of our domestic commerce. The restrictive regulations, which, in foreign markets, abridge the vent of the increasing surplus of our agricultural produce . . . beget an earnest desire that a more extensive demand for that surplus may be created at home. . . .

To affirm that the labor of the manufacturer is unproductive, because he consumes as much of the produce of land as he adds value to the raw material which he manufactures, is not better founded than it would be to affirm that the labor of the farmer, which furnishes materials to the manufacturer, is unproductive, because he consumes an equal value of manufactured articles. Each furnishes a certain portion of the produce of his labor to the other, and each destroys a corresponding portion of the produce of the labor of the other. In the meantime, the maintenance of two citizens, instead of one, is going on; the State has two members instead of one; and they, together, consume twice the value of what is produced from the land. . . .

It is now proper to proceed a step further, and to enumerate the principal circumstances from which it may be inferred that manufacturing establishments not only occasion a positive augmentation of the produce and revenue of the society, but that they contribute essentially to rendering them greater than they could possibly be without such establishments. These circumstances are:

1. The division of labor.
2. An extension of the use of machinery.
3. Additional employment to classes of the community not ordinarily engaged in the business.
4. The promoting of emigration from foreign countries.
5. The furnishing greater scope for the diversity of talents and dispositions, which discriminate men from each other.
6. The affording a more ample and various field for enterprise.
7. The creating, in some instances, a new, and securing, in all, a more certain and steady demand for the surplus produce of the soil.

Each of these circumstances has a considerable influence upon the total mass of industrious effort in a community; together, they add to it a degree of energy and effect which is not easily conceived. . .

1. As to the Division of Labor

It has justly been observed, that there is scarcely any thing of greater moment in the economy of a nation than the proper division of labor. The separation of occupations causes each to be carried to a much greater perfection than it could possibly acquire if they were blended. This arises principally from three circumstances:

1st. The greater skill and dexterity naturally resulting from a constant and undivided application to a single object.. . .
2d. The economy of time, by avoiding the loss of it, incident to a frequent transition from one operation to another of a different nature.. . .

3d. An extension of the use of machinery. A man occupied on a single object will have it more in his power, and will be more naturally led to exert his imagination, in devising methods to facilitate and abridge labor, than if he were perplexed by a variety of independent and dissimilar operations.. . .

2. As to an Extension of the Use of Machinery, a Point Which, Though Partly Anticipated, Requires to be Placed in One or Two Additional Lights

The employment of machinery forms an item of great importance in the general mass of national industry. It is an artificial force brought in aid of the natural force of man; and, to all the purposes of labor, is an increase of hands, an accession of strength, unencumbered too by the expense of maintaining the laborer. May it not, therefore, be fairly inferred, that those occupations which give greatest scope to the use of this auxiliary, contribute most to the general stock of industrious effort, and, in consequence, to the general product of industry?. . .

3. As to the Additional Employment of Classes of the Community not Originally Engaged in the Particular Business

This is not among the least valuable of the means by which manufacturing institutions contribute to augment the general stock of industry and production. In places where those institutions prevail, besides the persons regularly engaged in them, they afford occasional and extra employment to industrious individuals and families, who are willing to devote the leisure resulting from the intermissions of their ordinary pursuits to collateral labors, as a resource for multiplying their acquisitions or their enjoyments. The husbandman himself experiences a new source of profit and support from the increased industry of his wife and daughters, invited and stimulated by the demands of the neighboring manufactories.

It is worthy of particular remark that, in general, women and children are rendered more useful, and the latter more early useful, by manufacturing establishments, than they would otherwise be. Of the number of persons employed in the cotton manufactories of Great Britain, it is computed that four sevenths, nearly, are women and children, of whom the greatest proportion are children, and many of them of a very tender age.. . .

4. As to Promoting of Emigration from Foreign Countries

Men reluctantly quit one course of occupation and livelihood for another, unless invited to it by very apparent and proximate advantages. Many who would go from one country to another, if they had a prospect of continuing with more benefit the callings to which they have been educated, will often not be tempted to change their situation by the hope of doing better in some other way. Manufacturers who, listening to the powerful invitations of a better price for their fabrics or their labor, of greater cheapness of provisions and raw materials, of an exemption from the chief part of the taxes, burdens, and restraints which they endure in the Old World, of greater personal independence and consequence, under the operation of a more equal government, and of what is far more precious than mere religious toleration, a perfect equality of religious privileges, would probably flock from Europe to the United States, to pursue their own trades or professions, if they were once made sensible of the advantages they would enjoy, and were inspired with an assurance of encouragement and employment, will, with difficulty, be induced to transplant themselves, with a view to becoming cultivators of land.. . .

5. As to the Furnishing Greater Scope for the Diversity of Talents and Dispositions, Which Discriminate Men from Each Other

If there be any thing in a remark often to be met with, namely, that there is, in the genius of the people of this country, a peculiar aptitude for mechanic improvements, it would operate as a forcible reason for giving opportunities to the exercise of that species of talent, by the propagation of manufactures.

6. As to the Affording a More Ample and Various Field for Enterprise

The spirit of enterprise, useful and prolific as it is, must necessarily be contracted or expanded, in proportion to the simplicity or variety of the occupations and productions which are to be found in a society. It must be less in a nation of mere cultivators, than in a nation of cultivators and merchants; less in a nation of cultivators and merchants, than in a nation of cultivators, artificers, and merchants.

7. As to the Creating, In Some Instances, A New, and Securing, in all, a More Certain and Steady Demand for the Surplus Produce of the Soil

This is among the most important of the circumstances which have been indicated. It is a principal means by which the establishment of manufactures contributes to an augmentation of the produce or revenue of a country, and has an immediate and direct relation to the prosperity of agriculture.

It is evident that the exertions of the husbandman will be steady or fluctuating, vigorous or feeble, in proportion to the steadiness or fluctuation, adequateness or inadequateness, of the markets on which he must depend for the vent of the surplus which may be produced by his labor; and that such surplus, in the ordinary course of things, will be greater or less in the same proportion. . . .

This idea of an extensive domestic market for the surplus produce of the soil, is of the first consequence. It is, of all things, that which most effectually conduces to a flourishing state of agriculture. If the effect of manufactories should be to detach a portion of the hands which would otherwise be engaged in tillage, it might possibly cause a smaller quantity of lands to be under cultivation; but, by their tendency to procure a more certain demand for the surplus produce of the soil, they would, at the same time, cause the lands which were in cultivation to be better improved and more productive. And while, by their influence, the condition of each individual farmer would be meliorated, the total mass of agricultural production would probably be increased. For this must evidently depend as much upon the degree of improvement, if not more, than upon the number of acres under culture. . . .

The foregoing considerations seem sufficient to establish, as general propositions, that it is the interest of nations to diversify, the industrious pursuits of the individuals who compose them; that the establishment of manufactures is calculated not only to increase the general stock of useful and productive labor, but even to improve the state of agriculture in particular,—certainly to advance the interests of those who are engaged in it. . . .

NOTES ON THE STATE OF VIRGINIA (1785)

Query XIX

The present state of manufactures, commerce, interior and exterior trade?

Manufactures

We never had an interior trade of any importance. Our exterior commerce has suffered very much from the beginning of the present contest. During this time we have manufactured within our families the most necessary articles of cloathing. Those of cotton will bear some comparison with the same kinds of manufacture in Europe; but those of wool, flax and hemp are very coarse, unsightly, and unpleasant: and such is our attachment to agriculture, and such our preference for foreign manufactures, that be it wise or unwise, our people will certainly return as soon as they can, to the raising raw materials, and exchanging them for finer manufactures than they are able to execute themselves.

The political economists of Europe have established it as a principle that every state should endeavour to manufacture for itself. and this principle, like many others, we transfer to America, without calculating the difference of circumstance which should often produce a difference of result. In Europe the lands are either cultivated, or locked up against the cultivator. Manufacture must therefore be resorted to of necessity not of choice, to support the surplus of their people. But we have an immensity of land courting the industry of the husbandman. Is it best then that all our citizens should be employed in its improvement, or that one half should be called off from that to exercise manufactures and handicraft arts for the other? Those who labour in the earth are the chosen people of God, if ever he had a chosen people, whose breasts he has made his peculiar deposit for substantial and genuine virtue. It is the focus in which he keeps alive that sacred fire, which otherwise might escape from the face of the earth. Corruption of morals in the mass of cultivators is a phaenomenon of which no age nor nation has furnished an example. It is the mark set on those, who not looking up to heaven, to their own soil and industry, as does the husbandman, for their subsistence, depend for it on the casualties and caprice of customers. Dependance begets subservience and venality, suffocates the germ of virtue, and prepares fit tools for the designs of ambition. This, the natural progress and consequence of the arts, has sometimes perhaps been retarded by accidental circumstances: but, generally speaking, the proportion which the aggregate of the other classes of citizens bears in any state to that of its husbandman, is the proportion of its unsound to its healthy parts, and is a good-enough barometer whereby to measure its degree of corruption. While we have land to labour then, let us never wish to see our citizens occupied at a work-bench, or twirling a distaff. Carpenters, masons, smiths, are wanting in husbandry: but, for the general operations of manufacture, let our work-shops remain in Europe. It is better to carry provisions and materials to workmen there, than bring them to the provisions and materials, and with them their manners and principles. The loss by the transportation of commodities across the Atlantic will be made up in happiness and permanence of government. The mobs of great cities add just so much to the support of pure government, as sores do to the strength of the human body. It is the manners and spirit of a people which preserve a republic in vigour. A degeneracy in these is a canker which soon eats to the heart of its laws and constitution.

1. According to Hamilton's *Report*, what should be the relationship between agriculture and industry in the United States? How important is free enterprise and free trade in Hamilton's plan?
2. According to Thomas Jefferson, what is the danger inherent in an industrial economy?

7-5 George Washington, Farewell Address (1796)

Washington's Farewell Address was similar to one he had prepared with the help pf James Madison at the end of his first term, when he had contemplated retiring from public office. In May 1796, Washington wrote a first draft of a new address based on Madison's old notes, then presented manuscript to Alexander Hamilton for revisions. Hamilton rewrote the document, careful to preserve Washington's ideas or "sentiments," as he liked to call them. The result, rewritten again by Washington in a final version, was a product of adoption and adaption, but nonetheless representing the thoughts, ideas, and principles of the retiring president. Perhaps the most famous of his speeches, Washington's Farewell Address was never actually delivered orally. It first appeared in Philadelphia's *American Daily Advertiser* on September 19, 1796, and was later reprinted in other newspapers.

Observe good faith and justice toward all nations. Cultivate peace and harmony with all. Religion and morality enjoin this conduct. And can it be that good policy does not equally enjoin it? It will be worthy of a free, enlightened, and, at no distant period, a great nation to give to mankind the magnanimous and too novel example of a people always guided by an exalted justice and benevolence. . . .

In the execution of such a plan nothing is more essential than that permanent, inveterate antipathies against particular nations and passionate attachments for others should be excluded, and that, in place of them just and amicable feelings toward all should be cultivated. The nation which indulges toward another an habitual hatred or an habitual fondness is in some degree a slave. It is a slave to its animosity or to its affection either of which is sufficient to lead it astray from its duty and its interest. . . .

The nation prompted by ill will and resentment sometimes impels to war the government, contrary to the best calculations of policy. The government sometimes participates in the national propensity, and adopts through passion what reason would reject. . . .

So, likewise, a passionate attachment of one nation for another produces a variety of evils. Sympathy for the favorite nation, facilitating the illusion of an imaginary common interest in cases where no real common interest exists, and infusing into one the enmities of the other, betrays the former into a participation in the quarrels and wars of the latter without adequate inducement or justification. . . .

As avenues to foreign influence in innumerable ways, such attachments are particularly alarming to the truly enlightened and independent patriot. How many opportunities do they afford to tamper with domestic factions to practice the arts of seduction, to mislead public opinion, to influence or awe the public councils! Such an attachment of a small or weak toward a great and powerful nation dooms the former to be the satellite of the latter.

Against the insidious wiles of foreign influence (I conjure you to believe me, fellow citizens) the jealousy of a free people ought to be constantly awake, since history and experience prove that foreign influence is one of the most baneful foes of republican government. . . .

The great rule of conduct for us in regard to foreign nations is, in extending our commercial relation, to have with them as little political connection as possible. So far as we have already formed engagements, let them be fulfilled with perfect good faith. Here let us stop.

Europe has a set of primary interests which to us have no, or a very remote, relation. Hence she must be engaged in frequent controversies, the causes of which are essentially foreign to our concerns. Hence, therefore, it must be unwise in us to implicate ourselves by artificial ties in the ordinary vicissitudes of her politics, or the ordinary combinations and collisions of her friendships or enmities.

Our detached and distant situation invites and enables us to pursue a different course. If we remain one people, under an efficient government, the period is not far off when we may defy material injury from external annoyance; when we may take such an attitude as will cause the neutrality we may at any time resolve upon to be scrupulously respected; when belligerent nations, under the impossibility of making acquisitions upon us, will not lightly hazard the giving us provocation; when we may choose peace or war, as our interest, guided by justice, shall counsel.

Why forego the advantages of so peculiar a situation? Why quit our own to stand upon foreign ground? Why, by interweaving our destiny with that of any part of Europe, entangle our peace and prosperity in the toils of European ambition, rivalship, interest, humor, or caprice?

It is our true policy to steer clear of permanent alliances with any portion of the foreign world, so far, I mean, as we are now at liberty to do it. For let me not be understood as capable of patronizing infidelity to existing engagements. I hold the maxim of less applicable to public than to private affairs that honesty is always the best policy. I repeat, therefore, let those engagements be observed in their genuine sense. But in my opinion it is unnecessary and would be unwise to extend them.

Taking care always to keep ourselves by suitable establishments on a respectable defensive posture, we may safely trust to temporary alliances for extraordinary emergencies.

Harmony, liberal intercourse with all nations, are recommended by policy, humanity, and interest. But even our commercial policy should hold an equal an impartial hand, neither seeking nor granting exclusive favors or preference; . . . constantly keeping in view that it is folly in one nation to look for disinterested favors from another; that it must pay with a portion of its independence for whatever it may accept under that character; that by such acceptance it may place itself in the condition of having given equivalents for nominal favors, and yet of being reproached with ingratitude for not giving more. There can be no greater error than to expect or calculate upon real favors from nation to nation. It is an illusion which experience must cure, which a just pride ought to discard.

1. Explain.why Washington warns against habitual hatred or fondness for other countries?
2. Identify and explain the foreign policy for America proposed by Washington in this address.

7-6 The Alien and Sedition Acts (1798)

Written in response to fears of war with Revolutionary France, The Alien and Sedition Acts also sought to injure the new Jeffersonian Republican party which, it was thought, harbored support of the Revolutionary Government. The high number of recent immigrants active in the party was also seen as evidence of disloyalty. The acts triggered several constitutional disputes and some were imprisoned. The election of Thomas Jefferson to the Presidency ended the enforcement of these infamous laws, though elements of them were utilized years later.

The Alien Act

June 25, 1798. Statute II., Chap. LVIII.-An Act Concerning Aliens

SECTION I. *Be it enacted by the Senate and House of Representatives of the United States of America in Congress assembled,* That it shall be lawful for the President of the United States at any time during the continuance of this act, to *order* all such *aliens* as he shall judge dangerous to the peace and safety of the United States, or shall have reasonable grounds to suspect are concerned in any treasonable or secret machinations against the government thereof, to depart out of the territory of the United States, within such time as shall be expressed in such order, which order shall be served on such alien by delivering him a copy thereof, or leaving the same at his usual abode, and returned to the office of the Secretary of State, by the marshal or other person to whom the same shall be directed. And in case any alien, so ordered to depart, shall be found at large within the United States after the time limited in such order for his departure, and not having obtained a *license* from the President to reside therein, or having obtained such *license* shall not have conformed thereto, every such alien shall, on conviction thereof, be imprisoned for a term not exceeding three years, and shall never after be admitted to become a citizen of the United States. *Provided always and be it further enacted,* that if any alien so ordered to depart shall prove to the satisfaction of the President, by evidence to be taken before such person or persons as the President shall direct who are for that purpose hereby authorized to administer oaths, that no injury or danger to the United States will arise from suffering such alien to reside therein, the President may grant a *license* to such alien to remain within the United States for such time as he shall judge proper, and at such place as he may designate. And the President may also require of such alien to enter into a bond to the United States, in such penal sum as he may direct, with one or more sufficient sureties to the satisfaction of the person authorized by the President to take the same, conditioned for the good behavior of such alien during his residence in the United States, and not violating his license, which license the President may revoke whenever he shall think proper.

SEC. 2. *And be it further enacted,* That is shall be lawful for the President of the United States, whenever he may deem it necessary for the public safety, to order to be removed out of the territory thereof, any alien who may or shall be in prison in pursuance of this act; and to cause to be arrested and sent out of the United States such of those aliens as shall have been ordered to depart therefrom and shall not have obtained a license as aforesaid, in all cases where, in the opinion of the President, the public safety requires a speedy removal. And if any alien so removed or sent out of the United States by the President shall voluntarily return thereto, unless by permission of the President of the United States, such alien on conviction thereof, shall be imprisoned so long as, in the opinion of the President, the public safety may require.

SEC. 3. *And be it further enacted,* That every master or commander of any ship or vessel which shall come into any port of the United States after the first day of July next, shall immediately on his arrival make report in writing to the collector, or other chief officer of the customs of such port, of all aliens, if any, on board his vessel, specifying their names, age, the place of nativity, the country from which they shall have come, the nation to which they belong and owe allegiance, their occupation and a description of their persons, as far as he shall be informed thereof, and on failure, every such master and commander shall forfeit and pay three hundred dollars, for the payment whereof on default of such master or commander, such vessel shall also be holden, and may by such collector or other officer of the customs be detained. And it shall be the duty of such collector, or other officer of the customs, forthwith to transmit to the office of the department of state true copies of all such returns.

SEC. 4. *And be it further enacted,* That the circuit and district courts of the United States, shall respectively have cognizance of all crimes and offences against this act. And all marshals and other officers of the United States are required to execute all precepts and orders of the President of the United States issued in pursuance or by virtue of this act.

SEC. 5. *And be it further enacted*, That it shall be lawful for any alien who may be ordered to be removed from the United States, by virtue of this act, to take with him such part of his goods, chattels, or other property, as he may find convenient; and all property left in the United States by any alien, who may be removed, as aforesaid, shall be, and remain subject to his order and disposal, in the same manner as if this act had not been passed.

SEC. 6. *And be it further enacted*, That this act shall continue and be in force for and during the term of two years from the passing thereof.

APPROVED, June 25, 1798.-*Statutes at Large of the United States*, ed. 1850, Vol. I., pp. 570-572.

The Second Alien Act

July 6, 1798. Statute II., Chap. LXVI.-An Act respecting Alien Enemies

SECTION 1. *Be it enacted by the Senate and House of Representatives of the United States of America in Congress assembled*, That whenever there shall be a declared war between the United States and any foreign nation or government, or any invasion or predatory incursion shall be perpetrated, attempted, or threatened against the territory of the United States, by any foreign nation or government, and the President of the United States shall make public proclamation of the event, all natives, citizens, denizens, or subjects of the hostile nation or government, being males of the age of fourteen years and upwards, who shall be within the United States, and not actually naturalized, shall be liable to be apprehended, restrained, secured and removed, as alien enemies. And the President of the United States shall be, and he is hereby authorized, in any event, as aforesaid, by his proclamation thereof or other public act, to direct the conduct to be observed, on the part of the United States, towards the aliens who shall become liable, as aforesaid; the manner and degree of the restraint to which they shall be subject, and in what cases, and upon what security their residence shall be permitted, and to provide for the removal of those, who, not being permitted to reside within the United States, shall refuse or neglect to depart therefrom; and to establish any other regulations which shall be found necessary in the premises and for the public safety: Provided, that aliens resident within the United States, who shall become liable as enemies, in the manner aforesaid, and who shall not be chargeable with actual hostility, or other crime against the public safety, shall be allowed for the recovery, disposal, and removal of their goods and effects, and for their departure, the full time which is, or shall be stipulated by any treaty, where any shall have been between the United States and the hostile nation or government, of which they shall be natives, citizens, denizens or subjects: and when no such treaty shall have existed, the President of the United States may ascertain and declare such reasonable time as may be consistent with the public safety, and according to the dictates of humanity and national hospitality.

SEC. 2. *And be it further enacted*, That after any proclamation shall be made as aforesaid, it shall be the duty of the several courts of the United States, and of each state, having criminal jurisdiction, and of the several judges and justices of the courts of the United States, and they shall be, and are hereby respectively, authorized upon complaint, against any alien or alien enemies, as aforesaid, who shall be resident and at large within such jurisdiction or district, to the danger of the public peace or safety, and contrary to the tenor or intent of such proclamation, or other regulations which the President of the United States shall and may establish in the premises, to cause such alien or aliens to be duly apprehended and convened before such court, judge or justice; and after a full examination and hearing on such complaint, and sufficient cause therefor appearing, shall and may order such alien or aliens to be removed out of the territory of the United States, or to give such sureties for their good behaviour, or to be otherwise restrained, conformably to the proclamation or regulations which shall or may be established as aforesaid, and may imprison, or otherwise secure such alien or aliens, until the order which shall and may be made, as aforesaid, shall be performed.

SEC. 3. *And be it further enacted*, That it shall be the duty of the marshal of the district in which any alien enemy shall be apprehended, who by condemnment of the United States, or by the order of any court judge or justice, as aforesaid, shall be required to depart, and to be removed, as aforesaid, to provide therefor, and to execute such order, by himself or his deputy, or other discreet person or persons to be employed by him, by causing a removal of such alien out of the territory of the United States; and for such removal the marshal shall have the warrant of the President of the United States, or of the court, judge or justice ordering the same, as the case may be.

APPROVED, July 6, 1798.-*Statutes at Large of the United States,* ed. of 1850, Vol. I., p. 577.

The Sedition Act

July 14, 1798. Chap. LXXIV.-An Act in addition to the act, entitled ''An Act for the punishment of certain crimes against the United States''

SECTION I. *Be it enacted by the Senate and House of Representatives of the United States of America, in Congress assembled,* That if any persons shall unlawfully combine or conspire together, with intent to oppose any measure or measures of the government of the United States, which are or shall be directed by proper authority, or to impede the operation of any law of the United States, or to intimidate or prevent any person holding a place of office in or under the government of the United States, from undertaking, performing or executing, his trust or duty; and if any person or persons, with intent as aforesaid, shall counsel, advise or attempt to procure any insurrection, riot, unlawful assembly, or combination, whether such conspiracy, threatening, counsel, advice, or attempt shall have the proposed effect or not, he or they shall be deemed guilty of a high misdemeanor, and on conviction, before any court of the United States having jurisdiction thereof, shall be punished by a fine not exceeding five thousand dollars, and by imprisonment during a term not less than six months nor exceeding five years; and further, at the discretion of the court may be holden to find sureties for his good behaviour in such sum, and for such time, as the said court may direct.

SEC. 2. *And be it further enacted,* That if any person shall write, print, utter or publish, or shall cause or procure to be written, printed, uttered or published, or shall knowingly and willingly assist or aid in writing, printing, uttering or publishing any false, scandalous and malicious writing or writings against the government of the United States, or the President of the United States, with intent to defame the said government, or either house of the said Congress, or the said President, or to bring them, or either of them, into contempt or disrepute; or to excite against them, or either or any of them, the hatred of the good people of the United States, or to stir up sedition within the United States, or to excite any unlawful combinations therein, for opposing (or resisting any law of the United States,) or any act of the President of the United States, done in pursuance of any such law, or of the powers in him vested by the Constitution of the United States, or to resist, oppose, or defeat any such law or act, or to aid, encourage or abet any hostile designs of any foreign nation against the United States, their people or government, then such person, being thereof convicted before any court of the United States having jurisdiction thereof, shall be punished by a fine not exceeding two thousand dollars, and by imprisonment not exceeding two years.

SEC. 3. *And be it further enacted and declared,* That if any person shall be prosecuted under this act, for the writing or publishing any libel aforesaid, it shall be lawful for the defendant, upon the trial of the cause, to give in evidence in his defence, the truth of the matter contained in the publication charged as a libel. And the jury who shall try the cause, shall have a right to determine the law and the fact, under the direction of the court, as in other cases.

SEC. 4. *And be it further enacted,* That this act shall continue and be in force until the third day of March, one thousand eight hundred and one, and no longer: *Provided,* that the expiration of the act shall not prevent or defeat a prosecution and punishment of any offence against the law, during the time it shall be in force.

APPROVED, July 14, 1798.-*Statutes at Large of the United States,* ed., of 1850, Vol. I., p. 596.

1. Summarize rights that are given to the President in the First and Second Alien Acts. How are these acts intended to protect the nation?
2. Summarize the Sedition Act. What limits are placed on freedom of speech and press by this Act?

7-7   *Marbury v. Madison* (1803)

The Marbury versus Madison case revolved around William Marbury, who had been appointed a justice of the peace by President John Adams two days before Adams ended his term. The new President, Thomas Jefferson, denied Marbury the position by directing the Secretary of State James Madison not to deliver the commission. Marbury filed a lawsuit, asking the Supreme Court to issue a writ of mandamus, forcing Madison to deliver the commission. Chief Justice John Marshall ruled that the court was not authorized to issue writs of mandamus and more importantly, in the following excerpt from the decision, made it clear that the Supreme Court did, however, have the power to declare legislation unconstitutional, thereby maintaining the balance of power in government. This is one of the landmark decisions of the Supreme Court, giving them more authority than they had previously held.

[CHIEF JUSTICE MARSHALL DELIVERED THE OPINION OF THE COURT.]

In the order in which the Court has viewed this subject, the following questions have been considered and decided: 1st. Has the applicant a right to the commission he demands? 2d. If he has a right, and that right has been violated, do the laws of this country afford him a remedy? 3d. If they do afford him a remedy, is it a mandamus issuing from this court? . . .

It is . . . the opinion of the Court: 1st. That by signing the commission of Mr. Marbury, the President of the United States appointed him a justice of the peace for the county of Washington, in the District of Columbia; and that the seal of the United States, affixed thereto by the secretary of state, is conclusive testimony of the verity of the signature, and of the completion of the appointment; and that the appointment conferred on him a legal right to the office for the space of five years. 2d. That, having this legal title to the office, he has a consequent right to the commission; a refusal to deliver which is a plain violation of that right, for which the laws of his country afford him a remedy. 3d. It remains to be inquired whether he is entitled to the remedy for which he applies? . . .

This . . . is a plain case for a mandamus, either to deliver the commission, or a copy of it from the record; and it only remains to be inquired, whether it can issue from this court?

The act to establish the judicial courts of the United States authorizes the Supreme Court, "to issue writs of mandamus, in cases warranted by the principles and usages of law, to any courts appointed or persons holding office, under the authority of the United States." The secretary of state, being a person holding an office under the authority of the United States, is precisely within the letter of this description; and if this court is not authorized to issue a writ of mandamus to such an officer, it must be because the law is unconstitutional . . .

The Constitution vests the whole judicial power of the United States in one Supreme Court, and such inferior courts as Congress shall, from time to time, ordain and establish. . . .

In the distribution of this power, it is declared that "the Supreme Court shall have original jurisdiction in all cases affecting ambassadors, other public ministers and consuls, and those in which a state shall be a party. In all other cases, the Supreme Court shall have appellate jurisdiction." . . .

If it had been intended to leave it in the discretion of the legislature to apportion the judicial power between the supreme and inferior courts according to the will of that body, it would certainly have been useless to have proceeded further than to have defined the judicial power, and the tribunals in which it should be vested. The subsequent part of the section is mere surplusage, is entirely without meaning, . . .

It cannot be presumed that any clause in the Constitution is intended to be without effect . . .

To enable this court, then, to issue a mandamus, it must be shown to be an exercise of appellate jurisdiction . . .

The authority, therefore, given to the Supreme Court, by the Act establishing the judicial courts of the United States, to issue writs of mandamus to public officers, appears not to be warranted by the Constitution . . .

1. Summarize the reasoning and legal decision regarding whether or not withholding Marbury's commission was a violation of his right to appointment.
2. Summarize the relationship that exists among the Constitution, the legislative branch of government, and the Supreme Court as it is discussed in this document? What is the role of the Supreme court in relation to the Constitution?

PART EIGHT
JEFFERSON AND THE REPUBLIC

8-1 "Memoirs of a Monticello Slave, as Dictated to Charles Campbell by Isaac" (1847)

A man of many and diverse interests and accomplishments, Thomas Jefferson is one of the greatest of American figures. An enduring stain on his reputation, however, is the fact that he kept slaves until the end of his life. This document demonstrates his qualities but the very fact that it is written by a man who was his slave points to his shortcomings.

Old Master was never seen to come out before breakfast-about 8 o'clock. If it was warm weather he wouldn't ride out till evening: studied upstairs till bell ring for dinner. When writing he had a copyin' machine. While he was a-writin' he wouldn't suffer nobody to come in his room. Had a dumb-waiter; when he wanted anything he had nothin' to do but turn a crank and the dumb-waiter would bring him water or fruit on a plate or anything he wanted. Old Master had abundance of books; sometimes would have twenty of 'em down on the floor at once-read fust one, then tother. Isaac has often wondered how Old Master came to have such a mighty head; read so many of them books; and when they go to him to ax him anything, he go right straight to the book and tell you all about it. He talked French and Italian. Madzay talked with him; his place was called Colle. General Redhazel (Riedesel) stayed there. He (Mazzei) lived at Monticello with Old Master some time. Didiot, a Frenchman, married his daughter Peggy, a heavy chunky looking woman-mighty handsome. She had a daughter Frances and a son Francis; called the daughter Franky. Mazzei brought to Monticello Antonine, Jovanini, Francis, Modena, and Belligrini, all gardeners. My Old Master's garden was monstrous large: two rows of palings, all 'round ten feet high.

Mr. Jefferson had a clock in his kitchen at Monticello; never went into the kitchen except to wind up the clock. He never would have less than eight covers at dinner if nobody at table but himself. Had from eight to thirty-two covers for dinner. Plenty of wine, best old Antigua rum and cider; very fond of wine and water. Isaac never heard of his being disguised in drink. He kept three fiddles; played in the arternoons and sometimes arter supper. This was in his early time. When he begin to git so old, he didn't play. Kept a spinnet made mostly in shape of a harpsichord; his daughter played on it. Mr. Fauble, a Frenchman that lived at Mr. Walker's, a music man, used to come to Monticello and tune it. There was a *fortepiano* and a guitar there. Never seed anybody play on them but the French people. Isaac never could git acquainted with them; could hardly larn their names. Mr. Jefferson always singing when ridin' or walkin'; hardly see him anywhar outdoors but what he was a-singin'. Had a fine clear voice, sung minnits (minuets) and sich; fiddled in the parlor. Old Master very kind to servants.

The fust year Mr. Jefferson was elected President, he took Isaac on to Philadelphia. He was then about fifteen years old; traveled on horseback in company with a Frenchman named Joseph Rattiff and Jim Hemings, a body servant. Fust day's journey they went from Monticello to old Nat Gordon's, on the Fredericksburg road, next day to Fredericksburg, then to Georgetown, crossed the Potomac there, and so to Philadelphia-eight days a-goin'. Had two ponies and Mr. Jefferson's tother riding horse Odin. Mr. Jefferson went in the phaeton. Bob Hemings drove; changed horses on the road. When they got to Philadelphia, Isaac stayed three days at Mr. Jefferson's house. Then he was bound prentice to one Bringhouse, a tinner; he lived in the direction of the Waterworks. Isaac remembers seeing the image of a woman thar holding a goose in her hand-the water spouting out of the goose's mouth. This was the head of Market Street. Bringhouse was a short, mighty small, neat-made; treated Isaac very well. Went thar to larn the tinner's trade. Fust week larnt to cut out and sodder; make little pepper boxes and graters and sich, out of scraps of tin, so as not to waste any till he had larnt. Then to making cups. Every Sunday Isaac would go to the President's house-large brick house, many windows; same house Ginral Washington lived in before when he was President. Old Master used to talk to me mighty free and ax me, "How you come on Isaac, larning de tin business?" As soon as he could make cups pretty well, he carred three or four to show him. Isaac made four dozen pint cups a day and larnt to tin copper and sheets (sheet iron)-make 'em tin. He lived four years with Old Bringhouse. One time Mr. Jefferson sent to Bringhouse to tin his copper kittles and pans for kitchen use; Bringhouse sent Isaac and another prentice thar-a white boy named Charles; can't think of his other name. Isaac was the only black boy in Bringhouse's shop. When Isaac carred the cups to his Old Master to show him, he was mightily pleased. Said, "Isaac you are larnin mighty fast; I bleeve I must send you back to Vaginny to car on the tin business. You is growin too big; no use for you to stay here no longer."

1. Analyze Isaac's account of the "Old Master's" lifestyle. How would you characterize his leisure? What seems to be his demeanor toward his slaves?
2. What does this first hand account reveal about different aspects of the life of a slave?

8-2 Thomas Jefferson, "First Inaugural Address" (1801)

Years after his presidency, Thomas Jefferson would call the election of 1800 "as real a revolution in the principles of our government as that of 1776 was in its form." His view of an agrarian republic was in sharp contrast to what he saw as the Federalists trend towards increasing national power and the Alien and Sedition Acts were, he thought, threatening civil liberties. His First Inaugural Address advanced many of the notions of what would be called Jefferson Democracy.

Friends and Fellow Citizens:

Called upon to undertake the duties of the first executive office of our country, I avail myself of the presence of that portion of my fellow citizens which is here assembled to express my grateful thanks for the favor with which they have been pleased to look toward me, to declare a sincere consciousness that the task is above my talents, and that I approach it with those anxious and awful presentiments which the greatness of the charge and the weakness of my powers so justly inspire. A rising nation, spread over a wide and fruitful land, traversing all the seas with the rich productions of their industry, engaged in commerce with nations who feel power and forget right, advancing rapidly to destinies beyond the reach of mortal eye-when I contemplate these transcendent objects and see the honor, the happiness, and the hopes of this beloved country committed to the issue and the auspices of this day, I shrink from the contemplation and humble myself before the magnitude of the undertaking. Utterly indeed should I despair did not the presence of many whom I here see remind me that in the other high authorities provided by our Constitution I shall find resources of wisdom, of virtue, and of zeal on which to rely under all difficulties. To you then, gentlemen, who are charged with the sovereign functions of legislation, and to those associated with you, I look with encouragement for that guidance and support which may enable us to steer with safety the vessel in which we are all embarked amidst the conflicting elements of a troubled world.

During the contest of opinion through which we have passed, the animation of discussions and of exertions has sometimes worn an aspect which might impose on strangers unused to think freely and to speak and to write what they think. But this being now decided by the voice of the nation, enounced according to the rules of the Constitution, all will of course arrange themselves under the will of the law and unite in common efforts for the common good. All, too, will bear in mind this sacred principle that, though the will of the majority is in all cases to prevail, that will, to be rightful, must be reasonable; that the minority possess their equal rights, which equal laws must protect and to violate which would be oppression. Let us then, fellow citizens, unite with one heart and one mind; let us restore to social intercourse that harmony and affection without which liberty, and even life itself, are but dreary things. And let us reflect that, having banished from our land that religious intolerance under which mankind so long bled and suffered, we have yet gained little if we countenance a political intolerance as despotic, as wicked, and capable of as bitter and bloody persecutions. During the throes and convulsions of the ancient world, during the agonizing spasms of infuriated man, seeking through blood and slaughter his long-lost liberty, it was not wonderful that the agitation of the billows should reach even this distant and peaceful shore, that this should be more felt and feared by some and less by others, and should divide opinions as to measures of safety.

But every difference of opinion is not a difference of principle. We have called by different names brethren of the same principle. We are all republicans; we are all federalists. If there be any among us who would wish to dissolve this Union or to change its republican form, let them stand undisturbed as monuments of the safety with which error of opinion may be tolerated, where reason is left free to combat it. I know, indeed, that some honest men fear that a republican government cannot be strong; that this government is not strong enough. But would the honest patriot, in the full tide of successful experiment, abandon a government which has so far kept us free and firm, on the theoretic and visionary fear that this government, the world's best hope, may by possibility want energy to preserve itself? I trust not. I believe this, on the contrary, the strongest government on earth. I believe it the only one where every man, at the call of the law, would fly to the standard of the law and would meet invasions of the public order as his own personal concern. Sometimes it is said that man cannot be trusted with the government of himself. Can he then be trusted with the government of others? Or have we found angels, in the form of kings, to govern him? Let history answer this question.

Let us then, with courage and confidence, pursue our own federal and republican principles, our attachment to Union and representative government. Kindly separated by nature and a wide ocean from the exterminating havoc of one quarter of the globe; too high-minded to endure the degradations of the others; possessing a chosen country, with room enough for our descendants to the thousandth and thousandth generation; entertaining a due sense of our equal right to the use of our own faculties, to the acquisitions of our own industry, to honor and confidence from our fellow citizens, resulting not from birth but from our actions and their sense of them; enlightened by a benign religion, professed indeed and practiced in various forms, yet all of them including honesty, truth, temperance, gratitude, and the love of man; acknowledging and adoring an overruling Providence which, by all its dispensations, proves that It delights in the happiness of man here and his greater happiness hereafter; with all these blessings, what more is necessary to make us a happy and a prosperous people? Still one thing more, fellow citizens-a wise and frugal government which shall restrain men from injuring one another, shall leave them otherwise free to regulate their own pursuits of industry and improvement, and shall not take from the mouth of labor the bread it has earned. This is the sum of good government, and this is necessary to close the circle of our felicities.

About to enter, fellow citizens, on the exercise of duties which comprehend everything dear and valuable to you, it is proper you should understand what I deem the essential principles of our government and, consequently, those which ought to shape its administration. I will compress them within the narrowest compass they will bear, stating the general principle but not all its limitations: Equal and exact justice to all men, of whatever state or persuasion, religious or political; peace, commerce, and honest friendship with all nations, entangling alliances with none; the support of the State governments in all their rights, as the most competent administrations for our domestic concerns and the surest bulwarks against anti-republican tendencies; the preservation of the general government in its whole constitutional vigor, as the sheet anchor of our peace at home and safety abroad; a jealous care of the right of election by the people, a mild and safe corrective of abuses which are lopped by the sword of revolution where peaceable remedies are unprovided; absolute acquiescence in the decisions of the majority, the vital principle of republics from which there is no appeal but to force, the vital principle and immediate parent of despotism; a well-disciplined militia, our best reliance in peace and for the first moments of war till regulars may relieve them; the supremacy of the civil over the military authority; economy in the public expense, that labor may be lightly burdened; the honest payment of our debts and sacred preservation of the public faith; encouragement of agriculture, and of commerce as its handmaid; the diffusion of information, and arraignment of all abuses at the bar of the public person, under the protection of the habeas corpus; and trial by juries, impartially selected. These principles form the bright constellation which has gone before us and guided our steps through an age of revolution and reformation. The wisdom of our sages and blood of our heroes have been devoted to their attainment; they should be the creed of our political faith, the text of civic instruction, the touchstone by which to try the services of those we trust; and should we wander from them in moments of error or of alarm, let us hasten to retrace our steps and to regain the road which alone leads to peace, liberty, and safety.

I repair then, fellow citizens, to the post you have assigned me. With experience enough in subordinate offices to have seen the difficulties of this, the greatest of all, I have learned to expect that it will rarely fall to the lot of imperfect man to retire from this station with the reputation and the favor which bring him into it. Without pretensions to that high confidence you reposed in our first and great revolutionary character, whose pre-eminent services had entitled him to the first place in his country's love and destined for him the fairest page in the volume of faithful history, I ask so much confidence only as may give firmness and effect to the legal administration of your affairs. I shall often be thought wrong by those whose positions will not command a view of the whole ground. I ask your indulgence for my own errors, which will never be intentional, and your support against the errors of others who may condemn what they would not if seen in all its parts. The approbation implied by your suffrage is a great consolation to me for the past, and my future solicitude will be to retain the good opinion of those who have bestowed it in advance, to conciliate that of others by doing them all the good in my power, and to be instrumental to the happiness and freedom of all.

Relying then on the patronage of your good will, I advance with obedience to the work, ready to retire from it whenever you become sensible how much better choice it is in your power to make. And may that Infinite Power which rules the destinies of the universe lead our councils to what is best and give them a favorable issue for your peace and prosperity.

1. What encouragement does Jefferson offer regarding unification between people and politicians of divided opinions in his speech?
2. Identify and explain what Jefferson defines as the "sum of good government" and "the essential principles of our government."

8-3 Constitutionality of the Louisiana Purchase (1803)

The Louisiana Purchase doubled the size of the nation. The 828,000 square miles were purchased from France for fifteen million dollars or about four cents an acre. The circumstances of the purchase were sudden and the Federalists argued that the Constitution made no provision for the purchase of land. Jefferson, who was usually a strict constructionist, argued for a broad view of the Constitution in this case. These documents discuss the purchase and Jefferson's justification.

Thomas Jefferson to John C. Breckinridge

Monticello, Aug. 12, 1803

DEAR SIR,-The enclosed letter, tho' directed to you, was intended to me also, and was left open with a request, that when perused, I would forward it to you. It gives me occasion to write a word to you on the subject of Louisiana, which being a new one, an interchange of sentiments may produce correct ideas before we are to act on them.

Our information as to the country is very incompleat; we have taken measures to obtain it in full as to the settled part, which I hope to receive in time for Congress. The boundaries, which I deem not admitting question, are the high lands on the western side of the Mississippi enclosing all it's waters, the Missouri of course, and terminating in the line drawn from the northwestern point of the Lake of the Woods to the nearest source of the Missipi, as lately settled between Gr Britain and the U S. We have some claims to extend on the sea coast Westwardly to the Rio Norte or Bravo, and better, to go Eastwardly to the Rio Perdido, between Mobile & Pensacola, the antient boundary of Louisiana. These claims will be a subject of negociation with Spain, and if, as soon as she is at war, we push them strongly with one hand, holding out a price in the other, we shall certainly obtain the Floridas, and all in good time. In the meanwhile, without waiting for permission, we shall enter into the exercise of the natural right we have always insisted on with Spain, to wit, that of a nation holding the upper part of streams, having a right of innocent passage thro' them to the ocean. We shall prepare her to see us practise on this, & she will not oppose it by force.

Objections are raising to the Eastward against the vast extent of our boundaries, and propositions are made to exchange Louisiana, or a part of it, for the Floridas. But, as I have said, we shall get the Floridas without, and I would not give one inch of the waters of the Mississippi to any nation, because I see in a light very important to our peace the exclusive right to it's navigation, & the admission of no nation into it, but as into the Potomak or Delaware, with our consent & under our police. These federalists see in this acquisition the formation of a new confederacy, embracing all the waters of the Missipi, on both sides of it, and a separation of it's Eastern waters from us. These combinations depend on so many circumstances which we cannot foresee, that I place little reliance on them. We have seldom seen neighborhood produce affection among nations. The reverse is almost the universal truth. Besides, if it should become the great interest of those nations to separate from this, if their happiness should depend on it so strongly as to induce them to go through that convulsion, why should the Atlantic States dread it? But especially why should we, their present inhabitants, take side in such a question? When I view the Atlantic States, procuring for those on the Eastern waters of the Missipi friendly instead of hostile neighbors of it's Western waters, I do not view it as an Englishman would the procuring future blessing for the French nation, with whom he has no relations of blood or affection. The future inhabitants of the Atlantic & Missipi States will be our sons. We leave them in distinct but bordering establishments. We think we see their happiness in their union, & we wish it. Events may prove it otherwise; and if they see their interest in separation, why should we take side with our Atlantic rather than our Missipi descendants? It is the elder and the younger son differing. God bless them both, & keep them in union, if it be for their good, but separate them, if it be better. The inhabited part of Louisiana, from Point Coupe to the sea, will of course be immediately a territorial government, and soon a State. But above that, the best use we can make of the country for some time, will be to give establishments in it to the Indians on the East side of the Missipi, in exchange for their present country, and open land offices in the last, & thus make this acquisition the means of filling up the Eastern side, instead of drawing off it's population. When we shall be full on this side, we may lay off a range of States on the Western bank from the head to the mouth, & so, range after range, advancing compactly as we multiply.

This treaty must of course be laid before both Houses, because both have important functions to exercise respecting it. They, I presume, will see their duty to their country in ratifying & paying for it, so as to secure a good which would otherwise probably be never again in their power. But I suppose they must then appeal to *the nation* for an additional article to the Constitution, approving & confirming an act which the nation had not previously authorized. The constitution has made no provision for our holding foreign territory, still less for incorporating foreign nations into our Union. The Executive in seizing the fugitive occurrence which so much advances the good of their country, have done an act beyond the Constitution. The Legislature in casting behind them metaphysical subtleties, and risking themselves like faithful servants, must ratify & pay for it, and throw themselves on their country for doing for them unauthorized what we know they would have done for themselves had they been in a situation to do it. It is the case of a guardian, investing the money of his ward in purchasing an important adjacent territory; & saying to him when of age, I did this for your good;

I pretend to no right to bind you: you may disavow me, and I must get out of the scrape as I can: I thought it my duty to risk myself for you. But we shall not be disavowed by the nation, and their act of indemnity will confirm & not weaken the Constitution, by more strongly marking out its lines.

We have nothing later from Europe than the public papers give. I hope yourself and all the Western members will make a sacred point of being at the first day of the meeting of Congress; for *vestra res agitur.*

Accept my affectionate salutations & assurances of esteem & respect.

Thomas Jefferson to Wilson Cary Nicholas

Monticello, Sep. 7, 1803

DEAR SIR,-Your favor of the 3d was delivered me at court; but we were much disappointed at not seeing you here, Mr. Madison & the Gov. being here at the time. I enclose you a letter from Monroe on the subject of the late treaty. You will observe a hint in it, to do without delay what we are bound to do. There is reason, in the opinion of our ministers, to believe, that if the thing were to do over again, it could not be obtained, & that if we give the least opening, they will declare the treaty void. A warning amounting to that has been given to them, & an unusual kind of letter written by their minister to our Secretary of State, direct. Whatever Congress shall think it necessary to do, should be done with as little debate as possible, & particularly so far as respects the constitutional difficulty. I am aware of the force of the observations you make on the power given by the Constn to Congress, to admit new States into the Union, without restraining the subject to the territory then constituting the U S. But when I consider that the limits of the U S are precisely fixed by the treaty of 1783, that the Constitution expressly declares itself to be made for the U S, I cannot help believing the intention was to permit Congress to admit into the Union new States, which should be formed out of the territory for which, & under whose authority alone, they were then acting. I do not believe it was meant that they might receive England, Ireland, Holland, &c. into it, which would be the case on your construction. When an instrument admits two constructions, the one safe, the other dangerous, the one precise, the other indefinite, I prefer that which is safe & precise. I had rather ask an enlargement of power from the nation, where it is found necessary, than to assume it by a construction which would make our powers boundless. Our peculiar security is in possession of a written Constitution. Let us not make it a blank paper by construction. I say the same as to the opinion of those who consider the grant of the treaty making power as boundless. If it is, then we have no Constitution. If it has bounds, they can be no others than the definitions of the power which that instrument gives. It specifies & delineates the operations permitted to the federal government, and gives all the powers necessary to carry these into execution. Whatever of these enumerated objects is proper for a law, Congress may make the law; whatever is proper to be executed by way of a treaty, the President & Senate may enter into the treaty; whatever is to be done by a judicial sentence, the judges may pass the sentence. Nothing is more likely than that their enumeration of powers is defective. This is the ordinary case of all human works. Let us go on then perfecting it, by adding, by way of amendment to the Constitution, those powers which time & trial show are still wanting. But it has been taken too much for granted, that by this rigorous construction the treaty power would be reduced to nothing. I had occasion once to examine its effect on the French treaty, made by the old Congress, & found that out of thirty odd articles which that contained, there were one, two, or three only which could not now be stipulated under our present Constitution. I confess, then, I think it important, in the present case, to set an example against broad construction, by appealing for new power to the people. If, however, our friends shall think differently, certainly I shall acquiesce with satisfaction; confiding, that the good sense of our country will correct the evil of construction when it shall produce ill effects.

No apologies for writing or speaking to me freely are necessary. On the contrary, nothing my friends can do is so dear to me, & proves to me their friendship so clearly, as the information they give me of their sentiments & those of others on interesting points where I am to act, and where information & warning is so essential to excite in me that due reflection which ought to precede action. I leave this about the 21st, and shall hope the District Court will give me an opportunity of seeing you.

Accept my affectionate salutations, & assurances of cordial esteem & respect.

Thomas Paine to John C. Breckinridge

I know little and can learn but little of the extent and present population of Louisiana. After the cession be completed and the territory annexed to the United States it will, I suppose, be formed into states, one, at least, to begin with. The people, as I have said, are new to us and we to them and a great deal will depend on a right beginning. As they have been transferred backward and forward several times from one European Government to another it is natural to conclude they have no fixed prejudices with respect to foreign attachments, and this puts them in a fit disposition for their new condition. The established religion is roman; but in what state it is as to exterior ceremonies (such as processions and celebrations), I know not. Had the cession to France continued with her, religion I suppose would have been put on the same footing as it is in that country, and there no ceremonial of religion can appear on the streets or highways; and the same regulation is particularly necessary now or there will soon be quarrells and tumults between the old settlers and the new. The Yankees will not move out of the road for a little wooden Jesus stuck on a stick and carried in procession nor kneel in the dirt to a wooden Virgin Mary. As we do not govern the territory as provinces but incorporated as states, religion there must be on the same footing it is here, and Catholics have the same rights as Catholics have with us and no others. As to political condition the Idea proper to be held out is, that we have neither conquered them, nor bought them, but formed a Union with them and they become in consequence of that union a part of the national sovereignty.

The present Inhabitants and their descendants will be a majority for some time, but new emigrations from the old states and from Europe, and intermarriages, will soon change the first face of things, and it is necessary to have this in mind when the first measures shall be taken. Everything done as an expedient grows worse every day, for in proportion as the mind grows up to the full standard of sight it disclaims the expedient. America had nearly been ruined by expedients in the first stages of the revolution, and perhaps would have been so, had not *Common Sense* broken the charm and the Declaration of Independence sent it into banishment.

1. In Jefferson's opinion, of what importance is the Mississippi River to the safety, security, and unity of the American states?
2. What concerns are noted by Thomas Paine in terms of religious differences between the population of the existing Union and the inhabitants of the new territories?

8-4 Sacagawea Interprets for Lewis and Clark (1804)

In November 1804, Meriwether Lewis, William Clark, and the Corps of Discovery arrived at the Hidatsa-Mandan villages near present day Bismarck, North Dakota. There they met and hired Toussaint Charbonneau, a French-Canadian fur trader and Sacagawea ("Canoe Launcher"), one of his two Shoshone "wives." Lewis and Clark believed Sacagawea could be important in trading for horses when the Corps reached the Bitterroot mountains and the Shoshones. While Sacagawea did not speak English, she spoke Shoshone and Hidatsa. Charbonneau spoke Hidatsa and French. It was hoped that when the expedition met the Shoshones, Sacagawea would talk with them, then translate to Hidatsa for Charbonneau, who would translate into French. The Corps' Francois Labiche spoke French and English, and would make the final translation so that Lewis and Clark could understand.

Source: Meriwether Lewis and William Clark, *History of the Expedition of Captains Lewis and Clark*, 2 Vols. (Chicago: A. C. McClurg & Co., 1924), 1: 406–411.

SATURDAY, August 17. Captain Lewis rose very early and despatched Drewyer and the Indian down the river in quest of the boats. Shields was sent out at the same time to hunt, while M'Neal prepared a breakfast out of the remainder of the meat. Drewyer had been gone about two hours, and the Indians were all anxiously waiting for some news, when an Indian who had straggled a short distance down the river returned with a report that he had seen the white men, who were only a short distance below, and were coming on. The Indians were all transported with joy, and the chief in the warmth of his satisfaction renewed his embrace to Captain Lewis, who was quite as much delighted as the Indians themselves. The report proved most agreeably true. On setting out at seven o'clock, Captain Clark, with Charbonneau and his wife, walked on shore; but they had not gone more than a mile before Captain Clark saw Sacagawea, who was with her husband one hundred yards ahead, begin to dance and show every mark of the most extravagant joy, turning round him and pointing to several Indians, whom he now saw advancing on horseback, sucking her fingers at the same time to indicate that they were of her native tribe. As they advanced Captain Clark discovered among them Drewyer dressed like an Indian, from whom he learnt the situation of the party. While the boats were performing the circuit he went towards the forks with the Indians, who, as they went along, sang aloud with the greatest appearance of delight. We soon drew near to the camp, and just as we approached it a woman made her way through the crowd towards Sacagawea, and recognising each other, they embraced with the most tender affection. The meeting of these two young women had in it something peculiarly touching, not only in the ardent manner in which their feelings were expressed, but from the real interest of their situation. They had been companions in childhood; in the war with the Minnetarees they had both been taken prisoners in the same battle, they had shared and softened the rigours of their captivity, till one of them had escaped from the Minnetarees, with scarce a hope of ever seeing her friend relieved from the hands of her enemies. While Sacagawea was renewing among the women the friendships of former days, Captain Clark went on, and was received by Captain Lewis and the chief, who, after the first embraces and salutations were over, conducted him to a sort of circular tent or shade of willows. Here he was seated on a white robe, and the chief immediately tied in his hair six small shells resembling pearls, an ornament highly valued by these people, who procured them in the course of trade from the seacoast. The moccasins of the whole party were then taken off, and after much ceremony the smoking began. After this the conference was to be opened, and glad of an opportunity of being able to converse more intelligibly, Sacagawea was sent for; she came into the tent, sat down, and was beginning to interpret, when in the person of Cameahwait she recognised her brother; she instantly jumped up and ran and embraced him, throwing over him her blanket and weeping profusely; the chief was himself moved, though not in the same degree. After some conversation between them she resumed her seat, and attempted to interpret for us, but her new situation seemed to overpower her, and she was frequently interrupted by her tears. After the council was finished, the unfortunate woman learnt that all her family were dead except two brothers, one of whom was absent, and a son of her eldest sister, a small boy, who was immediately adopted by her. The canoes arriving soon after, we formed a camp in a meadow on the left side, a little below the forks, took out our baggage, and by means of our sails and willow poles formed a canopy for our Indian visitors. About four o'clock the chiefs and warriors were collected, and after the customary ceremony of taking off the moccasins and smoking a pipe, we explained to them in a long harangue the purposes of our visit, making themselves one conspicuous object of the good wishes of our government, on whose strength as well as its friendly disposition we expatiated. We told them of their dependence on the will of our government for all future supplies of whatever was necessary either for their comfort or defence; that as we were sent to discover the best route by which merchandise could be conveyed to them, and no trade would be begun before our return, it was mutually advantageous that we should proceed with as little delay as possible; that we were under the necessity of requesting them to furnish us with horses to transport our baggage across the mountains, and a guide to show us the route, but that they should be amply remunerated for their horses, as well as for every other service they should render us. In the meantime our first wish was, that they should immediately collect as many horses as were necessary to transport our baggage to their village, where, at our leisure, we would trade with them for as many horses as they could spare.

The speech made a favourable impression; the chief in reply thanked us for our expressions of friendship towards himself and his nation, and declared their willingness to render us every service. He lamented that it would be so long before they should be supplied with firearms, but that till then they could subsist as they had heretofore done. He concluded by saying that there were not horses here sufficient to transport our goods, but that he would return to the village tomorrow, and bring all his own horses, and encourage his people to come over with theirs. The conference being ended to our satisfaction, we now inquired of Cameahwait what chiefs were among the party, and he pointed out two of them. We then distributed our presents: to Cameahwait we gave a medal of the small size, with the likeness of President Jefferson, and on the reverse a figure of hands clasped with a pipe and tomahawk; to this was added a uniform coat, a shirt, a pair of scarlet leggings, a carrot of tobacco, and some small articles. Each of the other chiefs received a small medal struck during the presidency of General Washington, a shirt, handkerchief, leggings, a knife, and some tobacco. Medals of the same sort were also presented to two young warriors, who though not chiefs were promising youths and very much respected in the tribe. These honorary gifts were followed by presents of paint, moccasins, awls, knives, beads, and looking-glasses. We also gave them all a plentiful meal of Indian corn, of which the hull is taken off by being boiled in lye; and as this was the first they had ever tasted, they were very much pleased with it. They had indeed abundant sources of surprise in all they saw: the appearance of the men, their arms, their clothing, the canoes, the strange looks of the negro, and the sagacity of our dog, all in turn shared their admiration, which was raised to astonishment by a shot from the airgun; this operation was instantly considered as *a great medicine*, by which they as well as the other Indians mean something emanating directly from the Great Spirit, or produced by his invisible and incomprehensible agency. The display of all these riches had been intermixed with inquiries into the geographical situation of their country, for we had learnt by experience that to keep the savages in good temper their attention should not be wearied with too much business, but that the serious affairs should be enlivened by a mixture of what is new and entertaining. Our hunters brought in very seasonably four deer and an antelope, the last of which we gave to the Indians, who in a very short time devoured it. After the council was over, we consulted as to our future operations. The game does not promise to last here for a number of days, and this circumstance combined with many others to induce our going on as soon as possible. Our Indian information as to the state of the Columbia is of a very alarming kind, and our first object is of course to ascertain the practicability of descending it, of which the Indians discourage our expectations. It was therefore agreed that Captain Clark should set off in the morning with eleven men, furnished, besides their arms, with tools for making canoes; that he should take Charbonneau and his wife to the camp of the Shoshonees, where he was to leave them, in order to hasten the collection of horses; that he was then to lead his men down to the Columbia, and if he found it navigable, and the timber in sufficient quantity, begin to build canoes. As soon as he had decided as to the propriety of proceeding down the Columbia or across the mountains, he was to send back one of the men with information of it to Captain Lewis, who by that time would have brought up the whole party and the rest of the baggage as far as the Shoshonee village.

Preparations were accordingly made this evening for such an arrangement. The sun is excessively hot in the day time, but the nights very cold, and rendered still more unpleasant from the want of any fuel except willow brush. The appearances, too, of game for many days' subsistence are not very favourable.

1. The Shoshone were known to have horses that the Corps of Discovery would need to cross the western mountains. What do you think the expedition would have done had they not found a Shoshone band or been able to trade for horses?
2. What was the relationship between Sacagawea and the Shoshone band encountered by the Corps? Do you think this relationship aided in the trading process and the success of the expedition? Why or why not?

PART NINE
ECONOMIC AND SOCIAL CHANGE

9-1 The Cherokee Treaty of 1817

In the interest of promoting orderly white expansion in the years immediately following the War of 1812, the United States government sought to open up lands adjacent to existing settlement and discourage widespread dispersal into the more distant west. Between 1816 and 1828, seventeen treaties relating to land cessions or boundary adjustments were signed between the United States Government and the five major Indian nations in the South. In a treaty signed on July 8, 1817, the Cherokee Nation agreed to give up two large tracts of land in North Carolina and Georgia in exchange for one of equal size west of the Mississippi River. Although signed by a substantial number of chiefs, the treaty spawned factions within the Cherokee Nation that would intensify in the decades to come.

Source: The Treaty of Cherokee Agency, in *American State Papers, Indian Affairs* (Washington: GPO, 1934), 2:129–31.
http://members.nbci.com/histroll/treaties/treaty2.html

Articles of a treaty concluded, at the Cherokee Agency, within the Cherokee nation, between major general Andrew Jackson, Joseph M'Minn, governor of the state of Tennessee, and general David Meriwether, commissioners plenipotentiary of the United States of America, of the one part, and the chiefs, head men, and warriors, of the Cherokee nation, east of the Mississippi river, and the chiefs, head men, and warriors, of the Cherokees on the Arkansas river, and their deputies, John D. Chisholm and James Rogers, duly authorized by the chiefs of the Cherokees on the Arkansas river, in open council, by written power of attorney, duly signed and executed, in presence of Joseph Sevier and William Ware.

WHEREAS in the autumn of the year one thousand eight hundred and eight, a deputation from the Upper and Lower Cherokee towns, duly authorized by their nation, went on to the city of Washington, the first named to declare to the President of the United States their anxious desire to engage in the pursuits of agriculture and civilized life, in the country they then occupied, and to make known to the President of the United States the impracticability of inducing the nation at large to do this, and to request the establishment of a division line between the upper and lower towns, so as to include all the waters of the Hiwassee river to the upper town, that, by thus contracting their society within narrow limits, they proposed to begin the establishment of fixed laws and a regular government: The deputies from the lower towns to make known their desire to continue the hunter life, and also the scarcity of game where they then lived, and, under those circumstances, their wish to remove across the Mississippi river, on some vacant lands of the United States. And whereas the President of the United States, after maturely considering the petitions of both parties, on the ninth day of January, A.D. one thousand eight hundred and nine, including other subjects, answered those petitions as follows:

"The United States, my children, are the friends of both parties, and, as far as can be reasonably asked, they are willing to satisfy the wishes of both. Those who remain may be assured of our patronage, our aid, and good neighborhood. Those who wish to remove, are permitted to send an exploring party to reconnoiter the country on the waters of the Arkansas and White rivers, and the higher up the better, as they will be the longer unapproached by our settlements, which will begin at the mouths of those rivers. The regular districts of the government of St. Louis are already laid off to the St. Francis.

"When this party shall have found a tract of country suiting the emigrants, and not claimed by other Indians, we will arrange with them and you the exchange of that for a just portion of the country they leave, and to a part of which, proportioned to their numbers, they have a right. Every aid towards their removal, and what will be necessary for them there, will then be freely administered to them; and when established in their new settlements, we shall still consider them as our children, give them the benefit of exchanging their peltries for what they will want at our factories, and always hold them firmly by the hand."

And whereas the Cherokees, relying on the promises of the President of the United States, as above recited, did explore the country on the west side of the Mississippi, and made choice of the country on the Arkansas and White rivers, and settled themselves down upon United States' lands, to which no other tribe of Indians have any just claim, and have duly notified the President of the United States thereof, and of their anxious desire for the full and complete ratification of his promise, and, to that end, as notified by the President of the United States, have sent on their agents, with full powers to execute a treaty, relinquishing to the United States all the right, title, and interest, to all lands of right to them belonging, as part of the Cherokee nation, which they have left, and which they are about to leave, proportioned to their numbers, including, with those now on the Arkansas, those who are about to remove thither, and to a portion of which they have an equal right agreeably to their numbers.

Now, know ye, that the contracting parties, to carry into full effect the before recited promises with good faith, and to promote a continuation of friendship with their brothers on the Arkansas river, and for that purpose to make an equal distribution of the annuities secured to be paid by the United States to the whole Cherokee nation, have agreed and concluded on the following articles, viz:

ARTICLE 1

The chiefs, head men, and warriors, of the whole Cherokee nation, cede to the United States all the lands lying north and east of the following boundaries, viz: Beginning at the high shoals of the Appalachy river, and running thence, along the boundary line between the Creek and Cherokee nations, westwardly to the Chatahouchy river; thence, up the Chatahouchy river, to the mouth of Souque creek; thence, continuing with the general course of the river until it reaches the Indian boundary line, and, should it strike the Turrurar river, thence, with its meanders, down said river to its mouth, in part of the proportion of land in the Cherokee nation east of the Mississippi, to which those now on the Arkansas and those about to remove there are justly entitled.

ARTICLE 2

The chiefs, head men, and warriors, of the whole Cherokee nation, do also cede to the United States all the lands lying north and west of the following boundary lines, viz: Beginning at the Indian boundry line that runs from the north bank of the Tennessee river, opposite to the mouth of Hywassee river, at a point on the top of Walden's ridge, where it divides the waters of the Tennessee river from those of the Sequatchie river; thence, along the said ridge, southwardly, to the bank of the Tennessee river, at a point near to a place called the Negro Sugar Camp, opposite to the upper end of the first island above Running Water Town; thence, westwardly, a straight line to the mouth of Little Sequatchie river; thence, up said river, to its main fork; thence, up its northernmost fork, to its source; and thence, due west, to the Indian boundary line.

ARTICLE 3

It is also stipulated by the contracting parties, that a census shall be taken of the whole Cherokee nation, during the month of June, in the year of our Lord one thousand eight hundred and eighteen, in the following manner, viz: That the census of those on the east side of the Mississippi river, who declare their intention of remaining, shall be taken by a commissioner appointed by the President of the United States, and a commissioner appointed by the Cherokees on the Arkansas river; and the census of the Cherokees on the Arkansas river, and those removing there, and who, at that time, declare their intention of removing there, shall be taken by a commissioner appointed by the President of the United States, and one appointed by the Cherokees east of the Mississippi river.

ARTICLE 4

The contracting parties do also stipulate that the annuity due from the United States to the whole Cherokee nation for the year one thousand eight hundred and eighteen, is to be divided between the two parts of the nation in proportion to their numbers, agreeably to the stipulations contained in the third article of this treaty; and to be continued to be divided thereafter in proportion to their numbers; and the lands to be apportioned and surrendered to the United States agreeably to the aforesaid enumeration, as the proportionate part, agreeably to their numbers, to which those who have removed, and who declare their intention to remove, have a just right, including these with the lands ceded in the first and second articles of this treaty.

ARTICLE 5

The United States bind themselves, in exchange for the lands ceded in the first and second articles hereof, to give to that part of the Cherokee nation on the Arkansas as much land on said river and White river as they have or may hereafter receive from the Cherokee nation east of the Mississippi, acre for acre, as the just proportion due that part of the nation on the Arkansas agreeably to their numbers; which is to commence on the north side of the Arkansas river, at the mouth of Point Remove or Budwell's Old Place; thence, by a straight line, northwardly, to strike Chataunga mountain, or the hill first above Shield's Ferry on White river, running up and between said rivers for complement, the banks of which rivers to be the lines; and to have the above line, from the point of beginning to the point on White river, run and marked, which shall be done soon after the ratification of this treaty; and all citizens of the United States, except Mrs. P. Lovely, who is to remain where she lives during life, removed from within the bounds as above named. And it is further stipulated, that the treaties heretofore between the Cherokee nation and the United States are to continue in full force with both parts of the nation, and both parts thereof entitled to all the immunities and privilege which the old nation enjoyed under the aforesaid treaties; the United States reserving the right of establishing factories, a military post, and roads, within the boundaries above defined.

ARTICLE 6

The United States do also bind themselves to give to all the poor warriors who may remove to the western side of the Mississippi river, one rifle gun and ammunition, one blanket, and one brass kettle, or, in lieu of the brass kettle, a beaver trap, which is to be considered as a full compensation for the improvements which they may leave; which articles are to be delivered at such point as the President of the United States may direct: and to aid in the removal of the emigrants, they further agree to furnish flat bottomed boats and provisions sufficient for that purpose: and to those emigrants whose improvements add real value to their lands, the United States agree to pay a full valuation for the same, which is to be ascertained by a commissioner appointed by the President of the United States for that purpose, and paid for as soon after the ratification of this treaty as practicable. The boats and provisions promised to the emigrants are to be furnished by the agent on the Tennessee river, at such time and place as the emigrants may notify him of; and it shall be his duty to furnish the same.

ARTICLE 7

And for all improvements which add real value to the lands lying within the boundaries ceded to the United States, by the first and second articles of this treaty, the United States do agree to pay for at the time, and to be valued in the same manner, as stipulated in the sixth article of this treaty; or, in lieu thereof, to give in exchange improvements of equal value which the emigrants may leave, and for which they are to receive pay. And it is further stipulated, that all these improvements, left by the emigrants within the bounds of the Cherokee nation east of the Mississippi river, which add real value to the lands, and for which the United States shall give a consideration, and not so exchanged, shall be rented to the Indians by the agent, year after year, for the benefit of the poor and decrepit of that part of the nation east of the Mississippi river, until surrendered by the nation, or to the nation. And it is further agreed, that the said Cherokee nation shall not be called upon for any part of the consideration paid for said improvements at any future period.

ARTICLE 8

And to each and every head of any Indian family residing on the east side of the Mississippi river, on the lands that are now, or may hereafter be, surrendered to the United States, who may wish to become citizens of the United States, the United States do agree to give a reservation of six hundred and forty acres of land, in a square, to include their improvements, which are to be as near the centre thereof as practicable, in which they will have a life estate, with a reversion in fee simple to their children, reserving to the widow her dower, the register of whose names is to be filed in the office of the Cherokee agent, which shall be kept open until the census is taken as stipulated in the third article of this treaty. Provided, That if any of the heads of families, for whom reservations may be made, should remove therefrom, then, in that case, the right to revert to the United States. And provided further, That the land which may be reserved under this article, be deducted from the amount which has been ceded under the first and second articles of this treaty.

ARTICLE 9

It is also provided by the contracting parties, that nothing in the foregoing articles shall be construed so as to prevent any of the parties so contracting from the free navigation of all the waters mentioned therein.

ARTICLE 10

The whole of the Cherokee nation do hereby cede to the United States all right, title, and claim, to all reservations made to Doublehead and others, which were reserved to them by a treaty made and entered into at the city of Washington, bearing date the seventh of January, one thousand eight hundred and six.

ARTICLE 11

It is further agreed that the boundary lines of the lands ceded to the United States by the first and second articles of this treaty, and the boundary line of the lands ceded by the United States in the fifth article of this treaty, is to be run and marked by a commissioner or commissioners appointed by the President of the United States, who shall be accompanied by such commissioners as the Cherokees may appoint; due notice thereof to be given to the nation.

ARTICLE 12

The United States do also bind themselves to prevent the intrusion of any of its citizens within the lands ceded by the first and second articles of this treaty, until the same shall be ratified by the President and Senate of the United States, and duly promulgated.

ARTICLE 13

The contracting parties do also stipulate that this treaty shall take effect and be obligatory on the contracting parties so soon as the same shall be ratified by the President of the United States, by and with the advice and consent of the Senate of the United States.

In witness of all and every thing herein determined, by and between the before recited contracting parties, we have, in full and open council, at the Cherokee Agency, this eighth day of July, A.D. one thousand eight hundred and seventeen, set our hands and seals.

1. What conditions of this treaty might have been appealing to some Cherokee leaders? Why do you think a significant number of chiefs signed it?
2. In its quest for orderly white settlement, what other options might the United States Government have pursued short of displacing native peoples in the South?

9-2   The Case for the Erie Canal

In 1807, Jesse Hawley was imprisoned for debt in Canandaigua, New York, largely as result of his business expenditures in transporting flour from the mills in Geneva. Hoping to render himself "useful to society," Hawley wrote a series of essays published in the Genesee *Messenger* under the name "Hercules," on the wisdom and reality of building an overland canal across New York State. His essays materially contributed to enlighten public opinion with regard to a projected canal. In a letter written to Hawley in 1822, De Witt Clinton wrote "I have no hesitation in stating, that the first suggestion of a canal from Lake Erie to the Hudson River, which came to my knowledge, was communicated in essays under the signature of 'Hercules'."

> **Source:** David Hosack, *Memoir of De Witt Clinton* (New York: J. Seymour, 1829)
> http://www.history.rochester.edu/canal/bib/hosack/APPOT.html

In consequence of the difference and conflict of political sentiments which pervade the United States, respecting the administration of the government, and the appropriation of their resources, it is probable that it will be left to the future politician to duly appreciate and justly admire the ingenuity and patriotism of Mr. Jefferson, which devised and promulgated the idea of appropriating the surplus revenue of the United States, after the payment of the national debt, to the improvement of canals, roads, &c. which he threw out in his second inaugural speech.

It appears by the president's last message, that there is a greater surplus of revenue than was anticipated at the time the terms for the discharge of the national debt were stipulated; so as to leave a sum of money in the treasury without any appropriation; for the use of which he has suggested its application to the improvement of some great national object, the undertaking of which is to be immediately commenced.

I will presume to assert, that the president himself will agree that, if not even before, at least, next to the utility of a National Institute, is the improvement of the navigation of our fresh waters.

This admitted, the next inquiry is—where and what waters can be improved, to afford the most extensive and immediate benefits to the agricultural and commercial interests of the United States?

With due deference to the president of the United States, and the committees appointed by the national legislature, who now have the subject under consideration, I will presume to suggest to them, that improvement which would afford the most immediate, and consequently the most extensive advantages which any other in the United States can possibly do. It is the connecting the waters of Lake Erie and those of the Mohawk and Hudson rivers by means of a canal.

As this project is probably not more than twelve months old in human conception, but imperfect data can be furnished on the subject at present—such as I am possessed of, I will add.

It ought to commence at the foot of Lake Erie, as soon as a suitable place can be found to afford a draft on its waters—to gain and preserve a moderate descent of ground it will have to pursue a north-eastern course for some miles, it then may pursue an east course and cross the Genesee River, somewhere above its Falls, thence near to, and probably in the channel of, Mud Creek, an outlet of Canandaigua Lake, and follow them into Seneca River; but leaving that, up stream to Jack's Rifts, for the purpose of preserving the head of water—thence meandering along between the high and low grounds of Onondaga and Oneida counties, going south of their lakes, and let it fall into the Mohawk and mingle with its waters somewhere above Utica.

The distance from Buffalo village, at the foot of Lake Erie, to Canandaigua, is ninety miles according to the present road—from thence, on the Seneca turnpike to Utica, is one hundred and twelve miles—making two hundred and two miles from Lake Erie to Utica. It is possible that the angles of the roads are equal to the necessary meanderings of the canal through so extensive and level a country. By Ellicott's map of the Holland company's tract, the level of the waters of Lake Erie are four hundred and fifty feet above that of Ontario. The level of the Mohawk above that of Ontario is not correctly known, but we can approximate the fact from the following comparative statement. From the canal at Rome or Fort Stanwix, down Wood Creek to Oneida Lake, is twenty miles through a tract of very level land, say ten feet fall. Oneida Lake thirty miles in length, say three feet fall—from thence to Three River Point, eighteen miles, say twelve feet fall—thence to Oswego Falls, twelve miles, say ten feet fall. The Falls a quarter of a mile, say fifteen feet fall—thence to Lake Ontario twenty-four miles, say fifteen feet fall, makes the elevation of Rome sixty-five feet above the waters of Ontario. From Rome to Utica, sixteen miles by land, and twenty-eight by water with good current, say twenty-five feet fall, which deduct from sixty-five leaves forty feet, the elevation of the Mohawk at Utica above the Ontario. As the whole of this calculation is conjectured without ever seeing any part of the ground except the villages of Utica and Rome, it cannot be pretended that it is correct; yet it is presumed to be sufficiently large. Deduct the difference between Utica and Ontario (forty feet) from the difference between Erie and Ontario (four hundred and fifty feet) and it leaves four hundred and ten feet fall, between the waters of Erie and the Mohawk at Utica, which will average two feet a mile on the whole distance.

The result of this crude calculation is sufficient, and merely intended to demonstrate the possibility, and even practicability, of the undertaking. When we consider the Herculean task performed on sundry canals in Europe, the crossing Genesee river and other streams which intersect the course of the route, cannot be admitted as insuperable obstacles to the undertaking.

Pretending to no knowledge in the science of canalling, consequently no calculation on the probable expenses will be hazarded—but the level country through which it would take its course, is such, that more than half the distance would require no further digging than to sink the ditch sufficient for the depth of water and its necessary banks; and it is obvious that it would require but few stone. The western part of the Genesee county and Onondaga county afford a sufficient supply. Other tracts no doubt would furnish at least partial supplies by occasional beds and quarried. The principal use of stone contemplated here is to wall the banks of the ditch. Where stone was scarce, timber could be substituted in the first essay, and stone could be boated to supply its place when decayed.

The magnitude of this improvement is far beyond the reach of individual capital in America, for the present age, and probably for a century to come. The present governor of the state of New-York has indeed suggested the idea of calling into its aid British capitalists; but as their object, by vesting their capital in foreign stock, would be the double consideration of having that stock permanent, and to receive from it a rate of interest above that which they can obtain for their capital in their own market; consequently both the immense agricultural and commercial interests of America, flowing through this channel, must for ever, by an inexhaustible load of taxes, be tributary to foreign capitalists.

America already suffers by foreign capitalists drawing from her resources large sums, in premiums, from her stocks and new lands; from which she can have no possible reciprocity of interest, except merely in the contemplation of redressing at some future day, the wrongs of foreign nations, in spoliations on her commerce, by a sequestration of this foreign capital. And unless the government holds the idea of sequestration in reserve, as the dernier resort for the redress of foreign aggressions, there can scarcely be a palliative argument offered by them for their toleration to foreigners, of foreign residence, by their superior wealth drawing a private revenue from our best resources. We, therefore, can alone, with confidence, turn our attention and our best hopes to a patriotic government, whose treasury must in a few years, be amply competent to the undertaking; which, when finished, may be given to us for an insignificant tax.

When completed, this would afford a course of navigation from New-York, by sloop navigation to Albany, 160 miles—from Albany to Buffalo, by boat navigation, 300 miles—from Buffalo to Chicago by sloop navigation, 1200 miles; making a distance of 1600 miles of inland navigation up stream, where the cargo has to be shifted but three times.

The probable charges of freight would be—from New-York to Albany (the present price on small packages of merchandise up freight is about) five dollars per ton, from thence to Buffalo (full large enough, including no charge for lockage) fifty dollars a ton, from thence to Chicago, say large fifty dollars per ton—is equal to 105 dollars per ton, or five cents per pound nearly. From Chicago harbour it might be continued up its river, by portage, into and down the Illinois, and up the Mississippi; and into, as yet, almost unknown regions.

The navigation of the four largest lakes in the known world, together with all their tributary streams—the agricultural products and the commerce of all the surrounding country, would pass through this canal—and even the fifth (Ontario) would become its tributary.—The additional duty on the Canadian trade alone would defray the annual repairs of the canal.

The vast extension of and facility to commerce, together with the additional spur to industry which this canal would give, would in twenty years redeem the principal and interest of their expenditure, at the rate of their present imposts, by its additional increase.

Its invitation to the culture of the fertile soil surrounding these extensive navigable waters, would be such, that in a few generations the exhibition of their improvements and the display of their wealth, would even scarcely be equaled by the old world.

—HERCULES

1. According to Hawley, how should a canal of this magnitude be funded? What does he think of the prospect of using foreign investors?
2. What benefits would this canal bring to the state of New York—other than lowering the cost of transportation?

9-3 John Marshall Affirms the Power of the Federal Government

In the case of *McCulloch v. Maryland*, Chief Justice John Marshall delivered arguably his most important interpretation of the Constitution—endorsing the doctrine of broad construction and implied powers. The case focused on the right of the state of Maryland to levy a tax on the Baltimore branch of the Bank of the United States and thereby assert its sovereignty over the federal institution. The Supreme Court's decision was unanimous—upholding the power of Congress to charter the bank and stating that the state's (Maryland) right to tax it was contrary to the supreme law of the land.

Source: *The American Revolution—an HTML Project*
http://odur.let.rug.nl/~usa/D/1801-1825/marshallcases/mar02.htm
also in Henry Steele Commanger, ed., *Documents of American History* (New York: Appleton-Century-Crofts, 1949), 213–220.

In the case now to be determined, the defendant, a sovereign State, denies the obligation of a law enacted by the legislature of the Union, and the plaintiff, on his part, contests the validity of an act which has been passed by the legislature of that State. The Constitution of our country, in its most interesting and vital parts, is to be considered; the conflicting powers of the government of the Union and of its members, as marked in that constitution, are to be discussed; and an opinion given, which may essentially influence the great operations of the government. No tribunal can approach such a question without a deep sense of its importance, and of the awful responsibility involved in its decision. But it must be decided peacefully, or remain a source of hostile legislation, perhaps of hostility of a still more serious nature; and if it is to be so decided, by this tribunal alone can the decision be made. On the Supreme Court of the United States has the constitution of our country devolved this important duty.

The first question made in the cause is, has Congress power to incorporate a bank?

It has been truly said that this can scarcely be considered as an open question, entirely unprejudiced by the former proceedings of the nation respecting it. The principle now contested was introduced at a very early period of our history, has been recognized by many successive legislatures, and has been acted upon by the judicial department, in cases of peculiar delicacy, as a law of undoubted obligation. . . .

The power now contested was exercised by the first Congress elected under the present constitution. The bill for incorporating the bank of the United States did not steal upon an unsuspecting legislature, and pass unobserved. Its principle was completely understood, and was opposed with equal zeal and ability. After being resisted, first in the fair and open field of debate, and afterwards in the executive cabinet, with as much persevering talent as any measure has ever experienced, and being supported by arguments which convinced minds as pure and as intelligent as this country can boast, it became a law. The original act was permitted to expire; but a short experience of the embarrassments to which the refusal to revive it exposed the government, convinced those who were most prejudiced against the measure of its necessity, and induced the passage of the present law. It would require no ordinary share of intrepidity to assert that a measure adopted under these circumstances was a bold and plain usurpation, to which the constitution gave no countenance.

These observations belong to the cause; but they are not made under the impression that, were the question entirely new, the law would be found irreconcilable with the constitution.

In discussing this question, the counsel for the State of Maryland have deemed it of some importance, in the construction of the constitution, to consider that instrument not as emanating from the people, but as the act of sovereign and independent States. The powers of the general government, it has been said, are delegated by the States, who alone are truly sovereign; and must be exercised in subordination to the States, who alone possess supreme dominion.

It would be difficult to sustain this proposition. The Convention which framed the constitution was indeed elected by the State legislatures. But the instrument, when it came from their hands, was a mere proposal, without obligation, or pretensions to it. It was reported to the then existing Congress of the United States, with a request that it might "be submitted to a convention of delegates, chosen in each State by the people thereof, under the recommendation of its legislature, for their assent and ratification." This mode of proceeding was adopted; and by the convention, by Congress, and by the State legislatures, the instrument was submitted to the people. They acted upon it in the only manner in which they can act safely, effectively, and wisely, on such a subject, by assembling in convention. It is true, they assembled in their several States—and where else should they have assembled? No political dreamer was ever wild enough to think of breaking down the lines which separate the States, and of compounding the American people into one common mass. Of consequence, when they act, they act in their States. But the measures they adopt do not, on that account, cease to be the measures of the people themselves, or become the measures of the State governments.

From these conventions the constitution derives its whole authority. The government proceeds directly from the people; is "ordained and established" in the name of the people; and is declared to be ordained, "in order to form a more perfect union, establish justice, ensure domestic tranquility, and secure the blessings of liberty to themselves and to their posterity." The assent of the States, in their sovereign capacity, is implied in calling a convention, and thus submitting that instrument to the people. But the people were at perfect liberty to accept or reject it; and their act was final. It required not the affirmance, and could not be negatived, by the State governments. The constitution, when thus adopted, was of complete obligation, and bound the State sovereignties. . . . of this fact on the case), is, emphatically, and truly, a government of the people. In form and in substance it emanates from them. Its powers are granted by them, and are to be exercised directly on them, and for their benefit.

This government is acknowledged by all to be one of enumerated powers. The principle, that it can exercise only the powers granted to it, [is] now universally admitted. But the question respecting the extent of the powers actually granted, is perpetually arising, and will probably continue to arise, as long as our system shall exist. . . .

Among the enumerated powers, we do not find that of establishing a bank or creating a corporation. But there is no phrase in the instrument which, like the articles of confederation, excludes incidental or implied powers; and which requires that everything granted shall be expressly and minutely described. Even the 10th amendment, which was framed for the purpose of quieting the excessive jealousies which had been excited, omits the word "expressly," and declares only that the powers "not delegated to the United States, nor prohibited to the States, are reserved to the States or to the people"; thus leaving the question, whether the particular power which may become the subject of contest has been delegated to the one government, or prohibited to the other, to depend on a fair construction of the whole instrument. The men who drew and adopted this amendment had experienced the embarrassments resulting from the insertion of this word in the articles of confederation, and probably omitted it to avoid those embarrassments. A constitution, to contain an accurate detail of all the subdivisions of which its great powers will admit, and of all the means by which they may be carried into execution, would partake of the prolixity of a legal code, and could scarcely be embraced by the human mind. It would probably never be understood by the public. Its nature, therefore, requires, that only its great outlines should be marked, its important objects designated, and the minor ingredients which compose those objects be deduced from the nature of the objects themselves. That this idea was entertained by the framers of the American constitution, is not only to be inferred from the nature of the instrument, but from the language. Why else were some of the limitations, found in the ninth section of the 1st article, introduced? It is also, in some degree, warranted by their having omitted to use any restrictive term which might prevent its receiving a fair and just interpretation. In considering this question, then, we must never forget that it is a constitution we are expounding.

Although, among the enumerated powers of government, we do not find the word "bank," or "incorporation," we find the great powers to lay and collect taxes; to borrow money; to regulate commerce; to declare and conduct a war; and to raise and support armies and navies. The sword and the purse, all the external relations, and no inconsiderable portion of the industry of the nation, are entrusted to its government. It can never be pretended that these vast powers draw after them others of inferior importance, merely because they are inferior. Such an idea can never be advanced. But it may with great reason be contended, that a government, entrusted with such ample powers, on the due execution of which the happiness and prosperity of the nation so vitally depends, must also be entrusted with ample means for their execution. The power being given, it is the interest of the nation to facilitate its execution. It can never be their interest, and cannot be presumed to have been their intention, to clog and embarrass its execution by withholding the most appropriate means . . . require it) which would impute to the framers of that instrument, when granting these powers for the public good, the intention of impeding their exercise by withholding a choice of means? If, indeed, such be the mandate of the constitution, we have only to obey; but that instrument does not profess to enumerate the means by which the powers it confers may be executed; nor does it prohibit the creation of a corporation, if the existence of such a being be essential to the beneficial exercise of those powers. It is, then, the subject of fair inquiry, how far such means may be employed.

It is not denied, that the powers given to the government imply the ordinary means of execution. That, for example, of raising revenue, and applying it to national purposes, is admitted to imply the power of conveying money from place to place, as the exigencies of the nation may require, and of employing the usual means of conveyance. But it is denied that the government has its choice of means; or, that it may employ the most convenient means, if, to employ them, it be necessary to erect a corporation. . . .

The government which has a right to do an act, and has imposed on it the duty of performing that act, must, according to the dictates of reason, be allowed to select the means; and those who contend that it may not select any appropriate means, that one particular mode of effecting the object is excepted, take upon themselves the burden of establishing that exception. . . . The power of creating a corporation, though appertaining to sovereignty, is not like the power of making war, or levying taxes, or of regulating commerce, a great substantive and independent power, which cannot be implied as incidental to other powers, or used as a means of executing them. It is never the end for which other powers are exercised, but a means by which other objects are accomplished. . . . The power of creating a corporation is never used for its own sake, but for the purpose of effecting something else. No sufficient reason is, therefore, perceived, why it may not pass as incidental to those powers which are expressly given, if it be a direct mode of executing them.

But the constitution of the United States has not left the right of Congress to employ the necessary means, for the execution of the powers conferred on the government, to general reasoning. To its enumeration of powers is added that of making "all laws which shall be necessary and proper for carrying into execution the foregoing powers, and all other powers vested by this constitution, in the government of the United States, or in any department thereof."

The counsel for the State of Maryland have urged various arguments, to prove that this clause, though in terms a grant of power, is not so in effect; but is really restrictive of the general right, which might otherwise be implied, of selecting means for executing the enumerated powers. . . .

Almost all compositions contain words, which, taken in their rigorous sense, would convey a meaning different from that which is obviously intended. It is essential to just construction, that many words which import something excessive should be understood in a more mitigated sense—in that sense which common usage justifies. The word "necessary" is of this description. It has not a fixed character peculiar to itself. It admits of all degrees of comparison; and is often connected with other words, which increase or diminish the impression the mind receives of the urgency it imports. A thing may be necessary, very necessary, absolutely or indispensably necessary. To no mind would the same idea be conveyed by these several phrases. This comment on the word is well illustrated by the passage cited at the bar, from the 20th section of the 1st article of the constitution. It is, we think, impossible to compare the sentence which prohibits a State from laying "imposts, or duties on imports or exports, except what may be absolutely necessary for executing its inspection laws," with that which authorizes Congress "to make all laws which shall be necessary and proper for carrying into execution" the powers of the general government, without feeling a conviction that the convention understood itself to change materially the meaning of the word "necessary," by prefixing the word "absolutely." This word, then, like others, is used in various senses; and, in its construction, the subject, the context, the intention of the person using them, are all to be taken into view.

Let this be done in the case under consideration. The subject is the execution of those great powers on which the welfare of a nation essentially depends. It must have been the intention of those who gave these powers, to insure, as far as human prudence could insure, their beneficial execution. This could not be done by confiding the choice of means to such narrow limits as not to leave it in the power of Congress to adopt any which might be appropriate, and which were conducive to the end. This provision is made in a constitution intended to endure for ages to come, and, consequently, to be adapted to the various crises of human affairs. To have prescribed the means by which government should, in all future time, execute its powers, would have been to change, entirely, the character of the instrument, and give it the properties of a legal code. It would have been an unwise attempt to provide, by immutable rules, for exigencies which, if foreseen at all, must have been seen dimly, and which can be best provided for as they occur. To have declared that the best means shall not be used, but those alone without which the power given would be nugatory, would have been to deprive the legislature of the capacity to avail itself of experience, to exercise its reason, and to accommodate its legislation to circumstances. If we apply this principle of construction to any of the powers of the government, we shall find it so pernicious in its operation that we shall be compelled to discard it. . . .

The result of the most careful and attentive consideration bestowed upon this clause is, that if it does not enlarge, it cannot be construed to restrain the powers of Congress, or to impair the rights of the legislature to exercise its best judgment in the selection of measures to carry into execution the constitutional powers of the government. If no other motive for its insertion can be suggested, a sufficient one is found in the desire to remove all doubts respecting the right to legislate on that vast mass of incidental powers which must be involved in the constitution, if that instrument be not a splendid bauble.

We admit, as all must admit, that the powers of the government are limited, and that its limits are not to be transcended. But we think the sound construction of the constitution must allow to the national legislature that discretion, with respect to the means by which the powers it confers are to be carried into execution, which will enable that body to perform the high duties assigned to it, in the manner most beneficial to the people. Let the end be legitimate, let it be within the scope of the constitution, and all means which are appropriate, which are plainly adapted to that end, which are not prohibited, but consist with the letter and spirit of the constitution, are constitutional. . . .

Should Congress, in the execution of its powers, adopt measures which are prohibited by the constitution; or should Congress, under the pretext of executing its powers, pass laws for the accomplishment of objects not entrusted to the government; it would become the painful duty of this tribunal, should a case requiring such a decision come before it, to say that such an act was not the law of the land. But where the law is not prohibited, and is really calculated to effect any of the objects entrusted to the government, to undertake here to inquire into the degree of its necessity, would be to pass the line which circumscribes the judicial department, and to tread on legislative ground. This court disclaims all pretensions to such a power.

After this declaration, it can scarcely be necessary to say that the existence of State banks can have no possible influence on the question. No trace is to be found in the constitution of an intention to create a dependence of the government of the Union on those of the States, for the execution of the great powers assigned to it. Its means are adequate to its ends; and on those means alone was it expected to rely for the accomplishment of its ends. To impose on it the neces-

107

sity of resorting to means which it cannot control, which another government may furnish or withhold, would render its course precarious, the result of its measures uncertain, and create a dependence on other governments, which might disappoint its most important designs, and is incompatible with the language of the constitution. But were it otherwise, the choice of means implies a right to choose a national bank in preference to State banks, and Congress alone can make the election.

After the most deliberate consideration, it is the unanimous and decided opinion of this Court, that the act to incorporate the Bank of the United States is a law made in pursuance of the constitution, and is a part of the supreme law of the land. . . .

It being the opinion of the Court, that the act incorporating the bank is constitutional; and that the power of establishing a branch in the State of Maryland might be properly exercised by the bank itself, we proceed to inquire—

2. Whether the State of Maryland may, without violating the constitution, tax that branch?

That the power of taxation is one of vital importance; that it is retained by the States; that it is not abridged by the grant of a similar power to the government of the Union; that it is to be concurrently exercised by the two governments: are truths which have never been denied. But, such is the paramount character of the constitution, that its capacity to withdraw any subject from the action of even this power, is admitted. The States are expressly forbidden to lay any duties on imports or exports, except what may be absolutely necessary for executing their inspection laws. If the obligation of this prohibition must be conceded, the same paramount character would seem to restrain, as it certainly may restrain, a State from such other exercise of this power; as is in its nature incompatible with, and repugnant to, the constitutional laws of the Union. . . .

On this ground the counsel for the bank place its claim to be exempted from the power of a State to tax its operations. There is no express provision for the case, but the claim has been sustained on a principle which so entirely pervades the constitution, is so intermixed with the materials which compose it, so interwoven with its web, so blended with its texture, as to be incapable of being separated from it, without rending it into shreds.

This great principle is, that the constitution and the laws made in pursuance thereof are supreme; that they control the constitution and laws of the respective States, and cannot be controlled by them. From this, which may be almost termed an axiom, other propositions are deduced as corollaries, on the truth or error of which, and on their application to this case, the cause has been supposed to depend. These are, 1st. that a power to create implies a power to preserve. 2nd. That a power to destroy, if wielded by a different hand, is hostile to, and incompatible with these powers to create and to preserve. 3d. That where this repugnancy exists, that authority which is supreme must control, not yield to that over which it is supreme. . . .

That the power of taxing by the States may be exercised so as to destroy it, is too obvious to be denied. But taxation is said to be an absolute power, which acknowledges no other limits than those expressly prescribed in the constitution, and like sovereign power of every other description, is trusted to the discretion of those who use it. But the very terms of this argument admit that the sovereignty of the State, in the article of taxation itself, is subordinate to, and may be controlled by, the constitution of the United States. How far it has been controlled by that instrument must be a question of construction. In making this construction, no principle not declared, can be admissible, which would defeat the legitimate operations of a supreme government. It is of the very essence of supremacy to remove all obstacles to its action within its own sphere, and so to modify every power vested in subordinate governments, as to exempt its own operations from their own influence. This effect need not be stated in terms. It is so involved in the declaration of supremacy, so necessarily implied in it, that the expression of it could not make it more certain. We must, therefore, keep it in view while construing the constitution.

The argument on the part of the State of Maryland is, not that the States may directly resist a law of Congress, but that they may exercise their acknowledged powers upon it, and that the constitution leaves them this right in the confidence that they will not abuse it.

Before we proceed to examine this argument, and to subject it to the test of the constitution, we must be permitted to bestow a few considerations on the nature and extent of this original right of taxation, which is acknowledged to remain with the States. It is admitted that the power of taxing the people and their property is essential to the very existence of government, and may be legitimately exercised on the objects to which it is applicable, to the utmost extent to which the government may choose to carry it. The only security against the abuse of this power, is found in the structure of the government itself. In imposing a tax the legislature acts upon its constituents. . . .

The sovereignty of a State extends to everything which exists by its own authority, or is so introduced by its permission; but does it extend to those means which are employed by Congress to carry into execution powers conferred on that body by the people of the United States? We think it demonstrable that it does not. Those powers are not given by the people of a single State. They are given by the people of the United States, to a government whose laws, made in pursuance of the constitution, are declared to be supreme. Consequently, the people of a single State cannot confer a sovereignty which will extend over them.

If we measure the power of taxation residing in a State, by the extent of sovereignty which the people of a single State possess, and can confer on its government, we have an intelligible standard, applicable to every case to which the power may be applied. We have a principle which leaves the power of taxing the people and property of a State unimpaired; which leaves to a State the command of all its resources, and which places beyond its reach, all those powers which are conferred by the people of the United States on the government of the Union, and all those means which are given for the purpose of carrying those powers into execution. We have a principle which is safe for the States, and safe for the Union. We are relieved, as we ought to be, from clashing sovereignty; from interfering powers; from a repugnancy between a right in one government to pull down what there is an acknowledged right in another to build up; from the incompatibility of a right in one government to destroy what there is a right in another to preserve. We are not driven to the perplexing inquiry, so unfit for the judicial department, what degree of taxation is the legitimate use, and what degree may amount to the abuse of the power. The attempt to use it on the means employed by the government of the Union, in pursuance of the constitution, is itself an abuse, because it is the usurpation of a power which the people of a single State cannot give.

We find, then, on just theory, a total failure of this original right to tax the means employed by the government of the Union, for the execution of its powers. The right never existed, and the question whether it has been surrendered, cannot arise.

But, waiving this theory for the present, let us resume the inquiry, whether this power can be exercised by the respective States, consistently with a fair construction of the constitution?

That the power to tax involves the power to destroy; that the power to destroy may defeat and render useless the power to create; that there is a plain repugnance, in conferring on one government a power to control the constitutional measures of another, which other, with respect to those very measures, is declared to be supreme over that which exerts the control, are propositions not to be denied. But all inconsistencies are to be reconciled by the magic of the word CONFI-DENCE. Taxation, it is said, does not necessarily and unavoidably destroy. To carry it to the excess of destruction would be an abuse, to presume which, would banish that confidence which is essential to all government.

But is this a case of confidence? Would the people of any one State trust those of another with a power to control the most insignificant operations of their State government? We know they would not. Why, then, should we suppose that the people of any one State should be willing to trust those of another with a power to control the operations of a government to which they have confided their most important and most valuable interests? In the legislature of the Union alone, are all represented. The legislature of the Union alone, therefore, can be trusted by the people with the power of controlling measures which concern all, in the confidence that it will not be abused. This, then, is not a case of confidence, and we must consider it as it really is.

If we apply the principle for which the State of Maryland contends, to the constitution generally, we shall find it capable of changing totally the character of that instrument. We shall find it capable of arresting all the measures of the government, and of prostrating it at the foot of the States. The American people have declared their constitution, and the laws made in pursuance thereof, to be supreme; but this principle would transfer the supremacy, in fact, to the States.

If the States may tax one instrument, employed by the government in the execution of its powers, they may tax any and every other instrument. They may tax the mail; they may tax the mint; they may tax patent rights; they may tax the papers of the custom-house; they may tax judicial process; they may tax all the means employed by the government, to an excess which would defeat all the ends of government. This was not intended by the American people. They did not design to make their government dependent on the States. . . .

The Court has bestowed on this subject its most deliberate consideration. The result is a conviction that the States have no power, by taxation or otherwise, to retard, impede, burden, or in any manner control, the operations of the constitutional laws enacted by Congress to carry into execution the powers vested in the general government. This is, we think, the unavoidable consequence of that supremacy which the constitution has declared.

We are unanimously of opinion, that the law passed by the legislature of Maryland, imposing a tax on the Bank of the United States, is unconstitutional and void.

This opinion does not deprive the States of any resources which they originally possessed. It does not extend to a tax paid by the real property of the bank, in common with the other real property within the State, nor to a tax imposed on the interest which the citizens of Maryland may hold in this institution, in common with other property of the same description throughout the State. But this is a tax on the operations of the bank, and is, consequently, a tax on the operation of an instrument employed by the government of the Union to carry its powers into execution. Such a tax must be unconstitutional.

1. How can it be argued that the case of *McCulloch v. Maryland* is perhaps the best representation of judicial nationalism?
2. What might be the long-term consequences of the Marshall Court's decision? What future issues or concerns could be affected by this ruling?

9-4 The Monroe Doctrine and a Reaction (1823)

One of the most important foreign policy statements in American History, The Monroe Doctrine declared the Americas off limits to future European colonization. Most immediately proclaimed in reaction to Russian statements and Spanish and British activities in Central and South America, the Doctrine was a foreign policy declaration of independence and became a cornerstone of American Policy for many years.

In the discussion to which this interest [Russia's on the northwest coast] has given rise, the occasion has been judged proper for asserting, as a principle in which the rights and interests of the United States are involved, that the American continents, by the free and independent condition which they have assumed and maintain, are henceforth not to be considered as subjects for the future colonization by any European powers. . . .

The political system of the Allied Powers [Holy Alliance] is essentially different . . . from that of America. This difference proceeds from that which exists in their prospective [monarchical] governments; and to the defence of our own . . . this whole nation is devoted. We owe it, therefore, to candor and to the amicable relations existing between the United States and those powers to declare that we should consider any attempt on their part to extend their system to any portion of this hemisphere as dangerous to our peace and safety.

With the existing colonies or dependencies of any European power, we have not interfered and shall not interfere. But with the governments [of Spanish America] who have declared their independence and maintained it, and whose independence we have, on great consideration and on just principles, acknowledged, we could not view any interposition for the purpose of oppressing them, or controlling in any other light than as the manifestation of an unfriendly disposition toward the United States. . . .

Our policy in regard to Europe, which was adopted at an early stage of the wars which have so long agitated that quarter of the globe, nevertheless remains the same, which is, not to interfere in the internal concerns of any of its powers; to consider the government *de facto* as the legitimate government for us; to cultivate friendly relations with it, and to preserve those relations by a frank, firm, and manly policy, meeting in all instances the just claims of every power, submitting to injuries from none.

But in regard to those [American] continents, circumstances are eminently and conspicuously different. It is impossible that the Allied Powers should extend their political system to a portion of either continent without endangering our peace and happiness. Nor can anyone believe that our southern brethren, if left to themselves, would adopt it of their own accord. It is equally impossible, therefore, that we should behold such interposition in any form with indifference.

[Baltimore *Chronicle*, Editorial]

We can tell . . . further that this high-toned, independent, and dignified message will not be read by the crowned heads of Europe without a revolting stare of astonishment. The conquerors of Bonaparte, with their laurels still green and blooming on their brows, and their disciplined animal machines, called armies, at their backs, could not have anticipated that their united force would so soon be defied by a young republic, whose existence, as yet, cannot be measured with the ordinary life of man.

This message itself constitutes an era in American history, worthy of commemoration. . . . We are confident that, on this occasion, we speak the great body of American sentiment, such as exulting millions are ready to re-echo. . . . We are very far from being confident that, if Congress occupy the high and elevated ground taken in the Message, it may not, under the smiles of Divine Providence, be the means of breaking up the Holy Alliance.

Of this we are positively sure: that all timidity, wavering imbecility, an backwardness on our part will confirm these detested tyrants in their confederacy; paralyze the exertions of freedom in every country; accelerate the fall of those young sister republics whom we have recently recognized; and, perhaps, eventually destroy our own at the feet of absolute monarchy.

1. In general, what does the Monroe Doctrine prescribe in regard to American foreign policy? What is the rationale for this policy?
2. Summarize the tone and message of the response to this doctrine published in the Baltimore Chronicle.

9-5 Henry Clay, "Defense of the American System" (1832)

Henry Clay was an American statesman for over 40 years, serving as Secretary of State, Speaker of the House and Senate Leader. He ran, unsuccessfully, for President five times. The focus of Clay's efforts was the so called "American System" which is the subject of this document. The system was designed to reduce dependence and develop American resources and included tariffs, a national bank and federal subsidies for transportation. With these measures Clay sought economic development and a more unified America.

I have now to perform the more pleasing task of exhibiting an imperfect sketch of the existing state of the unparalleled prosperity of the country. On a general survey, we behold cultivation extended, the arts flourishing, the face of the country improved; our people fully and profitably employed, and the public countenance exhibiting tranquility, contentment and happiness. And if we descend into particulars, we have the agreeable contemplation of a people out of debt, land rising slowly in value, but in a secure and salutary degree; a ready though not extravagant market for all the surplus productions of our industry; innumerable flocks and herds browsing and gamboling on ten thousand hills and plains, covered with rich and verdant grasses; our cities expanded, and whole villages springing up, as it were, by enchantment; our exports and imports increased and increasing; our tonnage, foreign and coastwise, swelling and fully occupied; the rivers of our interior animated by the perpetual thunder and lightning of countless steam-boats; the currency sound and abundant; the public debt of two wars nearly redeemed; and, to crown all, the public treasury overflowing, embarrassing Congress, not to find subjects of taxation, but to select the objects which shall be liberated from the impost. If the term of seven years were to be selected, of the greatest prosperity which this people have enjoyed since the establishment of their present constitution, it would be exactly that period of seven years which immediately followed the passage of the tariff of 1824.

This transformation of the condition of the country from gloom and distress to brightness and prosperity, has been mainly the work of American legislation, fostering American industry, instead of allowing it to be controlled by foreign legislation, cherishing foreign industry. The foes of the American System, in 1824, with great boldness and confidence, predicted, 1st. The ruin of the public revenue, and the creation of a necessity to resort to direct taxation. The gentleman from South Carolina, (General Hayne,) I believe, thought that the tariff of 1824 would operate a reduction of revenue to the large amount of eight millions of dollars. 2d. The destruction of our navigation. 3d. The desolation of commercial cities. And 4th. The augmentation of the price of objects of consumption, and further decline in that of the articles of our exports. Every prediction which they made has failed-utterly failed. Instead of the ruin of the public revenue, with which they then sought to deter us from the adoption of the American System, we are now threatened with its subversion, by the vast amount of the public revenue produced by that system. . . .

If the system of protection be founded on principles erroneous in theory, pernicious in practice-above all if it be unconstitutional, as is alledged, it ought to be forthwith abolished, and not a vestage of it suffered to remain. But, before we sanction this sweeping denunciation, let us look a little at this system, its magnitude, its ramifications, its duration, and the high authorities which have sustained it. We shall see that its foes will have accomplished comparatively nothing, after having achieved their present aim of breaking down our iron-founderies, our woollen, cotton, and hemp manufactories, and our sugar plantations. The destruction of these would, undoubtedly, lead to the sacrifice of immense capital, the ruin of many thousands of our fellow citizens, and incalculable loss to the whole community. But their prostration would not disfigure, nor produce greater effect upon the *whole* system of protection, in all its branches, than the destruction of the beautiful domes upon the capitol would occasion to the magnificent edifice which they surmount. Why, sir, there is scarcely an interest, scarcely a vocation in society, which is not embraced by the beneficence of this system.

It comprehends our coasting tonnage and trade, from which all foreign tonnage is absolutely excluded.

It includes all our foreign tonnage, with the inconsiderable exception made by the treaties of reciprocity with a few foreign powers.

It embraces our fisheries, and all our hardy and enterprising fishermen.

It extends to almost every mechanic and: to tanners, cordwainers, tailors, cabinet-makers, hatters, tinners, brass-workers, clock-makers, coach-makers, tallow-chandlers, trace-makers, rope-makers, cork-cutters, tobacconists, whip-makers, paper-makers, umbrella-makers, glass-blowers, stocking-weavers, butter-makers, saddle and harness-makers, cutlers, brush-makers, book-binders, dairy-men, milk-farmers, black-smiths, type-founders, musical instrument-makers, basket-makers, milliners, potters, chocolate-makers, floor-cloth-makers, bonnet-makers, hair-cloth-makers, copper-smiths, pencil-makers, bellows-makers, pocket book-makers, card-makers, glue-makers, mustard-makers, lumber-sawyers, saw-makers, scale-beam-makers, scythe-makers, wood-saw-makers, and many others. The mechanics enumerated, enjoy a measure of protection adapted to their several conditions, varying from twenty to fifty per cent. The extent and importance of some of these artizans may be estimated by a few particulars. The tanners, curriers, boot and shoe-makers, and other workers in hides, skins and leather, produce an ultimate value per annum of forty millions of dollars; the manufacturers of hats and caps produce an annual value of fifteen millions; the cabinet-makers twelve millions; the manufacturers of bonnets and hats for the female sex, lace, artificial flowers, combs, &c. seven millions; and the manufacturers of glass, five millions.

It extends to all lower Louisiana, the Delta of which might as well be submerged again in the Gulf of Mexico, from which it has been a gradual conquest, as now to be deprived of the protecting duty upon is great staple.

It effects the cotton planter himself, and the tobacco planter, both of whom enjoy protection.

The total amount of the capital vested in sheep, the land to sustain them, wool, woollen manufacturers, and woollen fabrics, and the subsistence of the various persons directly or indirectly employed in the growth and manufacture of the article of wool, is estimated at one hundred and sixty-seven millions of dollars, and the number of persons at one hundred and fifty thousand.

The value of iron, considered as a raw material, and of its manufacturers, is estimated at twenty-six millions of dollars per annum. Cotton goods, exclusive of the capital vested in the manufacture, and of the cost of the raw material, are believed to amount annually, to about twenty millions of dollars.

These estimates have been carefully made, by practical men of undoubted character, who have brought together and embodied their information. Anxious to avoid the charge of exaggeration, they have sometimes placed their estimates below what was believed to be the actual amount of these interests. With regard to the quantity of bar and other iron annually produced, it is derived from the known works themselves; and I know some in western States which they have omitted in their calculations. . . .

When gentlemen have succeeded in their design of an immediate or gradual destruction of the American System, what is their substitute? Free trade? Free trade! The call for free trade is as unavailing as the cry of a spoiled child, in its nurse's arms, for the moon, or the stars that glitter in the firmament of heaven. It never has existed, it never will exist. Trade implies, at least two parties. To be free, it should be fair, equal and reciprocal. But if we throw our ports wide open to the admission of foreign productions, free of all duty, what ports of any other foreign nation shall we find open to the free admission of our surplus produce? We may break down all barriers to free trade on our part, but the work will not be complete until foreign powers shall have removed theirs. There would be freedom on one side, and restrictions, prohibitions and exclusions on the other. The bolts, and the bars, and the chains of all other nations will remain undisturbed. It is, indeed, possible, that our industry and commerce would accommodate themselves to this unequal and unjust, state of things; for, such is the flexibility of our nature, that it bends itself to all circumstances. The wretched prisoner incarcerated in a jail, after a long time becomes reconciled to his solitude, and regularly notches down the passing days of his confinement.

Gentlemen deceive themselves. It is not free trade that they are recommending to our acceptance. It is in effect, the British colonial system that we are invited to adopt; and, if their policy prevail, it will lead substantially to the re-colonization of these States, under the commercial dominion of Great Britain. . . .

Gentlemen are greatly deceived as to the hold which this system has in the affections of the people of the United States. They represent that it is the policy of New England, and that she is most benefitted by it. If there be any part of this Union which has been most steady, most unanimous, and most determined in its support, it is Pennsylvania. Why is not that powerful State attacked? Why pass her over, and aim the blow at New England? New England came reluctantly into the policy. In 1824 a majority of her delegation was opposed to it. From the largest State of New England there was but a solitary vote in favor of the bill. That enterprising people can readily accommodate their industry to any policy, provided it be *settled*. They supposed this was fixed, and they submitted to the decrees of government. And the progress of public opinion has kept pace with the developments of the benefits of the system. Now, all New England, at least in this house (with the exception of one small still voice) is in favor of the system. In 1824 all Maryland was against it; now the majority is for it. Then, Louisiana, with one exception, was opposed to it; now, without any exception, she is in favor of it. The march of public sentiment is to the South. Virginia will be the next convert; and in less than seven years, if there be no obstacles from political causes, or prejudices industriously instilled, the majority of eastern Virginia will be, as the majority of western Virginia now is, in favor of the American System. North Carolina will follow later, but not less certainly. Eastern Tennessee is now in favor of the system. And finally, its doctrines will pervade the whole Union, and the wonder will be, that they ever should have been opposed.

1. What is the state of the "American System" as it is described in this document?
2. Explain the opinion expressed in this document regarding "Free Trade."

9-6 *The Harbinger,* Female Workers of Lowell (1836)

The famous Lowell system of factory management attracted young farm girls to work in the fully mechanized factories of Lowell. The system was paternalistic and included, at first, good wages, clean places to live and close supervision. The response was great but as economic times declined, so did wages and working conditions. This document explores the life of Lowell factory workers during this time.

We have lately visited the cities of Lowell [Mass.] and Manchester [N.H.] and have had an opportunity of examining the factory system more closely than before. We had distrusted the accounts which we had heard from persons engaged in the labor reform now beginning to agitate New England. We could scarcely credit the statements made in relation to the exhausting nature of the labor in the mills, and to the manner in which the young women-the operatives-lived in their boardinghouses, six sleeping in a room, poorly ventilated.

We went through many of the mills, talked particularly to a large number of the operatives, and ate at their boardinghouses, on purpose to ascertain by personal inspection the facts of the case. We assure our readers that very little information is possessed, and no correct judgments formed, by the public at large, of our factory system, which is the first germ of the industrial or commercial feudalism that is to spread over our land. . . .

In Lowell live between seven and eight thousand young women, who are generally daughters of farmers of the different states of New England. Some of them are members of families that were rich in the generation before. . . .

The operatives work thirteen hours a day in the summer time, and from daylight to dark in the winter. At half past four in the morning the factory bell rings, and at five the girls must be in the mills. A clerk, placed as a watch, observes those who are a few minutes behind the time, and effectual means are taken to stimulate to punctuality. This is the morning commencement of the industrial discipline (should we not rather say industrial tyranny?) which is established in these associations of this moral and Christian community.

At seven the girls are allowed thirty minutes for breakfast, and at noon thirty minutes more for dinner, except during the first quarter of the year, when the time is extended to forty-five minutes. But within this time they must hurry to their boardinghouses and return to the factory, and that through the hot sun or the rain or the cold. A meal eaten under such circumstances must be quite unfavorable to digestion and health, as any medical man will inform us. After seven o'clock in the evening the factory bell sounds the close of the day's work.

Thus thirteen hours per day of close attention and monotonous labor are extracted from the young women in these manufactories. . . . So fatigued-we should say, exhausted and worn out, but we wish to speak of the system in the simplest language-are numbers of girls that they go to bed soon after their evening meal, and endeavor by a comparatively long sleep to resuscitate their weakened frames for the toil of the coming day.

When capital has got thirteen hours of labor daily out of a being, it can get nothing more. It would be a poor speculation in an industrial point of view to own the operative; for the trouble and expense of providing for times of sickness and old age would more than counterbalance the difference between the price of wages and the expenses of board and clothing. The far greater number of fortunes accumulated by the North in comparison with the South shows that hireling labor is more profitable for capital than slave labor.

Now let us examine the nature of the labor itself, and the conditions under which it is performed. Enter with us into the large rooms, when the looms are at work. The largest that we saw is in the Amoskeag Mills at Manchester. . . . The din and clatter of these five hundred looms, under full operation, struck us on first entering as something frightful and infernal, for it seemed such an atrocious violation of one of the faculties of the human soul, the sense of hearing. After a while we became somewhat used to it, and by speaking quite close to the ear of an operative and quite loud, we could hold a conversation and make the inquiries we wished.

The girls attended upon an average three looms; many attended four, but this requires a very active person, and the most unremitting care. However, a great many do it. Attention to two is as much as should be demanded of an operative. This gives us some idea of the application required during the thirteen hours of daily labor. The atmosphere of such a room cannot of course be pure; on the contrary, it is charged with cotton filaments and dust, which, we are told, are very injurious to the lungs.

On entering the room, although the day was warm, we remarked that the windows were down. We asked the reason, and a young woman answered very naively, and without seeming to be in the least aware that this privation of fresh air was anything else than perfectly natural, that "when the wind blew, the threads did not work well." After we had been in the room for fifteen or twenty minutes, we found ourselves, as did the persons who accompanied us, in quite a perspiration, produced by a certain moisture which we observed in the air, as well as by the heat. . . .

113

The young women sleep upon an average six in a room, three beds to a room. There is no privacy, no retirement, here. It is almost impossible to read or write alone, as the parlor is full and so many sleep in the same chamber. A young woman remarked to us that if she had a letter to write, she did it on the head of a bandbox, sitting on a trunk, as there was no space for a table.

So live and toil the young women of our country in the boardinghouses and manufactories which the rich an influential of our land have built for them.

1. Summarize this accounts description of living conditions in Lowell. What is the daily life of a Lowell worker like?
2. Describe the working conditions presented in this account? What hazards and unhealthful conditions are observed?

PART TEN
JACKSONIAN DEMOCRACY

10-1 A "Corrupt Bargain" or Politics as Usual? (1824)

The immediate outcome of the election of 1824 was inconclusive—both in the electoral college and in the popular vote—yet it was clearly a defeat for Henry Clay and his American System. With the election thrown into the House of Representatives, Speaker Clay's influence was nevertheless decisive. Clay's support for John Quincy Adams carried the New Englander to victory. Soon, Adams appointed Clay to the office of secretary of state, the proving ground for three successive presidents, triggering accusations of political maneuvering. The following excerpt is from Adams's diary during the months following the election when his future was uncertain.

> **Source:** Charles Francis Adams, ed. *Memoirs of John Quincy Adams*, 12 Volumes (Philadelphia: J. B. Lippincott & Co., 1875).

17th. At the office. Visits from W. Kelly, Senator from Louisiana, Letcher, member of H. R. from Kentucky, and G. B. English. Letcher came ostensibly with a claim of an assistant to the Marshal of Kentucky for additional compensation for his service in taking the census of 1820. But his apparent main object was to talk about the Presidential election. The account was yesterday received of the choice of electors in Louisiana by the Legislature, from which it is rendered almost certain that three of the votes have been for General Jackson, probably four, and perhaps all five—but certainly none for Mr. Clay. This leaves Mr. Crawford with forty-one, and Mr. Clay with thirty-seven, electoral votes. Mr. Crawford, therefore, will, and Mr. Clay will not, be one of the three persons from whom the House of Representatives, voting by States, will be called to choose a President. Mr. Letcher is an intimate friend of Mr. Clay's, and lodges at the same house with him. He expects that after the result is known, that Mr. Clay cannot be voted for in the House, there will be meetings of the people in the several counties instructing their members to vote for Jackson, and perhaps that similar instructions will be sent on by their Legislature. These, he supposes, will be gotten up by what they call the *Relief* party in the politics of the State, and by men like Rowan, Barry, and Bibb, secondary leaders of the State, not daring to oppose Clay openly, on account of his own popularity in the State, but seizing upon the first opportunity afforded them indirectly to put him down. Letcher is evidently alarmed at this, and, in the midst of strong professions of indepdnence, and of indifference about retaining his seat, is plainly not prepared to act definitively in opposition to the will of his constituents. He intimated that the Relief party were in fact hostile to Mr. Clay; that of the Kentucky delegation here, a large portion were warmly attached to him; that lately, speaking of what might ensue here, he had expressed the wish to go in harmony with his friends—which Letcher said he interpreted as a wish that his friends would go in harmony with him. Colonel R. M. Johnson, Letcher thinks, is warmly of the Relief party, and as to the Presidency, determined to be at all events on the strongest side. I observed to Letcher that Colonel R. M. had candidly told me so himself.

Letcher wished to know what my sentiments toward Clay were, and I told him without disguise that I harbored no hostility against him; that whatever of difference there had been between us had arisen altogether from him, and not from me. I adverted to Jonathan Russell's attack upon me, which, I said, I believed Mr. Clay had been privy to and countenanced. But, having completely repelled that attack, I felt no animosity against any person concerned in it.

Letcher said Clay's friends thought he had been wrong in his letter against me concerning that affair. It was written in a moment of excitement. He was sure Clay felt now no hostility to me. He had spoken respectfully of me, and was a man of sincerity. Of the fourteen electors of Kentucky, seven voted for Calhoun as Vice-President; and this vote I thought, and Letcher fully concurred in the opinion, was more hostile to Clay than any vote for Jackson as President could be. It held up Calhoun as a future competitor against Clay, and thereby postponed all his prospects indefinitely. The drift of all Letcher's discourse was much the same as Wyer had told me, that Clay would willingly support me if he could thereby serve himself, and the substance of his *meaning* was, that if Clay's friends could *know* that he would have a prominent share in the Administration, that might induce them to vote for me, even in the face of instructions. But Letcher did not profess to have any authority from Clay for what he said, and he made no definite propositions. He spoke of his interview with me as altogether confidential, and in my answers to him I spoke in mere general terms.

* * *

23d . . . R. P. Letcher had a long conversation with me upon the subject which he had broached the other day. The object appeared to me to be to convince me of the importance of obtaining an election in the House of Representatives at the first ballot, and that it would be obtainable by securing the votes of the States of Kentucky, Ohio, Indiana, Illinois, Missouri, and Louisiana. I told him candidly that, however desirable this might be, it would be utterly impracticable, and that I had no expectation of receiving the vote of his own State of Kentucky. He seemed anxious to convince me that I *might* receive it, and enumerated the whole delegation, stating how each of them was now disposed—a majority of them being *uncommitted*. I consider Letcher as moving for Mr. Clay; and this anxiety of a friend of Clay's, that I should obtain the election at the first ballot in the House, is among the whimsical results of political combination at this time—"Incedo super ignes."

* * *

. . . At noon I went to the President's drawing-room, which was much crowded. Mrs. Adams, being quite unwell, did not go. I presented to the President, with Mr. Rebello, the Brazilian Chargé d'Affaires, Mr. Oliveira, Secretary of Legation, whom he had yesterday introduced to me at the Department of State. Robert P. Letcher, a member of the House of Representatives from Kentucky, asked me if I should go to the Department after the drawing-room. I said I should. He said he would call there, and did. He told me he had received from home many letters lately, and several this morning; that the members of the Kentucky Legislature would, in their private capacities, and not by Legislative Act, recommend to the members from the State in the House to vote for General Jackson as President, and popular meetings to pass similar resolutions had been, and would be, got up. But I might rely upon it they would have no effect. The vote of Kentucky in the House was fixable and unalterable. He spoke of the difference between Mr. Clay and me as giving concern to some of the members of the delegation, and intimated a wish that I should have some conversation with Mr. Clay upon the subject. I told him I would very readily, and whenever it might suit the convenience of Mr. Clay. . . .

I attended the dinner given by the members of both Houses of Congress to General La Fayette, at Williamson's Hotel. It was attended also by the President. About one hundred and fifty members of the two Houses were present, and about thirty officers of the Government—civil and military. . . . Mr. Clay made a speech about Bolivar and the cause of South America, and seemed very desirous of eliciting speeches from me and Mr. Calhoun. He told me that he should be glad to have with me soon some confidential conversation upon public affairs. I said I should be happy to have it whenever it might suit his convenience.

9th. . . . Mr. Clay came at six, and spent the evening with me in a long conversation explanatory of the past and prospective of the future. He said that the time was drawing near when the choice must be made in the House of Representatives of a President from the three candidates presented by the electoral colleges; that he had been much urged and solicited with regard to the part in that transaction that he should take, and had not been five minutes landed at his lodgings before he had been applied to by a friend of Mr. Crawford's, in a manner so gross that it had disgusted him; that some of my friends also, disclaiming, indeed, to have any authority from me, had repeatedly applied to him, directly or indirectly, urging considerations personal to himself as motives to his cause. He had thought it best to reserve for sometime his determination to himself: first, to give a decent time for his own funeral solemnities as a candidate; and, secondly, to prepare and predispose all his friends to a state of neutrality between the three candidates who would be before the House, so that they might be free ultimately to take that course which might be most conducive to the public interest. The time had now come at which he might be explicit in his communication with me, and he had for that purpose asked this confidential interview. He wished me, as far as I might think proper, to satisfy him with regard to some principles of great public importance, but without any personal considerations for himself. In the question to come before the House between General Jackson, Mr. Crawford, and myself, he had no hesitation in saying that his preference would be for me.

* * *

15th. Horatio Seymour, S. U. S. from Vermont, in great concern about the instructions, from the Kentucky House of Representatives to the members of that delegation here, to vote for General Jackson as President. He is alarmed for its probable effect on the votes of all the Western States. I advised him to see and converse with Mr. Clay.

Colonel R. M. Johnson, S. U. S. from Kentucky, who told me there was an article in the Lexington Reporter stating that it was said the instructions had been given by the advice of one of the Senators of the State at Washington; and, as it was known Talbot took no part in the election, the imputation was upon him (Johnson). But he solemnly protested that he had not written any such letter, and intimated that the instructions were given in consequence of Mr. Clay's own partisans having taken so much pains to make me unpopular in the State, for which he believed they were now very sorry. Johnson professed neutrality between General Jackson and me, and said he should be well satisfied if either of us should be elected.

* * *

17th. W. C. Bradley, member from Vermont, was here, and afterwards W. Plumer, Jr., of New Hampshire, much concerned about these instructions from the Legislature of Kentucky. Bradley said he had seen Clay this morning, who told him the resolutions would confirm the majority of the delegation in their determination to vote otherwise, but who spoke of the event of the election as exceedingly uncertain—of Missouri and Illinois particularly, the votes of both the States being in single persons. Bradley said he had urged Clay to see me, but Clay had told him it was altogether unnecessary—that his course was fixed, and he should consider the elevation of the Hero as the greatest calamity which could befall the country.

* * *

18th. Dr. Thornton called this morning to give me some information respecting the prospects of the election. It respected the Kentucky and Ohio delegations, and concurred with what I had heard before.

Mr. S. L. Southard came, to ask for the papers he had left with me yesterday, of which Mr. Kirkpatrick wishes to take copies. I gave them to him. He then asked me some questions respecting the election, upon which I spoke to him with entire confidence. I asked him if he wished me so to speak to him, and he said he did. I told him of the present state of things, so far as it is known to myself; of the present prospect, that a majority of the friends of Mr. Clay and Mr. Crawford would finally vote for me, but that the whole of the aspect may be changed from day to day.

* * *

20th. Morning visits at my house from A. H. Everett, J. Sloane, member from Ohio, with a Mr. Bissell, from that State, D. P. Cook, member from Illinois, and W. Plumer, Jr., from New Hampshire. J. Reed, member from Massachusetts, came, but, finding company with me, promised to call again. Cook told me that some time since he had been informed by three persons of weight in the Western delegations that they would all vote for General Jackson. He had received also letters from some of his warmest friends in Illinois, and of those who had been my warmest friends, advising him, in that event, to vote with the other Western members, as by standing out alone

Scott then proceeded to speak of the approaching election, and said that he had made up his mind to vote with the other Western delegates, but intimated that he should incur great opposition for it in his own State. He spoke of himself as being entirely devoted to Mr. Clay, and of his hope that he would be a member of the next Administration.

I told him that he would not expect me to enter upon details with regard to the formation of an Administration, but that if I should be elected by the suffrages of the West I should naturally look to the West for much of the support that I should need.

He parted from me apparently satisfied.

Reed came to speak about Webster, Louis McLane, and the federalists. His own disposition is favorable to me; but Webster is specially apprehensive that the federalists will be excluded from office by me.

I told Reed that I should exclude no person for political opinions, or for personal opposition to me; that my great object would be to break up the remnant of old party distinctions, and bring the whole people together in sentiment as much as possible.

Bradley told me that General Jackson had yesterday, or the day before, paid a visit to Mr. Crawford, and they had been reconciled together, with mutual assurances that there had never been any *personal* hostility towards each other. I have expected this movement ever since the development of the Western phalanx, and if, as is highly probable, it brings all the Crawford force in the House to bear in favor of Jackson, it will be decisive of the election.

* * *

29th. . . . I dined with Mr. George Sullivan. The party consisted of Mr. Clay, the Speaker, Mr. Salazar, the Colombian Minister, J. S. Johnston, Senator, and E. Livingston, member from Louisiana, T. Newton, W. Archer, and J. Taliaferro, members from Virginia, James Hamilton, member from South Carolina, A. H. Everett, and Miss Stockton, who is residing with Mrs. Sullivan. The party, though variously selected, was exceedingly good-humored and jovial, and it was past nine in the evening when we broke up.

On my return home, Mr. Clay came in, and sat with me a couple of hours, discussing all the prospects and probabilities of the Presidential election. He spoke to me with the utmost freedom of men and things; intimated doubts and prepossessions concerning individual friends of mine, to all which I listened with due consideration. He was anxious for the conciliation of Webster and Louis McLane, and expressed some jealousy as from Webster of the persons by whom he supposed me to be surrounded.

I told him the sources of Webster's anxieties, and my own earnest desire to conciliate him; the manner in which my overtures had been received by him, and my own high opinion of his talents and capacities for service.

* * *

31st. . . . I called at the President's, and found Messrs. Calhoun and Southard with him, but they immediately withdrew. I delivered to him two or three dispatches received from R. Rush, and the letter last received from S. Mullowny. I also read to him the note received from S. Rebello, Chargé d'Affaires from Brazil, proposing an alliance offensive and defensive; which, he said, must be declined. He soon began to speak, however, of the nominations, and said he believed he should send them in immediately.

117

I observed that I should be perfectly satisfied if he would determine upon his selection of the persons now, and prepare the nominations; but I was convinced it would much increase the excitement, already great and every day inflaming, if he should send in the nominations *now* or before the election. I asked him if he had been advised to this measure by Mr. Calhoun.

He said he had, and by Mr. Southard, by Mr. Elliott, Senator from Georgia, and by Mr. Taliaferro, member from Virginia.

I said that the motives of all these gentlemen, or of those by whom they were instigated, were suspicions of me—suspicions that I was using these vacant missions as lures to promote my own election in the House. They wished to take this weapon out of my hands. They were mistaken. The only person whom I wished to recommend to him was one of those whom he proposed to nominate. I was willing he should fix all his nominations *now*. It would disconcert no arrangements of mine, and I had no suspicion that General Jackson would use the suspension of them to promote *his* election.

* * *

Feb. 2nd. . . . I called at the president's with dispatches from H. Allen, in Chili, and from R. Rush, at London. The last answers to letters from me of 27th November last—the sixty-eighth day. Referring to the conversation that I had with the President yesterday, I asked if I had understood him correctly that he had determined not to make the nominations to the vacant offices at all.

He said I had.

I said I had understood the alternative was, that he should make them before or after the election. So far as I was personally concerned, I should prefer that even now he would make the nominations before the election, rather than that he should omit to make them altogether. I had wished him to determine upon his choice now, without making it known, but not leave the nominations as prizes to be held out by, or to, any one to purchase votes. Among the candidates whom he had mentioned to me were two members of Congress, one holding, the other supposed to influence, votes. It would be difficult for the successor to nominate either of them, especially if the votes in question should be for him. The nominations belonged properly to his Administration, and my wish was that it should be really his Administration to the last moment of its existence. If the election should fall upon me, I should therefore entreat of him, as a favor, that he would make the nominations as his own, and as he would have made them at any other period of his Administration. If, as was more probable, General Jackson should be chosen, I should of course have nothing further to say; but, having no suspicion that he would anticipate his power of nomination by pledges, I presumed he would equally acquiesce in Mr. Monroe's making the nominations. . . .

* * *

3d. The flood of visitors is unceasing. Mr. Webster called and spent the evening with me. The excitement of electioneering is kindling into fury. George Kremer's "Another Card," in answer to that of H. Clay on Monday, appeared in the Intelligencer this morning. Mr. Clay called upon the House to institute an investigation. Kremer did the same, and a debate ensued upon it in the House, which is postponed till to-morrow.

* * *

Webster's talk was about the election. He read to me a letter from Warfield, of Maryland, to him, concerning the election, and asking advice of him with regard to his vote; and the draft of an answer which he had prepared; and said he would send it or not, as I should think proper. He said that J. Lee, also of Maryland, had consulted him too, and was under impressions similar to those of Warfield. Their concern was lest, in the event of my election, the federalists should be treated as a proscribed party. Webster's answer to Warfield expressed entire confidence that I should be governed by no such considerations, and said that he should show this confidence by his vote. It intimated a hope that the object of the Administration would be to promote harmony among the people, and that the disposition would be marked by conferring some one prominent appointment upon a person of that party.

I observed that if that referred to the formation of an Administration, it would imply more than I could confirm.

He said it did not—but to an appointment perhaps of a Judge.

I said I approved altogether of the general spirit of his answer, and should consider it as one of the objects nearest to my heart to bring the whole people of the Union to harmonize together. I must, however, candidly tell him that I believed either General Jackson or Mr. Crawford would pursue precisely the same principle, and that no Administration could possibly succeed upon any other.

* * *

Feb. 4. . . . I delivered to the President the letter I had written him yesterday upon the subject of the nominations to the foreign missions, and told him that I wished to put it as a deposit in his hands, for a testimonial that I had not used those missions to promote any purpose of my own.

He took the paper, and said he would not communicate it to any one; that he was aware of the extreme circumspection with which it was necessary for me at this moment to act; that his own situation was also one of great difficulty; that his impression at the beginning of the present session of Congress had been to leave these appointments to be made by his successor, whose confidential officers the persons receiving them would be. He had been afterwards urged to make the nominations, but had yielded to the consideration presented by me, in which he had thought there was great weight, that these nominations could scarcely have been made at this crisis without having some improper effect on the pending election. But, in determining upon the postponement, he had thought best to put it on the other ground, of leaving the appointments to his successor, because that, operating equally upon both, could not be attributed to the influence of either. He said he had no doubt of my kind and friendly disposition to himself, and not the most distant suspicion that I had used, or would use, those appointments for any electioneering purpose.

* * *

5th. D. P. Cook called this morning, as he had promised. I reminded him of what he had told me of Ingham's conversations with him respecting the Government of Arkansas, and of McDuffie's talk with him in Ingham's chamber; and I asked him to put in writing the substance of all those conversations. I said I did not ask him to do this for me, but for himself. I told him that all this would be history hereafter, and that those conversations would be an important part of history. He said he regretted not having written them down at the time. I said it would have been better then, but, the time being still very recent, little would now be lost of the substance, and the longer it should be delayed, the less full and correct would the statement be.

He said he would write it. The substance was, that Ingham, knowing Cook to be a candidate for the appointment of Governor of Arkansas, urged him to declare openly that he would vote for Jackson, and intimated that he should then have the appointment. Cook says he offended Ingham by his answer to this proffer, and Ingham has said nothing of it since. McDuffie's argument was to the same purpose; that General Jackson's election would depend upon his (Cook's) vote; that there was a moral obligation to vote for Jackson, who had the greatest number of electoral votes; that if I should be elected, it would only be by Clay's corrupt coalition with me, and that the people would be so disgusted with this that there would be a systematic and determined opposition from the beginning, so that the Administration could not get along. It would be overthrown, and he would be involved in its ruin.

* * *

Tracy and Crowninshield were here this morning, and gave accounts of the attempt at accommodation. An apology was drawn up disclaiming any intention of imputing corruption to Clay, and declaring that he knew no fact ascertaining that any bargain had been made, which Kremer professed himself ready to sign, and which Clay declared would be satisfactory to him.

* * *

9th. May the blessing of God rest upon the event of this day!—the second Wednesday in February, when the election of a President of the United States for the term of four years, from the 4th of March next, was consummated. Of the votes in the electoral colleges, there were ninety-nine for Andrew Jackson, of Tennessee; eighty-four for John Quincy Adams, of Massachusetts; forty-one for William Harris Crawford, of Georgia; and thirty-seven for Henry Clay, of Kentucky: in all, two hundred and sixty-one. This result having been announced, on opening and counting the votes in joint meeting of the two Houses, the House of Representatives immediately proceeded to the vote by ballot from the three highest candidates, when John Quincy Adams received the votes of thirteen, Andrew Jackson of seven, and William H. Crawford of four States. The election was thus completed, very unexpectedly, by a single ballot. Alexander H. Everett gave me the first notice, both of the issue of the votes of the electoral colleges as announced in the joint meeting, and of the final vote as declared.

* * *

10th. Mr. Southard called, as I had requested, at ten. I invited him to remain at the head of the Navy Department; to which he consented. I told him that I should offer the Department of State to Mr. Clay, and should invite Mr. Crawford to remain in the Department of the Treasury.

* * *

Feb. 11. . . . I was at the President's, and again repeated the request that he would make the nominations which had been postponed till after the election. He said he would take it into consideration. I told the President I had invited Mr. Crawford to remain at the head of the Treasury Department, and showed him the letter I had received from him this morning, in very friendly terms declining the offer. I then said that I should offer the Department of State to Mr. Clay, considering it due to his talents and services, to the Western section of the Union, whence he comes, and to the confidence in me manifested by their delegations; that for the Treasury and War Departments I should be glad to take his advice, and to consult him with reference to other objects of public interest, if it would be agreeable to him.

    Feb. 12. . . . General Brown entered this morning into an argument to convince me that it would not be expedient that Mr. Clay should be Secretary of State. He had a high opinion of Mr. Clay, but if I should offer him the Department he hoped he would not accept it, and he believed it would be better if I should not offer it to him. General Brown wished that De Witt Clinton should be the Secretary of State. I listened to what he said, and then told him I had already made the offer to Mr. Clay. Brown's next wish is that Clinton should be Secretary of the Treasury. The members of Congress all advise variously for the formation of a Cabinet, and many are anxious to be treated confidentially.

1. Is there any evidence in Adams's writings that he bargained with Henry Clay to win the presidency? What dangers are there in using memoirs as sources?
2. Whether true or not, how do you think accusations of a "corrupt bargain" would affect Adams's presidency? How might his family background make the matter worse?

10-2 The "Commoner" Takes Office (1828)

The inauguration of Andrew Jackson in 1829 marked a new era in American politics and economic opportunity as the new president's supporters sought to democratize both during what some historians have called "the age of the common man." Although the sixty-one-year-old Jackson, suffering from a severe headache and chronic cough, could barely be heard by those in attendance, Jackson's inaugural was the first in which the "people" played an important role and which they attended en masse. Although vague on particulars, the new president outlined his agenda for the country, emphasizing the need for reform.

Source: *American Treasures of the Library of Congress*
http://lcweb.loc.gov/exhibits/treasures/trr075a.html

Fellow-Citizens:

About to undertake the arduous duties that I have been appointed to perform by the choice of a free people, I avail myself of this customary and solemn occasion to express the gratitude which their confidence inspires and to acknowledge the accountability which my situation enjoins. While the magnitude of their interests convinces me that no thanks can be adequate to the honor they have conferred, it admonishes me that the best return I can make is the zealous dedication of my humble abilities to their service and their good.

As the instrument of the Federal Constitution it will devolve on me for a stated period to execute the laws of the United States, to superintend their foreign and their confederate relations, to manage their revenue, to command their forces, and, by communications to the Legislature, to watch over and to promote their interests generally. And the principles of action by which I shall endeavor to accomplish this circle of duties it is now proper for me briefly to explain.

In administering the laws of Congress I shall keep steadily in view the limitations as well as the extent of the Executive power trusting thereby to discharge the functions of my office without transcending its authority. With foreign nations it will be my study to preserve peace and to cultivate friendship on fair and honorable terms, and in the adjustment of any differences that may exist or arise to exhibit the forbearance becoming a powerful nation rather than the sensibility belonging to a gallant people.

In such measures as I may be called on to pursue in regard to the rights of the separate States I hope to be animated by a proper respect for those sovereign members of our Union, taking care not to confound the powers they have reserved to themselves with those they have granted to the Confederacy.

The management of the public revenue—that searching operation in all governments—is among the most delicate and important trusts in ours, and it will, of course, demand no inconsiderable share of my official solicitude. Under every aspect in which it can be considered it would appear that advantage must result from the observance of a strict and faithful economy. This I shall aim at the more anxiously both because it will facilitate the extinguishment of the national debt, the unnecessary duration of which is incompatible with real independence, and because it will counteract that tendency to public and private profligacy which a profuse expenditure of money by the Government is but too apt to engender. Powerful auxiliaries to the attainment of this desirable end are to be found in the regulations provided by the wisdom of Congress for the specific appropriation of public money and the prompt accountability of public officers.

With regard to a proper selection of the subjects of impost with a view to revenue, it would seem to me that the spirit of equity, caution and compromise in which the Constitution was formed requires that the great interests of agriculture, commerce, and manufactures should be equally favored, and that perhaps the only exception to this rule should consist in the peculiar encouragement of any products of either of them that may be found essential to our national independence.

Internal improvement and the diffusion of knowledge, so far as they can be promoted by the constitutional acts of the Federal Government, are of high importance.

Considering standing armies as dangerous to free governments in time of peace, I shall not seek to enlarge our present establishment, nor disregard that salutary lesson of political experience which teaches that the military should be held subordinate to the civil power. The gradual increase of our Navy, whose flag has displayed in distant climes our skill in navigation and our fame in arms; the preservation of our forts, arsenals, and dockyards, and the introduction of progressive improvements in the discipline and science of both branches of our military service are so plainly prescribed by prudence that I should be excused for omitting their mention sooner than for enlarging on their importance. But the bulwark of our defense is the national militia, which in the present state of our intelligence and population must render us invincible.

As long as our Government is administered for the good of the people, and is regulated by their will; as long as it secures to us the rights of person and of property, liberty of conscience and of the press, it will be worth defending; and so long as it is worth defending a patriotic militia will cover it with an impenetrable aegis. Partial injuries and occasional mortifications we may be subjected to, but a million of armed freemen, possessed of the means of war, can never be conquered by a foreign foe. To any just system, therefore, calculated to strengthen this natural safeguard of the country I shall cheerfully lend all the aid in my power.

It will be my sincere and constant desire to observe toward the Indian tribes within our limits a just and liberal policy, and to give that humane and considerate attention to their rights and their wants which is consistent with the habits of our Government and the feelings of our people.

The recent demonstration of public sentiment inscribes on the list of Executive duties, in characters too legible to be overlooked, the task of reform, which will require particularly the correction of those abuses that have brought the patronage of the Federal Government into conflict with the freedom of elections, and the counteraction of those causes which have disturbed the rightful course of appointment and have placed or continued power in unfaithful or incompetent hands.

In the performance of a task thus generally delineated I shall endeavor to select men whose diligence and talents will insure in their respective stations able and faithful cooperation, depending for the advancement of the public service more on the integrity and zeal of the public officers than on their numbers.

A diffidence, perhaps too just, in my own qualifications will teach me to look with reverence to the examples of public virtue left by my illustrious predecessors, and with veneration to the lights that flow from the mind that founded and the mind that reformed our system. The same diffidence induces me to hope for instruction and aid from the coordinate branches of the Government, and for the indulgence and support of my fellow-citizens generally. And a firm reliance on the goodness of that Power whose providence mercifully protected our national infancy, and has since upheld our liberties in various vicissitudes, encourages me to offer up my ardent supplications that He will continue to make our beloved country the object of His divine care and gracious benediction.

1. What does Jackson say about the relationship between the Federal government and the various states? What does he imply about his administration's future relations with Indian nations/tribes?
2. What does Jackson identify as the catalyst for his "task of reform"? To whom might he directing his comments? Why?

10-3 "Memorial of the Cherokee Nation" (1830)

The Washington administration had established a policy designed to "civilize" the Indians, and the Cherokee, more than any other Native American group, had done so-by codifying their own legal system, printing their own newspapers, and even owning slaves. However, no amount of assimilation helped the Cherokee when the state of Georgia demanded their land. During the "trail of tears," when the Cherokee were forced to march to Oklahoma, more than 4,000 Cherokee died. The "Memorial of the Cherokee Nation" appeared in Nile's Weekly Register in 1830.

We are aware that some persons suppose it will be for our advantage to remove beyond the Mississippi. We think otherwise. Our people universally think otherwise. Thinking that it would be fatal to their interests, they have almost to a man sent their memorial to Congress, deprecating the necessity of a removal. . . . It is incredible that Georgia should ever have enacted the oppressive laws to which reference is here made, unless she had supposed that something extremely terrific in its character was necessary in order to make the Cherokees willing to remove. We are not willing to remove; and if we could be brought to this extremity, it would be not by argument, nor because our judgment was satisfied, not because our condition will be improved; but only because we cannot endure to be deprived of our national and individual rights and subjected to a process of intolerable oppression.

We wish to remain on the land of our fathers. We have a perfect and original right to remain without interruption or molestation. The treaties with us, and laws of the United States made in pursuance of treaties, guaranty our residence and our privileges, and secure us against intruders. Our only request is, that these treaties may be fulfilled, and these laws executed.

But if we are compelled to leave our country, we see nothing but ruin before us. The country west of the Arkansas territory is unknown to us. From what we can learn of it, we have no prepossessions in its favor. All the inviting parts of it, as we believe, are preoccupied by various Indian nations, to which it has been assigned. They would regard us as intruders. . . . The far greater part of that region is, beyond all controversy, badly supplied with wood and water; and no Indian tribe can live as agriculturists without these articles. All our neighbors . . . would speak a language totally different from ours, and practice different customs. The original possessors of that region are now wandering savages lurking for prey in the neighborhood. . . . Were the country to which we are urged much better than it is represented to be, . . . still it is not the land of our birth, nor of our affections. It contains neither the scenes of our childhood, nor the graves of our fathers.

. . . We have been called a poor, ignorant, and degraded people. We certainly are not rich; nor have we ever boasted of our knowledge, or our moral or intellectual elevation. But there is not a man within our limits so ignorant as not to know that he has a right to live on the land of his fathers, in the possession of his immemorial privileges, and that this right has been acknowledged by the United States; nor is there a man so degraded as not to feel a keen sense of injury, on being deprived of his right and driven into exile. . . .

1. Identify and summarize the Cherokee Tribe's objections to moving west beyond the Arkansas Territory. How is American expansion westward impacting the lives of the Cherokee?
2. What rights are claimed in this Memorial?

10-4 Andrew Jackson, Veto of the Bank Bill (1832)

Few presidents have had such ardent admirers and staunch critics. Jackson had a varied political career before becoming a hero in the War of 1812. His reputation as an Indian Fighter made him a popular favorite. He built on this reputation, returned to the Senate and eventually was elected President as a champion of the "common man". His fight against the Second Bank was a very important element of this "Jacksonian Democracy". Jackson's violent opposition to the bank is reflected in this veto message.

To the Senate:

The bill "to modify and continue" the act entitled "An act to incorporate the subscribers to the Bank of the United States" was presented to me on the 4th July instant. Having considered it with that solemn regard to the principles of the Constitution which the day was calculated to inspire, and come to the conclusion that it ought not to become a law, I herewith return it to the Senate, in which it originated, with my objections.

A bank of the United States is in many respects convenient for the Government and useful to the people. Entertaining this opinion, and deeply impressed with the belief that some of the powers and privileges possessed by the existing bank are unauthorized by the Constitution, subversive of the rights of the States, and dangerous to the liberties of the people, I felt it my duty at an early period of my Administration to call the attention of Congress to the practicability of organizing an institution combining all its advantages and obviating these objections. I sincerely regret that in the act before me I can perceive none of those modifications of the bank charter which are necessary, in my opinion, to make it compatible with justice, with sound policy, or with the Constitution of our country.

The present corporate body, denominated the president, directors, and company of the Bank of the United States, will have existed at the time this act is intended to take effect twenty years. It enjoys an exclusive privilege of banking under the authority of the General Government, a monopoly of its favor and support, and, as a necessary consequence, almost a monopoly of the foreign and domestic exchange. The powers, privileges, and favors bestowed upon it in the original character, by increasing the value of the stock far above its par value, operated as a gratuity of many millions to the stockholders. . . .

It is not our own citizens only who are to receive the bounty of our Government. More than eight millions of the stock of this bank are held by foreigners. By this act the American Republic proposes virtually to make them a present of some millions of dollars. For these gratuities to foreigners and to some of our own opulent citizens the act secures no equivalent whatever. . . .

It is not conceivable how the present stockholders can have any claim to the special favor of the Government. The present corporation has enjoyed its monopoly during the period stipulated in the original contract. If we must have such a corporation, why should not the Government sell out the whole stock and thus secure to the people the full market value of the privileges granted? Why should not Congress create and sell twenty-eight millions of stock, incorporating the purchasers with all the powers and privileges secured in this act and putting the premium upon the sales into the Treasury?

But this act does not permit competition in the purchase of this monopoly. It seems to be predicated on the erroneous idea that the present stockholders have a prescriptive right not only to the favor but to the bounty of Government. It appears that more than a fourth part of the stock is held by foreigners and the residue is held by a few hundred of our own citizens, chiefly of the richest class. For their benefit does this act exclude the whole American people from competition in the purchase of this monopoly and dispose of it for many millions less than it is worth. This seems the less excusable because some of our citizens not now stockholders petitioned that the door of competition might be opened, and offered to take a charter on terms much more favorable to the Government and country. . . .

It is to be regretted that the rich and powerful too often bend the acts of government to their selfish purposes. Distinctions in society will always exist under every just government. Equality of talents, of education, or of wealth can not be produced by human institutions. In the full enjoyment of the gifts of Heaven and the fruits of superior industry, economy, and virtue, every man is equally entitled to protection by law; but when the laws undertake to add to these natural and just advantages artificial distinctions, to grant titles, gratuities, and exclusive privileges, to make the rich richer and the potent more powerful, the humble members of society-the farmers, mechanics, and laborers-who have neither the time nor the means of securing like favors to themselves, have a right to complain of the injustice of their Government. There are no necessary evils in government. Its evils exist only in its abuses. If it would confine itself to equal protection, and, as Heaven does its rains, shower its favors alike on the high and the low, the rich and the poor, it would be an unqualified blessing. In the act before me there seems to be a wide and unnecessary departure from these just principles.

124

Nor is our Government to be maintained or our Union preserved by invasions of the rights and powers of the several States. In thus attempting to make our General Government strong we make it weak. Its true strength consists in leaving individuals and States as much as possible to themselves-in making itself felt, not in its power, but in its beneficence; not in its control, but in its protection; not in binding the States more closely to the center, but leaving each to move unobstructed in its proper orbit.

Experience should teach us wisdom. Most of the difficulties our Government now encounters and most of the dangers which impend over our Union have sprung from an abandonment of the legitimate objects of Government by our national legislation, and the adoption of such principles as are embodied in this act. Many of our rich men have not been content with equal protection and equal benefits, but have besought us to make them richer by act of Congress. By attempting to gratify their desires we have in the results of our legislation arrayed section against section, interest against interest, and man against man, in a fearful commotion which threatens to shake the foundations of our Union. It is time to pause in our career to review our principles, and if possible revive that devoted patriotism and spirit of compromise which distinguished the sages of the Revolution and the fathers of our Union. If we can not at once, in justice to interests vested under improvident legislation, make our Government what it ought to be, we can at least take a stand against all new grants of monopolies and exclusive privileges, against any prostitution of our Government to the advancement of the few at the expense of the many, and in favor of compromise and gradual reform in our code laws and system of political economy.

1. Summarize and explain Jackson's reasoning for vetoing the Bank Bill.

10-5   The Force Bill (1833)

A key issue in the fight over nullification, Andrew Jackson desired this clause to assert the right of the national government to force compliance and payment of taxes by force of arms if necessary, over a possible nullification. Passed with a compromise tariff bill, which sought to head off sectional trouble, it was later "nullified" by the state of South Carolina.

An Act further to provide for the collection of duties on imports.

Be it enacted by the Senate and House of Representatives of the United States of America, in Congress assembled, That whenever, by reason of unlawful obstructions, combinations, or assemblages of persons, it shall become impracticable, in the judgment of the President, to execute the revenue laws, and collect the duties on imports in the ordinary way, in any collection district, it shall and may be lawful for the President to direct that the custom-house for such district be established and kept in any secure place within some port or harbour of such district, either upon land or on board any vessel; and, in that case, it shall be the duty of the collector to reside at such place, and there to detain all vessels and cargoes arriving within the said district until the duties imposed on said cargoes, by law, be paid in cash, deducting interest according to existing laws; and in such cases it shall be unlawful to take the vessel or cargo from the custody of the proper officer of the customs, unless by process from some court of the United States; and in case of any attempt otherwise to take such vessel or cargo by any force, or combination, or assemblage of persons too great to be overcome by the officers of the customs, it shall and may be lawful for the President of the United States, or such person or persons as he shall have empowered for that purpose, to employ such part of the land or naval forces, or militia of the United States, as may be deemed necessary for the purpose of preventing the removal of such vessel or cargo, and protecting the officers of the customs in retaining the custody thereof.

SEC. 2. *And be it further enacted,* That the jurisdiction of the circuit courts of the United States shall extend to all cases, in law or equity, arising under the revenue laws of the United States, for which other provisions are not already made by law; and if any person shall receive any injury to his person or property for or on account of any act by him done, under any law of the United States, for the protection of the revenue or the collection of duties on imports, he shall be entitled to maintain suit for damage therefor in the circuit court of the United States in the district wherein the party doing the injury may reside, or shall be found. And all property taken or detained by any officer or other person under authority of any revenue law of the United States, shall be irrepleviable, and shall be deemed to be in the custody of the law, and subject only to the orders and decrees of the courts of the United States having jurisdiction thereof. And if any person shall dispossess or rescue, or attempt to dispossess or rescue, any property so taken or detained as aforesaid, or shall aid or assist therein, such person shall be deemed guilty of a misdemeanour . . .

SEC. 5. *And be it further enacted,* That whenever the President of the United States shall be officially informed, by the authorities of any state, or by a judge of any circuit or district court of the United States, in the state, that, within the limits of such state, any law or laws of the United States, or the execution thereof, or of any process from the courts of the United States, is obstructed by the employment of military force, or by any other unlawful means, too great to be overcome by the ordinary course of judicial proceeding, or by the powers vested in the marshal by existing laws, it shall be lawful for him, the President of the United States, forthwith to issue his proclamation, declaring such fact or information, and requiring all such military and other force forthwith to disperse; and if at any time after issuing such proclamation, any such opposition or obstruction shall be made, in the manner or by the means aforesaid, the President shall be, and hereby is, authorized, promptly to employ such means to suppress the same, and to cause the said laws or process to be duly executed . . .

SEC. 6. *And be it further enacted*, That in any state where the jails are not allowed to be used for the imprisonment of persons arrested or committed under the laws of the United States, or where houses are not allowed to be so used, it shall and may be lawful for any marshal, under the direction of the judge of the United States for the proper district, to use other convenient places, within the limits of said state, and to make such other provision as he may deem expedient and necessary for that purpose.

SEC. 8. *And be it further enacted*, That the several provisions contained in the first and fifth sections of this act, shall be in force until the end of the next session of Congress, and no longer.

APPROVED, March 2, 1833.

1. What provisions are made under this bill to assist in the collection of duties and imports and to overcome "unlawful obstructions, combinations, or assemblages of persons" in the pursuit of these collections?

PART ELEVEN
REFORMING THE NATION

11-1 Lyman Beecher, Six Sermons on Intemperance (1828)

The patriarch of what would become a very influential American family, Lyman Beecher was educated at Yale and become a minister in several churches before coming to Boston in 1826. He started preaching revivals with intemperance a major theme. He saw drunkenness as the primary sin of America and became a noted speaker for temerence. He later become the President of Lane Seminary in Cincinnati where his "new school" Calvinism came into conflict with the old school. Beecher was a leading figure in the Second Great Awakening.

But of all the ways to hell, which the feet of deluded mortals tread, that of the intemperate is the most dreary and terrific. The demand for artificial stimulus to supply the deficiencies of healthful aliment, is like the rage of thirst, and the ravenous demand of famine. It is famine: for the artificial excitement has become as essential now to strength and cheerfulness, as simple nutrition once was. But nature, taught by habit to require what once she did not need, demands gratification now with a decision inexorable as death, and to most men as irresistible. The denial is a living death. The stomach, the head, the heart, and arteries, and veins, and every muscle, and every nerve, feel the exhaustion, and the restless, unutterable wretchedness which puts out the light of life, and curtains the heavens, and carpets the earth with sackcloth. All these varieties of sinking nature, call upon the wretched man with trumpet tongue, to dispel this darkness, and raise the ebbing tide of life, by the application of the cause which produced these woes, and after a momentary alleviation will produce them again with deeper terrors, and more urgent importunity; for the repetition, at each time renders the darkness deeper, and the torments of self-denial more irresistible and intolerable.

At length, the excitability of nature flags, and stimulants of higher power, and in greater quantities, are required to rouse the impaired energies of life, until at length the whole process of dilatory murder, and worse than purgatorial suffering, having been passed over, the silver cord is loosed, the golden bowl is broken, the wheel at the cistern stops, and the dust returns to the earth as it was, and the spirit to God who gave it.

These sufferings, however, of animal nature, are not to be compared with the moral agonies which convulse the soul. It is an immortal being who sins, and suffers; and as his earthly house dissolves, he is approaching the judgment seat, in anticipation of a miserable eternity. He feels his captivity, and in anguish of spirit clanks his chains and cries for help. Conscience thunders, remorse goads, and as the gulf opens before him, he recoils, and trembles, and weeps, and prays, and resolves, and promises, and reforms, and "seeks it yet again,"-again resolves, and weeps, and prays, and "seeks it yet again!" Wretched man, he has placed himself in the hands of a giant, who never pities, and never relaxes his iron gripe. He may struggle, but he is in chains. He may cry for release, but it comes not; and lost! lost! may be inscribed upon the door posts of his dwelling.

In the mean time these paroxsyms of his dying moral nature decline, and a fearful apathy, the harbinger of spiritual death, comes on. His resolution fails, and his mental energy, and his vigorous enterprise; and nervous irritation and depression ensue. The social affections lose their fulness and tenderness, and conscience loses its power, and the heart its sensibility, until all that was once lovely and of good report, retires and leaves the wretch abandoned to the appetites of a ruined animal. In this deplorable condition, reputation expires, business falters and becomes perplexed, and temptations to drink multiply as inclination to do so increases, and the power of resistance declines. And now the vortex roars, and the struggling victim buffets the fiery wave with feebler stroke, and warning supplication, until despair flashes upon his soul, and with an outcry that pierces the heavens, he ceases to strive, and disappears. . . .

Upon national industry the effects of intemperance are manifest and mischievous.

The results of national industry depend on the amount of well-directed intellectual and physical power. But intemperance paralyses and prevents both these springs of human action.

In the inventory of national loss by intemperance, may be set down-the labor prevented by indolence, by debility, by sickness, by quarrels and litigation, by gambling and idleness, by mistakes and misdirected effort, by improvidence and wastefulness, and by the shortened date of human life and activity. Little wastes in great establishments constantly occurring may defeat the energies of a mighty capital. But where the intellectual and muscular energies are raised to the working point daily by ardent spirits, until the agriculture, and commerce, and arts of a nation move on by the power of artificial stimulus, that moral power cannot be maintained, which will guaranty fidelity, and that physical power cannot be preserved and well directed, which will ensure national prosperity. The nation whose immense enterprise is thrust forward by the stimulus of ardent spirits, cannot ultimately escape debility and bankruptcy. . . .

The prospect of a destitute old age, or of a suffering family, no longer troubles the vicious portion of our community. They drink up their daily earnings, and bless God for the poor-house, and begin to look upon it as, of right, the drunkard's home, and contrive to arrive thither as early as idleness and excess will give them a passport to this sinecure of vice. Thus is the insatiable destroyer of industry marching through the land, rearing poor-houses, and augmenting taxation: night and day, with sleepless activity, squandering property, cutting the sinews of industry, undermining vigor, engendering disease, paralysing intellect, impairing moral principle, cutting short the date of life, and rolling up a national debt, invisible, but real and terrific as the debt of England: continually transferring larger and larger bodies of men, from the class of contributors to the national income, to the class of worthless consumers. . . .

The effects of intemperance upon civil liberty may not be lightly passed over.

It is admitted that intelligence and virtue are the pillars of republican institutions, and that the illumination of schools, and the moral power of religious institutions, are indispensable to produce this intelligence and virtue.

But who are found so uniformly in the ranks of irreligion as the intemperate? Who like these violate the Sabbath, and set their mouth against the heavens-neglecting the education of their families-and corrupting their morals? Almost the entire amount of national ignorance and crime is the offspring of intemperance. Throughout the land, the intemperate are hewing down the pillars, and undermining the foundations of our national edifice. Legions have besieged it, and upon every gate the battle-axe rings; and still the sentinels sleep.

Should the evil advance as it has done, the day is not far distant when the great body of the laboring classes of the community, the bones and sinews of the nation, will be contaminated; and when this is accomplished, the right of suffrage becomes the engine of self-destruction. For the laboring classes constitute an immense majority, and when these are perverted by intemperance, ambition needs no better implements with which to dig the grave of our liberties, and entomb our glory.

Such is the influence of interest, ambition, fear, and indolence, that one violent partisan, with a handful of disciplined troops, may overrule the influence of five hundred temperate men, who act without concert. Already is the disposition to temporize, to tolerate, and even to court the intemperate, too apparent, on account of the apprehended retribution of their perverted suffrage. The whole power of law, through the nation, sleeps in the statute book, and until public sentiment is roused and concentrated, it may be doubted whether its execution is possible.

Where is the city, town, or village, in which the laws are not openly violated, and where is the magistracy that dares to carry into effect the laws against the vending or drinking of ardent spirits? Here then an aristocracy of bad influence has already risen up, which bids defiance to law, and threatens the extirpation of civil liberty. As intemperance increases, the power of taxation will come more and more into the hands of men of intemperate habits and desperate fortunes; of course the laws gradually will become subservient to the debtor, and less efficacious in protecting the rights of property. This will be a vital stab to liberty-to the security of which property is indispensable. For money is the sinew of war-and when those who hold the property of a nation cannot be protected in their rights, they will change the form of government, peaceably if they may, by violence if they must.

1. Identify the physical effects of intemperance discussed in this sermon. What is the ultimate end of a lack of temperance? Compare these effects to the "moral agonies" that are alleged to be the results of intemperance. How does intemperance affect man's spirit?
2. What affect does intemperance have on industry, society, and civil Liberty? In what way is this sermon a plea for personal improvement as well as an attempt at wide social reform for the common good?

11-2 Temperance and the Washingtonians (1836)

At the 1836 spring convention of the American Temperance Union, the society's leadership decided the organization should promote total abstinence from all alcoholic beverages. This step required an entirely new orientation for many of the union's members who had chosen moderation over complete denial. It is not surprising that many individuals were not ready to go along with this new policy, including wealthy contributors who were unwilling to forgo wine. As a result, the temperance movement fell upon lean years. By 1840, many reformers were wondering what could be done to restore the momentum of the years preceding 1836. The stage was set for the emergence of the Washingtonian movement.

Source: History of Alcoholics Anonymous; Text and Articles on the Washingtonian Temperance Society: *The Foundation, Progress and Principles of the Washington Temperance Society of Baltimore, 1842.* http://www.historyofaa.com/Washingtonians/wash1.html

CHAPTER I

Foundation of the Society

The 5th of April, 1840, was an eventful day. Influences were set at work then, which have been developing and extending ever since, and which promise to accomplish much for the good of mankind. On the evening of that day, half a dozen men met in the bar-room of a tavern in Baltimore. They had often met there before, spent their hours in friendly converse, and mingled in the mutual drowning of care in the bowl. It was a place of usual resort to them. And now they had met there as before, to drink together from the poisonous cup, to which they were all too much addicted. Without having become outcasts or sots, they had all confessedly suffered severely from the frequent and intemperate use of intoxicating drinks,—suffered in their health, suffered in their estates, suffered in their families, their habits, their feelings and their reputation.

But though these were plain men, they were men of unusual energy. It is true that alcohol had made its ravages on their characters, their minds, and their hearts. But the energy of manhood still survived. They were the victims, rather than merely the votaries of the pleasures of the bowl. They were in business, and five of them had families. They cared for their business and loved their families. They had all started out in life when young, with the hopes which usually beat high in the hearts of youth in every branch of business, or situation in life, when first entering upon the world. For a time they ran well. Business was fair. Friends were not few. They had married, and were happy.

Had any man told either of them at eighteen, nineteen, or twenty years of age, that twenty-five or thirty would find them drunkards,—that, like thousands around them, they would suffer from the poison of the serpent, and the sting of the adder in the cup, they would have laughed the insinuation to scorn, and honestly too. They never dreamed then of being drunkards. They drank moderately, and freely too. The habits of society at that time,—of all classes of society, even religious, sanctioned the free use of alcoholic drinks; and they went with the multitude never for a moment thinking of evil. But the love of drink particularly of the "social glass," grew upon them gradually and insensibly, until habit was fixed and appetite strong; and ere they had suspected it, they found themselves in the power of a monster, bound hand and foot in chains,—the slaves of their own appetites. And now they frequented the public taverns; and oft at night, or during the day, and even on the Sabbath, instead of being at their business, or with their families, or at church, they were to be found at the Hotel or Grogshop. They knew it was wrong. They saw the evil; they felt it; they lamented it; and times without number did they promise wife and friend and self, that they would drink no more. They were sincere. They meant to be sober. But at some fatal hour they would take one glass again, "just one glass;" and they found themselves as powerless and debased as ever.

It was on the evening of the day on which we have introduced them to the reader, that these six men were once more together at the tavern. Their families were forsaken at home. Their business for the day was done. But neither was entirely forgotten. The bar with its temptations was near them. Their habits were to contend with. And the cravings of an unnatural appetite within were against all good resolves. But these men had not lost all their principle, their energy, or their feeling. They looked to their homes, and they saw that much of domestic bliss, which should gather round the fireside, was banished by the inebriating cup. They looked to their business, and they knew they had suffered there. They counted the cost, and they were astonished at the amount of money they threw away in visiting the dram-shop. They looked back to the days of their youth, when with free hearts and bounding hopes, they had leaped into life, and had looked forward into the future never dreaming of such a slavery. They looked to their reputation, their influence, their health, their feelings, and their energy of character; and they felt that they would lose all these, if they prosecuted much longer the way in which they were hurrying down to death. They looked into the future, and all was clouds and darkness. They deliberately weighed the movement about to be made; and then rising in the energy of their still surviving manhood, they resolved that hour they would drink no more of the poisonous draught forever; and that to carry out their resolutions, they would form a society with a pledge to that effect, and bind themselves under it to each other for life.

This is no fancy sketch. The circumstances have often been stated by the founders of the society, just as we have detailed them. We do not pretend to say, that the feelings and reflections above stated were matters of grave deliberation and discussion among them. The movement had more of a spontaneous character, and was at once and rather impulsively approved as soon as suggested. But these were the silent meditations and reflections, which were working in each individual breast, so that it needed but that the proper chord should be touched, under the circumstances, and their hearts all vibrated together: the matter needed but a proposal to meet the approbation of all. It should also be remarked that the idea of reformation had been suggested among them at a former meeting, but no conclusion had been arrived at, as to either the certainty or the manner of the accomplishment of their purpose.

And now the deed was done. A constitution was agreed upon; and as the movement was a great and important one, a great name was proposed to be affixed as the title of the society. It was adopted. And this was the foundation of the Washington Temperance Society of Baltimore.

From the character of the deed itself, and the extraordinary results, which have proceeded and are yet proceeding from it, justice requires that the names of the founders of this association should be recorded, that they may be handed down in all the future annals of the Temperance cause. William K. Mitchell, John F. Loss, David Anderson, George Stears, Archibald Campbell and James McCurley were the "original six," who founded the Washington Temperance Society of Baltimore, and of course the originators of that new system of Temperance operations, which has of late attracted the attention of the country.

Previous to the evening on which the society was formed, we have intimated that the subject of reformation had been in contemplation among them for several days. When the adoption of a society and pledge was proposed, several difficulties were in the way of their successful organization. These difficulties were mainly the apprehensions of evil influences being introduced into the action of the society, to divert them from their simple purpose, if, as might be, the society should ever become efficient and numerous. Upon suggestion therefore it was resolved among themselves, that they would place the temperance cause, so far as they were concerned, in the position of a unit: that the society, as such, was to recognize no creed of religion, nor party in politics; and that neither political nor religious action of any kind, should ever be introduced into the society's operations. Personal abstinence from all intoxicating drinks was to be the basis, and only requisite of membership. Moral suasion was to be the only means by which they, as a body, were to induce others to adopt their principles. As a society, their whole business was to induce others not to drink intoxicating liquors. They would thus be less likely to excite the suspicions or prejudices of any class of men, and have free access to all; this would render Temperance a simple principle of personal abstinence. It would be, in the language of Father Matthew, "a green spot in the desert of life, where all could meet in peace and harmony."

Moreover they determined that the regular meetings of the society should be meetings for the detail of personal experience, and not for debates, lectures and speeches; that even on matters of necessary business, as few remarks as possible only would be tolerated. Thus all temperance addresses were to be in the form of the individual experience of the several members. The spirit of this rule and common sense were to guide them how far any should be allowed to go in his remarks. The society was thus based on facts, and not on an abstraction, and the principle of common honesty was to direct them in all their movements.

These difficulties being out of the way—the society being now organized, and the constitution and pledge adopted and signed, the founders resolved to hold weekly experience meetings for their own encouragement and benefit, and for the good of others who might be induced to attend.

CHAPTER II

Progress and Influence of the Society

Immediately after the organization of the society, the several members went privately to their friends, especially their former drinking associates, and persuaded them in the spirit of kindness, to abandon strong drink, and join the society. To every excuse and plea that they could not reform, they would reply by referring to their own experience. And they generally clung to a man until they had persuaded him to give up the bottle forever, or at least to go with them to the next meeting of their society. When such was the condition or promise, true to his man, each member on the evening of meeting, instead of going alone and waiting for his friend, would go to his house, or to the Grogshop, and, if necessary, lead him by the arm away from the bar, and conduct him in person to the meeting. This has often been done. When the individual was once within their hall, they regarded him as a easy convert. The experience of others who had been like him, and the good influences set to work upon him, soon led him to feel, think and act aright. Such exertions, judiciously made in the spirit of kindness, have rarely failed of entire success.

In the course of some months, the society gradually increased in numbers and interest.

The aggressive principle, or missionary spirit, once at work, grew and spread with the growth and extension of the society. In the meantime, the members had the benefit of several months' experience in the use of cold water. They began to feel better, to look better, and in every respect to be satisfied with the change in their habits. As some of them expressed it: "They were just waking up from a long sleep of many years, and now only beginning to live." The "experiences" of the members were now more and more interesting, and began to attract somewhat the attention of the public; and through their influence many of the most desperate and hopeless subjects of intemperance were redeemed. By the truly Samaritan conduct of these sacrificing men, many a poor inebriate, whose friends had long given him over as beyond the reach of hope, was rescued from his chains, and elevated from the depths of degradation, to which strong drink had reduced him. Each of these was not only a new experience man, but virtually another missionary.

In six months after its formation, the society numbered eighty or ninety, many of whom were reformed drunkards. And no man could attend their meetings, as the author then first did without seeing that there was a spirit among them which would not die—a principle which would diffuse itself abroad in the community, and pour the richest blessings on the heads of many a family in Baltimore;—and even spread to the farthest borders of the land. As yet, however, their meetings were held in their own private hall, which they had rented for the purpose. The citizens did not generally know of the movement; and such as did, hardly had confidence in the permanency of the reformations.

In November, 1840, their first public meeting was held in the Masonic Hall, which was crowded on the occasion. As this was their first public effort however, and as the object was rather intended to be an introduction to the public, very little experience was given. In addition to these remarks made by gentlemen invited to address the meeting, the President simply stated the principles of the society, that they might be understood by the community. Not long after this another public meeting was called in one of the churches of the city, on which occasion several of the members of the society publicly told their tale of woe and warning, counsel and advice, and with thrilling effect. Numbers were induced to sign the pledge; many of them victims of intemperance. And in the bosom of the society they found a home, and friends to counsel and defend them.

Frequent public experience meetings now followed, and were continued week after week during the entire winter. Public attention was now fully arrested. The meetings, though held in the largest churches of the city, were crowded to excess. Every family that had a poor miserable inebriate connected with it, hailed with joy and hope the influence which this society was exerting in reforming the intemperate, and used every exertion to induce such persons to attend the meetings of the Washington Society, and sign the pledge. And many a good-hearted, yea, noble-hearted man, who had long found the chains of appetite galling to him, and had often wished and tried in vain to shake them off, now went to this society, signed the pledge, and found him-self a free man. Many reformed, whose friends and the community had long since given them over as irrecoverable,—many even from the lowest depths of disgrace and reproach. Some were almost literally dug up out of the earth,—who had not only been abandoned as beyond hope, but who had been forgotten by their early friends, or reckoned among the dead. Many such were brought out of their hiding-places, and to the surprise of their friends, soon after their reformation, they were found "clothed and in their right mind," and prepared to occupy that position in society, which they had forfeited only by dissipation. Insomuch that the society was familiarly known by the expressive title of the "Resurrection Society."

The society was now increasing in numbers so fast, that their regular place of meeting was becoming too small to accommodate them all. A division was contemplated. But it was at length resolved, the branches should be formed in the various sections of the city; this was accordingly done. In the meantime other societies began to spring up in the city, on the same general principles with the Washington; some auxiliary, and others independent. All of these societies under their present organization, (with two or three exceptions,) owe their origin directly or indirectly to the influence of the parent Washington Society, and have borrowed most of their features, as well as obtained most of their life from it. Many of these associations have been very prosperous, and have done incalculable good in reclaiming the intemperate, confirming the temperate, and advancing the common cause. If our assigned limits would allow, it would afford us pleasure to make honourable mention of some of these societies; but as it is, we can not go into any detail respecting them. We hail them as fellow-labourers in a common cause, take them by the hand, and bid them "God speed." We call upon them to rival us in good works, and in adhering to first principles,—and then our motto is: "We be brethren; let us not fall out by the way."

It should be observed that most of the Temperance societies, in existence in this city previous to the formation of the Washington, have either been remodeled or discontinued, and their places filled up by more energetic ones. Many of the societies admit only of grown men as members; but there are others connected with the various churches, or composed entirely of female or youth, where such may join as choose to do so. . . .

CONCLUSION

From the preceding pages we learn that the principal causes of the extraordinary influence of the Washington Temperance Society, are as follow:

1. The drunkard is now regarded in a new light by the Washingtonians. Instead of being considered a cruel monster—a loathsome brute—an object of ridicule, contempt and indignation, as formerly, we are now taught to look upon him as a brother—as more weak perhaps than wicked—as a slave to appetite, and debased by passion—yet still as a man, our own brother. Thus all the sympathies of the public are excited in his behalf.

2. The substitution of personal experience for addresses and lectures, has had the same effect of exciting the sympathy of the community in behalf of the intemperate. A reformed drunkard's experience touches a chord, that vibrates in every human breast. Moreover the drunkard when reformed best knows how to reach the drunkard's heart; for he best understands his feelings.

3. Another cause lies in the simplicity and unity of the pledge, requiring but one thing—personal abstinence. To this add the neutrality of the society, as we have explained it in the preceding pages, and the whole matter is explained on the common principles of human nature.

1. How would you describe the original membership of the Washingtonian Society? Did their overall goal differ from that of the American Temperance Union?
2. What methods and techniques did the members of the Washingtonian Society employ to attract new members? How do you account for their success?

11-3 A Lowell Mill Girl Tells her Story (1836)

Harriet Hanson Robinson worked in the textile mills of Lowell, Massachusetts from the age of ten in 1834 until 1848. Later, as the wife of a newspaper editor, Robinson wrote an account of her earlier life as female factory worker and a description of the strike of 1836. Deeply involved in the political culture of her time, Robinson explained some of the family dynamics involved, and portrayed women as active participants in their own lives.

Source: *Internet Modern History Sourcebook* http://www.fordham.edu/halsall/mod/robinson-lowell.html

In what follows, I shall confine myself to a description of factory life in Lowell, Massachusetts, from 1832 to 1848, since, with that phase of Early Factory Labor in New England, I am the most familiar—because I was a part of it.

In 1832, Lowell was little more than a factory village. Five "corporations" were started, and the cotton mills belonging to them were building. Help was in great demand and stories were told all over the country of the new factory place, and the high wages that were offered to all classes of workpeople; stories that reached the ears of mechanics' and farmers' sons and gave new life to lonely and dependent women in distant towns and farmhouses. . . . Troops of young girls came from different parts of New England, and from Canada, and men were employed to collect them at so much a head, and deliver them at the factories.

* * *

At the time the Lowell cotton mills were started the caste of the factory girl was the lowest among the employments of women. In England and in France, particularly, great injustice had been done to her real character. She was represented as subjected to influences that must destroy her purity and self-respect. In the eyes of her overseer she was but a brute, a slave, to be beaten, pinched and pushed about. It was to overcome this prejudice that such high wages had been offered to women that they might be induced to become mill girls, in spite of the opprobrium that still clung to this degrading occupation. . . .

The early mill girls were of different ages. Some were not over ten years old; a few were in middle life, but the majority were between the ages of sixteen and twenty-five. The very young girls were called "doffers." They "doffed," or took off, the full bobbins from the spinning frames, and replaced them with empty ones. These mites worked about fifteen minutes every hour and the rest of the time was their own. When the overseer was kind they were allowed to read, knit, or go outside the mill yard to play. They were paid two dollars a week. The working hours of all the girls extended from five o'clock in the morning until seven in the evening, with one half hour each, for breakfast and dinner. Even the doffers were forced to be on duty nearly fourteen hours a day. This was the greatest hardship in the lives of these children. Several years later a ten hour law was passed, but not until long after some of these little doffers were old enough to appear before the legislative committee on the subject, and plead, by their presence, for a reduction of the hours of labor.

Those of the mill girls who had homes generally worked from eight to ten months in the year; the rest of the time was spent with parents or friends. A few taught school during the summer months. Their life in the factory was made pleasant to them. In those days there was no need of advocating the doctrine of the proper relation between employer and employed. Help was too valuable to be ill-treated. . . .

* * *

The most prevailing incentive to labor was to secure the means of education for some male member of the family. To make a gentleman of a brother or a son, to give him a college education, was the dominant thought in the minds of a great many of the better class of mill girls. I have known more than one to give every cent of her wages, month after month, to her brother, that he might get the education necessary to enter some profession. I have known a mother to work years in this way for her boy. I have known women to educate young men by their earnings, who were not sons or relatives. There are many men now living who were helped to an education by the wages of the early mill girls.

It is well to digress here a little, and speak of the influence the possession of money had on the characters of some of these women. We can hardly realize what a change the cotton factory made in the status of the working women. Hitherto woman had always been a money saving rather than a money earning, member of the community. Her labor could command but small return. If she worked out as servant, or "help," her wages were from 50 cents to $1.00 a week; or, if she went from house to house by the day to spin and weave, or do tailoress work, she could get but 75 cents a week and her meals. As teacher, her services were not in demand, and the arts, the professions, and even the trades and industries, were nearly all closed to her.

As late as 1840 there were only seven vocations outside the home into which the women of New England had entered. At this time woman had no property rights. A widow could be left without her share of her husband's (or the family) property, an " encumbrance" to his estate. A father could make his will without reference to his daughter's share of the inheritance. He usually left her a home on the farm as long as she remained single. A woman was not supposed to be capable of spending her own, or of using other people's money. In Massachusetts, before 1840, a woman could not, legally, be treasurer of her own sewing society, unless some man were responsible for her. The law took no cognizance of woman as a money spender. She was a ward, an appendage, a relict. Thus it happened that if a woman did not choose to marry, or, when left a widow, to remarry, she had no choice but to enter one of the few employments open to her, or to become a burden on the charity of some relative.

* * *

One of the first strikes that ever took place in this country was in Lowell in 1836. When it was announced that the wages were to be cut down, great indignation was felt, and it was decided to strike or "turn out" en masse. This was done. The mills were shut down, and the girls went from their several corporations in procession to the grove on Chapel Hill, and listened to incendiary speeches from some early labor reformers.

One of the girls stood on a pump and gave vent to the feelings of her companions in a neat speech, declaring that it was their duty to resist all attempts at cutting down the wages. This was the first time a woman had spoken in public in Lowell, and the event caused surprise and consternation among her audience.

It is hardly necessary to say that, so far as practical results are concerned, this strike did no good. The corporation would not come to terms. The girls were soon tired of holding out, and they went back to their work at the reduced rate of wages. The ill-success of this early attempt at resistance on the part of the wage element seems to have made a precedent for the issue of many succeeding strikes.

1. According to Harriet Hanson Robinson, what was one of the primary reasons why women worked in the mills?
2. Describe the life of a mill girl as depicted by Robinson. What is her assessment of the efficacy of the strike in 1836?

11-4 Ralph Waldo Emerson, "Self-Reliance" (1841)

Ralph Waldo Emerson was one of America's greatest philosophers. His rejection of organized religion if favor of "self reliance" Was embraced by many who became transcendentalists. Born into a long line of ministers, Emerson resigned from the pulpit because he could no longer give communion in good conscience. He became an essayist and a lecturer on the Lyceum circuit and his revolutionary addresses including The Divinity School Address, and The American Scholar sought to liberate Americans from European and orthodox influence. He was, however, best known as the "apostle of self-reliance" and his influence on rising generations can hardly be underestimated.

Whoso would be a man, must be a nonconformist. He who would gather immortal palms must not be hindered by the name of goodness, but must explore if it be goodness. Nothing is at last sacred but the integrity of your own mind. Absolve you to yourself, and you shall have the suffrage of the world. I remember an answer which when quite young I was prompted to make to a valued adviser who was wont to importune me with the dear old doctrines of the church. On my saying, "What have I to do with the sacredness of traditions, if I live wholly from within?" my friend suggested,-"But these impulses may be from below, not from above." I replied, "They do not seem to me to be such; but if I am the Devil's child, I will live then from the Devil." No law can be sacred to me but that of my nature. Good and bad are but names very readily transferable to that or this; the only right is what is after my constitution; the only wrong what is against it. A man is to carry himself in the presence of all opposition as if every thing were titular and ephemeral but he. I am ashamed to think how easily we capitulate to badges and names, to large societies and dead institutions. Every decent and well-spoken individual affects and sways me more than is right. I ought to go upright and vital, and speak the rude truth in all ways. If malice and vanity wear the coat of philanthropy, shall that pass? If an angry bigot assumes this bountiful cause of Abolition, and comes to me with his last news from Barbadoes, why should I not say to him, 'Go love thy infant; love thy woodchopper; be good-natured and modest; have that grace; and never varnish your hard, uncharitable ambition with this incredible tenderness for black folk a thousand miles off. Thy love afar is spite at home.' Rough and graceless would be such greeting, but truth is handsomer than the affection of love. Your goodness must have some edge to it,-else it is none. The doctrine of hatred must be preached, as the counteraction of the doctrine of love, when that pules and whines. I shun father and mother and wife and brother when my genius calls me. I would write on the lintels of the door-post, *Whim*. I hope it is somewhat better than whim at last, but we cannot spend the day in explanation. Expect me not to show cause why I seek or why I exclude company. Then again, do not tell me, as a good man did to-day, of my obligation to put all poor men in good situations. Are they my poor? I tell thee, thou foolish philanthropist, that I grudge the dollar, the dime, the cent I give to such men as do not belong to me and to whom I do not belong. There is a class of persons to whom by all spiritual affinity I am bought and sold; for them I will go to prison if need be; but your miscellaneous popular charities; the education at college of fools; the building of meeting-houses to the vain end to which many now stand; alms to sots, and the thousand-fold Relief Societies;-though I confess with shame I sometimes succumb and give the dollar, it is a wicked dollar, which by and by I shall have the manhood to withhold. . . .

What I must do is all that concerns me, not what the people think. This rule, equally arduous in actual and in intellectual life, may serve for the whole distinction between greatness and meanness. It is the harder because you will always find those who think they know what is your duty better than you know it. It is easy in the world to live after the world's opinion; it is easy in solitude to live after our own; but the great man is he who in the midst of the crowd keeps with perfect sweetness the independence of solitude. . . .

A foolish consistency is the hobgoblin of little minds, adored by little statesmen and philosophers and divines. With consistency a great soul has simply nothing to do. He may as well concern himself with his shadow on the wall. Speak what you think now in hard words and to-morrow speak what to-morrow thinks in hard words again, though it contradict every thing you said to-day.-'Ah, so you shall be sure to be misunderstood.'-Is it so bad then to be misunderstood? Pythagoras was misunderstood, and Socrates, and Jesus, and Luther, and Copernicus, and Galileo, and Newton, and every pure and wise spirit that ever took flesh. To be great is to be misunderstood.

1. What does this excerpt suggest regarding the importance and sovereignty of the individual?
2. In what ways does this document propose modes of living quite different than what would be considered proper social behavior?

11-5   Declaration of Sentiments and Resolutions, Woman's Rights Convention, Seneca Falls, New York (1848)

Organized by Lucretia Mott and Elizabeth Cady Stanton, the Seneca Falls Convention was the first national women's rights convention in the United States. This document, obviously modeled on the Declaration of Independence listed the ways in which women had been denied the basic rights inherent in the American idea. Though 40 men attended (including Fredrick Douglass) the convention blamed men for the unjust treatment of women and stated that women must earn independence for themselves. The meeting become the first of many and provided impetus for the burgeoning women' movement.

> **Source:** E. C. Stanton, S. B. Anthony, and Matilda Joslyn Gage, eds., *History of Woman Suffrage,* vol. 1 (Rochester, NY: Charles Mann, 1881), pp. 70–72.

We hold these truths to be self-evident: that all men and women are created equal; that they are endowed by their Creator with certain inalienable rights; that among these are life, liberty, and the pursuit of happiness; that to secure these rights governments are instituted, deriving their just powers from the consent of the governed. . ... But when a long train of abuses and usurpations, pursuing invariably the same object evinces a design to reduce them under absolute despotism, it is their duty to throw off such government, and to provide new guards for their future security. Such has been the patient sufferance of the women under this government, and such is now the necessity which constrains them to demand the equal station to which they are entitled.

The history of mankind is a history of repeated injuries and usurpations on the part of man toward woman, having in direct object the establishment of an absolute tyranny over her. To prove this, let facts be submitted to a candid world.

He has never permitted her to exercise her inalienable right to the elective franchise.

He has compelled her to submit to laws, in the formation of which she had no voice.

He has withheld from her rights which are given to the most ignorant and degraded menÑboth natives and foreigners.

Having deprived her of this first right of a citizen, the elective franchise, thereby leaving her without representation in the halls of legislation, he has oppressed her on all sides.

He has made her, if married, in the eye of the law, civilly dead.

He has taken from her all right in property, even to the wages she earns.

He has made her, morally, an irresponsible being, as she can commit many crimes with impunity, provided they be done in the presence of her husband. In the covenant of marriage, she is compelled to promise obedience to her husband, he becoming, to all intents and purposes, her masterÑthe law giving him power to deprive her of her liberty, and to administer chastisement.

He has so framed the laws of divorce, as to what shall be the proper causes, and in case of separation, to whom the guardianship of the children shall be given, as to be wholly regardless of the happiness of womenÑthe law, in all cases, going upon a false supposition of the supremacy of man, and giving all power into his hands.

After depriving her of all rights as a married woman, if single, and the owner of property, he has taxed her to support a government which recognizes her only when her property can be made profitable to it.

He has monopolized nearly all the profitable employments, and from those she is permitted to follow, she receives but a scanty remuneration. He closes against her all the avenues to wealth and distinction which he considers most honorable to himself. As a teacher of theology, medicine, or law, she is not known.

He has denied her the facilities for obtaining a thorough education, all colleges being closed against her.

He allows her in Church, as well as State, but a subordinate position, claiming Apostolic authority for her exclusion from the ministry, and, with some exceptions, from any public participation in the affairs of the Church.

He has created a false public sentiment by giving to the world a different code of morals for men and women, by which moral delinquencies which exclude women from society, are not only tolerated, but deemed of little account in man.

He has usurped the prerogative of Jehovah himself, claiming it as his right to assign for her a sphere of action, when that belongs to her conscience and to her God.

He has endeavored, in every way that he could, to destroy her confidence in her own powers, to lessen her self-respect, and to make her willing to lead a dependent and abject life.

Now, in view of this entire disfranchisement of one-half the people of this country, their social and religious degradationÑin view of the unjust laws above mentioned, and because women do feel themselves aggrieved, oppressed, and fraudulently deprived of their most sacred rights, we insist that they have immediate admission to all the rights and privileges which belong to them as citizens of the United States.

In entering upon the great work before us, we anticipate no small amount of misconception, misrepresentation, and ridicule; but we shall use every instrumentality within our power to effect our object. We shall employ agents, circulate tracts, petition the State and National legislatures, and endeavor to enlist the pulpit and the press in our behalf. We hope this Convention will be followed by a series of Conventions embracing every part of the country.

The following resolutions were adopted:

Resolved, That such laws as conflict, in any way, with the true and substantial happiness of woman, are contrary to the great precept of nature and of no validity, for this is "superior in obligation to any other."

Resolved, That all laws which prevent woman from occupying such a station in society as her conscience shall dictate, or which place her in a position inferior to that of man, are contrary to the great precept of nature, and therefore of no force or authority.

Resolved, That woman is man's equalÑwas intended to be so by the Creator, and the highest good of the race demands that she should be recognized as such.

Resolved, That the women of this country ought to be enlightened in regard to the laws under which they live, that they may no longer publish their degradation by declaring themselves satisfied with their present position, nor their ignorance, by asserting that they have all the rights they want.

Resolved, That inasmuch as man, while claiming for himself intellectual superiority, does accord to woman moral superiority, it is pre-eminently his duty to encourage her to speak and teach, as she has an opportunity, in all religious assemblies.

Resolved, That the same amount of virtue, delicacy, and refinement of behavior that is required of woman in the social state, should also be required of man, and the same transgressions should be visited with equal severity on both man and woman.

Resolved, That the objection of indelicacy and impropriety, which is so often brought against woman when she addresses a public audience, comes with a very ill-grace from those who encourage, by their attendance, her appearance on the stage, in the concert, or in feats of the circus.

Resolved, That woman has too long rested satisfied in the circumscribed limits which corrupt customs and a perverted application of the Scriptures have marked out for her, and that it is time she should move in the enlarged sphere which her great Creator has assigned her.

Resolved, That it is the duty of the women of this country to secure to themselves their sacred right to the elective franchise.

Resolved, That the equality of human rights results necessarily from the fact of the identity of the race in capabilities and responsibilities.

Resolved, therefore, That, being invested by the Creator with the same capabilities, and the same consciousness of responsibility for their exercise, it is demonstrably the right and duty of woman, equally with man, to promote every righteous cause by every righteous means; and especially in regard to the great subjects of morals and religion, it is self-evidently her right to participate with her brother in teaching them, both in private and in public, by writing and by speaking, by any instrumentalities proper to be used, and in any assemblies proper to be held; and this being a self-evident truth growing out of the divinely implanted principles of human nature, any custom or authority adverse to it, whether modern or wearing the hoary sanction of antiquity, is to be regarded as a self-evident falsehood, and at war with mankind.

Resolved, That the speedy success of our cause depends upon the zealous and untiring efforts of both men and women, for the overthrow of the monopoly of the pulpit, and for the securing to woman an equal participation with men in the various trades, professions, and commerce.

1. In the "Resolutions" at the end of the document, how does Lucretia Mott attempt to persuade men to agree to equal rights for women?
2. 2. Even though the women's rights movement followed closely on the heels of abolitionism, slaves gained emancipation over fifty years before women won the right to vote in national elections. Why do you think this was the case?

11-6   Horace Mann on Education and National Welfare

In 1837, Horace Mann accepted the position of First Secretary of the State Board of Education in Massachusetts, the first of its kind in the nation, and inaugurated a new era in the history of American education. Over a period of twelve years, Mann transformed the state's assortment of common schools into a system of free public schools, organized on sound educational principles. He also sponsored the first state-supported "normal school" for the training of teachers, a state teachers' association, and a minimum school year of six months. In his twelve annual reports to the board, Mann discussed the larger implications of education in a democracy. His *Twelfth Annual Report*, included here, expounds a rationale for the support of public education through taxation.

Source: United States Department of State, International Information Programs
http://usinfo.state.gov/usa/infousa/facts/democrac/16.htm

Under the Providence of God, our means of education are the grand machinery by which the "raw material" of human nature can be worked up into inventors and discoverers, into skilled artisans and scientific farmers, into scholars and jurists, into the founders of benevolent institutions, and the great expounders of ethical and theological science. By means of early education, these embryos of talent may be quickened, which will solve the difficult problems of political and economical law; and by them, too, the genius may be kindled which will blaze forth in the Poets of Humanity. Our schools, far more than they have done, may supply the Presidents and Professors of Colleges, and Superintendents of Public Instruction, all over the land; and send, not only into our sister states, but across the Atlantic, the men of practical science, to superintend the construction of the great works of art. Here, too, may those judicial powers be developed and invigorated, which will make legal principles so clear and convincing as to prevent appeals to force; and, should the clouds of war ever lower over our country, some hero may be found,—the nursling of our schools, and ready to become the leader of our armies,—that best of all heroes, who will secure the glories of a peace, unstained by the magnificent murders of the battlefield. . . .

Without undervaluing any other human agency, it may be safely affirmed that the Common School, improved and energized, as it can easily be, may become the most effective and benignant of all the forces of civilization. Two reasons sustain this position. In the first place, there is a universality in its operation, which can be affirmed of no other institution whatever. If administered in the spirit of justice and conciliation, all the rising generation may be brought within the circle of its reformatory and elevating influences. And, in the second place, the materials upon which it operates are so pliant and ductile as to be susceptible of assuming a greater variety of forms than any other earthly work of the Creator. The inflexibility and ruggedness of the oak, when compared with the lithe sapling or the tender germ, are but feeble emblems to typify the docility of childhood, when contrasted with the obduracy and intractableness of man. It is these inherent advantages of the Common School, which, in our own State, have produced results so striking, from a system so imperfect, and an administration so feeble. In teaching the blind, and the deaf and dumb, in kindling the latent spark of intelligence that lurks in an idiot's mind, and in the more holy work of reforming abandoned and outcast children, education has proved what it can do, by glorious experiments. These wonders, it has done in its infancy, and with the lights of a limited experience; but, when its faculties shall be fully developed, when it shall be trained to wield its mighty energies for the protection of society against the giant vices which now invade and torment it;—against intemperance, avarice, war, slavery, bigotry, the woes of want and the wickedness of waste,—then, there will not be a height to which these enemies of the race can escape, which it will not scale, nor a Titan among them all, whom it will not slay.

Now I proceed, then, in endeavoring to show how the true business of the schoolroom connects itself, and becomes identical, with the great interests of society. The former is the infant, immature state of those interests; the latter, their developed, adult state. As "the child is father to the man," so may the training of the schoolroom expand into the institutions and fortunes of the State. . . .

INTELLECTUAL EDUCATION, AS A MEANS OF REMOVING POVERTY, AND SECURING ABUNDANCE

Another cardinal object which the government of Massachusetts, and all the influential men in the State should propose to themselves, is the physical well-being of all the people,—the sufficiency, comfort, competence, of every individual, in regard to food, raiment, and shelter. And these necessaries and conveniences of life should be obtained by each individual for himself, or by each family for themselves, rather than accepted from the hand of charity, or extorted by poor-laws. It is not averred that this most desirable result can, in all instances, be obtained; but it is, nevertheless, the end to be aimed at. True statesmanship and true political economy, not less than true philanthropy, present this perfect theory as the goal, to be more and more closely approximated by our imperfect practice. The desire to achieve such a result cannot be regarded as

139

an unreasonable ambition; for, though all mankind were well-fed, well-clothed, and well-housed, they might still be but half-civilized. . . .

According to the European theory, men are divided into classes,—some to toil and earn, others to seize and enjoy. According to the Massachusetts theory, all are to have an equal chance for earning, and equal security in the enjoyment of what they earn. The latter tends to equality of condition; the former to the grossest inequalities. Tried by any Christian standard of morals, or even by any of the better sort of heathen standards, can any one hesitate, for a moment, in declaring which of the two will produce the greater amount of human welfare; and which, therefore, is the more conformable to the Divine will? The European theory is blind to what constitutes the highest glory, as well as the highest duty, of a State. . . .

I suppose it to be the universal sentiment of all those who mingle any ingredient of benevolence with their notions on Political Economy, that vast and overshadowing private fortunes are among the greatest dangers to which the happiness of the people in a republic can be subjected. Such fortunes would create a feudalism of a new kind; but one more oppressive and unrelenting than that of the Middle Ages. The feudal lords in England, and on the continent, never held their retainers in a more abject condition of servitude, than the great majority of foreign manufacturers and capitalists hold their operatives and laborers at the present day. The means employed are different, but the similarity in results is striking. What force did then, money does now. The villein of the Middle Ages had no spot of earth on which he could live, unless one were granted to him by his lord. The operative or laborer of the present day has no employment, and therefore no bread, unless the capitalist will accept his services. The vassal had no shelter but such as his master provided for him. Not one in five thousand of English operatives, or farm laborers, is able to build or own even a hovel; and therefore they must accept such shelter as Capital offers them. The baron prescribed his own terms to his retainers; those terms were peremptory, and the serf must submit or perish. The British manufacturer or farmer prescribes the rate of wages he will give to his work-people; he reduces these wages under whatever pretext he pleases; and they too have no alternative but submission or starvation. In some respects, indeed, the condition of the modern dependant is more forlorn than that of the corresponding serf class in former times. Some attributes of the patriarchal relation did spring up between the lord and his lieges, to soften the harsh relations subsisting between them. Hence came some oversight of the condition of children, some relief in sickness, some protection and support in the decrepitude of age. But only in instances comparatively few, have kindly offices smoothed the rugged relation between British Capital and British Labor. The children of the work-people are abandoned to their fate; and, notwithstanding the privations they suffer, and the dangers they threaten, no power in the realm has yet been able to secure them an education; and when the adult laborer is prostrated by sickness, or eventually worn out by toil and age, the poor-house, which has all along been his destination, becomes his destiny.

Now two or three things will doubtless be admitted to be true, beyond all controversy, in regard to Massachusetts. By its industrial condition, and its business operations, it is exposed, far beyond any other state in the Union, to the fatal extremes of overgrown wealth and desperate poverty. Its population is more dense than that of any other state. It is four or five times more dense than the average of all the other states, taken together; and density of population has always been one of the proximate causes of social inequality. According to population and territorial extent, there is far more capital in Massachusetts,—capital which is movable, and instantaneously available,—than in any other state in the Union; and probably both these qualifications respecting population and territory could be omitted without endangering the truth of the assertion. It has been recently stated, in a very respectable public journal, on the authority of a writer conversant with the subject, that, from the last of June, 1846, to the 1st of August, 1848, the amount of money invested, by the citizens of Massachusetts, "in manufacturing cities, railroads, and other improvements," is "fifty-seven millions of dollars, of which more than fifty has been paid in and expended." The dividends to be received by the citizens of Massachusetts from June, 1848, to April, 1849, are estimated, by the same writer, at ten millions, and the annual increase of capital at "little short of twenty-two millions." If this be so, are we not in danger of naturalizing and domesticating among ourselves those hideous evils which are always engendered between Capital and Labor, when all the capital is in the hands of one class, and all the labor is thrown upon another?

Now, surely, nothing but Universal Education can counter-work this tendency to the domination of capital and the servility of labor. If one class possesses all the wealth and the education, while the residue of society is ignorant and poor, it matters not by what name the relation between them may be called; the latter, in fact and in truth, will be the servile dependents and subjects of the former. But if education be equably diffused, it will draw property after it, by the strongest of all attractions; for such a thing never did happen, and never can happen, as that an intelligent and practical body of men should be permanently poor. Property and labor, in different classes, are essentially antagonistic; but property and labor, in the same class, are essentially fraternal. The people of Massachusetts have, in some degree, appreciated the truth, that the unexampled prosperity of the State,—its comfort, its competence, its general intelligence and virtue,—is attributable to the education, more or less perfect, which all its people have received; but are they sensible of a fact equally important?—namely, that it is to this same education that two thirds of the people are indebted for not being, to-day, the vassals of as severe a tyranny, in the form of capital, as the lower classes of Europe are bound to in the form of brute force.

Education, then, beyond all other devices of human origin, is the great equalizer of the conditions of men—the balance-wheel of the social machinery. I do not here mean that it so elevates the moral nature as to make men disdain and abhor the oppression of their fellow-men. This idea pertains to another of its attributes. But I mean that it gives each man the independence and the means, by which he can resist the selfishness of other men. It does better than to disarm the poor of their hostility towards the rich; it prevents being poor. Agrarianism is the revenge of poverty against wealth. The wanton destruction of the property of others,—the burning of hay-ricks and corn-ricks, the demolition of machinery, because it supersedes hand-labor, the sprinkling of vitriol on rich dresses,—is only agrarianism run mad. Education prevents both the revenge and the madness. On the other hand, a fellow-feeling for one's class or caste is the common instinct of hearts not wholly sunk in selfish regards for person, or for family. The spread of education, by enlarging the cultivated class or caste, will open a wider area over which the social feelings will expand; and, if this education should be universal and complete, it would do more than all things else to obliterate factitious distinctions in society.

The main idea set forth in the creeds of some political reformers, or revolutionizers, is that some people are poor because others are rich. This idea supposes a fixed amount of property in the community, which, by fraud or force, or arbitrary law, is unequally divided among men; and the problem presented for solution is, how to transfer a portion of this property from those who are supposed to have too much, to those who feel and know that they have too little. At this point, both their theory and their expectation of reform stop. But the beneficent power of education would not be exhausted, even though it should peaceably abolish all the miseries that spring from the coexistence, side by side, of enormous wealth and squalid want. It has a higher function. Beyond the power of diffusing old wealth, it has the prerogative of creating new. It is a thousand times more lucrative than fraud; and adds a thousandfold more to a nation's resources than the most successful conquests. Knaves and robbers can obtain only what was before possessed by others. But education creates or develops new treasures,—treasures not before possessed or dreamed of by any one. . . .

If a savage will learn how to swim, he can fasten a dozen pounds' weight to his back, and transport it across a narrow river, or other body of water of moderate width. If he will invent an axe, or other instrument, by which to cut down a tree, he can use the tree for a float, and one of its limbs for a paddle, and can thus transport many times the former weight, many times the former distance. Hollowing out his log, he will increase, what may be called, its tonnage,—or, rather, its poundage,—and, by sharpening its ends, it will cleave the water both more easily and more swiftly. Fastening several trees together, he makes a raft, and thus increases the buoyant power of his embryo water-craft. Turning up the ends of small poles, or using knees of timber instead of straight pieces, and grooving them together, or filling up the interstices between them, in some other way, so as to make them water-tight, he brings his rude raft literally into ship-shape. Improving upon hull below and rigging above, he makes a proud merchantman, to be wafted by the winds from continent to continent. But, even this does not content the adventurous naval architect. He frames iron arms for his ship; and, for oars, affixes iron wheels, capable of swift revolution, and stronger than the strong sea. Into iron-walled cavities in her bosom, he puts iron organs of massive structure and strength, and of cohesion insoluble by fire. Within these, he kindles a small volcano; and then, like a sentient and rational existence, this wonderful creation of his hands cleaves oceans, breasts tides, defies tempests, and bears its living and jubilant freight around the globe. Now, take away intelligence from the ship-builder, and the steamship,—that miracle of human art,—falls back into a floating log; the log itself is lost; and the savage swimmer, bearing his dozen pounds on his back, alone remains.

And so it is, not in one department only, but in the whole circle of human labors. The annihilation of the sun would no more certainly be followed by darkness, than the extinction of human intelligence would plunge the race at once into the weakness and helplessness of barbarism. To have created such beings as we are, and to have placed them in this world, without the light of the sun, would be no more cruel than for a government to suffer its laboring classes to grow up without knowledge. . .

For the creation of wealth, then,—for the existence of a wealthy people and a wealthy nation,—intelligence is the grand condition. The number of improvers will increase, as the intellectual constituency, if I may so call it, increases. In former times, and in most parts of the world even at the present day, not one man in a million has ever had such a development of mind, as made it possible for him to become a contributor to art or science. Let this development precede, and contributions, numberless, and of inestimable value, will be sure to follow. That Political Economy, therefore, which busies itself about capital and labor, supply and demand, interest and rents, favorable and unfavorable balances of trade; but leaves out of account the element of a wide-spread mental development, is nought but stupendous folly. The greatest of all the arts in political economy is, to change a consumer into a producer; and the next greatest is to increase the producer's producing power;—an end to be directly attained, by increasing his intelligence. . .

POLITICAL EDUCATION

The necessity of general intelligence,—that is, of education, (for I use the terms as substantially synonymous; because general intelligence can never exist without general education, and general education will be sure to produce general intelligence,)—the necessity of general intelligence, under a republican form of government, like most other very important truths, has become a very trite one. It is so trite, indeed, as to have lost much of its force by its familiarity. Almost all the champions of education seize upon this argument, first of all; because it is so simple as to be understood by the ignorant, and so strong as to convince the skeptical. Nothing would be easier than to follow in the train of so many writers, and to demonstrate, by logic, by history, and by the nature of the case, that a republican form of government, without intelligence in the people, must be, on a vast scale, what a mad-house, without superintendent or keepers, would be, on a small one;— the despotism of a few succeeded by universal anarchy, and anarchy by despotism, with no change but from bad to worse. Want of space and time alike forbid me to attempt any full development of the merits of this theme; but yet, in the closing one of a series of reports, partaking somewhat of the nature of a summary of former arguments, an omission of this topic would suggest to the comprehensive mind the idea of incompleteness.

That the affairs of a great nation or state are exceedingly complicated and momentous, no one will dispute. Nor will it be questioned that the degree of intelligence that superintends, should be proportioned to the magnitude of the inter-ests superintended. He who scoops out a wooden dish needs less skill than the maker of a steam-engine or a telescope. The dealer in small wares requires less knowledge than the merchant who exports and imports to and from all quarters of the globe. An ambassador cannot execute his functions with the stock of attainments or of talents sufficient for a parish clerk. Indeed, it is clear, that the want of adequate intelligence,—of intelligence commensurate with the nature of the duties to be performed,—will bring ruin or disaster upon any department. A merchant loses his intelligence, and he becomes a bankrupt. A lawyer loses his intelligence, and he forfeits all the interests of his clients. Intelligence abandons a physician, and his patients die, with more than the pains of natural dissolution. Should judges upon the bench be bereft of this guide, what havoc would be made of the property and the innocence of men! Let this counsellor be taken from executive officers, and the penalties due to the wicked would be visited upon the righteous, while the rewards and immunities of the righteous would be bestowed upon the guilty. And so, should intelligence desert the halls of legislation, weakness, rashness, contra-diction, and error would glare out from every page of the statute book. Now, as a republican government represents almost all interests, whether social, civil or military, the necessity of a degree of intelligence adequate to the due administration of them all, is so self-evident, that a bare statement is the best argument.

But in the possession of this attribute of intelligence, elective legislators will never far surpass their electors. By a natural law, like that which regulates the equilibrium of fluids, elector and elected, appointer and appointee, tend to the same level. It is not more certain that a wise and enlightened constituency will refuse to invest a reckless and profligate man with office, or discard him if accidentally chosen, than it is that a foolish or immoral constituency will discard or eject a wise man. This law of assimilation, between the choosers and the chosen, results, not only from the fact that the voter orig-inally selects his representative according to the affinities of good or of ill, of wisdom or of folly, which exist between them; but if the legislator enacts or favors a law which is too wise for the constituent to understand, or too just for him to approve, the next election will set him aside as certainly as if he had made open merchandise of the dearest interests of the people, by perjury and for a bribe. And if the infinitely Just and Good, in giving laws to the Jews, recognized the "hard-ness of their hearts," how much more will an earthly ruler recognize the baseness or wickedness of the people, when his heart is as hard as theirs! In a republican government, legislators are a mirror reflecting the moral countenance of their con-stituents. And hence it is, that the establishment of a republican government, without well-appointed and efficient means for the universal education of the people, is the most rash and fool-hardy experiment ever tried by man. Its fatal results may not be immediately developed,—they may not follow as the thunder follows the lightning,—for time is an element in maturing them, and the calamity is too great to be prepared in a day; but, like the slow-accumulating avalanche, they will grow more terrific by delay, and, at length, though it may be at a late hour, will overwhelm with ruin whatever lies athwart their path. It may be an easy thing to make a Republic; but it is a very laborious thing to make Republicans; and woe to the republic that rests upon no better foundations than ignorance, selfishness, and passion. Such a Republic may grow in numbers and in wealth. As an avaricious man adds acres to his lands, so its rapacious government may increase its own darkness by annexing provinces and states to its ignorant domain. Its armies may be invincible, and its fleets may strike terror into nations on the opposite sides of the globe, at the same hour. Vast in its extent, and enriched with all the prodi-gality of nature, it may possess every capacity and opportunity of being great, and of doing good. But if such a Republic be devoid of intelligence, it will only the more closely resemble an obscene giant who has waxed strong in his youth, and grown wanton in his strength; whose brain has been developed only in the region of the appetites and passions, and not in the organs of reason and conscience; and who, therefore, is boastful of his bulk alone, and glories in the weight of his heel and in the destruction of his arm. Such a Republic, with all its noble capacities for beneficence, will rush with the speed of a whirlwind to an ignominious end; and all good men of after-times would be fain to weep over its downfall, did not their scorn and contempt at its folly and its wickedness, repress all sorrow for its fate. . . .

However elevated the moral character of a constituency may be; however well informed in matters of general sci-ence or history, yet they must, if citizens of a Republic, understand something of the true nature and functions of the gov-ernment under which they live. That any one who is to participate in the government of a country, when he becomes a man, should receive no instruction respecting the nature and functions of the government he is afterwards to administer, is a political solecism. In all nations, hardly excepting the most rude and barbarous, the future sovereign receives some training which is supposed to fit him for the exercise of the powers and duties of his anticipated station. Where, by force of law, the government devolves upon the heir, while yet in a state of legal infancy, some regency, or other substitute, is appointed, to act in his stead, until his arrival at mature age; and, in the meantime, he is subjected to such a course of study and discipline, as will tend to prepare him, according to the political theory of the time and the place, to assume the reins of authority at the appointed age. If, in England, or in the most enlightened European monarchies, it would be a proof of restored barbarism, to permit the future sovereign to grow up without any knowledge of his duties,—and who can doubt that it would be such a proof,—then, surely, it would be not less a proof of restored, or of never-removed barbarism, amongst us, to empower any individual to use the elective franchise, without preparing him for so momentous a trust. Hence, the constitution of the United States, and of our own State, should be made a study in our Public Schools. The partition of the powers of government into the three co-ordinate branches,—legislative, judicial, and executive,—with the duties appropriately devolving upon each; the mode of electing or of appointing all officers, with the reason on which it was founded; and, especially, the duty of every citizen, in a government of laws, to appeal to the courts for redress, in all cases of alleged wrong, instead of undertaking to vindicate his own rights by his own arm; and, in a government where the people are the acknowledged sources of power, the duty of changing laws and rulers by an appeal to the ballot, and not by rebellion, should be taught to all the children until they are fully understood.

Had the obligations of the future citizen been sedulously inculcated upon all the children of this Republic, would the patriot have had to mourn over so many instances, where the voter, not being able to accomplish his purpose by voting, has proceeded to accomplish it by violence; where, agreeing with his fellow-citizens, to use the machinery of the ballot, he makes a tacit reservation, that, if that machinery does not move according to his pleasure, he will wrest or break it? If the responsibleness and value of the elective franchise were duly appreciated, the day of our State and National elections would be among the most solemn and religious days in the calendar. Men would approach them, not only with preparation and solicitude, but with the sobriety and solemnity, with which discreet and religious-minded men meet the great crises of life. No man would throw away his vote, through caprice or wantonness, any more than he would throw away his estate, or sell his family into bondage. No man would cast his vote through malice or revenge, any more than a good surgeon would amputate a limb, or a good navigator sail through perilous straits, under the same criminal passions.

But, perhaps, it will be objected, that the constitution is subject to different readings, or that the policy of different administrations has become the subject of party strife; and, therefore, if any thing of constitutional or political law is introduced into our schools, there is danger that teachers will be chosen on account of their affinities to this or that political party; or that teachers will feign affinities which they do not feel, in order that they may be chosen; and so each school-room will at length become a miniature political club-room, exploding with political resolves, or flaming out with political addresses, prepared, by beardless boys, in scarcely legible hand-writing, and in worse grammar.

With the most limited exercise of discretion, all apprehensions of this kind are wholly groundless. There are different readings of the constitution, it is true; and there are partisan topics which agitate the country from side to side; but the controverted points, compared with those about which there is no dispute, do not bear the proportion of one to a hundred. And what is more, no man is qualified, or can be qualified, to discuss the disputable questions, unless previously and thoroughly versed in those questions, about which there is no dispute. In the terms and principles common to all, and recognized by all, is to be found the only common medium of language and of idea, by which the parties can become intelligible to each other; and there, too, is the only common ground, whence the arguments of the disputants can be drawn.

It is obvious, on the other hand, that if the tempest of political strife were to be let loose upon our Common Schools, they would be overwhelmed with sudden ruin. Let it be once understood, that the schoolroom is a legitimate theatre for party politics, and with what violence will hostile partisans struggle to gain possession of the stage, and to play their parts upon it! Nor will the stage be the only scene of gladiatorial contests. These will rage in all the avenues that lead to it. A preliminary advantage, indispensable to ultimate success, will be the appointment of a teacher of the true faith. As the great majority of the schools in the State are now organized, this can be done only by electing a prudential committee, who will make what he calls political soundness paramount to all other considerations of fitness. Thus, after petty skirmishings among neighbors, the fierce encounter will begin in the district's primary assembly,—in the schoolroom itself. This contest being over, the election of the superintending, or town's committee, must be determined in the same way, and this will bring together the combustibles of each district, to burn with an intenser and a more devouring flame, in the town meeting. It is very possible, nay, not at all improbable, that the town may be of one political complexion, while a majority of the districts are of the opposite. Who shall moderate the fury of these conflicting elements, when they rage against each other; and who shall save the dearest interests of the children from being consumed in the fierce combustion? If parents find that their children are indoctrinated into what they call political heresies, will they not withdraw them from the school; and, if they withdraw them from the school, will they not resist all appropriations to support a school from which they derive no benefit?

But, could the schools, themselves, survive these dangers for a single year, it would be only to encounter others still more perilous. Why should not the same infection that poisons all the relations of the schoolroom, spread itself abroad, and mingle with all questions of external organization and arrangement? Why should not political hostility cause the dismemberment of districts, already too small; or, what would work equal injury, prevent the union of districts, whose power of usefulness would be doubled by a combination of their resources? What better could be expected, than that one set of school books should be expelled, and another introduced, as they might be supposed, however remotely, to favor one party or the other; or, as the authors of the books might belong to one party or the other? And who could rely upon the reports, or even the statistics of a committee, chosen by partisan votes, goaded on by partisan impulses, and responsible to partisan domination; and this, too, without any opportunity of control or check from the minority? Nay, if the schools could survive long enough to meet the crisis, why should not any and every measure be taken, either to maintain an existing political ascendancy, or to recover a lost one, in a school district, or in a town, which has even been taken by unscrupulous politicians, to maintain or to recover an ascendancy at the polls? Into a district, or into a town, voters may be introduced from abroad, to turn the scale. An employer may dismiss the employed, for their refusal to submit to his dictation; or make the bread that is given to the poor man's children, perform the double office of payment for labor to be performed, and of a bribe for principle to be surrendered. And, beyond all this, if the imagination can conceive any thing more deplorable than this, what kind of political doctrines would be administered to the children, amid the vicissitudes of party domination,—their alternations of triumph and defeat? This year, under the ascendancy of one side, the constitution declares one thing: and commentaries, glosses, and the authority of distinguished names, all ratify and confirm its decisions. But victory is a fickle goddess. Next year, the vanquished triumph; and constitution, gloss, and authority, make that sound doctrine, which was pestilent error before, and that false, which was true. Right and wrong have changed sides. The children must now join in chorus to denounce what they had been taught to reverence before, and to reverence what they had been taught to denounce. In the mean time, those great principles, which, according to Cicero, are the same at Rome and at Athens, the same now and forever;—and which, according to Hooker, have their seat in the bosom of God, become the fittest emblems of chance and change.

Long, however, before this series of calamities would exhaust itself upon our schools, these schools themselves would cease to be. The plough-share would have turned up their foundations. Their history would have been brought to a close,—a glorious and ascending history, until struck down by the hand of political parricide; then, suddenly falling with a double ruin,—with death, and with ignominy. But to avoid such a catastrophe, shall all teaching, relative to the nature of our government, be banished from our schools; and shall our children be permitted to grow up in entire ignorance of the political history of their country? In the schools of a republic, shall the children be left without any distinct knowledge of the nature of a republican government; or only with such knowledge as they may pick up from angry political discussions, or from party newspapers; from caucus speeches, or Fourth of July orations,—the Apocrypha of Apocrypha?

Surely, between these extremes, there must be a medium not difficult to be found. And is not this the middle course, which all sensible and judicious men, all patriots, and all genuine republicans, must approve?—namely, that those articles in the creed of republicanism, which are accepted by all, believed in by all, and which form the common basis of our political faith, shall be taught to all. But when the teacher, in the course of his lessons or lectures on the fundamental law, arrives at a controverted text, he is either to read it without comment or remark; or, at most, he is only to say that the passage is the subject of disputation, and that the schoolroom is neither the tribunal to adjudicate, nor the forum to discuss it.

Such being the rule established by common consent, and such the practice, observed with fidelity under it, it will come to be universally understood, that political proselytism is no function of the school; but that all indoctrination into matters of controversy between hostile political parties is to be elsewhere sought for, and elsewhere imparted. Thus, may all the children of the Commonwealth receive instruction in the great essentials of political knowledge,—in those elementary ideas without which they will never be able to investigate more recondite and debatable questions;—thus, will the only practicable method be adopted for discovering new truths, and for discarding,—instead of perpetuating,—old errors; and thus, too, will that pernicious race of intolerant zealots, whose whole faith may be summed up in two articles,—that they, themselves, are always infallibly right, and that all dissenters are certainly wrong,—be extinguished,—extinguished, not by violence, nor by proscription, but by the more copious inflowing of the light of truth.

1. What does Horace Mann mean when he states that education is the "great equalizer of the conditions of men"?
2. According to Mann, what role does education play in the overall health of the Republic?

11-7 Sojourner Truth, Address to the Woman's Rights Convention, Akron, Ohio (1851)

Frances D. Gage, a pioneer in the Women's Rights Movement during the early nineteenth century, recorded her impressions of Sojourner Truth's speech at the Woman's Rights Convention in Akron, Ohio in 1851. Gage wrote this reminiscence some twelve years after the fact, and tried to capture Truth's speech as she remembered it, complete with what Gage perceived to be Truth's manner of speech and actions before the audience.

Source: E. C. Stanton, S. B. Anthony, and Matilda Joslyn Gage, eds., *History of Woman Suffrage*, vol. 1 (Rochester, NY: Charles Mann, 1881), pp. 115–117.

Reminiscences by Frances D. Gage

The leaders of the movement trembled upon seeing a tall, gaunt black woman in a gray dress and white turban, surmounted with an uncouth sun-bonnet, march deliberately into the church, walk with the air of a queen up the aisle, and take her seat upon the pulpit steps. A buzz of disapprobation was heard all over the house and there fell on the listening ear, "An abolition affair!" "Woman's rights and niggers!" "I told you so! "Go it, darkey!" . . .When, slowly from her seat in the corner rose Sojourner Truth, who, till now, had scarcely lifted her head. "Don't let her speak!" gasped half a dozen in my ear. She moved slowly and solemnly to the front, laid her old bonnet at her feet, and turned her great speaking eyes to me. There was a hissing sound of disapprobation above and below. I rose and announced "Sojourner Truth," and begged the audience to keep silence for a few moments. . . .

"Wall, chilern, whar dar is so much racket dar must be somethin' out o' kilter. I tink dat 'twixt de niggers of de Souf and de womin at de Norf, all talkin' 'bout rights, de white men will be in a fix pretty soon. But what's all dis here talkin' 'bout?

"Dat man ober dar say dat womin needs to be helped into carriages, and lifted ober ditches, and to hab de best place everywhar. Nobody eber helps me into carriages, or ober mud-puddles, or gibs me any best place!" . . ."And a'n't I a woman? Look at me! Look at my arm! (and she bared her right arm to the shoulder, showing her tremendous muscular power). "I have ploughed, and planted, and gathered into barns, and no man could head me! And a'n't I a woman? I could work as much and eat as much as a manÑwhen I could get itÑand bear de lash as well! And a'n't I a woman? I have borne thirteen chilern, and seen 'em mos' all sold off to slavery, and when I cried out with my mother's grief, none but Jesus heard me! And a'n't I a woman?

"Den dey talks 'bout dis ting in de head; what dis dey call it?" ("Intellect," whispered some one near.) "Dat's it, honey. What's dat got to do wid womin's rights or nigger's rights? If my cup won't hold but a pint, and yourn holds a quart, wouldn't ye be mean not to let me have my little half-measure full?" And she pointed her significant finger, and sent a keen glance at the minister who had made the argument. The cheering was long and loud.

"Den dat little man in black dar, he say women can't have as much rights as men, 'cause Christ wan't a woman! Whar did your Christ come from?" Rolling thunder couldn't have stilled that crowd, as did those deep, wonderful tones, as she stood there with outstretched arms and eyes of fire. Raising her voice still louder, she repeated, "Whar did your Christ come from? From God and a woman! Man had nothin' to do wid Him." Oh, what a rebuke that was to that little man.

Turning again to another objector, she took up the defense of Mother Eve. I can not follow her through it all. It was pointed, and witty, and solemn; eliciting at almost every sentence deafening applause; and she ended by asserting: "If de fust woman God ever made was strong enough to turn de world upside down all alone, dese women togedder (and she glanced her eye over the platform) ought to be able to turn it back, and get it right side up again! And now dey is asking to do it, de men better let 'em." Long-continued cheering greeted this. "'Bleeged to ye for hearin' on me, and now ole Sojourner han't got nothin' more to say."

Amid roars of applause, she returned to her corner, leaving more than one of us with streaming eyes, and hearts beating with gratitude. She had taken us up in her arms and carried us safely over the slough of difficulty turning the whole tide in our favor. I have never in my life seen anything like the magical influence that subdued the mobbish spirit of the day, and turned the sneers and jeers of an excited crowd into notes of respect and admiration. Hundreds rushed up to shake hands with her, and congratulate the glorious old mother, and bid her God-speed on her mission of "testifyin' agin concerning the wickedness of this 'ere people."

1. Describe Gage's impression of the audience's different responses to Sojourner Truth's manner and message. What does Gage's impression seem to be?
2. Summarize Sojourner Truth's message to the Woman's Rights Convention. How is this message similar to and different from the message the reader and the crowd might expect from her?

PART TWELVE
MANIFEST DESTINY

12-1 John L. O'Sullivan, "The Great Nation of Futurity" (1845)

The journalist John L. O'Sullivan (1813-1895), an enthusiastic Jacksonian Democrat, first coined the phrase "manifest destiny" in this article supporting the Annexation of Texas, printed in the Democratic Review for July 1845. O'Sullivan was later involved in other movements to annex additional territories, such as the Spanish colony of Cuba in the Caribbean.

The American people having derived their origin from many other nations, and the Declaration of National Independence being entirely based on the great principle of human equality, these facts demonstrate at once our disconnected position as regards any other nation; that we have, in reality, but little connection with the past history of any of them and still less with all antiquity, its glories, or its crimes. On the contrary, our national birth was the beginning of a new history, the formation and progress of an untried political system, which separates us from the past and connects us with the future only; and so far as regards the entire development of the natural rights of man, in moral, political, and national life, we may confidently assume that our country is destined to be the great nation of futurity.

It is so destined, because the principle upon which a nation is organized fixes its destiny, and that of equality is perfect, is universal. It presides in all the operations of the physical world, and it is also the conscious law of the soul-the self-evident dictate of morality, which accurately defines the duty of man to man, and consequently man's rights as man. Besides, the truthful annals of any nation furnish abundant evidence that its happiness, its greatness, its duration, were always proportionate to the democratic equality in its system of government.

How many nations have had their decline and fall because the equal rights of the minority were trampled on by the despotism of the majority; or the interests of the many sacrificed to the aristocracy of the few; or the rights and interests of all given up to the monarchy of one? These three kinds of government have figured so frequently and so largely in the ages that have passed away that their history, through all time to come, can only furnish a resemblance. Like causes produce like effects, and the true philosopher of history will easily discern the principle of equality, or of privilege, working out its inevitable result. The first is regenerative, because it is natural and right; and the latter is destructive to society, because it is unnatural and wrong.

What friend of human liberty, civilization, and refinement can cast his view over the past history of the monarchies and aristocracies of antiquity, and not deplore that they ever existed? What philanthropist can contemplate the oppressions, the cruelties, and injustice inflicted by them on the masses of mankind and not turn with moral horror from the retrospect?

America is destined for better deeds. It is our unparalleled glory that we have no reminiscences of battlefields, but in defense of humanity, of the oppressed of all nations, of the rights of conscience, the rights of personal enfranchisement. Our annals describe no scenes of horrid carnage, where men were led on by hundreds of thousands to slay one another, dupes and victims to emperors, kings, nobles, demons in the human form called heroes. We have had patriots to defend our homes, our liberties, but no aspirants to crowns or thrones; nor have the American people ever suffered themselves to be led on by wicked ambition to depopulate the land, to spread desolation far and wide, that a human being might be placed on a seat of supremacy.

We have no interest in the scenes of antiquity, only as lessons of avoidance of nearly all their examples. The expansive future is our arena and for our history. We are entering on its untrodden space with the truths of God in our minds, beneficent objects in our hearts, and with a clear conscience unsullied by the past. We are the nation of human progress, and who will, what can, set limits to our onward march? Providence is with us, and no earthly power can. We point to the everlasting truth on the first page of our national declaration, and we proclaim to the millions of other lands that "the gates of hell"-the powers of aristocracy and monarchy-"shall not prevail against it."

The far-reaching, the boundless future, will be the era of American greatness. In its magnificent domain of space and time, the nation of many nations is destined to manifest to mankind the excellence of divine principles; to establish on earth the noblest temple ever dedicated to the worship of the Most High, the Sacred, and the True. Its floor shall be a hemisphere, roof the firmament of the star-studded heavens, and its congregation of Union of many Republics, comprising hundreds of happy millions, calling owning no man master, but governed by God's natural and moral law of equality, the law of brotherhood-of "peace and good will amongst men."

Yes, we are the nation of progress, of individual freedom, of universal enfranchisement. Equality of rights is the cynosure of our union of states, the grand exemplar of the correlative equality of individuals; and, while truth sheds its effulgence, we cannot retrograde without dissolving the one and subverting the other. We must onward to the fulfillment of our mission-to the entire development of the principle of our organization-freedom of conscience, freedom of person, freedom of trade and business pursuits, universality of freedom and equality. This is our high destiny, and in nature's eternal, inevitable decree of cause and effect we must accomplish it. All this will be our future history, to establish on earth the moral dignity and salvation of man-the immutable truth and beneficence of God. For this blessed mission to the nations of the world, which are shut out from the lifegiving light of truth, has America been chosen; and her high example shall smite unto death the tyranny of kings, hierarchs, and oligarchs and carry the glad tidings of peace and good will where myriads now endure in existence scarcely more enviable than that of beasts of the field. Who, then, can doubt that our country is destined to be the great nation of futurity?

1. What reasoning does O'Sullivan use to support his claim that America "is destined to be the great nation of futurity"?
2. Explain the author's attitude toward history.

12-2 Thomas Corwin, Against the Mexican War (1847)

The Mexican-American war began in early 1846 and ended abruptly — after Americans had marched all the way to Mexico City — less than a year later. The question of who would win the war was never really seriously debated. What was in debate was the character of the American expansion and the question of slavery. Corwin, a Whig senator from Ohio, questioned expansionism and feared that the South would carry slavery wherever it went.

> From *The American Reader: Words That Moved a Nation*, ed. Diane Ravitch
> (New York: HarperCollins, 1991), 77-79.

What is the territory, Mr. President, which you propose to wrest from Mexico? It is consecrated to the heart of the Mexican by many a well-fought battle with his old Castilian master. His Bunker Hills, and Saratogas, and Yorktowns are there! The Mexican can say, "There I bled for liberty! and shall I surrender that consecrated home of my affections to the Anglo-Saxon invaders? What do they want with it? They have Texas already. They have possessed themselves of the territory between the Nueces and the Rio Grande. What else do they want? To what shall I point my children as memorials of that independence which I bequeath to them, when those battlefields shall have passed from my possession?"

Sir, had one come and demanded Bunker Hill of the people of Massachusetts, had England's lion ever showed himself there, is there a man over thirteen and under ninety who would not have been ready to meet him? Is there a river on this continent that would not have run red with blood? Is there a field but would have been piled high with the unburied bones of slaughtered Americans before these consecrated battlefields of liberty should have been wrested from us? But this same American goes into a sister republic, and says to poor, weak Mexico, "Give up your territory, you are unworthy to possess it; I have got one half already, and all I ask of you is to give up the other!" ....

Sir, look at this pretense of want of room. With twenty millions of people, you have about one thousand millions of acres of land, inviting settlement by every conceivable argument, bringing them down to a quarter of a dollar an acre, and allowing every man to squat where the pleases....

There is one topic connected with this subject which I tremble when I approach, and yet I cannot forbear to notice it. It meets you in every step you take; it threatens you which way soever you go in the prosecution of this war. I allude to the question of slavery. Opposition to its further extension, it must be obvious to everyone, is a deeply rooted determination with men of all parties in what we call the nonslaveholding states. New York, Pennsylvania, and Ohio, three of the most powerful, have already sent their legislative instructions here. So it will be, I doubt not, in all the rest. It is vain now to speculate about the reasons for this. Gentlemen of the South may call it prejudice, passion, hypocrisy, fanaticism. I shall not dispute with them now on that point. You and I cannot alter or change this opinion, if we would. These people only say we will not, cannot consent that you shall carry slavery where it does not already exist. They do not seek to disturb you in that institution as it exists in your states. Enjoy it if you will and as you will. This is their language; this their determination. How is it in the South? Can it be expected that they should expend in common their blood and their treasure in the acquisition of immense territory, and then willingly forgo the right to carry thither their slaves, and inhabit the conquered country if they please to do so? Sir, I know the feelings and opinions of the South too well to calculate on this. Nay, I believe they would even contend to any extremity for the mere right, had they no wish to exert it. I believe (and I confess I tremble when the conviction presses upon me) that there is equal obstinacy on both sides of this fearful question.

If, then, we persist in war, which, if it terminates in anything short of a mere wanton waste of blood as well as money, must end (as this bill proposes) in the acquisition of territory, to which at once this controversy must attach-this bill would seem to be nothing less than a bill to produce internal commotion. Should we prosecute this war another moment, or expend one dollar in the purchase or conquest of a single acre of Mexican land, the North and the South are brought into collision on a point where neither will yield. Who can foresee or foretell the result! Who so bold or reckless as to look such a conflict in the face unmoved! I do not envy the heart of him who can realize the possibility of such a conflict without emotions too painful to be endured. Why, then, shall we, the representatives of the sovereign states of the Union-the chosen guardians of this confederated Republic, why should we precipitate this fearful struggle, by continuing a war the result of which must be to force us at once upon a civil conflict? Sir, rightly considered, this is treason, treason to the Union, treason to the dearest interests, the loftiest aspirations, the most cherished hopes of our constituents. It is a crime to risk the possibility of such a contest. It is a crime of such infernal hue that every other in the catalogue of iniquity, when compared with it, whitens into virtue.... Let us abandon all idea of acquiring further territory and by consequence cease at once to prosecute this war. Let us call home our armies, and bring them at once within our own acknowledged limits. Show Mexico that you are sincere when you say you desire nothing by conquest. She has learned that she cannot encounter you in war, and if she had not, she is too weak to disturb you here. Tender her peace, and, my life on it, she will then accept it. But whether she shall or not, you will have peace without her consent. It is your invasion that has made war; your retreat will restore peace. Let us then close forever the approaches of internal feud, and so return to the ancient concord and the old ways of national prosperity and permanent glory. Let us here, in this temple consecrated to the Union, perform a solemn lustration; let us wash Mexican blood from our hands, and on these altars, and in the presence of that image of the Father of his Country that looks down upon us, swear to preserve honorable peace with all the world and eternal brotherhood with each other.

1. What is the author's reasoning as he argues in favor of Mexican freedom and against further American seizure of Mexican territory?
2. Summarize the author's argument that continuing the war effort against Mexico would be tantamount to treason. How does public opinion regarding slavery relate to this point?

PART THIRTEEN
ANTEBELLUM SOUTH

13-1 Nat Turner, Confession (1831)

This is a selection from Nat Turner's confessions, collected by his white lawyer after he had been apprehended for leading a revolt that culminated in the murder of fifty-five whites and the death of at least that many African Americans from white retaliation. The revolt, intended, in Turner's words, to "carry terror and devastation," was spurred by his divine vision. This selection describes the origins of Turner's sense of his own uniqueness and his divine revelation.

> From Thomas R. Gray, *The Confessions of Nat Turner, The Leader of the Late Insurrection in Southamton Virginia* (Baltimore, 1831).

...To a mind like mine, restless, inquisitive and observant of every thing that was passing, it
is easy to suppose that religion was the subject to which it would be directed, and although this subject principally occupied my thoughts-there was nothing that I saw or heard of to which my attention was not directed-The manner in which I learned to read and write, not only had great influence on my own mind, as I acquired it with the most perfect ease, so much so, that I have no recollection whatever of learning the alphabet-but to the astonishment of the family, one day, when a book was shewn to me to keep me from crying, I began spelling the names of different objects-this was a source of wonder to all in the neighborhood, particularly the blacks-and this learning was constantly improved at all opportunities-when I got large enough to go to work, while employed, I was reflecting on many things that would present themselves to my imagination, and whenever an opportunity occurred of looking at a book, when the school children were getting their lessons, I would find many things that the fertility of my own imagination had depicted to me before....

All my time, not devoted to my master's service, was spent either in prayer, or in making experiments in casting different things in moulds made of earth, in attempting to make paper, gun-powder, and many other experiments, that although I could not perfect, yet convinced me of its practicability if I had the means.

I was not addicted to stealing in my youth, nor have ever been-Yet such was the confidence of the negroes in the neighborhood, even at this early period of my life, in my superior judgment, that they would often carry me with them when they were going on any roguery, to plan for them. Growing up among them, with this confidence in my superior judgment, and when this, in their opinions, was perfected by Divine inspiration, from the circumstances already alluded to in my infancy, and which belief was ever afterwards zealously inculcated by the austerity of my life and manners, which became the subject of remark by white and black.

-Having soon discovered to be great, I must appear so, and therefore studiously avoided mixing in society, and wrapped myself in mystery, devoting my time to fasting and prayer-by this time, having arrived to man's estate, and hearing the scriptures commented on at meetings, I was struck with that particular passage which says: "Seek ye the kingdom of Heaven and all things shall be added unto you." I reflected much on this passage, and prayed daily for light on this subject-As I was praying one day at my plough, the spirit spoke to me, saying "Seek ye the kingdom of Heaven and all things shall be added unto you."

Question-what do you mean by the Spirit? Ans.-The Spirit that spoke to the prophets in former days-and I was greatly astonished, and for two years prayed continually, whenever my duty would permit-and then again I had the same revelation, which fully confirmed me in the impression that I was ordained for some great purpose in the hands of the Almighty.

Several years rolled round, in which many events occurred to strengthen me in this my belief. At this time I reverted in my mind to the remarks made of me in my childhood, and the things that had been shewn me-and as it had been said of me in my childhood by those by whom I had been taught to pray, both white and black, and in whom I had the greatest confidence, that I had too much sense to be raised, and if I was, I would never be of any use to any one as a slave. Now finding I had arrived to man's estate, and was a slave, and these revelations being made known to me, I began to direct my attention to this great object, to fulfill the purpose for which, by this time, I felt
assured I was intended.

Knowing the influence I had obtained over the minds of my fellow servants (not by the means of conjuring and such like tricks-for to them I always spoke of such things with contempt) but by the communion of the Spirit whose revelations I often communicated to them, and they believed and said my wisdom came from God. I now began to prepare them for my purpose, by telling them something was about to happen that would terminate in fulfilling the great promise that had been made to me- ....

1. Summarize the evidence provided of Nat Turner's natural genius. How do others react to his intellectual abilities?
2. What are Turner's beliefs regarding his intellect? Describe the process whereby he determines the future course of his life.

13-2 An Abolitionist Defends the *Amistad* Mutineers (1839)

The *Amistad* case brought international attention to the issue of slavery in America. A group of American abolitionists formed the Amistad Committee to defend the ship's captives and their right to return to Africa. The following passage is a letter written by Lewis Tappan, a leading abolitionist and organizer of the committee, who recounts an interview with the leader of the captured Mendi tribesman, Joseph Cinque. Tappan soon became actively involved in the case by planning the strategy for the court trials, raising money for the defense, writing letters to the *New York Journal of Commerce* presenting the captive's side of the mutiny, and helping to argue their case before the U. S. Supreme Court. In the year following the release of the Africans, Tappan devoted his energy to arranging for their return home to Sierra Leone.

Source: Exploring *Amistad* at Mystic Seaport
http://amistad.mysticseaport.org/library/news/journal.of.commerce.html

To the Committee on Behalf of the African Prisoners and To the Marshal of the District of Connecticut. *New York Journal of Commerce* 10 Sept., 1839: 2.

Communicated for the Journal of Commerce
New Haven, Sept. 9, 1839.
To the Committee on behalf of the African prisoners:

I arrived here last Friday evening, with three men who are natives of Africa, and who were joined the next day by two others, to act as interpreters in conversing with Joseph Cinquez and his comrades. On going to the jail, the next morning, we found to our great disappointment, that only one of the men, J. F. was able to converse with the prisoners. He is about 30 years of age, a native of Geshee or Gishe, which is about 100 or 150 miles from the mouth of the river Gallinas, in the interior, which is about a day's journey south of Sierra Leone. He was kidnapped when about 12 years of age, and was liberated in Colombia, by Bolivar. He is able to converse a little in the Mandingo dialect, but understands better that of Gallinao, which some of the prisoners can speak. Most of the prisoners can understand him, although none of them can speak his Geshee dialect. You may imagine the joy manifested by these poor Africans, when they heard one of their own color address them in a friendly manner, and in a language they could comprehend!

The prisoners are in comfortable rooms.—They are well clothed in dark striped cotton trowsers, called by some of the manufacturers "hard times," and in striped cotton shirts. The girls are in calico frocks, and have made the little shawls that were given them into turbans. The prisoners eyed the clothes some time, and laughed a good deal among themselves before they put them on. Their food is brought to them in separate tin pans, and they eat it in an orderly manner. In general, they are in good health. One of their number, however, died on Tuesday last, and two or three more are on the sick list and considered dangerous. They probably suffer for want of exercise in the open air. The four children are apparently from 10 to 12 years of age. The boy and two of the girls (who appeared to be sisters) are Mandingos, and the other girl is from Congo. They are robust, are full of hilarity, especially the Mandingos. The sheriff of the county took them to ride in a wagon on Friday. At first their eyes were filled with tears, and they seemed to be afraid, but soon they enjoyed themselves very well, and appeared to be greatly delighted. The children speak only their native dialects. Neither Cinquez nor any of his comrades have been manacled since they have been here. Their demeanor is altogether quiet, kind, and orderly.

Most of the prisoners told the interpreter that they are from Mandingo. The district of Mandingo, in the Senegambia country, is bounded by the Atlantic Ocean, and is directly north of Liberia. Two or three of the men, besides one of the little girls, are natives of Congo, which is on the coast just south of the equator. The man with some of his teeth like tusks, is from Gahula in Congo. The teeth are said to be sharpened and made thus prominent by artificial means. One of the men from Mandingo, named Dama, talks Mandingo, and is a good looking and intelligent man. Cinquez is about 5 feet 8 inches high, of fine proportions, with a noble air. Indeed, the whole company, although thin in flesh, and generally of slight forms, and limbs, especially, are as good looking and intelligent a body of men as we usually meet with. All are young, and several are quite striplings. The Mandingos are described in books as being a very gentle race, cheerful in their dispositions, inquisitive, credulous, simple hearted, and much given to trading propensities. The Mandingo dialects are spoken extensively, and it is said to be the commercial language of nearly the whole coast of West Africa. We found that the following words are nearly the same in the Gallinas of the interpreter, in the Mandingo of the prisoners, in the Mandingo of Mungo Park, and in Jallowka of the German author Adeburg, viz:—Sun, moon, woman, child, father, head, hand, and foot. The numerals do not agree so well. If any person, who reads this statement, can furnish the Committee information concerning the Mandingo language, and its different dialects, particularly for vocabularies, they may render important service in the future examination of these unfortunate Africans. Professor Gibbs, of Yale College, has Adeburg's Mithridates, Park's Travels, and Mollien's Travels in Africa, and Professor Silliman has Prichard's Physical History of Mankind, which are at the service of the Committee.

Senegambia extends 800 miles in length, and where widest is about 700 miles. It is inhabited by different tribes, all negroes, living under petty sovereigns. Among these nations, the Foulahs, Jalcops, and Mandingoes, are the most numerous. Others less prominent are the Feloops, Naloes, Pagoes, Susoos, Timmancis, &c. The Foulahs are Mahomedans. The Mandingoes are the most numerous people of this region. These are partly Mahomedans and partly Pagans. Their original country is Manding, of which the government is said to be a species of republicanism. Nearly all the prisoners appear to be people of this description. The physician says they have nearly all been circumcised. No person will be able to converse with them well until he can speak the dialect of Manding. Persons, however, born on the Gallinas river may be able to converse with some of them. Although there are many native Africans in New York, and some of them came probably from places not remote from the native places of most of these prisoners, yet it is difficult to find an interpreter who can converse with them readily and intelligently. The tribes in Africa are very numerous, almost every tribe has a distinct language, and it often varies, it is said, from village to village.

After conversing awhile, through the interpreter with the men, who are in three different rooms, and with the four children, who are in a room by themselves, we went to the door of the room where Joseph Cinquez is confined: He is with several savage looking fellows, black and white, who are in jail on various charges. Visitors are not allowed to enter this strong hold of the jail, and the inmates can only be seen and conversed with through the aperture of the door. The jailer is fearful that some of them would escape if the door was opened in frequently. Even the other African prisoners are not permitted to hold converse with their Chief. Before they and he were deprived of this privilege, and when he occasionally came among them, they gathered around him, all talking at once, and shaking hands, as if they rejoiced to see him among them. They appeared to look up to him, I am told, with great respect. We found Cinquez stretched upon his bedding on the floor, wholly unclothed, with a single blanket partly wrapped around him. He arose at the call of the jailer, rather reluctantly, and came towards us with a good degree of gracefulness and native dignity. Afterwards we saw him well clothed; but he does not seem to like the tight dress of this country. At first he seemed adverse to answering the questions of the interpreter, and made the impression that he could not speak the Mandingo dialect. But after the interpreter had told him that he had conversed freely with his comrades, he conversed very freely, and with much energy of expression and action. R. S. Baldwin, Esq., of counsel for the prisoners, and Professor Gibbs having accompanied the interpreter.

Joseph Cinquez, as the Spaniards have named him, but who pronounces his name in his own language, Shinquau, says he is a native of the Mandingo country. His father is neither a king nor a chief, but one of the principal men. Shinquau was kidnapped and sent down to the town of Gendema or Geduma, in the Gallina country. The interpreter knows the place, says it is from ten to fifteen miles from the ocean. It is a small town on an inconsiderable river. Here he was put into the hands of King Sharka, and after staying a while was delivered by this king "to a great man" named Fulekower, belonging to Manu, near the mouth of the river Gambia, who disposed of him to the Spaniards. By them he was sent on board a ship, where he met, for the first time, the persons who are now with him in prison. From Shinquau and his comrades we gathered the following statements, nearly in their very words, as translated by the interpreter:—They demanded of the slavers where they were going to take them, but got no satisfactory answer. In one and a half moons, they said, we arrived at Havana. Here they were put ashore, and confined one moon in a house very close. Then they were put on board the schooner which brought them to this country, and continued on board of her about one moon or a month. After being on board the schooner some time, they agreed to take the schooner and go back to their own country. Previous to this the Captain was very cruel and beat them severely. They would not take it, to use their own expression, and therefore turned to and fought for it. After this they did not know which way to go. But at length they told the Spaniards to take them to Sierra Leone. "They made fools of us," said Shinquau, "and did not go to Sierra Leone." In the day time, they said they could tell very well which way to go by the sun, but at night the Spaniards deceived them, and put the vessel the other way. After this said they, we got here, and did not know where we were.

Captain Green, of Sag Harbor, who was one of the first men the prisoner met ashore, before their capture by Lieut. Gedney, of the U.S. brig Washington, and who has given me a circumstantial account, differing in many respects from what has been published, of all that took place, says that the Africans asked him, by one of their number who speaks a little broken English, "What country is this?" He replied, this is America. They immediately asked, "Is it a slave country?" Captain Green answered, it is free here, and safe, and there are no Spanish laws here. Shinquau then gave a sort of whistle, when they all sprang upon their feet and shouted. Captain Green and his associates sprang to their wagon for their guns, supposing the Africans were about to attack them. But Shinquau came up, delivered his cutlass and gun, and even offered his hat, &c, and the rest did the same, indicating that they would give all up, that Capt. G. might take charge of the schooner and everything on board. They however begged of him to take them to Sierre Leone. Shinquau positively assured Capt. G. at the time, and he repeats it now, that they threw nothing overboard. The stories about his loosening his girdle, and letting three or four hundred doubloons drop into the sea, and of diving and keeping under water forty minutes, are considered fabulous. The Africans assert that there was a quantity of doubloons in the trunks that were carried on shore on

Long Island, and Captain Green says he heard the money rattle as the trunks were returned to the schooner by order of Lieut. Gedney. On examining the contents of the trunks afterwards no gold was found! Some person, or persons, are supposed to have the money, but who, is a secret. While on shore, at Long Island, Shinquau and his companions, although hungry, and with arms in their hands, would not kill a single animal, or take an article even to satisfy their hunger, without paying generously for it. They appeared, it is true, to know very little about the value of money, and gave a doubloon for a dog, and a small gold piece for some victuals.

The African prisoners are orderly and peaceable among themselves. Some of them sing well, and appear to be in good spirits and grateful for the kindness shown them. Col. Stanton Pendleton, at whose house I stop, is the jailer, and is kind and attentive to the prisoners. He provides them wholesome food in sufficient quantities, and gives every reasonable indulgence to the numerous visitors, from the neighboring towns and elsewhere, who throng the prison continually to see these interesting strangers from a distant land. Col. P. has allowed me to take copies of the warrants of commitment. The little girls, and the negro boy, Antonio, are committed as witnesses, "for neglecting to become recognized to the United States with surety," and Shinquau and his comrades are bound over "for murder on the high seas."

I have read an ingenious and well written article in the Evening Post signed Veto, in which the learned writer presents a pretty full examination of the case of the schooner Amistad. He says that it seems but too probable that the slave holders, Messrs. Ruez and Montez, conscious of the invalidity of their claim in the Civil Courts, have drawn this criminal prosecution (the charge of murder) to give time to their government to make a demand: and he rather singularly says "this raises a far more difficult question." If Veto will turn to Niles' Register for 1823, he will find an elegantly written and very able opinion of Chief Justice Tilghman, of Pa., on this subject, in which that eminent jurist, in giving his own judgment against the claim of a foreign government in the case of a fugitive charged with treason or murder, where there exists no treaty stipulation, as there does not at present between the United States and Spain, refers also to the corroborative opinions of all the preceding Presidents of the United States, (with the exception of the elder Adams, who had not given an opinion) very clearly and satisfactorily shows that the government of this country ought not to surrender persons situated as are Joseph Shinquau and his unfortunate countrymen, who are, by the act of God, thrown upon these shores to find, I trust, that protection and relief of which they had been, probably, forever deprived had it not been for this remarkable and providential interposition.

I remain, very truly, yours,
LEWIS TAPPAN.

P. S. Sabbath evening. The Rev. H. G. Ludlow prayed for the poor Africans this forenoon, very feelingly, at the service in his church. The outer door of the jail was closed today, and visitors generally were not admitted. I distributed some religious tracts, in the morning, to the convicts, and attempted to instruct the African prisoners, especially the children. They pronounce words in English very distinctly, and have already nearly the numerals. In showing them some books containing pictures of tropical animals, birds, &c., they seemed much pleased to recognize those with whose appearance they were acquainted, endeavoring to imitate their voices and actions. With suitable instruction these intelligent and docile Africans would soon learn to read and speak our language, and I cannot but hope that some of the benevolent inhabitants of this city will diligently continue to improve the opportunity to impart instruction to these pagans, brought by the providence of God to their very doors. Towards evening we made a visit to Shinquau, and conversed with him a considerable time. He drew his hand across his throat, as his room mates said he had done frequently before, and asked whether the people here intended to kill him. He was assured that probably no harm would happen to him—that we were his friends—and that he would be sent across the ocean towards the rising sun, home to his friends. His countenance immediately lost the anxious and distressed expression it had before, and beamed with joy. He says he was born about two days travelling from the ocean; that he purchased some goods, and being unable to pay for only two thirds of the amount, he was seized by the traders, his own countrymen, and sold to king Sharka for the remaining third. "I don't tell a bit of a lie about it," he said. He says he left in Africa both his parents, a wife and three children. Two of the children, he remarked, are a little larger than the African girls who are prisoners, and the other about as large. We endeavored to ascertain what his ideas were about a Supreme Being, if he had any. He said, "God is good." His countrymen, he says, know nothing about reading or writing. Tomorrow we expect to have him taken out of his cell, and examined, through the interpreter, by Messrs. Staples and Baldwin.

L. T.

1. From the text of the letter, what can you infer were the arguments under consideration to return the Mendis to slavery?
2. Why do you think prominent individuals such as United States senators and a former president rallied to the defense of the Mendis? What defense do you think would be made for the *Amistad* captives today?

13-3 De Bow's Review, "The Stability of the Union," (1850)

The economic and social differences between the north and south are illuminated in this document and the relative well being of slaves in relation to those differences explored. Many in the south saw the industrial north as a different planet with different values. They also saw, in the north, a hypocritical view of slavery, which the south justified as a way of elevating the slave from his condition in Africa.

The South is now with its institutions and capabilities, possessed of that on which half the manufacturing and commercial interests of the world depends. It is the source whence the only means of employing and feeding at least 5,000,000 whites can be drawn, and without which, nearly $1,000,000,000 of active capital in ships and factory would be valued less. A country and institutions so important to the welfare of humanity at large, are not to be trifled with. This country forms one-half of our glorious Union, on terms agreed upon by those immortal men who separated from England, because they would no longer suffer the continuance of the African slave-trade; but, in its independent position, the South holds the welfare of other nations almost entirely within its keeping. The capital and laboring abilities of England are such as to afford the South an outlet for its staple, should it exclude all other customers. The result of such a movement, would be to force other countries to draw their goods from England only. On the other hand, the manufacturing progress of the North is such, that in a few years she may absorb the whole of the southern staple, and place herself at the head of the manufacturing interest for the supply of the world. To the South, it is comparatively of small importance, whether England or the North obtains this mastery. Between the North and England, it is a mortal duel; and yet, in the crisis of this struggle, there are to be found persons at the North so destitute of all moral sense and political acuteness as to attack, in violation of the sacred pledge of the constitution, those institutions which it guarantees, and which are so necessary to the interests of humanity.

The continued harmony of the United States, permitting the industry of each section to furnish materials for the enterprise of the others, the reciprocity of benefits and uninterrupted interchange of mutual productions, facilitated by continually increasing means of intercourse and accumulation of capital, are laying the foundation for an empire of which the world's history not only affords no example, but the magnitude of which the wildest dream of the most imaginative of the world's statesmen has failed to conceive. In this undisturbed progress, the condition of the black race is being elevated on the swelling tide of white progress. Inasmuch as that the first slaves imported were, under their new masters, vastly superior in condition to the nude cannibals by whom they were sold, only because avarice triumphed over appetite so is the condition of the slave of the present day far above that of his progenitor a few generations back. The black race, in its servitude to the whites, has undergone an improvement, which the same race, in its state of African freedom, has failed to manifest. By whatever degree, physically and morally, the blacks of the United States are superior to the nude cannibals of Africa, are they indebted to the white race for its active, though not disinterested agency. That process of improvement has not ceased, but is ever progressive in the train of white advancement. The huge lumber-car has no vitality of itself, but, attached to the resistless locomotive, moves forward with a vigor not its own. To cast off that race, in dependence on its own resources, is a singular manifestation of desire for its progress. As an indication of the progress in respect of freedom, which that race makes as it is trained to endure it, we may take the numbers classified upon the continent, for three periods, according to the United States census:

Slave States	Free States	Slaves	Free Blacks
1800,	857,095	61,441	73,100
1830,	2,005,475	182,070	137,525
1840,	2,486,226	215,568	172,509

In 1800 there were 36,946 slaves in what are now free States. The emancipation of these increased the free blacks in the free States; but the multiplication of the free blacks in the slave States is much more rapid, and is increasing on the proportion of slaves. Thus, the free blacks in those States, in forty years, reached 25 per cent of the original number of slaves-the emancipation being always 10 per cent of the increase. This has been greatly retarded by the abolition excitement. It is observable that the free blacks do not emigrate from the southern States. Their social position there is less onerous than the nominal freedom of the North. The increase of free blacks at the South, in forty years, was 250 per cent, and, at the North, 140 per cent. It is, undoubtedly, true, that the unconquerable repugnance of the North to permit the presence of blacks, if they can possibly be excluded, has, to a very great extent, checked emancipation. Thus, the constitution passed by Ohio on its organization as a State, with the black laws, passed by its Legislature, by preventing the ingress of slaves, greatly retarded emancipation. To suppose that the ordinance of 1787 stopped slave migration is a great mistake. It was the opposition of the white settlers to the presence of negroes that alone prevented it. Had any number of slaves been settled in Ohio, they would, ultimately, as in New York, have been emancipated, and would, by so much, have reduced the existing number of slaves. Thus, notwithstanding all the false sympathies of the North, the progress of emancipation at the South is quite as rapid as it should be, to avoid convulsions. It is more than probable, that, when the body of free blacks shall have become more considerable, they will supplant slaves as domestic servants, until slavery becomes, in those States, almost entirely predial. There is no comparison between the well-trained free black, subject to dismissal for misconduct as a domestic servant, and the slothful slave who has no fear of loss of place before his eyes. The free blacks must, necessarily, crowd out the slaves by a gradual and regular process, as the latter become more fitted for freedom. It is an inevitable law of political economy, that slavery must cease where trade is free and the population of freemen becomes more dense. This process is gradually and surely elevating the black race; and, to disturb it by any means, is at once to plunge this incapable race into hopeless barbarism, as complete as that which pervades Africa. An earnest desire for progress, political and social, for both races, as well on this continent as upon that of Europe, will find, in a firm adherence to the compromises of the constitution, the only sure mode of accomplishing that double end. To preserve the harmony of the several sections, by refraining from an attack upon that state of things which we may wish did not exist, but which we cannot remedy, is the only mode of ameliorating them. Those political schemers who seek for their own advancement amid the ruins of an empire, the desolation of a continent and the barbarizing of a race of men, will find, in the awakening intelligence of the people, the fiat of their own destruction.

1. Describe the kind of reciprocal and interdependent relationship between the North and the South that is described in this document.
2. What, according to this document, is the best way to secure the stability of the Union, and to ensure the improvement of the black race?

13-4 George Fitzhugh, "The Blessings of Slavery" (1857)

The descendent of an old southern family that had suffered hard times, Fitzhugh became a lawyer and planter. He became famous for his books "Sociology for the South" and "Cannibals All" which sought to elevate slavery to a higher plane. His call for an end to world capitalism and a society based on servile labor made him an infamous figure. In this document, Fitzhugh explores the idea that slaves are happier than competing "free" laborers and that a society that has embraced slavery is a stable and happy one.

The negro slaves of the South are the happiest, and in some sense, the freest people in the world. The children and the aged and infirm work not at all, and yet have all the comforts and necessaries of life provided for them. They enjoy liberty, because they are oppressed neither by care or labor. The women do little hard work, and are protected from the despotism of their husbands by their masters. The negro men and stout boys work, on the average, in good weather, no more than nine hours a day. The balance of their time is spent in perfect abandon. Besides, they have their Sabbaths and holidays. White men, with som muh of license and abandon, would die of ennui; but negroes luxuriate in corporeal and mental repose. With their faces upturned to the sun, they can sleep at any hour; and quiet sleep is the gretest of human enjoyments. "Blessed be the man who invented sleep." 'Tis happiness in itself-and results from contentment in the present, and confident assurance of the future. We do not know whether free laborers ever sleep. They are fools to do so; for, whilst they sleep, the wily and watchful capitalist is devising means to ensnare and exploit them. The free laborer must work or starve. He is more of a slave than the negro, because he works longer and harder for less allowance than the slave, and has no holiday, because the cares of life with him begin when its labors end. He has no liberty and not a single right. . . .

Until the lands of America are appropriated by a few, population becomes dense, competition among laborers active, employment uncertain, and wages low, the personal liberty of all the whites will continue to be a blessing. We have vast unsettled territories; population may cease to increase slowly, as in most countries, and many centuries may elapse before the question will be practically suggested, whether slavery to capital be preferable to slavery to human masters. But the negro has neither energy nor enterprise, and, even in our sparser populations, finds with his improvident habits, that his liberty is a curse to himself, and a greater curse to the society around him. These considerations, and others equally obvious, have induced the South to attempt to defend negro slavery as an exceptional institution, admitting, nay asserting, that slavery, in the general or in the abstract, is morally wrong, and against common right. With singular inconsistency, after making this admission, which admits away the authority of the Bible, of profane history, and of the almost universal practice of mankind-they turn around and attempt to bolster up the cause of negro slavery by these very exploded authorities. If we mean not to repudiate all divine, and almost all human authority in favor of slavery, we must vindicate that institution in the abstract.

To insist that a status of society, which has been almost universal, and which is expressly and continually justified by Holy Writ, is its natural, normal, and necessary status, under the ordinary circumstances, is on its face a plausible and probable proposition. To insist on less, is to yield our cause, and to give up our religion; for if white slavery be morally wrong, be a violation of natural rights, the Bible cannot be true. Human and divine authority do seem in the general to concur, in establishing the expediency of having masters and slaves of different races. In very many nations of antiquity, and in some of modern times, the law has permitted the native citizens to become slaves to each other. But few take advantage of such laws; and the infrequency of the practice establishes the general truth that master and slave should be of different national descent. In some respects the wider the difference the better, as the slave will feel less mortified by his position. In other respects, it may be that too wide a difference hardens the hearts and brutalizes the feeling of both master and slave. The civilized man hates the savage, and the savage returns the hatred with interest. Hence West India slavery of newly caught negroes is not a very humane, affectionate, or civilizing institution. Virginia negroes have become moral and intelligent. They love their master and his family, and the attachment is reciprocated. Still, we like the idle, but intelligent house-servants, better than the hard-used, but stupid outhands; and we like the mulatto better than the negro; yet the negro is generally more affectionate, contented, and faithful.

The world at large looks on negro slavery as much the worst form of slavery; because it is only acquainted with West India slavery. But our Southern slavery has become a benign and protective institution, and our negroes are confessedly better off than any free laboring population in the world. How can we contend that white slavery is wrong, whilst all the great body of free laborers are starving; and slaves, white or black, throughout the world, are enjoying comfort? . . .

The aversion to negroes, the antipathy of race, is much greater at the North than at the South; and it is very probable that this antipathy to the person of the negro, is confounded with or generates hatred of the institution with which he is usually connected. Hatred to slavery is very generally little more than hatred of negroes.

There is one strong argument in favor of negro slavery over all other slavery; that he, being unfitted for the mechanic arts, for trade, and all skillful pursuits, leaves those pursuits to be carried on by the whites; and does not bring all industry into disrepute, as in Greece and Rome, where the slaves were not only the artists and mechanics, but also the merchants.

Whilst, as a general and abstract question, negro slavery has no other claims over other forms of slavery, except that from inferiority, or rather peculiarity, of race, almost all negroes require masters, whilst only the children, the women, and the very weak, poor, and ignorant, &c., among the whites, need some protective and governing relation of this kind; yet as a subject of temporary, but worldwide importance, negro slavery has become the most necessary of all human institutions.

The African slave trade to America commenced three centuries and a half since. By the time of the American Revolution, the supply of slaves had exceeded the demand for slave labor, and the slaveholders, to get rid of a burden, and to prevent the increase of a nuisance, became violent opponents of the slave trade, and many of them abolitionists. New England, Bristol, and Liverpool, who reaped the profits of the trade, without suffering from the nuisance, stood out for a long time against its abolition. Finally, laws and treaties were made, and fleets fitted out to abolish it; and after a while, the slaves of most of South America, of the West Indies, and of Mexico were liberated. In the meantime, cotton, rice, sugar, coffee, tobacco, and other products of slave labor, came into universal use as necessaries of life. The population of Western Europe, sustained and stimulated by those products, was trebled, and that of the North increased tenfold. The products

of slave labor became scarce and dear, and famines frequent. Now, it is obvious, that to emancipate all the negroes would be to starve Western Europe and our North. Not to extend and increase negro slavery, *pari passu*, with the extension and multiplication of free society, will produce much suffering. If all South America, Mexico, the West Indies, and our Union south of Mason and Dixon's line, of the Ohio and Missouri, were slaveholding, slave products would be abundant and cheap in free society; and their market for their merchandise, manufactures, commerce, &c., illimitable. Free white laborers might live in comfort and luxury on light work, but for the exacting and greedy landlords, bosses, and other capitalists.

We must confess, that overstock the world as you will with comforts and with luxuries, we do not see how to make capital relax its monopoly-how to do aught but tantalize the hireling. Capital, irresponsible capital, begets, and ever will beget, the *immedicabile vulnus* of so-called Free Society. It invades every recess of domestic life, infects its food, its clothing, its drink, its very atmosphere, and pursues the hireling, from the hovel to the poor-house, the prison and the grave. Do what he will, go where he will, capital pursues and persecutes him. *"Haeret lateri lethalis arundo!"*

Capital supports and protects the domestic slave; taxes, oppresses, and persecutes the free laborer.

1. How does Fitzhugh support his claim that, "The negro slaves of the South are the happiest, and in some sense, the freest people in the world"?
2. Identify and explain the author's arguments in favor of the institution of slavery.

PART FOURTEEN
THE SECTIONAL CRISIS

14-1 William Lloyd Garrison, from *The Liberator* (1831)

William Lloyd Garrison was among the most prominent abolitionists and his long running paper "The Liberator" was a bastion of abolitionist thought and agitation. An opponent of gradual emancipation of slaves, Garrison spoke for immediate abolition. Often threatened, harassed, and abused, Garrison continued his fiery rhetoric even to the point of burning copies of the Constitution at public meetings. This document reveals the general apathy an even hostility of most northerners on the issue of slavery.

During my recent tour for the purpose of exciting the minds of the people by a series of discourses on the subject of slavery, every place that I visited gave fresh evidence of the fact that a great revolution in public sentiment was to be effected in the free states-and particularly in New England-than at the South. I find contempt more bitter, opposition more active, detraction more relentless, prejudice more stubborn, and apathy more frozen, than among slaveowners themselves. Of course, there were individual exceptions to the contrary.

    This state of things afflicted but did not dishearten me. I determined, at every hazard, to lift up the standard of emancipation in the eyes of the nation, within sight of Bunker Hill and in the birthplace of liberty. That standard is now unfurled; and long may it float, unhurt by the spoliations of time or the missiles of a desperate foe-yea, till every chain be broken, and every bondman set free! Let Southern oppressors tremble-let all the enemies of the persecuted blacks tremble.
. . .

    Assenting to the "self-evident truth" maintained in the American Declaration of Independence "that all men are created equal, and endowed by their Creator with certain inalienable rights-among which are life, liberty, and the pursuit of happiness," I shall strenuously contend for the immediate enfranchisement of our slave population. . . . In Park Street Church, on the Fourth of July, 1829, in an address on slavery, I unreflectingly assented to the popular but pernicious doctrine of gradual abolition. I seize this opportunity to make a full and unequivocal recantation, and thus publicly to ask pardon of my God, of my country, and of my brethren the poor slaves, for having uttered a sentiment so full of timidity, injustice, and absurdity. . . .

    I am aware that many object to the severity of my language; but is there not cause for severity? I will be as harsh as truth, and as uncompromising as justice. On this subject I do not wish to think, or speak, or write, with moderation. No! No! Tell a man whose house is on fire to give a moderate alarm; tell him to moderately rescue his wife from the hands of the ravisher; tell the mother to gradually extricate her babe from the fire into which it has fallen-but urge me not to use moderation in a cause like the present. I am in earnest-will not equivocate-I will not excuse-I will not retreat in a single inch-and I will be heard. The apathy of the people is enough to make every statue leap from its pedestal, and to hasten the resurrection of the dead.

    It is pretended that I am retarding the cause of emancipation by the coarseness of my invective and the precipitancy of my measures. The charge is not true. On this question my influence-humble as it is-is felt at this moment to a considerable extent, and shall be felt in coming years-not perniciously, but beneficially-not as a curse, but as a blessing. And posterity will bear testimony that I was right.

1. What are Garrison's observations regarding public sentiment about slavery in America?
2. How does Garrison justify his bold stand on slavery and his proposal for immediate abolition?

14-2   Harriet Beecher Stowe, from *Uncle Tom's Cabin* (1852)

Although she authored several books on New England, Harriet Beacher Stowe was best known for her portrayal of slavery in Uncle Tom's Cabin. The daughter of the most important Puritan preacher of her day, Stowe had a long concern with humanitarian causes. The death of one of Stowe's children prompted her to become involved with the abolitionist movement. Uncle Tom's Cabin outraged the south and solidified the anti-slavery movement in the north. Some even feel the book was one of the factors that brought on the Civil war. The following section finds Uncle Tom, recently purchased by the cruel Simon Legree, on his way to Legree's plantation.

"And now," said Legree, "come here, you Tom. You see, I told ye I didn't buy ye jest for the common work. I mean to promote ye, and make a driver of ye; and tonight ye may jest as well begin to get ye hand in. Now, ye jest take this yer gal and flog her; ye've seen enough on't [of it] to know how." "I beg Mas'r' pardon," said Tom; "hopes Mas'r won't set me at that. It's what I an't used to-never did-and can't do, no way possible."

"Ye'll larn a pretty smart chance of things ye never did know, before I've done with ye!" said Legree, taking up a cowhide and striking Tom a heavy blow across the cheek, and following up the infliction by a shower of blows.

"There!" he said, as he stopped to rest; "now, will ye tell me ye can't do it?"

"Yes, Mas'r," said Tom, putting up his hand, to wipe the blood that trickled down his face. "I'm willin' to work, night and day, and work while there's life and breath in me. But this yer thing I can't feel it right to do; and, Mas'r, I never shall do it-never!"

Tom had a remarkably smooth, soft voice, and a habitually respectful manner that had given Legree an idea that he would be cowardly and easily subdued. When he spoke these last words, a thrill of amazement went through everyone. The poor woman clasped her hands and said, "O Lord!" and everyone involuntarily looked at each other and drew in their breath, as if to prepare for the storm that was about to burst.

Legree looked stupefied and confounded; but at last burst forth: "What! Ye blasted black beast! Tell me ye don't think it right to do what I tell ye! What have any of you cussed cattle to do with thinking what's right? I'll put a stop to it! Why, what do ye think ye are? May be ye think ye're a gentleman, master Tom, to be a telling your master what's right, and what an't! So you pretend it's wrong to flog the gal!"

"I think so, Mas'r," said Tom; "the poor crittur's sick and feeble; 'twould be downright cruel, and it's what I never will do, nor begin to. Mas'r, if you mean to kill me, kill me; but, as to my raising my hand again any one here, I never shall-I'll die first!"

Tom spoke in a mild voice, but with a decision that could not be mistaken. Legree shook with anger; his greenish eyes glared fiercely, and his very whiskers seemed to curl with passion. But, like some ferocious beast, that plays with its victim before he devours it, he kept back his strong impulse to proceed to immediate violence, and broke out into bitterly raillery.

"Well, here's a pious dog, at last, let down among us sinners-a saint, a gentleman, and no less, to talk to us sinners about our sins! Powerful holy crittur, he must be! Here, you rascal, you make believe to be so pious-didn't you never hear, out of yer Bible, 'Servants, obey yer masters'? An't I yer master? Didn't I pay down twelve hundred dollars, cash, for all there is inside yer old cussed black shell? An't yer mine, now, body and soul?" he said, giving Tom a violent kick with his heavy boot; "tell me!"

In the very depth of physical suffering, bowed by brutal oppression, this question shot a gleam of joy an triumph through Tom's soul. He suddenly stretched himself up, and, looking earnestly to heaven, while the tears and blood that flowed down his face mingled, he exclaimed, " No! no! no! my soul an't yours, Mas'r! You haven't bought it-ye can't buy it! It's been bought and paid for by One that is able to keep it. No matter, no matter, you can't harm me!"

"I can't!" said Legree, with a sneer; "we'll see-we'll see! Here Sambo, Quimbo, give this dog such a breakin' in as he won't get over this month!"

The two gigantic Negroes that now laid hold of Tom, with fiendish exultation in their faces, might have formed no unapt personification of powers of darkness. The poor woman screamed with apprehension, and all rose, as by a general impulse, while they dragged him unresisting from the place.

1. Describe the view of slavery portrayed in this selection from Uncle Tom's Cabin.
2. What characteristics does Legree possess and what actions does he do that are symbolic of the practice of slavery?
3. How is Tom a symbol of the moral strength and spirit of slaves?

14-3 Frederick Douglass, Independence Day Speech (1852)

The most important African American leader of his time, Fredrick Douglass had a profound impact on American notions of slavery. Born in slavery, Douglass escaped at the age of 20 and began writing and speaking against slavery. His volumes of autobiography including "Narrative of the Life of Fredrick Douglass, an American Slave" (1845) were among the greatest of the slave narratives and are now considered classic examples of American autobiography. As a speaker, newspaper editor and writer, Douglass' influence was great. He knew and aided John Brown in his efforts, welcomed the Civil War and until his death in 1895, spoke against Jim Crow laws and lynching. This famous speech is a masterful example of Douglass' use of irony in illuminating the hypocrisy of the celebration of Independene day.

Fellow citizens above your national, tumultuous joy, I hear the mournful wail of millions! whose chains, heave and grievous yesterday, are, today, rendered more intolerable by the jubilee shouts that reach them. If I do forget, it I do not faithfully remember those bleeding children of sorrow this day, "may my right hand forger her cunning, and may ny tongue cleave to the roof of my mouth"! To forget them, to pass lightly over their wrongs, and to chime in with the popular theme would be treason most scandalous and shocking, and would make me a reproach before God and the world. My subject, them, fellow citizens, is *American Slavery*. I shall see this day and its popular characteristics from the slav;s point of view. Standing there identified with the American bondman, making his wrongs mine. I do not hesitate to declare with all my soul that the character and conduct of this nation never looked blacker to me than on this Fourth of July! Whether we turn to the declarations of the past or to the professions of the present, the conduct of the nation seems equally hideous and revolting. America is false to the past, false to the present, and solemnly binds herself to be false to the future. Standing with God and the crushed and bleeding slave on this occasion, I will,in the name of humanity which is outraged, in the name of liberty which is fettered, in the name of the Constitution and the Bible which are disregarded and trampled upon, All the emphasis I can command, everything that serves to perpetuate slavery the great sin and shame of America! "I will not equivocate, I will not excuse"; I will use the severest of language I can command; and yet not one word shall escape that any man, whose judgment is not blinded by prejudice, or who is not at heart a slaveholder, shall not confess to be right and just.

But I fancy I hear someone of my audience say, "It is just in this circumstance that your and your brother abolitionists fail to make a favorable impression on the public mind. Would you argue more and denounce less, would you persuade more and rebuke less, your cause would be much more likely to succeed." But, I submit, where all is plain, there is nothing to be argued. What point in the antislavery creed would you have me argue? On what branch of the subject do the people of this country need light? Must I undertake to prove that the slave is a man? That point is conceded already. Nobody doubts it. The slaveholders themselves acknowledge it the enactment of laws for their government. They acknowledge it when they punish disobedience on the part of the slave. There are seventy-two crimes in the state of Virginia which, if committed by a black man (no matter how ignorant he be), subject him to the punishment of death, while only two of the same crimes will subject a white man to the like punishment. What is this but the acknowledgment that the slave is a moral, intellectual, and responsible being? The manhood of the slave is conceded. It is admitted in the fact that the Southern statute books are covered with enactments forbidding, under severe fines and penalties, the teaching of the slave to read or to write. When you can point to any such laws in reference to the beasts of the field, then I may consent to argue the manhood of the slave. When the dogs in your streets, when the fowls of the air, when the cattle on your hills, when the fish of the sea and the reptiles that crawl shall be unable to distinguish the slave from a brute, then will I argue with you that the slave is a man!

For the present, it is enough to affirm the equal manhood of the Negro race. It is not stonishing that, while we are plowing, planting, and reaping, using all kinds of mechanical tools erecting houses, constructing bridges, building ships, working in metals of brass, iron, copper and silver, and gold; that, while we are reading, writing, and ciphering, acting as clerks, merchants and secretaries, having among us lawyers, doctors, ministers, poets, authors, editors, orators, and teachers; that, while we are engaged in all manner of enterprises common to other men, digging gold in California, capturing the whale in the Pacific, feeding sheep and cattle on the hillside, living, moving, acting, thinking, planning, living in families as husbands, wives, and children, and, above all, confessing and worshipping the Christian's God, and looking hopefully for life and immortality beyond the grave, we are called upon to prove that we are men!

Would you have me argue that man is entitled to liberty? That he is the rightful owner of his own body? You have already declared it. Must I argue the wrongfulness of slavery? Is that a question for republicans? Is it to be settled by the rules of logic and argumentation, as a matter beset with great difficulty, involving a doubtful application of the principle of justice, hart to be understood? How should I look today, in the presence of Americans, dividing and subdividing a discourse, to show that men have a natural right to freedom? speaking of it relatively and positively, negatively and affirmatively? To do so would be to make myself ridiculous and to offer an insult to your understanding. There is not a man beneath the canopy of heaven that does not know that slaver is wrong for him.

What, am I to argue that is wrong to make men brutes, to rob them of their liberty, to work them without wages, to keep them ignorant of their relations to their fellow men, to beat them with sticks, to flay their flesh with the last, to load their limbs with irons, to hunt them with dogs, to sell them at auction, to sunder their families, to knock out their teeth, to burn their flesh, to starve them into obedience and submission to their masters? Must I argue that a system them marked with blood, and stained with pollution, is wrong? No! I will not. I have better employment for my time and strength than such arguments would imply.

What, then remains to be argued? Is it that slavery is not divine; that God did not establish it; that our doctors of divinity are mistaken? There is blasphemy in the thought. That which is inhuman cannot be divine? Who can reason on such a proposition? They that can may; I cannot. The time for such argument is past.

At a time like this, scorching iron, not convincing argument, is needed. O! had I the ability, and could I reach the nation's ear, I would today pour out a fiery stream of biting ridicule, blasting reproach, withering sarcasm, and stern rebuke. For it is not light that is needed, but fire; it is not the gentle shower, but thunder. We need the storm, the whirlwind, and the earthquake. The feeling of the nation must be quickened, the conscience of the nation must be startled; the hypocrisy of the nation must be exposed; and its crimes against God and man must be proclaimed and denounced.

What, to the American slave is your Fourth of July? I answer: a day that reveals to him, more than all other days in the year, the gross injustice and cruelty to which he s the constant victim. To him, your celebration is a sham; your boasted liberty an unholy license; your national greatness, swelling vanity; your sound of rejoicing are empty and heart-less; your denunciation of tyrants, brass-fronted impudence; your shouts of liberty and equality, hollow mockery; your prayers and hymns, your sermons and thanksgivings with all your religious parade and solemnity, are, to Him, mere bom-bast, fraud, deception, impiety, and hypocrisy a thin veil to cover up crimes which would disgrace a nation of savages. There is not a nation of savages. There is not a nation on earth guilty of practices more shocking and bloody than are the people of the United States at this very hour.

Go where you may, search where you will, roam through all the monarchies and despotisms of the Old World, travel through South America, search out every abuse, and when you have found the last, lay your facts by the side of the everyday practices of this nation, and you will say with that, for revolting barbarity and shameless hypocrisy, America reigns without a rival.

1. How does Douglass use the celebration of the Fourth of July as a foundation for his argument against slavery? Describe his tone in this piece.
2. What are the contradictions and injustices of slavery that Douglass brings to light in this speech?

14-4 Kansas Begins to Bleed (1856)

As proslavery and Free State factions struggled for political control over the Territory of Kansas, tensions increased between devotees of the two opposing points of view until they erupted into outright violence. Individuals on both sides were tarred and feathered, kidnapped, and occasionally killed. On May 21, 1856, the violence escalated dramatically as a group of proslavery men entered Lawrence, a Free State stronghold, and wreaked havoc. This "sack of Lawrence" was followed three days later by a brutal attack led by John Brown upon proslavery settlers at Pottawatomie Creek. In September, a new territorial governor, John W. Geary, arrived and began to restore order to "Bleeding Kansas." Geary's strong antislavery views, however, forced his resignation six months later. Many of the details of this violent period in the history of Kansas can be found in a book written in 1857 by Dr. John Gihon, the governor's private secretary. The excerpt that follows relates the events surrounding the attack on Lawrence.

> **Source:** John H. Gihon, *Geary and Kansas: Governor Geary's Administration in Kansas With a Complete History of the Territory Until July 1857* (Philadelphia: Chas. C. Rhodes, 1857). The Kansas Collection Website, Lynn Nelson, Professor of History at the University of Kansas.
> http://www.ukans.edu/carrie/kancoll/books/gihon/g_intro.htm

On the 5th of May, Judge Lecompte delivered a charge, highly partisan in its character, to the grand jury of Douglas county, of which, the following extract is in his own words:

This territory was organized by an act of Congress, and so far its authority is from the United States. It has a Legislature elected in pursuance of that organic act. This Legislature, being an instrument of Congress, by which it governs the territory, has passed laws; these laws, therefore, are of United States authority and making, and all that resist these laws, resist the power and authority of the United States, and are, therefore, guilty of high treason. Now, gentlemen, if you find that any persons have resisted these laws, then must you, under your oaths, find bills against such persons for high treason. If you find that no such resistance has been made, but that combinations have been formed for the purpose of resisting them, and individuals of influence and notoriety have been aiding and abetting in such combinations, then must you still find bills for constructive treason, as the courts have decided that to constitute treason the blow need not be struck, but only the intention be made evident.

The grand jury accordingly made a presentment, as follows:

The grand jury, sitting for the adjourned term of the First District Court in and for the county of Douglas, in the Territory of Kansas, beg leave to report to the honorable court that, from evidence laid before them, showing that the newspaper known as *The Herald of Freedom*, published at the town of Lawrence, has from time to time issued publications of the most inflammatory and seditious character, denying the legality of the territorial authorities, addressing and commanding forcible resistance to the same, demoralizing the popular mind, and rendering life and property unsafe, even to the extent of advising assassination as a last resort; Also, that the paper known as *The Kansas Free State* has been similarly engaged, and has recently reported the resolutions of a public meeting in Johnson county, in this territory, in which resistance to the territorial laws even unto blood has been agreed upon; and that we respectfully recommend their abatement as a nuisance. Also, that we are satisfied that the building known as the 'Free-State Hotel' in Lawrence has been constructed with the view to military occupation and defence, regularly parapeted and port-holed for the use of cannon and small arms, and could only have been designed as a stronghold of resistance to law, thereby endangering the public safety, and encouraging rebellion and sedition in this country; and respectfully recommend that steps be taken whereby this nuisance may be removed.

OWEN C. STEWART, Foreman.

In order to accomplish the objects of this presentment, which was simply a declaration of war against Lawrence, a number of writs were made out and placed in the hands of the marshal for the arrest of prominent citizens of that place. Although it is asserted that no attempts were made to resist the marshal's deputies in serving these writs, the marshal, on the 11th of May, issued the following proclamation:

TO THE PEOPLE OF KANSAS TERRITORY:

Whereas, certain judicial writs of arrest have been directed to me by the First District Court of the United States, etc., to be executed within the county of Douglas, and whereas an attempt to execute them by the United States Deputy Marshal was evidently resisted by a large number of the citizens of Lawrence, and as there is every reason to believe that any attempt to execute these writs will be resisted by a large body of armed men; now, therefore, the law-abiding citizens of the territory are commanded to be and appear at Lecompton, as soon as practicable, and in numbers sufficient for the execution of the law. Given under my hand, this 11th day of May, 1856.

I. B. DONALSON, United States Marshal for Kansas Territory.

Previous to the publication of this proclamation, Buford's regiment, and other armed bands, had taken up positions in the vicinity of Lawrence, who were not only committing depredations upon the property of the settlers, but were intercepting, robbing, and imprisoning travellers on the public thoroughfares, and threatening to attack the town, in consequence of which a meeting was held, and a committee appointed to address Governor Shannon, stating the facts in gentle terms, and asking his protection against such bands by the United States troops at his disposal.

To this respectful application the committee received the following reply:

Executive Office, May 12, 1856,

Lecompton, K. T.

Gentlemen: Your note of the eleventh inst. is received, and, in reply, I have to state that there is no force around or approaching Lawrence, except the legally constituted posse of the United States Marshal and Sheriff of Douglas county, each of whom, I am informed, have a number of writs in their hands for execution against persons now in Lawrence. I shall in no way interfere with either of these officers in the discharge of their official duties.

If the citizens of Lawrence submit themselves to the territorial laws, and aid and assist the marshal and sheriff in the execution of processes in their hands, as all good citizens are bound to do when called on, they, or all such will entitle themselves to the protection of the law. But so long as they keep up a military or armed organization to resist the territorial laws and the officers charged with their execution, I shall not interpose to save them from the legitimate consequences of their illegal acts.

I have the honor to be yours, with great respect,

WILSON SHANNON.

Messrs. C. W. Toplief, John Hutchinson, W. Y. Roberts

Still desirous of averting the impending difficulties, the citizens of Lawrence held another meeting on the 13th, when the following preamble and resolution were adopted, copies of which were immediately forwarded to Marshal Donalson and Governor Shannon:

Whereas by a proclamation to the people of Kansas Territory, by I. B. Donalson, United States Marshal for said territory, issued on the 11th day of May, 1856, it is alleged that Certain judicial writs of arrest have been directed to him by the First District Court of the United States, etc., to be executed within the county of Douglas, and that an attempt to execute them by the United States Deputy Marshal was violently resisted by a large number of the citizens of Lawrence, and that there is every reason to believe that any attempt to execute said writs will be resisted by a large body of armed men; therefore,

Resolved, By this public meeting of the citizens of Lawrence, held this thirteenth day of May, 1856, that the allegations and charges against us, contained in the aforesaid proclamation, are wholly untrue in fact, and the conclusion which is drawn from them. The aforesaid deputy marshal was resisted in no manner whatever, nor by any person whatever, in the execution of said writs, except by him whose arrest the said deputy marshal was seeking to make. And that we now, as we have done heretofore, declare our willingness and determination, without resistance, to acquiesce in the service upon us of any judicial writs against us by the United States Deputy Marshal for Kansas Territory, and will furnish him with a posse for that purpose, if so requested; but that we are ready to resist, if need be, unto death, the ravages and desolations of an invading mob.

J. A. WAKEFIELD, President.

On the 14th, still another meeting was held at Lawrence, and a letter, signed by a large and respectable committee appointed for the purpose, was sent to the marshal, in which it was affirmed "that no opposition will now, or at any future time, be offered to the execution of any legal process by yourself, or any person acting for you. We also pledge ourselves to assist you, if called upon, in the execution of any legal process.

We declare ourselves to be order-loving and law-abiding citizens; and only await an opportunity to testify our fidelity to the laws of the country, the constitution, and the Union.

We are informed, also, that those men collecting about Lawrence openly declare that it is their attention to destroy the town and drive off the citizens. Of course we do not believe you give any countenance to such threats; but, in view of the excited state of the public mind, we ask protection of the constituted authorities of the government, declaring ourselves in readiness to co-operate with them for the maintenance of the peace, order, and quiet, of the community in which we live.

In reply to this the marshal sends a lengthy communication, intended to be bitterly sarcastic, which he closes with these words:

You say you call upon the constituted authorities of the government for protection. This, indeed, sounds strange from a large body of men armed with Sharpe's rifles, and other implements of war, bound together by oaths and pledges, to resist the laws of the government they call on for protection. All persons in Kansas Territory, without regard to location, who honestly submit to the constituted authorities, will ever find me ready to aid in protecting them; and all who seek to resist the laws of the land, and turn traitors to their country, will find me aiding and enforcing the laws, if not as an officer as a citizen.

Whilst these documents were passing, the roads were blockaded by the marshal's posse of southern volunteers, upon which no man without a passport could safely venture. Captain Samuel Walker, who had carried one of the above-mentioned letters to Lecompton, was fired upon on his return to Lawrence. Mr. Miller, who with two others had gone up to negotiate with the governor for an amicable adjustment of the pending troubles, was taken prisoner by a detachment of Buford's South Carolinians near Lecompton, who knowing him to have been from their own state, tried him for treason and sentenced him to be hung. He contrived, somehow, to get away with the loss of his horse and purse. Mr. Weaver, a sergeant-at-arms of the Congressional Committee, was arrested while in the discharge of his duty, and carried across the Kansas River, to the South Carolinian camp, where after a critical examination of his papers, he was discovered to be in the service of the United States, and released, the officer in command giving him a pass, and kindly advising him to answer promptly, if challenged, otherwise he might be shot. Outrages of this kind became so frequent that all travel was at last suspended.

On the 17th of May the citizens of Lawrence, through a committee, again addressed the United States Marshal, in the words of the following letter:

Lawrence, K. T., May 17, 1866
I. B. DONALSON, U. S. MARSHAL OF K. T.

Dear Sir: We desire to call your attention, as citizens of Kansas, to the fact that a large force of armed men have collected in the vicinity of Lawrence, and are engaged in committing depredations upon our citizens; stopping wagons, arresting, threatening and robbing unoffending travellers upon the highway, breaking open boxes of merchandise, and appropriating their contents; have slaughtered cattle, and terrified many of the women and children.

We have also learned from Governor Shannon, 'that there are no armed forces in the vicinity of this place but the regularly constituted militia of the territory—this is to ask if you recognise them as your posse, and feel responsible for their acts. If you do not, we hope and trust you will prevent a repetition of such acts, and give peace to the settlers.

On behalf of the citizens,

C. W. BABCOCK,
LYMAN ALLEN,
J. A. PERRY

To this communication no reply was given. In the mean time, preparations were going forward, and vigorously prosecuted, for the sacking of Lawrence. The pro-slavery people were to "wipe out" this ill-fated town under authority of law. They had received the countenance of the president—the approbation of the chief justice—the favorable presentment of the grand jury—the concurrence of the governor—the orders of the marshal,—and were prepared to consummate their purpose with the arms of the government, in the hands of a militia force gathered from the remotest sections of the Union.

They concentrated their troops in large numbers around the doomed city, stealing, or, as they termed it, "pressing into the service," all the horses they could find belonging to free-state men, whose cattle were also slaughtered, without remuneration, to feed the marshal's forces; and their stores and dwellings broken open and robbed of arms, provisions, blankets and clothing. And all this under the pretence of "law and order," and in the name and under the sanction of the government of the United States.

The marshal's army had a gallant host of commanders. There was General Atchison, with the Missouri Platte County Rifles, and two pieces of artillery; Captain Dunn, with the Kickapoo Rangers; General Stringfellow, and Colonel Abel, his law-partner, aided by Doctor John H. Stringfellow and Robert S. Kelly, editors of the Squatter Sovereign, with the forces from Doniphan, Atchison and Leavenworth; Colonel Boone, with sundry aids, at the head of companies from Westport, Liberty and Independence; Colonels Wilkes and Buford, with the Carolinians, Georgians and Mississippians; Colonel H. T. Titus, in command of the Douglas County Militia; and many others, too numerous to mention.

The heart of the marshal must have swelled with triumphant pride when he looked upon this posse comitatus, comprising in all not less than eight hundred warlike men. The governor must have reviewed them with that satisfaction which governors only can feel when about to accomplish a mighty undertaking, with the certainty of success. This patriotic host was about to engage in an enterprise that was to redound to their everlasting glory—of the most noble actions that ever called warriors to the field of battle. But where, all this time, was Sheriff Jones, the life and spirit and power of all this chivalric host? Why had he not made his appearance, to encourage with his presence, and cheer with his voice and smiles, these patriotic forces? By some it was still supposed that he was either dead or dying of the wound in his back. Jones was still behind the scenes. The time for his appearance upon the stage had not arrived, and he patiently awaited his proper cue.

On the 19th of May, while these forces were collecting for the destruction of Lawrence, a young man from Illinois, named Jones, had been to a store near Blanton's Bridge, to purchase flour, when he was attacked by two of the marshal's party, who were out as scouts. To escape these men, Jones dismounted and entered the store, into which they followed, and there abused him. He again mounted his horse and left for home, the others following, and swearing that the d---d abolitionist should not escape. When near the bridge, they levelled their guns (United States muskets), and fired. Jones fell mortally wounded, and soon expired.

On the following morning, the 20th, several young men, hearing of this transaction, left Lawrence to visit the scene of the tragedy. One of these was named Stewart, who had but recently arrived from the State of New York. They had gone about a mile and a half, when they met two men, armed with Sharpe's rifles. Some words passed between them, when the two strangers raised their rifles, and, taking deliberate aim at Stewart, fired. One of the balls entered his temple. The work of death was instantly accomplished, and another accusing spirit stood before the bar of God.

Soon after sunrise, on the morning of the 21st, an advanced guard of the marshal's army, consisting of about two hundred horsemen, appeared on the top of Mount Oread, on the outskirts of the town of Lawrence, where their cannon had been stationed late on the preceding night. The town was quiet, and the citizens had resolved to submit without resistance to any outrage that might be perpetrated. About seven o'clock, Doctor Robinson's house, which stood on the side of the hill, was taken possession of, and used as the headquarters of the invaders. At eight o'clock, the main body of the army posted themselves on the outer edge of the town. Deputy Marshal Fain, with ten men, entered Lawrence, and, without molestation, served the writs in his possession, and arrested Judge G. W. Smith and G. W. Deitzler. Fain and his companions dined at the free-state hotel, and afterwards returned to the army on Mount Oread. The marshal then dismissed his monster posse, telling them he had no further use for them.

It was nearly three o'clock in the afternoon, when suddenly another actor appeared upon the stage. The "dead" and "dying,"—immortal Sheriff Jones,—rode rapidly into Lawrence, at the head of twenty-five mounted men; and as he passed along the line of the troops, he was received with deafening shouts of applause. His presence was the signal for action, and a sanction for the outrages that ensued.

Atchison then addressed his forces, in language not sufficiently well selected for ears polite, and then marched the whole column to within a short distance of the hotel, where they halted. Jones now informed Col. Eldridge, the proprietor, that the hotel must be destroyed; he was acting under orders; he had writs issued by the First District Court of the United States to destroy the Free-State Hotel, and the offices of the *Herald of Freedom* and Free Press. The grand jury at Lecompton had indicted them as nuisances, and the court had ordered them to be destroyed. He gave Col. Eldridge an hour and a half to remove his family and furniture, after which time the demolition commenced, and was prosecuted with an earnestness that would have done credit to a better cause.

In the mean time the newspaper offices had been assailed, the presses broken to pieces, and these, with the type and other material, thrown into the Kansas River. The following extract from the report of these transactions, given in the columns of the Lecompton Union, the most rabid pro-slavery paper in Kansas, the Squatter Sovereign excepted, is too significant not to be read with interest:

During this time appeals were made to Sheriff Jones to save the Aid Society's Hotel. This news reached the company's ears, and was received with one universal cry of 'No! no! Blow it up! blow it up!'

About this time a banner was seen fluttering in the breeze over the office of *The Herald of Freedom*. Its color was a blood-red, with a lone star in the centre, and South Carolina above. This banner was placed there by the Carolinians—Messrs. Wrights and a Mr. Cross. The effect was prodigious. One tremendous and long-continued shout burst from the ranks. Thus floated in triumph the banner of South Carolina,—that single white star, so emblematic of her course in the early history of our sectional disturbances. When every southern state stood almost upon the verge of ceding their dearest rights to the north, Carolina stood boldly out, the firm and unwavering advocate of southern institutions.

Thus floated victoriously the first banner of southern rights over the abolition town of Lawrence, unfurled by the noble sons of Carolina, and every whip of its folds seemed a death-stroke to Beecher propagandism and the fanatics of the east. O! that its red folds could have been seen by every southern eye!

Mr. Jones listened to the many entreaties, and finally replied that it was beyond his power to do anything, and gave the occupants so long to remove all private property from it. He ordered two companies into each printing office to destroy the press. Both presses were broken up and thrown into the street, the type thrown in the river, and all the material belonging to each office destroyed. After this was accomplished, and the private property removed from the hotel by the different companies, the cannon were brought in front of the house and directed their destructive blows upon the walls. The building caught on fire, and soon its walls came with a crash to the ground. Thus fell the abolition fortress; and we hope this will teach the Aid Society a good lesson for the future.

Whilst the work of destruction was going on at the printing-offices, the bombardment of the hotel, a strongly constructed three-story stone building, commenced. Kegs of gunpowder had been placed inside and the house fired in numerous places; and whilst the flames were doing their destructive work within, heavy cannon were battering against the walls without; and amid the crackling of the conflagration, the noise of falling walls and timbers, and the roar of the artillery, were mingled the almost frantic yells of satisfaction that constantly burst from the "law and order" lovers of Kansas Territory. Jones himself was in ecstasies. He sat upon his horse, contemplating the havoc he was making, and rubbing his hands with wild delight, exclaimed: "This is the happiest day of my life. I determined to make the fanatics bow before me in the dust, and kiss the territorial laws; and I have done it--by G--d, I have done it!"

And then followed scenes of reckless pillage and wanton destruction in all parts of that ill-fated town. Stores were broken into and plundered of their contents. Bolts and bars were no obstacles to the entrance of drunken and infuriated men into private dwellings, from which most of the inhabitants had fled in terror. From these everything of value was stolen, and much that was useless to the marauders was destroyed.

The closing act of this frightful drama was the burning of the house of Dr. Robinson on the brow of Mount Oread. This was set on fire after the sun had gone down, and the bright light which its flames shed over the country illuminated the paths of the retreating army, as they proceeded toward their homes, pillaging houses, stealing horses, and violating the persons of defenceless women. All these dreadful deeds were done by human authority. There is yet an account to render to a Higher Power!

During the perpetration of these atrocities, one of the pro-slavery intruders accidentally shot himself on Mount Oread, another was killed by the falling of a brick from the free-state hotel, and a third had his leg crushed and broken by falling from his horse when gallopping in pursuit of an unoffending man, whom he had mistaken for Governor Reeder.

1. Based upon John Gihon's account, and its supporting documents, of the legal and martial proceedings prior to the attack on Lawrence on May 21st, do you think the devastation to the town was preventable?
2. How can it be argued that the events in Kansas during 1856 represent the American Civil War in microcosm?

14-5 *Dred Scott v. Sanford* (1857)

The Dred Scott case had a dramatic impact on the sectional divide over slavery and inflamed the passions of abolitionists. The decision by Chief Justice Taney, who became a figure of hatred for many, declared that ex-slave Dred Scott, who was suing for Missouri citizenship, was not a recognized citizen under the Constitution of the United States. The case had direct impact on the several of the compromises put in place to avoid sectional conflict and the new Republican Party viewed it as an attempt to eliminate them.

The Question is simply this: Can a negro, whose ancestors were imported into this country, and sold as slaves, become a member of the political community formed and brought into existence by the Constitution of the United States, and as such become entitled to all the rights, and privileges, and immunities, guarantied [*sic*] by that instrument to the citizen? One of which rights is the privilege of suing in a court of the United States in the cases specified in the constitution.

. . . The only matter in issue before the Court, therefore, is, whether the descendants of such slaves, when they shall be emancipated, or who are born of parents who had become free before their birth, are citizens of a State, in the sense which the word citizen is used in the Constitution. . . .

The words "people of the United States" and "citizens" are synonymous terms. . . . They both describe the political body who, according to our republican institutions, form the sovereignty, and who hold the power and conduct the government through their representatives. . . . The question before us is, whether the class of persons described in the plea in abatement compose a portion of this people, and are constituent members of this sovereignty? We think they are not, under the word "citizens" in the Constitution, and can therefore claim none of the rights and privileges which

that instrument provides for and secures to citizens of the United States. On the contrary, they were at that time considered as a subordinate and inferior class of beings, who had been subjugated

by the dominant race, and whether emancipated or not, yet remained subject to their authority, and had no rights or privileges but such as those who held the power and the government might choose to grant them. . . .

In discussing the question, we must not confound the rights of citizenship which a State may confer within its own limits, and the rights of citizenship as a member of the Union. It does not by any means follow, because he has all the rights and privileges of a citizen of a State, that he must be a citizen of the United States. . . .

In the opinion of the court, the legislation and histories of the times, and the language used in the Declaration of Independence, show, that neither the class of persons who had been imported as slaves, nor their descendants, whether they had become free or not, were then acknowledged as a part of the people, nor intended to be included in the general words used in that memorable instrument. . . .

They had for more than a century before been regarded as beings of an inferior order, and altogether unfit to associate with the white race, either in social or political relations, and so far inferior, that they had no rights which the white man was bound to respect; and that the negro might justly and lawfully be reduced to slavery for his benefit. . . .

. . . there are two clauses in the constitution which point directly and specifically to the negro race as a separate class of persons, and show clearly that they were not regarded as a portion of the people or citizens of the government then formed.

. . . upon full and careful consideration of the subject, the court is of opinion, that, upon the facts stated. . . , Dred Scott was not a citizen of Missouri within the meaning of the constitution of the United States and not entitled as such to sue in its courts. . . .

1. Summarize the reasoning behind the argument that former slaves are not "constituent members of this sovereignty."
2. Identify and characterize the view of the court regarding "the class of persons who had been imported as slaves" and their descendants?

14-6 Abraham Lincoln, "A House Divided" (1858)

Considered America's greatest president, Lincoln was a little know politician and lawyer from Illinois when he entered into his famous debates with Stephen Douglas. He was the first of the new Republicans to be elected President which event precipitated the Southern secession movement. A moderate on the slavery question, Lincoln argued against western expansion of slavery but sought to leave it alone where it already existed. He insisted that the Civil War was a war to preserve the union but his Emancipation Proclamation changed that for many into a moral war against slavery. A master at political oratory, Lincoln is famous for many speeches and phrases which defined the issues so dramatically. One is reproduced here in "A house Divided"

If we could first know where we are, and whither we are tending, we could better judge what to do and how to do it. We are now far into the fifth year since a policy was initiated with the avowed object, and confident promise, of putting an end to slavery agitation. Under the operation of that policy, that agitation has not only not ceased but has constantly augmented. In my opinion, it will not cease until a crisis shall have been reached and passed. "A house divided against itself cannot stand." I believe this government cannot endure permanently half-slave and half-free. I do not expect the Union to be dissolved-I do not expect the house to fall-but I do expect it will cease to be divided. It will become all one thing or all the other. Either the opponents of slavery will arrest the further spread of it and place it where the public mind shall rest in the belief that it is in the course of ultimate extinction or its advocates will push it forward, till it shall become alike lawful in all the states, old as well as new-North as well as South.

1. What is Lincoln's view of America's options as it deals with slavery? Compare/Contrast his perspective with the secession of the South.
2. How do Lincoln's attitudes and actions just before and just after his inaugeration compare or contrast with his resolve that America could not exist as "a house divided" and with his desire to keep the Union together?

PART FIFTEEN
THE CIVIL WAR

15-1 Jefferson Davis, Address to the Provisional Congress of the Confederate States of America (1861)

Jefferson Davis had a long and varied career before reluctantly becoming the first and only President of the Confederacy. A West Point graduate, he was a congressman before becoming a hero in the Mexican War. That success led to his appointment as United States Senator from Mississippi. Davis later became a very able Secretary of War in the administration of Franklin Pierce. He later returned to the Senate where he was a supporter of the extension of slavery. Though he sought to avoid secession, when it happened he resigned from the Senate and was made the President of the Confederate States of America. In this document Davis justifies the Confederacy on historical and constitutional grounds.

The declaration of war made against this Confederacy by Abraham Lincoln, the President of the United States, in his proclamation issued on the 15th day of the present month, rendered it necessary, in my judgment, that you should convene at the earliest practicable moment to devise the measures necessary for the defense of the country. The occasion is indeed an extraordinary one. It justifies me in a brief review of the relations heretofore existing between us and the States which now unite in warfare against us and in a succinct statement of the events which have resulted in this warfare, to the end that mankind may pass intelligent and impartial judgment on its motives and objects. During the war waged against Great Britain by her colonies on this continent a common danger impelled them to a close alliance and to the formation of a Confederation, by the terms of which the colonies, styling themselves States, entered "*severally* into a firm league of friendship with each other for their common defense, the security of their liberties, and their mutual and general welfare, binding themselves to assist each other against all force offered to or attacks made upon them, or any of them, on account of religion, sovereignty, trade, or any other pretense whatever." In order to guard against any misconstruction of their compact, the several States made explicit declaration in a distinct article-that "*each* State *retains its* sovereignty, freedom, and independence, and every power, jurisdiction, and right which is not by this Confederation *expressly delegated* to the United States in Congress assembled." . . .

Strange, indeed, must it appear to the impartial observer, but it is none the less true that all these carefully worded clauses proved unavailing to prevent the rise and growth in the Northern States of a political school which has persistently claimed that the government thus formed was not a compact *between* States, but was in effect a national government, set up *above* and *over* the States. An organization created by the States to secure the blessings of liberty and independence against *foreign* aggression, has been gradually perverted into a machine for their control in their *domestic* affairs. The *creature* has been exalted above its *creators*; the *principles* have been made subordinate to the *agent* appointed by themselves. The people of the Southern States, whose almost exclusive occupation was agriculture, early perceived a tendency in the Northern States to render the common government subservient to their own purposes by imposing burdens on commerce as a protection to their manufacturing and shipping interests. Long and angry controversies grew out of these attempts, often successful, to benefit one section of the country at the expense of the other. And the danger of disruption arising from this cause was enhanced by the fact that the Northern population was increasing, by immigration and other causes, in a greater ratio than the population of the South. By degrees, as the Northern States gained preponderance in the National Congress, self-interest taught their people to yield ready assent to any plausible advocacy of their right as a majority to govern the minority without control. They learned to listen with impatience of their will, and so utterly have the principles of the Constitution been corrupted in the Northern mind that, in the inaugural address delivered by President Lincoln in March last, he asserts as an axiom, which he plainly deems to be undeniable, that the theory of the Constitution requires that in all cases the majority shall govern; and in another memorable instance the same Chief Magistrate did not hesitate to liken the relations between a State and the United States to those which exist between a county and the State in which it is situated and by which it was created. This is the lamentable and fundamental error on which rests the policy that has culminated in his declaration of war against these Confederate States. In addition to the long-continued and deep-seated resentment felt by the Southern States at the persistent abuse of the powers they had delegated to the Congress, for the purpose of enriching the manufacturing and shipping classes of the North at the expense of the South, there has existed for nearly half a century another subject of discord, involving interests of such transcendent magnitude as at all times to create the apprehension in the minds of many devoted lovers of the Union that its permanence was impossible. When the several States delegated certain powers to the United States Congress, a large portion of the laboring population consisted of African slaves imported into the colonies by the mother country. In twelve out of the thirteen States negro slavery existed, and the right of property in slaves was protected by law. This property was recognized in the Constitution, and provision was made against its loss by the escape of the slave. The increase in the number of slaves by further importation from Africa was also secured by a clause forbidding Congress to prohibit the slave trade anterior to a certain date, and in no clause can there be found any delegation of power to the Congress authorizing it in any manner to legislate to the prejudice, detriment, or discouragement of the owners of that species of property, or excluding it from the protection of the Government.

The climate and soil of the Northern States soon proved unpropitious to the continuance of slave labor, whilst the converse was the case at the South. Under the unrestricted free intercourse between two sections, the Northern States consulted their own interests by selling their slaves to the South and prohibiting slavery within their limits. The South were willing purchasers of a property suitable to their wants, and paid the price of the acquisition without harboring a suspicion that their quiet possession was to be disturbed by those who were inhibited not only by want of constitutional authority, but by good faith as vendors, from disquieting a title emanating from themselves. As soon, however, as the Northern States that prohibited African slavery within their limits had reached a number sufficient to give their representation a controlling voice in the Congress, a persistent and organized system of hostile measures against the rights of the owners of slaves in the Southern States was inaugurated and gradually extended. A continuous series of measures was devised and prosecuted for the purpose of rendering insecure the tenure of property in slaves. Fanatical organizations, supplied with money by voluntary subscriptions, were assiduously engaged in exciting amongst the slaves a spirit of discontent and revolt; means were furnished for their escape from their owners, and agents secretly employed to entice them to abscond; the constitutional provision for their rendition to their owners was first evaded, then openly denounced as a violation of conscientious obligation and religious duty; men were taught that it was a merit to elude, disobey, and violently oppose the execution of the laws enacted to secure the performance of the promise contained in the constitutional compact; owners of slaves were mobbed and even murdered in open day solely for applying to a magistrate for the arrest of a fugitive slave; the dogmas of these voluntary organizations soon obtained control of the Legislatures of many of the Northern States, and laws were passed providing for the punishment, by ruinous fines and long-continued imprisonment in jails and penitentiaries, of citizens of the Southern States who should dare to ask aid of the officers of the law for the recovery of their property. Emboldened by success, the theater of agitation and aggression against the clearly expressed constitutional rights of the Southern States was transferred to the Congress; Senators and Representatives were sent to the common councils of the nation, whose chief title to this distinction consisted in the display of a spirit of ultra fanaticism, and whose business was not "to promote the general welfare or insure domestic tranquility," but to awaken the bitterest hatred against the citizens of sister States by violent denunciation of their institutions; the transaction of public affairs was impeded by repeated efforts to usurp powers not delegated by the Constitution, for the purpose of impairing the security of property in slaves, and reducing those States which held slaves to a condition of inferiority. Finally a great party was organized for the purpose of obtaining the administration of the Government, with the avowed object of using its power for the total exclusion of the slave States from all participation in the benefits of the public domain acquired by all the States in common, whether by conquest or purchase; of surrounding them entirely by States in which slavery should be prohibited; of thus rendering the property in slaves so insecure as to be comparatively worthless, and thereby annihilating in effect property worth thousands of millions of dollars. This party, thus organized, succeeded in the month of November last in the election of its candidate for the Presidency of the United States.

1. Summarize Davis' argument regarding the rights of states and the rights of the United States as they pertain to the declaration of war by the North. Explain the "fundamental error" that has resulted in the war Davis is now confronted with.
2. What actions have been taken by the North to undermine and destroy the successful existence of the southern states according to Davis?
3. Summarize Davis' point of view on the causes of the civil war? What factors are largely responsible for the South's need to defend itself?

15-2 Mary Boykin Chesnut, A Confederate Lady's Diary (1861)

Born into the political and social elite of southern society, Chesnut was the daughter of a Senator and Governor of South Carolina. She married James Chesnut, one of the largest land owners in the state and soon to be Senator. After secession, he became a confederate congressman and later aide to Jefferson Davis. Mary Chesnut's house became a salon for leading members of Confederate society. During the war, Chesnut kept a diary that became famous for its portrayal of the Confederacy. This selection reveals the ambivalence that many in the South had towards slavery.

I wonder if it be a sin to think slavery a curse to any land. Sumner said not one word of this hated institution which is not true. Men & women are punished when their masters & mistresses are brutes & not when they do wrong-& then we live surrounded by prostitutes. An abandoned woman is sent out of any decent house elsewhere. Who thinks any worse of a Negro or Mulatto woman for being a thing we can't name. God forgive *us*, but ours is a *monstrous* system & wrong & iniquity. Perhaps the rest of the world is as bad. This is *only* what I see: like the patriarchs of old, our men live all in one house with their wives & their concubines, & the Mulattos one sees in every family exactly resemble the white children-& every lady tells you who is the father of all the Mulatto children in everybody's household, but those in her own, she seems to think drop from the clouds or pretends so to think-. Good women we have, *but* they talk of *nastiness tho* they never do wrong; they talk day & night of -. My disgust sometimes is boiling over-but they are, I believe, in conduct the purest women God ever made. Thank God for my countrywomen-alas for the men! No worse than men everywhere, but the lower their mistresses, the more degraded they must be.

My mother-in-law told me when I was first married not to send my female servants in the street on errands. They were there tempted, led astray-& then she said placidly, "So they told *me* when I came here-& I was very particular, *but you see with what* result." Mr. Harris said it was so patriarchal. So it is-flocks & herds & slaves-& wife Leah does not suffice. Rachel must be *added*, if not *married* & all the time they seem to think themselves patterns-models of husbands & fathers.

Mrs. Davis told me "everybody described my husband's father as an odd character, a Millionaire who did nothing for his son whatever, left him to struggle with poverty," &c. I replied, "Mr. Chesnut Senior thinks himself the best of fathers-& his son thinks likewise. I have nothing to say-but it is true, he has no money but what he makes as a lawyer," &c. Again I say, my countrywomen are as pure as angels-tho surrounded by another race who are-the social evil!

1. What are Chesnut's sentiments and chief concerns in this account? In what ways does this diary entry reveal a "pre-war" sense of awareness? In other words, identify the events and thoughts that make up this entry? How might these concerns change in the coming months?

15-3   Why They Fought (1861)

Samuel Storrow was born in Boston, Massachusetts, July 24, 1843. When the war broke out, Samuel was seventeen years old and in college. Although desiring to join the army, his wish met with objections from his parents, who considered him too young for military service. In the spring of 1862, Storrow was forced to obtain a leave of absence from college to recover from an eye infection and sailed for the Azores. He found, on his return, that his father was in Europe, and that his elder brother, Charles, had just entered the army with a commission as captain in the Forty-Fourth Massachusetts—then mustering for immediate service. Samuel returned to college, but immediately wrote the following letter to his father to ask his permission to join the regiment.

Captain George E. Pickett was stationed at Fort Bellingham on Puget Sound in the northwest when the news came about his native Virginia's secession from the Union. Faced with the need to make a quick decision about his future, Pickett's destiny was determined by his notion of loyalty. Writing to his fiancé, Sally Corbell, the future Confederate general explained his decision to resign his commission and cast his lot with the Confederacy. Pickett would later participate in the fateful charge at the Battle of Gettysburg that today bears his name.

Source: Harvard Memorial Biographies
http://www.geocities.com/Pentagon/2126/hmb.storrow.html
George Edward Pickett, *The Heart of a Soldier, As Revealed in the Intimate Letters of Genl. George E. Pickett C.S.A.:* Electronic Edition.
http://docsouth.unc.edu/pickett/pickett.html#pick33

As soon as I landed I heard of the formation of the 44th, and Charles's commission. I at once wished to join this; but mother and Charles both opposed it, saying that it was your intention and desire that I should rejoin my Class at once, and expressed themselves so strongly against my enlisting, that on the following Monday I went to Cambridge, and resumed my studies with what zeal I could. . . .The excitement and intensity of feeling, the daily agony of doubt and suspense, is a thing scarcely to be appreciated in full by one who was not here at the time, and who did not pass through it. I assure you, my dear father, I know nothing in the course of my life which has caused me such deep and serious thought as this trying crisis in the history of our nation. What is the worth of this man's life or of that man's education, if this great and glorious fabric of our Union, raised with such toil and labor by our forefathers, and transmitted to us in value increased tenfold, is to be shattered to pieces by traitorous hands, and allowed to fall crumbling into the dust? If our country and our nationality is to perish, better that we should all perish with it, and not survive to see it a laughing-stock for all posterity to be pointed at as the unsuccessful trial of republicanism. It seems to me the part of a coward to stay at home and allow others to fight my battles and incur dangers for me. What shame, what mortification would it cause me years hence to be obliged to confess that, in the great struggle for our national existence, I stood aloof, an idle spectator, without any peculiar ties to retain me at home, and yet not caring or not daring to do anything in the defense of my country. . . .The only reason which could at all deter me from enlisting was your absence. I felt reluctant to take so important a step without your advice and consent; and yet I felt that, had you been here, you would have given me your blessing and bade me go.

Here was a regiment formed and commanded by friends and kinsmen, and surpassing others in the material of which it was composed. If I embraced this opportunity, I should be among friends and equals, instead of being forced to accept as my associates any with whom I might be placed. If I did not make my decision quickly, the chance would be lost; and I knew that if I went, you would agree with mother in much preferring that Charles and I should be together in the same regiment. At that time, too, a draft seemed almost certain; and, as several thousand were said to be wanting to complete the quota of Boston, the chance of being drawn was by no means small. . . .

Poor mother, she has had a hard time during your absence, especially in coming to a decision about me. . . .Assure her fully of your approval of the course she has taken, and I shall be happy too. . . .Everybody thinks that she has acted nobly, and that you have reason to be proud of your wife was we have of our mother.

I have tried as well as I can, and I find that it is but poorly to give you some idea of my feelings on this subject. I feel well satisfied that I have done what, upon careful deliberation, has seemed to me most in accordance with all my duties. I have looked at the matter from every point of view; and if I shall seem to you to have arrived at a wrong conclusion, believe me, it was not from any hasty impulse of the moment, but from the sober dictates of my best judgment. If I have unwittingly made the wrong choice, God forgive me; I did what I thought was for the best.

Ever you affectionate son,
Samuel Storrow

SEVERAL weeks ago I wrote quite a long letter from far-away San Francisco to a very dear little girl, and told her that a certain soldier who wears one of her long, silken ringlets next his heart was homeward bound and that he hoped a line of welcome would meet him on his arrival in his native state. He told her of the difficulties he had experienced in being relieved from his post, of how sorry he was to sheathe the sword which had helped to bring victory to the country for which he had fought, and how sorry he was to say good-by to his little command and to part from his faithful and closest companion, his dog, and his many dear friends; but sorrier still for the existing circumstances which made this severance necessary. He told her many things for which, with him, she will be sorry, and some of which he hopes will make her glad. He is troubled by finding no answer to this long letter which, having at that time no notion of the real conditions here, he is afraid was written too freely by far.

No, my child, I had no conception of the intensity of feeling, the bitterness and hatred toward those who were so lately our friends and are now our enemies. I, of course, have always strenuously opposed disunion, not as doubting the right of secession, which was taught in our text-book at West Point, but as gravely questioning its expediency. I believed that the revolutionary spirit which infected both North and South was but a passing phase of fanaticism which would perish under the rebuke of all good citizens, who would surely unite in upholding the Constitution; but when that great assembly, composed of ministers, lawyers, judges, chancellors, statesmen, mostly white haired men of thought, met in South Carolina and when their districts were called crept noiselessly to the table in the center of the room and affixed their signatures to the parchment on which the ordinance of secession was inscribed, and when in deathly silence, spite of the gathered multitude, General Jamison arose and without preamble read: "The ordinance of secession has been signed and ratified; I proclaim the State of South Carolina an independent sovereignty," and lastly, when my old boyhood's friend called for an invasion, it was evident that both the advocates and opponents of secession had read the portents aright.

You know, my little lady, some of those cross-stitched mottoes on the cardboard samplers which used to hang on my nursery wall, such as, "He who provides not for his own household is worse than an infidel" and "Charity begins at home," made a lasting impression upon me; and while I love my neighbor, i.e., my country, I love my household, i.e., my state, more, and I could not be an infidel and lift my sword against my own kith and kin, even though I do believe, my most wise little counselor and confidante, that the measure of American greatness can be achieved only under one flag, and I fear, alas, there can never again reign for either of us the true spirit of national unity whether divided under two flags or united under one.

We did not tarry even for a day in 'Frisco, but under assumed names my friend, Sam Barron, and I sailed for New York, where we arrived on the very day that Sam's father, Commodore Barron, was brought there a prisoner, which fact was proclaimed aloud by the pilot amid cheers of the passengers and upon our landing heralded by the newsboys with more cheers. Poor Sam had a hard fight to hide his feelings and to avoid arrest. We separated as mere ship acquaintances, and went by different routes to meet again, as arranged, at the house of Doctor Paxton, a Southern sympathizer and our friend.

On the next day we left for Canada by the earliest train. Thence we made our perilous way back south again, barely escaping arrest several times, and finally arrived in dear old Richmond, September 13th, just four days ago. I at once enlisted in the army and the following day was commissioned Captain. But so bitter is the feeling here that my being unavoidably delayed so long in avowing my allegiance to my state has been most cruelly and severely criticized by friends—yes, and even relatives, too.

Now, little one, if you had the very faintest idea how happy a certain captain in the C.S.A. (My, but that "C" looks queer!) would be to look into your beautiful, soul-speaking eyes and hear your wonderfully musical voice, I think you would let him know by wire where he could find you. I shall almost listen for the electricity which says, "I am at —. Come." I know that you will have mercy on your devoted SOLDIER.

1. What factors led Samuel Storrow to desire military service? Why do you think his parents submitted in 1862 when they had refused to grant their permission the previous year?
2. What made George E. Pickett, who was personally opposed to disunion, resign his commission and side with the Confederacy? How do you think he would define "loyalty"? How do Pickett's motives differ from Storrow's?

15-4 Abraham Lincoln, Gettysburg Address (1863)

Perhaps the most famous speech in American history, the Gettysburg Address was considered a failure by many at the time it was given. Presented at the dedication of the Battlefield at Gettysburg, Lincoln was not even the featured speaker. His very short speech (only 10 sentences) was overlooked by many. Edward Everett (who gave a two hour oration just before) summed up the power of Lincoln's speech, however, when he said "I should be glad if I could flatter myself that I came as near to the central idea of the occasion in two hours as you did in two minutes."

Four score and seven years ago our fathers brought forth on this continent a new nation, conceived in liberty, and dedicated to the proposition that all men are created equal.

Now we are engaged in a great civil war, testing whether that nation, or any nation so conceived and so dedicated, can long endure. We are met on a great battlefield of that war. We have come to dedicate a portion of that field as a final resting-place for those who here gave their lives that nation might live. It is altogether fitting and proper that we should do this.

But, in a larger sense, we cannot dedicate-we cannot consecrate-we cannot hallow-this ground. The brave men, living and dead, who struggled here, have consecrated it far above our poor power to add or detract. The world will little note nor long remember what we say here, but it can never forget what they did here. It is for us, the living, rather, to be dedicated here to the unfinished work which they who fought here have thus far so nobly advanced. It is rather for us to be here dedicated to the great task remaining before us-that from these honored dead we take increased devotion to that cause for which they gave the last full measure of devotion; that we here highly resolve that these dead shall not have died in vain; that this nation, under God, shall have a new birth of freedom; and that government of the people, by the people, for the people, shall not perish from the earth.

1. How does Lincoln honor the battle of Gettysburg in his address? What did the soldiers fight for in his opinion?
2. How does Lincoln connect the Battle of Gettysburg, the civil war, and the independence of America? How does his view of America in this speech differ from that of the southern leadership?

15-5   General William Tecumseh Sherman on War (1864)

Following the withdrawal of Confederate troops from Atlanta, Georgia, on September 1, 1864, General William Tecumseh Sherman issued Special Field Order No. 67 directing that Atlanta be evacuated by all civilians except those necessary for "the proper departments of government." The order met with a chorus of disapproval. Mayor James Calhoun and the city council asked the general to reconsider on the grounds that many citizens were too weak or infirm to travel and assume the role of refugee. Although sympathetic to a degree, Sherman was unyielding. In his response to Calhoun (included below), Sherman put into words his view of war and, in the months to come, further translated his ideas into practice during his "March to the Sea." In so doing, Sherman became the personification of "hard war."

Source: The United States War Department, *The War of the Rebellion: A Compilation of the Official Records of the Union and Confederate Armies*, 128 vols. (Washington: Government Printing Office, 1880–1901), Series I, vol. 39, pt. II, pp. 837-838; The Sage Page for American History and Literature, http://www.nv.cc.va.us/home/nvsageh/Hist121/Part4/ShermanAtl.htm

Special Field Orders, No. 67.
Hdqrs. Mil. Div. of the Mississippi,
In the Field, Atlanta, Ga.,
September 8, 1864.

I. The city of Atlanta, being exclusively required for warlike purposes, will at once be vacated by all except the armies of the United States and such civilian employés as may be retained by the proper departments of government.

II. The chief quartermaster, Colonel Easton, will at once take possession of buildings of all kinds, and of all staple articles, such as cotton, tobacco, & c., and will make such disposition of them as is required by existing regulations, or such orders as he may receive from time to time from the proper authorities.

III. The chief engineer will promptly reconnoiter the city and suburbs, and indicate the sites needed for the permanent defense of the place, together with any houses, sheds, or shanties that stand in his way, that they may be set apart for destruction. Colonel Easton will then, on consultation with the proper officers of the ordinance, quartermaster, commissary, medical, and railroad departments, set aside such buildings and lots of ground as will be needed for them, and have them suitably marked and set apart. He will then, on consultation with Generals Thomas and Slocum, set apart such as may be necessary to the proper administration of the military duties of the Department of the Cumberland and of the post of Atlanta, and all buildings and materials not thus embraced will be held subject to the use of the Government as may hereafter arise, according to the just rules of the quartermaster's department.

IV. No general, staff, or other officers, or any soldier will on any pretense occupy any house or shanty, unless it be embraced in the limits assigned as the camp of the troops to which such general or staff belongs, but the chief quartermaster may allow the troops to use boards, shingles, or materials of buildings, barns, sheds, warehouses, and shanties, not needed by the proper departments of government, to be used in the reconstruction of such shanties and bivouacs as the troops and officers serving with them require, and he will also provide as early as practicable the proper allowance of tents for the use of the officers and men in their encampments.

V. In proper time just arrangements will be made for the supply to the troops of all articles they may need over and above the clothing, provisions, & c., furnished by Government, and on no pretense whatever will traders, manufacturers, or sutlers be allowed to settle in the limits of fortified places, and if these manage to come in spite of this notice, the quartermaster will seize their stores and appropriate them to the use of the troops, and deliver the parties or other unauthorized citizens who thus place their individual interests above that of the United States, in the hands of some provost marshal, to be put to labor on the forts or conscripted into one of the regiments or batteries already in service.

VI. The same general principles will apply to all military posts south of Chattanooga.

By order of Maj. Gen. W. T. Sherman:

L. M. DAYTON,
Aide-de-Camp.

Notice.   Atlanta, Ga., *September 8, 1864.*

To the Citizens of Atlanta:

Major-General Sherman instructs me to say to you that you must all leave Atlanta; that as many of you as want to go North can do so, and that as many as want to go South can do so, and that all can take with them their movable property, servants included, if they want to go, but that no force is to be used, and that he will furnish transportation for persons and property as far as Rough and Ready, from whence it is expected General Hood will assist in carrying it on. Like transportation will be furnished for people and property going North, and it is required that all things contemplated by this notice will be carried into execution as soon as possible.

All persons are requested to leave their names and number in their families with the undersigned as early as possible, that estimates may be made of the quantity of transportation required.

JAMES M. CALHOUN,
Mayor.

HEADQUARTERS MILITARY DIVISION
OF THE MISSISSIPPI, IN THE FIELD, ATLANTA, GEORGIA
September 12, 1864

JAMES M. CALHOUN, Mayor, E. E. PAWSON and S. C. WELLS, representing City Council of Atlanta.

GENTLEMEN: I have your letter of the 11th, in the nature of a petition to revoke my orders removing all the inhabitants from Atlanta. I have read it carefully, and give full credit to your statements of the distress that will be occasioned, and yet shall not revoke my orders, because they were not designed to meet the humanities of the case, but to prepare for the future struggles in which millions of good people outside of Atlanta have a deep interest. We must have peace, not only at Atlanta, but in all America. To secure this, we must stop the war that now desolates our once happy and favored country. To stop war, we must defeat the rebel armies which are arrayed against the laws and Constitution that all must respect and obey. To defeat those armies, we must prepare the way to reach them in their recesses, provided with the arms and instruments which enable us to accomplish our purpose.

Now, I know the vindictive nature of our enemy, that we may have many years of military operations from this quarter; and, therefore, deem it wise and prudent to prepare in time. The use of Atlanta for warlike purposes is inconsistent with its character as a home for families. There will be no manufactures, commerce, or agriculture here, for the maintenance of families, and sooner or later want will compel the inhabitants to go. Why not go now, when all the arrangements are completed for the transfer, instead of waiting till the plunging shot of contending armies will renew the scenes of the past month? Of course, I do not apprehend any such thing at this moment, but you do not suppose this army will be here until the war is over. I cannot discuss this subject with you fairly, because I cannot impart to you what we propose to do, but I assert that our military plans make it necessary for the inhabitants to go away, and I can only renew my offer of services to make their exodus in any direction as easy and comfortable as possible.

You cannot qualify war in harsher terms than I will. War is cruelty, and you cannot refine it; and those who brought war into our country deserve all the curses and maledictions a people can pour out. I know I had no hand in making this war, and I know I will make more sacrifices today than any of you to secure peace. But you cannot have peace and a division of our country. If the United States submits to a division now, it will not stop, but will go on until we reap the fate of Mexico, which is eternal war. The United States does and must assert its authority, wherever it once had power; for, if it relaxes one bit to pressure, it is gone, and I believe that such is the national feeling. This feeling assumes various shapes, but always comes back to that of Union. Once admit the Union, once more acknowledge the authority of the national Government, and, instead of devoting your houses and streets and roads to the dread uses of war, I and this army become at once your protectors and supporters, shielding you from danger, let it come from what quarter it may. I know that a few individuals cannot resist a torrent of error and passion, such as swept the South into rebellion, but you can point out, so that we may know those who desire a government, and those who insist on war and its desolation.

You might as well appeal against the thunderstorm as against these terrible hardships of war. They are inevitable, and the only way the people of Atlanta can hope once more to live in peace and quiet at home, is to stop the war, which can only be done by admitting that it began in error and is perpetuated in pride.

We don't want your negroes, or your horses, or your houses, or your lands, or any thing you have, but we do want and will have a just obedience to the laws of the United States. That we will have, and, if it involves the destruction of your improvements, we cannot help it.

You have heretofore read public sentiment in your newspapers, that live by falsehood and excitement; and the quicker you seek for truth in other quarters, the better. I repeat then that, by the original compact of Government, the United States had certain rights in Georgia, which have never been relinquished and never will be; that the South began war by seizing forts, arsenals, mints, customhouses, etc., etc., long before Mr. Lincoln was installed, and before the South had one jot or tittle of provocation. I myself have seen in Missouri, Kentucky, Tennessee, and Mississippi, hundreds and thousands of women and children fleeing from your armies and desperadoes, hungry and with bleeding feet. In Memphis, Vicksburg, and Mississippi, we fed thousands upon thousands of the families of rebel soldiers left on our hands, and whom we could not see starve.

Now that war comes home to you, you feel very different. You deprecate its horrors, but did not feel them when you sent car-loads of soldiers and ammunition, and moulded shells and shot, to carry war into Kentucky and Tennessee, to desolate the homes of hundreds and thousands of good people who only asked to live in peace at their old homes, and under the Government of their inheritance. But these comparisons are idle. I want peace, and believe it can only be reached through union and war, and I will ever conduct war with a view to perfect and early success.

But, my dear sirs, when peace does come, you may call on me for any thing. Then will I share with you the last cracker, and watch with you to shield your homes and families against danger from every quarter.

Now you must go, and take with you the old and feeble, feed and nurse them, and build for them, in more quiet places, proper habitations to shield them against the weather until the mad passions of men cool down, and allow the Union and peace once more to settle over your old homes at Atlanta.

Yours in haste,

W. T. SHERMAN, Major-General commanding.

1. What was General Sherman's justification for demanding the evacuation of civilians from Atlanta? Do you find his explanation reasonable? What rights should civilians have in times of war?
2. How does Sherman define war? What was his goal in warfare other than victory?

PART SIXTEEN
RECONSTRUCTION

16-1 Mississippi Black Code (1865)

In the aftermath of Emancipation, southern states passed a variety of laws known as "Black Codes". Although these codes varied from state to state, they were all aimed at tightly controlling the lives and labor of newly freed people. The codes angered Congress and the northern pubic, who viewed them as southern attempts to roll back Emancipation and subvert Reconstruction. The Civil Rights Act of 1866, the Fourteenth Amendment, and the Military Reconstitution Act of 1867 were all designed in part to counter the Black Codes.

The Civil Rights of Freedmen in Mississippi

Section 1. Be it enacted by the legislature of the State of Mississippi, That all freedmen, free Negroes, and mulattoes may sue and be sued, implead and be impleaded in all the courts of law and equity of this state, and may acquire personal property and choses in action, by descent or purchase, any may dispose of the same, in the same manner, and to the same extent that white persons may: Provided that the provisions of this section shall not be so construed as to allow any freedman, free Negro, or mulatto to rent or lease any lands or tenements, except in incorporated town or cities in which places the corporate authorities shall control the same.

Sec. 2. Be it further enacted, That all freedmen, free Negroes, and mulattoes may intermarry with each other, in the same manner and under the same regulations that are provided by law for white persons: Provided, that the clerk of probate shall keep separate records of the same.

Sec. 3. Be it further enacted, That all freedmen, free Negroes, and mulattoes, who do now and have heretofore lived and cohabited together as husband and wife shall be taken and held in law as legally married, and the issue shall be taken and held as legitimate for all purposes. That it shall not be lawful for any freedman, free Negro, or mulatto to intermarry with any white person; nor for any white person to intermarry with any freedman, free Negro, or mulatto; any person who shall so intermarry shall be deemed guilty of felony and, on conviction thereof, shall be confined in the state penitentiary for life; and those shall be deemed freedmen, free Negroes, and mulattoes who are of pure Negro blood, and those descended from a Negro to the third generation inclusive, though one ancestor of each generation may have been a white person.

Sec. 4. Be it further enacted, That in addition to cases in which freedmen, free Negroes, and mulattoes are now by law competent witnesses, freedmen, free Negroes, or mulattoes shall be competent in civil cases when a party or parties to the suit, either plaintiff or plaintiffs, defendant or defendants, also in cases where freedmen, free Negroes, and mulattoes is or are either plaintiff or plaintiffs, defendant or defendants, and a white person or white persons is or are the opposing party or parties, plaintiff or plaintiffs, defendant or defendants. They shall also be competent witnesses in all criminal prosecutions where the crime charged is alleged to have been committed by a white person upon or against the person or property of a freedman, free Negro, or mulatto: Provided that in all cases said witnesses shall be examined in open court on the stand, except, however, they may be examined before the grand jury, and shall in all cases be subject to the rules and tests of the common law as to competency and credibility.

Sec. 5. Be it further enacted, That every freedman, free Negro, and mulatto shall, on the second Monday of January, one thousand eight hundred and sixty-six, and annually thereafter, have a lawful home or employment. . . .

Sec. 6. Be it further enacted, That all contracts for labor made with freedmen, free Negroes, and mulattoes for a longer period than one month shall be in writing and in duplicate, attested and read to said freedman, free Negro, or mulatto, by a beat, city or county officers, or two disinterested white persons of the country in which the labor is to be performed, of which each party shall have one; and said contracts shall be taken and held as entire contracts, and if the laborer shall quit the service of the employer, before expiration of his term of service, without good cause, he shall forfeit his wages for that year, up to the time of quitting.

Sec. 7. Be it further enacted, That every civil officer shall, and every person may, arrest and carry back to his or her legal employer any freedman, free Negro, or mulatto who shall have quit the service of his or her employer before the expiration of his or her term of service without good cause, and said officer and person shall be entitled to receive for arresting and carrying back every deserting employee aforesaid, the sum of five dollars, and ten cents per mile from the place of arrest to the place of delivery, and the same shall be paid by the employer, and held as a set-off for so much against the wages of said deserting employee.

Sec. 8. Be it further enacted, That upon affidavit made by the employer of any freedman, free Negro, or mulatto, or other credible person, before any justice of the peace or member of the board of police, that any freedman, free Negro, or mulatto, legally employed by said employer, has illegally deserted said employment, such justice of the peace or member of the board of police shall issue his warrant or warrants, returnable before himself, or other such officer, directed to any sheriff, constable, or special deputy, commanding him to arrest said deserter and return him or her to said employer, and the like proceedings shall be had as provided in the preceding section. . . .

Sec. 9. Be it further enacted, That if any person shall persuade or attempt to persuade, entice, or cause any freedman, free Negro, or mulatto to desert from the legal employment of any person, before the expiration of his or her term of service, or shall knowingly employ any such deserting freedman, free Negro, or mulatto, or shall knowingly give or sell to any such deserting freedman, free Negro, or mulatto, any food, raiment, or other thing, he or she shall be guilty of a misdemeanor and, upon conviction, shall be fined not less than twenty-five dollars and not more then two hundred dollars and the costs, and, if said fine and costs shall not be immediately paid, the court shall sentence said convict to not exceeding two months' imprisonment in the county jail, and he or she shall moreover be liable to the party injured in damages: . . . .

Sec. 10. Be it further enacted, That it shall be lawful for any freedman, free Negro, or mulatto to charge any white person, freedman, free Negro, or mulatto, by affidavit, with any criminal offense against his or her person or property and upon such affidavit the proper process shall be issued and executed as if said affidavit was made by a white person, and it shall be lawful for any freedman, free Negro, or mulatto, in any action, suit, or controversy pending, or about to be instituted, in any court of law or equity of this state, to make all needful and lawful affidavits, as shall be necessary for the institution, prosecution, or defense of such suit or controversy.

Sec. 11. Be it further enacted, That the penal laws of this state, in all cases not otherwise specially provided for, shall apply and extend to all freedmen, free Negroes, and mulattoes. . . .

Approved November 25, 1865

1. Identify and explain the actual freedoms and rights that are granted under the Mississippi Black Code.
2. What restrictions and laws enacted by the Black Code effectively extend the racist doctrines of pre-Civil War slavery? What freedoms are notably denied under the Code?

16-2 The Fourteenth Amendment (1868)

Southern attempts to deprive African Americans of their rights stimulated constitutional remedies. Congressional radical reconstruction hoped that constitutional guarantees of citizenship and federal protection of rights would alleviate oppressive state laws.

Sec. 1. All persons born or naturalized in the United States, and subject to the jurisdiction thereof, are citizens of the United States and of the State wherein they reside. No State shall make or enforce any law which shall abridge the privileges or immunities of citizens of the United States; nor shall any State deprive any person of life, liberty, or property, without due process of law; nor deny to any person within its jurisdiction the equal protection of the laws.

Sec. 2. Representatives shall be apportioned among the several States according to their respective numbers, counting the whole number of persons in each State, excluding Indians not taxed. But when the right to vote at any election for the choice of electors for President and Vice President of the United States, Representatives in Congress, the Executive and Judicial officers of a State, or the members of the Legislature thereof, is denied to any of the male inhabitants of such State, being twenty-one years of age, and citizens of the United States, or in any way abridged, except for participation in rebellion, or other crime, the basis of representation therein shall be reduced in the proportion which the number of such male citizens shall bear to the whole number of male citizens twenty-one years of age in such State.

Sec. 3. No person shall be a Senator or Representative in Congress, or elector of President and Vice President, or hold any office, civil or military, under the United States, or under any State, who, having previously taken an oath, as a member of Congress, or as an officer of the United States, or as a member of any State legislature, or as an executive or judicial officer of any State, to support the Constitution of the United States, shall have engaged in insurrection or rebellion against the same, or given aid or comfort to the enemies thereof. But Congress may by a vote of two-thirds of each House, remove such disability.

Sec. 4. The validity of the public debt of the United States, authorized by law, including debts incurred for payment of pensions and bounties for services in suppressing insurrection or rebellion, shall not be questioned. But neither the United States nor any State shall assume or pay any debt or obligation incurred in aid of insurrection or rebellion against the united States, or any claim for the loss or emancipation of any slave; but all such debts, obligations and claims shall be held illegal and void.

Sec. 5. The Congress shall have power to enforce, by appropriate legislation, the provisions of this article.

1. Explain the focus, scope, and effect of the Fourteenth Amendment.

16-3 Albion W. Tourgee, Letter on Ku Klux Klan Activities (1870)

Founded by former Confederate general Nathan Bedford Forrest in Tennessee, the Ku Klux Klan spread across the South. As this excerpt shows, southern whites in the Ku Klux Klan used brutality and violence against those who supported Reconstruction governments and efforts to improve conditions for African Americans.

Some of the Outrages-Letter from Judge Tourgee to Senator Abbott

Greensboro, N.C. May 24, 1870.
Gen. Jos. C. Abbott

My Dear General:

It is my mournful duty to inform you that our friend John W. Stephens, State Senator from Caswell, is dead. He was foully murdered by the Ku-Klux in the Grand Jury room of the Court House on Saturday or Saturday night last. The circumstances attending his murder have not yet fully come to light there. So far as I can learn, I judge these to have been the circumstances: He was one of the Justices of the Peace in that township, and was accustomed to hold court in that room on Saturdays. It is evident that he was set upon by some one while holding this court, or immediately after its close, and disabled by a sudden attack, otherwise there would have been a very sharp resistance, as he was a man, and always went armed to the teeth. He was stabbed five or six times, and then hanged on a hook in the Grand Jury room, where he was found on Sunday morning. Another brave, honest Republican citizen has met his fate at the hands of these fiends. Warned of his danger, and fully cognizant of the terrible risk which surrounded him, he still manfully refused to quit the field. Against the advice of his friends, against the entreaties of his family, he constantly refused to leave those who had stood by him in the day of his disgrace and peril. He was accustomed to say that 3,000 poor, ignorant, colored Republican voters in that county had stood by him and elected him, at the risk of persecution and starvation, and that he had no idea of abandoning them to the Ku-Klux. He was determined to stay with them, and either put an end to these outrages, or die with the other victims of Rebel hate and national apathy: Nearly six months ago I declared my belief that before the election in August next the Ku-Klux would have killed more men in the State than there would be members to be elected to the Legislature. A good beginning has been made toward the fulfillment of this prophecy. The following counties have already filled, or nearly so, their respective "quotas:" Jones County, quota full, excess 1; Orange County quota full; excess, 1. Caswell County quota full; excess, 2; Alamance County quota full; excess, 1. Chatham County quota nearly full. Or, to state the matter differently, there have been twelve murders in five counties of the district during the past eighteen months, by bands of disguised villains. In addition to this, from the best information I can derive, I am of the opinion that in this district alone there have been 1,000 outrages of a less serious nature perpetrated by the same masked fiends. Of course this estimate is not made from any absolute record, nor is it possible to ascertain with accuracy the entire number of beatings and other outrages which have been perpetrated. The uselessness, the utter futility of complaint from the lack of ability in the laws to punish is fully known to all. The danger of making such complaint is also well understood. It is therefore not unfrequently by accident that the outrage is found out, and unquestionably it is frequently absolutely concealed. Thus, a respectable, hard working white carpenter was working for a neighbor, when accidentally his shirt was torn, and disclosed his back scarred and beaten. The poor fellow begged for the sake of his wife and children that nothing might be said about it, as the Ku-Klux had threatened to kill him if he disclosed how he had been outraged. Hundreds of cases have come to my notice and that of my solicitor. . . .

Men and women come scarred, mangled, and bruised, and say: "The Ku-Klux came to my house last night and beat me almost to death, and my old woman right smart, and shot into the house, 'bust' the door down, and told me they would kill me if I made complaint;" and the bloody mangled forms attest the truth of their declarations. On being asked if any one knew any of the party it will be ascertained that there was no recognition, or only the most uncertain and doubtful one. In such cases as these nothing can be done by the court. We have not been accustomed to enter them on record. A man of the best standing in Chatham told me that he could count up 200 and upward in that county. In Alamance County, a citizen in conversation one evening enumerated upward of 50 cases which had occurred within his own knowledge, and in one section of the county. He gave it as his opinion that there had been 200 cases in that county. I have no idea that he exceeded the proper estimate. That was six months ago, and I am satisfied that another hundred would not cover the work done in that time.

These crimes have been of every character imaginable. Perhaps the most usual has been the dragging of men and women from their beds, and beating their naked bodies with hickory switches, or as witnesses in an examination the other day said, "sticks" between a "switch" and a "club." From 50 to 100 blows is the usual allowance, sometimes 200 and 300 blows are administered. Occasionally an instrument of torture is owned. Thus in one case two women, one 74 years old, were taken out, stripped naked, and beaten with a paddle, with several holes bored through it. The paddle was about 30 inches long, 3 or 4 inches wide, and 1/4 of an inch thick, of oak. Their bodies were so bruised and beaten that they were sickening to behold. They were white women and of good character until the younger was seduced, and swore her child to its father. Previous to that and so far as others were concerned her character was good.

Again, there is sometimes a fiendish malignity and cunning displayed in the form and character of the outrages. For instance, a colored man was placed astride of a log, and an iron staple driven through his person into the log. In another case, after a band of them had in turn violated a young negro girl, she was forced into bed with a colored man, their bodies were bound together face to face, and the fire from the hearth piled upon them. The K. K. K. rode off and left them, with shouts of laughter. Of course the bed was soon in flames, and somehow they managed to crawl out, though terribly burned and scarred. The house was burned.

I could give other incidents of cruelty, such as hanging up a boy of nine years old until he was nearly dead, to make him tell where his father was hidden, and beating an old negress of 103 years old with garden pallings because she would not own that she was afraid of the Ku-Klux. But it is unnecessary to go into further detail. In this district I estimate their offenses as follows, in the past ten months: Twelve murders, 9 rapes, 11 arsons, 7 mutilations, ascertained and most of them on record. In some no identification could be made.

Four thousand or 5,000 houses have been broken open, and property or persons taken out. In all cases all arms are taken and destroyed. Seven hundred or 800 persons have been beaten or otherwise maltreated. These of course are partly persons living in the houses which were broken into.

And yet the Government sleeps. The poor disarmed nurses of the Republican party-those men by whose ballots the Republican party holds power-who took their lives in their hands when they cast their ballots for U.S. Grant and other officials-all of us who happen to be beyond the pale of the Governmental regard-must be sacrificed, murdered, scourged, mangled, because some contemptible party scheme might be foiled by doing us justice. I could stand it very well to fight for Uncle Sam, and was never known to refuse an invitation on such an occasion; but this lying down, tied hand and foot with the shackles of the law, to be killed by the very dregs of the rebellion, the scum of the earth, and not allowed either the consolation of fighting or the satisfaction that our "fall" will be noted by the Government, and protection given to others thereby, is somewhat too hard. I am ashamed of the nation that will let its citizens be slain by scores, and scourged by thousands, and offer no remedy or protection. I am ashamed of a State which has not sufficient strength to protect its own officers in the discharge of their duties, nor guarantee the safety of any man's domicile throughout its length and breadth. I am ashamed of a party which, with the reins of power in its hands, has not nerve or decision enough to arm its own adherents, or to protect them from assassinations at the hands of their opponents. A General who in time of war would permit 2,000 or 3,000 of his men to be bushwhacked and destroyed by private treachery even in an enemy's country without any one being punished for it would be worthy of universal execration, and would get it, too. How much more worthy of detestation is a Government which in time of peace will permit such wholesale slaughter of its citizens? It is simple cowardice, inertness, and wholesale demoralization. The wholesale slaughter of the war has dulled our Nation's sense of horror at the shedding of blood, and the habit of regarding the South as simply a laboratory, where every demagogue may carry on his reconstructionary experiments at will, and not as an integral party of the Nation itself, has led our Government to shut its eyes to the atrocities of these times. Unless these evils are speedily remedied, I tell you, General, the Republican party has signed its death warrant. It is a party of cowards or idiots-I don't care which alternative is chosen. The remedy is in our hands, and we are afraid or too dull to bestir ourselves and use it.

But you will tell me that Congress is ready and willing to act if it only knew what to do. Like the old Irish woman it wrings its hands and cries, "O Lawk, O Lawk; if I only knew which way." And yet this same Congress has the control of the militia and can organize its own force in every county in the United States, and arm more or less of it. This same Congress has the undoubted right to guarantee and provide a republican government, and protect every citizen in "life, liberty, and the pursuit of happiness," as well as the power conferred by the XVth Amendment. And yet we suffer and die in peace and murderers walk abroad with the blood yet fresh upon their garments, unharmed, unquestioned and unchecked. Fifty thousand dollars given to good detectives would secure, if well used, a complete knowledge of all this gigantic organization of murderers. In connection with an organized and armed militia, it would result in the apprehension of any number of these Thugs *en masque* and with blood on their hands. What then is the remedy? *First:* Let Congress give to the U. S. Courts, or to Courts of the States under its own laws, cognizance of this class of crimes, as crimes against the nation, and let it provide that this legislation be enforced. Why not, for instance, make going armed and masked or disguised, or masked or disguised in the night time, an act of insurrection or sedition? *Second:* Organize militia, National-State militia is a nuisance-and arm as many as may be necessary in each county to enforce its laws. *Third:* Put detectives at work to get

182

hold of this whole organization. Its ultimate aim is unquestionably to revolutionize the Government. If we have not pluck enough for this, why then let us just offer our throats to the knife, emasculate ourselves, and be a nation of self-subjugated slaves at once.

And now, Abbott, I have but one thing to say to you. I have very little doubt that I shall be one of the next victims. My steps have been dogged for months, and only a good opportunity has been wanting to secure to me the fate which Stephens has just met, and I speak earnestly upon this matter. I feel that I have a right to do so, and a right to be heard as well, and with this conviction I say to you plainly that any member of Congress who, especially if from the South, does not support, advocate, and urge immediate, active, and thorough measures to put an end to these outrages, and make citizenship a privilege, is a coward, a traitor, or a fool. The time for action has come, and the man who has now only speeches to make over some Constitutional scarecrow, deserves to be damned.

1. Summarize some of the actions described in this letter that are attributed to the KKK? Why, do you think, Tourgee goes into such detail?
2. What is the tone of this letter? To whom does Tourgee turn in his plea?
3. Explain Tourgee's ultimate purpose in this letter. What remedy is suggested?

16-4 The Nation, "The State of the South" (1872)

The end of the Civil War left the South in dire economic straits. Despite efforts to revive the southern economy, by 1872, conditions had improved little. The Nation suggested the corrupt actions of carpet-baggers were exacerbating the situation.

The indolent excuse for our failure to understand the condition of the South is that nobody can very accurately comprehend it who has not been there to see for himself. With regard to troubles of a social character, this excuse is valid; but there are some plain statistical facts recently brought to light and published which it is our duty to recognize and confront. We must acknowledge that the condition of the South from almost every point of view is extremely wretched. The property of the eleven States in 1860, exclusive of slaves, was valued at $2,728,825,006. At the end of the war their increased liabilities and loss, exclusive of slaves, was $1,272,900,390, nearly one-half the assessed value of their property at the beginning of the war. This, however, was only the State loss. Secretary Belknap fixes the rebel debt, on the 1st of April, 1865, at $2,345,297,823. This estimate would make the total loss of the rebellious States by the war $5,262,303,554. This sum, it will be seen, is about twice the assessed value of all Southern property in 1860, exclusive of slaves. Five-eighths of Southern property is gone, and the taxes upon the remainder are four times that upon the original property before the war. How much of the money wrung from this impoverished country is expended upon public improvements, it is difficult to tell; but it is likely that most of it, and certain that much of it, goes to feed the vulgar and rapacious rogues who rob and rule a people helpless and utterly exhausted.

With the exception of Virginia and Tennessee, the debts of all the States have been increased since the end of the war. The near neighborhood of those communities to the Ohio may have had some influence in driving rogues further south. The real reason, however, is the comparative fewness of the negroes. The debt of Alabama in 1866 was $5,000,000; under the rule of the enlightened and disinterested economists who have undertaken to repair her finances, that debt has been increased to $24,000,000. In North Carolina the new government was established in 1868. In 1860, the State debt was $14,000,000; in 1865, $20,000,000; in 1868, $24,000,000; and in 1871, $34,000,000. Thus the increase of debt since the war has been more than twice the increase during the war-which looks as if war were a cheaper and more prosperous condition than peace. At any rate, reconstruction seems to be morally a more disastrous process than rebellion. Guile is the strength of the weak, and the carpet-baggers have taught the Southern people to meet rogues with trickery. The Ku-klux Committee, commenting upon their dreadful poverty at the close of the war, says that manifestly they must have at once succumbed under their loss of $5,000,000,000 had it not been for the benefactions of the North. It states that the Freedmen's Bureau has spent $13,000,000 upon Southern sufferers of both colors. This does not seem a considerable sum when we think that the increased debt since the war in North Carolina has been $14,000,000. Certainly, our charities have done less good than our carpet-baggers have done damage. The theory, of course, is that something remains from the enormous sums raised by taxation, that they have been expended upon needed public improvements. In North Carolina, it was alleged, the large subsidies given to railroads would encourage immigration. There has been no immigration, however; the bonds have been sold at a disadvantage; some of the money has been stolen, and a few of the rogues have been indicted. It is impossible to say how much of the sums raised remain to the States. The carpet-baggers have had it pretty much their own way. If they chose to rob, there was nothing to prevent them. Give men a chance to be tyrants or scamps, and there is no fear that some will not be found who will avail themselves of it. Here in New York, where we have all the rascals and all the plunderers within a radius of five miles, we know how long we have been in bringing the Ring to bay. The carpet-baggers have an immense extent of country to rifle; they do not buy the legislatures, they constitute them; they enact their own registration acts and vote their own supplies. The persons they rob are not of that apathetic and well-to-do class too indifferent to go to the polls, but people who could not go if they would.

All accounts agree as to the widespread misery and penury. In Mississippi, a large planter testified that it took all his cotton for the year 1871 to pay his taxes. It is South Carolina, however, that enjoys the unenviable eminence of being the worst-robbed State of the whole eleven. In the single county of Kershaw, possessing a population of only 11,000, there were 3,600 tax-executions issued. The taxation during 1870, $2,365,047, was more than the whole taxation on double the property for five years before the war. In order to change the fiscal year, they proposed to double this, and, in 1871, to levy a tax of $4,730,094; whether this law was executed we do not know, but the fact remains that it was enacted. Peculation and corruption are as universal as poverty and distress. In 1860, South Carolina paid for offices and salaries, $123,800; in 1871, the State expended on these $581,640. In two years, $1,208,577 67 have been paid out, for which no vouchers are to be found in the Treasury. According to the minority report of the Ku-klux Committee, the disbursements exceed the appropriations by $170,683. This report, though spoiled by some rather low allusions to "ebony legislators," "men and brothers," etc., brings to light some amusing facts. Money voted with which to fit up committee-rooms has been expended on the private apartments of the colored members of the legislatures. Their rooms were furnished with Brussels carpets, sofas, mirrors, etc. About seventy-five imported porcelain spittoons, bought for the South Carolina State-House, likewise adorned their private apartments. This fact seemed to affect the democratic minority of the committee even more profoundly than the vast robberies and excessive taxations. They remark, with rugged, Spartan simplicity, that they themselves, in "the splendid capital of the nation," had never had anything but "an article of common, plain brown earthenware, of domestic manufacture." This striking disparity between fortune and desert does not excite in us any feeling of indignation against the negroes. Emerging from a long night of slavery and cruel bondage, who can grudge them their fantastic lease of liberty and luxury? Did not graver considerations check us, our humor would be to vote them State barbers and the most delightful of oriental baths. We suspect the truth to be that in the distribution of spoils the poor African gets the gilt and plush, the porcelain spittoons, the barbaric upholstery, while the astuter Caucasian clings to the soldier and more durable advantages. The negroes by themselves would be but little to be feared; yet, in the hands of the carpet-baggers, they have been the unwitting instruments of most of the harm that has been done. The swindlers could not have so got the control of things without the help of the negroes. They have made numerically the largest part of the conventions and legislatures in South Carolina. The Convention of 1868, which drew up a State constitution, was composed of 72 negroes and 49 white men. This convention made provision for a levy of $2,230,950 upon the State, which would necessitate taxation at the rate of 6 per cent; yet but 13 of the 72 negroes paid taxes. In the Legislature of 1869, there were twelve black and twenty white senators; eight of the twelve black senators paid no taxes. In the House, there were 86 black and 37 white members; 68 of the 86 black members paid no taxes. As things are at present, there seems to be no limit to the power of the carpet-baggers to plunder the South as they choose. The only ray of hope is in the passage of an act of universal amnesty. We have given the negro the ballot to protect him against his old master; we need now to give the white citizen the vote to protect him against the carpet-bagger.

Seven years have gone over us since the close of the war, and, instead of occupying this precious season with endeavors to re-establish prosperity and to sow the seeds of a peace which, in another generation, would ripen into good-will and forgetfulness, we have averted our eyes from the whole problem, refused to listen to the complaints of men whose hands we have tied, and have fallen back upon the lazy belief that in some way this great country is bound to go through. The unconscious syllogism working in the indolent Northern mind seems to be: "Things are no doubt very bad-how bad, we haven't the time or the inclination to ascertain. Examination of such unpleasant matters, if a duty at all, is a disagreeable one. After all, the rebels have made their own bed, and they must lie in it." Perhaps their sufferings are only the just punishment of their crimes; but at any rate, there can be no reason for giving over the criminals into the hands of the carpet-baggers. What services have these persons rendered the country that we should grant them the monopoly of robbing rebels? It would be better to levy tribute-money, and get some national advantage from the merciless exactions inflicted upon the Southern people. Let us make up our minds one way or the other-do we or do we not propose further to punish the rebel States for their rebellion? If we do, let us at once proceed to devise some intelligent means for that purpose. If we do not, let us make haste to protect society from the ravages of ignorance and rapacity, or give society the means to protect itself. We thought it worth four years of war to retain the Southern States in the Union, now we hardly deem it worth an act of Congress to preserve them.

1. Summarize the South's economic situation as it is represented in this document.
2. What, in the opinion of the author, has been the effect of Reconstruction policies upon the South? What attitude is voiced in this document toward carpetbaggers? What have carpetbaggers done? What is the solution to this problem?

16-5   Susan B. Anthony and the "New Departure" for Women (1873)

During the early 1870s, Susan B. Anthony and Elizabeth Cady Stanton engaged in a strategy that they believed would secure the right to vote for women. This "New Departure" was based on the belief that the Fourteenth and Fifteenth Amendments guaranteed all citizens the right to vote regardless of gender. Anthony tested its constitutionality by casting a ballot in the 1872 presidential election. Anthony was arrested, indicted by a grand jury and placed on trial in June 1873 in Canandaigua, New York. The judge ordered the all-male jury to return a guilty verdict. In her comments to the court, Anthony exposed the trial for the travesty it was. She was fined $100 but refused to pay.

> **Source:** Ken Burns and Paul Barnes, *"Not For Ourselves Alone"*: The Story of Elizabeth Cady Stanton and Susan B. Anthony.
> http://www.pbs.org/stantonanthony/resources/index.html?body=04activity.html

Friends and Fellow-citizens: I stand before you to-night, under indictment for the alleged crime of having voted at the last Presidential election, without having a lawful right to vote. It shall be my work this evening to prove to you that in thus voting, I not only committed no crime, but, instead, simply exercised my citizen's right, guaranteed to me and all United States citizens by the National Constitution, beyond the power of any State to deny.

Our democratic-republican government is based on the idea of the natural right of every individual member thereof to a voice and a vote in making and executing the laws. We assert the province of government to be to secure the people in the enjoyment of their unalienable rights. We throw to the winds the old dogma that governments can give rights. Before governments were organized, no one denies that each individual possessed the right to protect his own life, liberty and property. And when 100 or 1,000,000 people enter into a free government, they do not barter away their natural rights; they simply pledge themselves to protect each other in the enjoyment of them, through prescribed judicial and legislative tribunals. They agree to abandon the methods of brute force in the adjustment of their differences, and adopt those of civilization.

Nor can you find a word in any of the grand documents left us by the fathers that assumes for government the power to create or to confer rights. The Declaration of Independence, the United States Constitution, the constitutions of the several states and the organic laws of the territories, all alike propose to protect the people in the exercise of their God-given rights. Not one of them pretends to bestow rights.

"All men are created equal, and endowed by their Creator with certain unalienable rights. Among these are life, liberty and the pursuit of happiness. That to secure these, governments are instituted among men, deriving their just powers from the consent of the governed."

Here is no shadow of government authority over rights, nor exclusion of any from their full and equal enjoyment. Here is pronounced the right of all men, and "consequently," as the Quaker preacher said, "of all women," to a voice in the government. And here, in this very first paragraph of the declaration, is the assertion of the natural right of all to the ballot; for, how can "the consent of the governed" be given, if the right to vote be denied. Again:

"That whenever any form of government becomes destructive of these ends, it is the right of the people to alter or abolish it, and to institute a new government, laying its foundations on such principles, and organizing its powers in such forms as to them shall seem most likely to effect their safety and happiness."

Surely, the right of the whole people to vote is here clearly implied, for however destructive in their happiness this government might become, a disfranchised class could neither alter nor abolish it, nor institute a new one, except by the old brute force method of insurrection and rebellion. One-half of the people of this nation to-day are utterly powerless to blot from the statute books an unjust law, or to write there a new and a just one. The women, dissatisfied as they are with this form of government, that enforces taxation without representation,—that compels them to obey laws to which they have never given their consent,—that imprisons and hangs them without a trial by a jury of their peers, that robs them, in marriage, of the custody of their own persons, wages and children,—are this half of the people left wholly at the mercy of the other half, in direct violation of the spirit and letter of the declarations of the framers of this government, every one of which was based on the immutable principle of equal rights to all. By those declarations, kings, priests, popes, aristocrats, were all alike dethroned, and placed on a common level politically, with the lowliest born subject or serf. By them, too, me, as such, were deprived of their divine right to rule, and placed on a political level with women. By the practice of those declarations all class and caste distinction will be abolished; and slave, serf, plebeian, wife, woman, all alike, bound from their subject position to the proud platform of equality. . . .

The preamble of the federal constitution says:

"We, the people of the United States, in order to form a more perfect union, establish justice, insure domestic tranquility, provide for the common defense, promote the general welfare and secure the blessings of liberty to ourselves and our posterity, do ordain and established this constitution for the United States of America."

It was we, the people, not we, the white male citizens, nor yet we, the male citizens; but we, the whole people, who formed this Union. And we formed it, not to give the blessings of liberty, but to secure them; not to the half of ourselves and the half of our posterity, but to the whole people-women as well as men. And it is downright mockery to talk to women of their enjoyment of the blessings of liberty while they are denied the use of the only means of securing them provided by this democratic-republican government-the ballot. . . .

For any State to make sex a qualification that must ever result in the disfranchisement of one entire half of the people, is to pass a bill of attainder, or an ex post facto law, and is therefore a violation of the supreme law of the land. By it, the blessings of liberty are forever withheld from women and their female posterity. . . .

There is no she, or her, or hers, in the tax laws. . . .

The same is true of all the criminal laws. . . .

The only question left to be settled, now, is: Are women persons? And I hardly believe any of our opponents will have the hardihood to say they are not. Being persons, then, women are citizens, and no state has a right to make any new law, or to enforce any old law, that shall abridge their privileges or immunities. Hence, every discrimination against women in the constitutions and laws of the several states, is to-day null and void, precisely as is every one against negroes.

Is the right to vote one of the privileges or immunities of citizens? I think the disfranchised ex-rebels, and the ex-state prisoners will agree with me, that it is not only one of the them, but the one without which all the others are nothing. Seek the first kingdom of the ballot, and all things else shall be given thee, is the political injunction.

Webster, Worcester and Bouvier all define citizen to be a person, in the United States, entitled to vote and hold office. . . .

Prior to the adoption of the thirteenth amendment, by which slavery was forever abolished, and black men transformed from property to persons, the judicial opinions of the country had always been in harmony with these definitions. To be a person was to be a citizen, and to be a citizen was to be a voter. . . .

If the fourteenth amendment does not secure to all citizens the right to vote, for what purpose was the grand old charter of the fathers lumbered with its unwieldy proportions? The republican party, and Judges Howard and Bingham, who drafted the document, pretended it was to do something for black men; and if that something was not to secure them in their right to vote and hold office, what could it have been? For, by the thirteenth amendment, black men had become people, and hence were entitled to all the privileges and immunities of the government, precisely as were the women of the country, and foreign men not naturalized. According to Associate Justice Washington, they already had the "Protection of the government, the enjoyment of life and liberty, with the right to acquire and possess property of every kind, and to pursue and obtain happiness and safety, subject to such restraints as the government may justly prescribe for the general welfare of the whole; the right of a citizen of one state to pass through or to reside in any other state for the purpose of trade, agriculture, professional pursuit, or otherwise; to claim the benefit of the writ of habeas corpus, to institute and maintain actions of any kind in the courts of the state; to take, hold, and dispose of property, either real or personal, and an exemption from higher taxes or impositions than are paid by the other citizens of the state."

Thus, you see, those newly freed men were in possession of every possible right, privilege and immunity of the government, except that of suffrage, and hence, needed no constitutional amendment for any other purpose. What right, I ask you, has the Irishman the day after he receives his naturalization papers that he did not possess the day before, save the right to vote and hold office? And the Chinamen, now crowding our Pacific coast, are in precisely the same position. What privilege or immunity has California or Oregon the constitutional right to deny them, save that of the ballot? Clearly, then if the fourteenth amendment was not to secure to black men their right to vote, it did nothing for them, since they possessed everything else before. But, if it was meant to be a prohibition of the states, to deny or abridge their right to vote-which I fully believe-then it did the same for all persons, white women included, born or naturalized in the United States; for the amendment does not say all male persons of African descent, but all persons are citizens. . . .

Clearly, then, the national government must not only define the rights of citizens, but it must stretch out its powerful hand and protect them in every state in this Union. . . .

But if you will insist that the fifteenth amendment's emphatic interdiction against robbing United States citizens of their right to vote," on account of race, color, or previous condition of servitude," is a recognition of the right, either of the United States, or any state, to rob citizens of that right, for any or all other reason, I will prove to you that the class of citizens for which I now plead, and to which I belong, may be, and sure, by all the principles of our government, and many of the laws of the states, included under the term "previous condition of servitude."

First, the married women and their legal status. What is servitude? "The condition of a slave," What is a slave? "A person who is robbed of the proceeds of his labor; a person who is subject to the will of another."

By the law of Georgia, South Carolina, and all the states of the South, the negro had no right to the custody and control of his person. He belonged to his master. If he was disobedient, the master had the right to use correction. If the negro didn't like the correction, and attempted to run away, the master had a right to use coercion to bring him back.

By the law of every state in this Union to-day, North as well as South, the married woman has no right to the custody and control of her person. The wife belongs to her husband; and if she refuses obedience to his will, he may use moderate correction, and if she doesn't like his moderate correction, and attempts to leave his "bed and board," the husband may use moderate coercion to bring her back. The little word "moderate," you see, is the saving clause for the wife, and would doubtless be overstepped should offended husband administer his correction with the "cat-o'-nine-tails," or accomplish his coercion with blood-hounds.

Again, the slave had no right to the earnings of his hands, they belonged to his master; no right to the custody of his children, they belonged to his master; no right to sue or be sued, or testify in the courts. If he committed a crime, it was the master who must sue or be sued.

In many of the states there has been special legislation, giving to married women the right to property inherited, or received by bequest, or earned by the pursuit of any avocation outside of the home; also, giving her the right to sue and be sued in matters pertaining to such separate property; but not a single state of this Union has ever secured the wife in the enjoyment of her right to the joint ownership of the joint earnings of the marriage copartnership. And since, in the nature of things, the vast majority of married women never earn a dollar, by work outside of their families, nor inherit a dollar from their fathers, it follows that from the day of their marriage to the day of the death of their husbands, not one of them ever has a dollar, except it shall please her husband to let her have it.

Is anything further needed to prove woman's condition of servitude sufficiently orthodox to entitle her to the guaranties of the fifteenth amendment?

Is there a man who will not agree with me, that to talk of freedom without the ballot, is mockery-is slavery-to the women of this Republic, precisely as New England's orator Wendell Phillips, at the close of the late war, declared it to be to the newly emancipated black men?

I admit that prior to the rebellion, by common consent, the right to enslave, as well as to disfranchise both native and foreign born citizens, was conceded to the States. But the one grand principle, settled by the war and the reconstruction legislation, is the supremacy of national power to protect the citizens of the United States in their right to freedom and the elective franchise, against any and every interference on the part of the several States. And again and again, have the American people asserted the triumph of this principle, by their overwhelming majorities for Lincoln and Grant.

The one issue of the last two Presidential elections was, whether the fourteenth and fifteenth amendments should be considered the irrevocable will of the people; and the decision was, they shall be—and that it is only the right, but the duty of the National Government to protect all United States citizens in the full enjoyment and free exercise of all their privileges and immunities against any attempt of any State to deny or abridge.

And in this conclusion Republican and Democrats alike agree.

Senator Frelinghuysen said:

"The heresy of State rights has been completely buried in these amendments, that as amended, the constitution confers not only national but State citizenship upon all persons born or naturalized within our limits."

The Call for the national Republican convention said:

"Equal suffrage has been engrafted on the national constitution; the privileges and immunities of American citizenship have become a part of the organic law."

The national Republican platform said:

"Complete liberty and exact quality in the enjoyment of all civil, political and public rights, should be established and maintained throughout the union by efficient and appropriate State and federal legislation."

If that means anything, it is that Congress should pass a law to require the States to protect women in their equal political rights, and that the States should enact laws making it the duty of inspectors of elections to receive women's votes on precisely the same conditions they do those of men.

Judge Stanley Mathews—a substantial Ohio democrat—in his preliminary speech at the Cincinnati convention, said most emphatically.

"The constitutional amendments have established the political equality of all citizens before the law."

President Grant, in his message to Congress March 30th 1870, on the adoption of the fifteenth amendment, said:

"A measure which makes at once four millions of people voters, is indeed a measure of greater importance than any act of the kind from the foundation of the Government to the present time."

How could four million negroes be made voter if two million were not included?

The California State Republican convention said:

"Among the many practical and substantial triumphs of the principles achieved by the Republican party during the past twelve years, it enumerated with pride and pleasure, the prohibiting of any State from abridging the privileges of any citizen of the Republic, the declaring the civil and political equality of every citizen, and the establishing all these principles in the federal constitution by amendments thereto, as the permanent law."

Benjamin F. Butler, in a recent letter to me, said:

"I do not believe anybody in Congress doubts that the Constitution authorizes the right of women to vote, precisely as it authorizes trial by jury and many other like rights guaranteed to citizens."

And again, General Butler said:

"It is not laws we want; there are plenty of laws—good enough, too. Administrative ability to enforce law is the great want of the age, in this country especially. Everybody talks of law, law. If everybody would insist on the enforcement of law, the government would stand on a firmer basis, and question would settle themselves."

And it is upon this just interpretation of the United States Constitution that our National Woman Suffrage Association which celebrates the twenty-fifth anniversary of the woman's rights movement in New York on the 6th of May next, has based all its arguments and action the past five years.

We no longer petition Legislature or Congress to give us the right to vote. We appeal to the women everywhere to exercise their too long neglected "citizen's right to vote." We appeal to the inspectors of election everywhere to receive the votes of all United States citizens as it is their duty to do. We appeal to United States commissioners and marshals to arrest the inspectors who reject the names and votes of United States citizens, as it is their duty to do, and leave those alone who, like our eighth ward inspectors, perform their duties faithfully and well.

We ask the juries to fail to return verdicts of "guilty" against honest, law-abiding, tax-paying United States citizens for offering their votes at our elections. Or against intelligent, worthy young men, inspectors of elections, for receiving and counting such citizens votes.

We ask the judges to render true and unprejudiced opinions of the law, and wherever there is room for a doubt to give its benefit on the side of liberty and equal rights to women, remembering that "the true rule of interpretation under our national constitution, especially since its amendments, is that anything for human rights is constitutional, everything against human right unconstitutional."

And it is on this line that we propose to fight our battle for the ballot-all peaceably, but nevertheless persistently through to complete triumph, when all United States citizens shall be recognized as equals before the law.

1. According to Anthony, what is the connection between citizenship and the right to vote? What example(s) did she use to prove her point?
2. According to Anthony, how do the Fourteenth and Fifteenth Amendments address the rights of women? How does she support her assertions?

16-6   A Sharecrop Contract (1882)

During the Reconstruction era, sharecropping emerged as the most common method of organizing and financing southern agriculture. Large plantations, no longer worked by gangs of slaves, were broken up into small plots worked by individual families. the following contract typifies the sort of formal arrangements that many thousands of poor black and white farmers made with local landowners

To every one applying to rent land upon shares, the following conditions must be read, and agreed to.

To every 30 and 35 acres, I agree to furnish the team, plow, and farming implements, except cotton planters, and I do not agree to furnish a cart to every cropper. The croppers are to have half of the cotton, corn, and fodder (and peas and pumpkins and potatoes if any are planted) if the following conditions are complied with, but-if not-they are to have only two-fifths ($^2/_5$). Croppers are to have no part or interest in the cotton seed raised from the crop planted and worked by them. No vine crops of any description, that is, no watermelons, muskmelons, . . . squashes or anything of that kind, except peas and pumpkins, and potatoes, are to be planted in the cotton or corn. All must work under my direction. All plantation work to be done by the croppers. My part of the crop to be housed by them, and the fodder and oats to be hauled and put in the house. All the cotton must be topped about 1st August. If any cropper fails from any cause to save all the fodder from his crop, I am to have enough fodder to make it equal to one-half of the whole if the whole amount of fodder had been saved.

For every mule or horse furnished by me there must be 1000 good sized rails. . . hauled, and the fence repaired as far as they will go, the fence to be torn down and put up from the bottom if I so direct. All croppers to haul rails and work on fence whenever I may order. Rails to be split when I may say. Each cropper to clean out every ditch in his crop, and where a ditch runs between two croppers, the cleaning out of that ditch is to be divided equally between them. Every ditch bank in the crop must be shrubbed down and cleaned off before the crop is planted and must be cut down every time the land is worked with his hoe and when the crop is "laid by," the ditch banks must be left clean of bushes, weeds, and seeds. The cleaning out of all ditches must be done by the first of October. The rails must be split and the fence repaired before corn is planted.

Each cropper must keep in good repair all bridges in his crop or over ditches that he has to clean out and when a bridge needs repairing that is outside of all their crops, then any one that I call on must repair it.

Fence jams to be done as ditch banks. If any cotton is planted on the land outside of the plantation fence, I am to have three-fourths of all the cotton made in those patches, that is to say, no cotton must be planted by croppers in their home patches.

All croppers must clean out stable and fill them with straw, and haul straw in front of stable whenever I direct. All the cotton must be manured, and enough fertilizer must be brought to manure each crop highly, the croppers to pay for one-half of all manure bought, the quantity to be purchased for each crop must be left to me.

No cropper is to work off the plantation when there is any work to be done on the land he has rented, or when his work is needed by me or other croppers. Trees to be cut down on Orchard, house field, & Evanson fences, leaving such as I may designate.

Road field is to be planted from the very edge of the ditch to the fence, and all the land to be planted close up to the ditches and fences. No stock of any kind belonging to croppers to run in the plantation after crops are gathered.

If the fence should be blown down, or if trees should fall on the fence outside of the land planted by any of the croppers, any one or all that I may call upon must put it up and repair it. Every cropper must feed or have fed, the team he works, Saturday nights, Sundays, and every morning before going to work, beginning to feed his team (morning, noon, and night every day in the week) on the day he rents and feeding it to including the 31st day of December. If any cropper shall from any cause fail to repair his fence as far as 1000 rails will go, or shall fail to clean out any part of his ditches, or shall fail to leave his ditch banks, any part of them, well shrubbed and clean when his crop is laid by, or shall fail to clean out stables, fill them up and haul straw in front of them whenever he is told, he shall have only two-fifths ($^2/_5$) of the cotton, corn, fodder, peas, and pumpkins made on the land he cultivates.

If any cropper shall fail to feed his team Saturday nights, all day Sunday and all the rest of the week, morning/noon, and night, for every time he so fails he must pay me five cents.

No corn or cotton stalks must be burned, but must be cut down, cut up and plowed in. Nothing must be burned off the land except when it is impossible to plow it in.

Every cropper must be responsible for all gear and farming implements placed in his hands, and if not returned must be paid for unless it is worn out by use.

Croppers must sow & plow in oats and haul them to the crib, but must have no part of them. Nothing to be sold from their crops, nor fodder nor corn to be carried out of the fields until my rent is all paid, and all amounts they owe me and for which I am responsible are paid in full.

I am to gin & pack all the cotton and charge every cropper an eighteenth of his part, the cropper to furnish his part of the bagging, ties, & twine. The sale of every cropper's part of the cotton to be made by me when and where I choose to sell, and after deducting all they owe me and all sums that I may be responsible for on their accounts, to pay them their half of the net proceeds. Work of every description, particularly the work on fences and ditches, to be done to my satisfaction, and must be done over until I am satisfied that it is done as it should be.

No wood to burn, nor light wood, nor poles, nor timber for boards, nor wood for any purpose whatever must be gotten above the house occupied by Henry Beasley-nor must any trees be cut down nor any wood used for any purpose, except for firewood, without my permission.

1. Identify and explain the stipulations of this contract that result in virtual slavery for the sharecropper.

13 Colonies

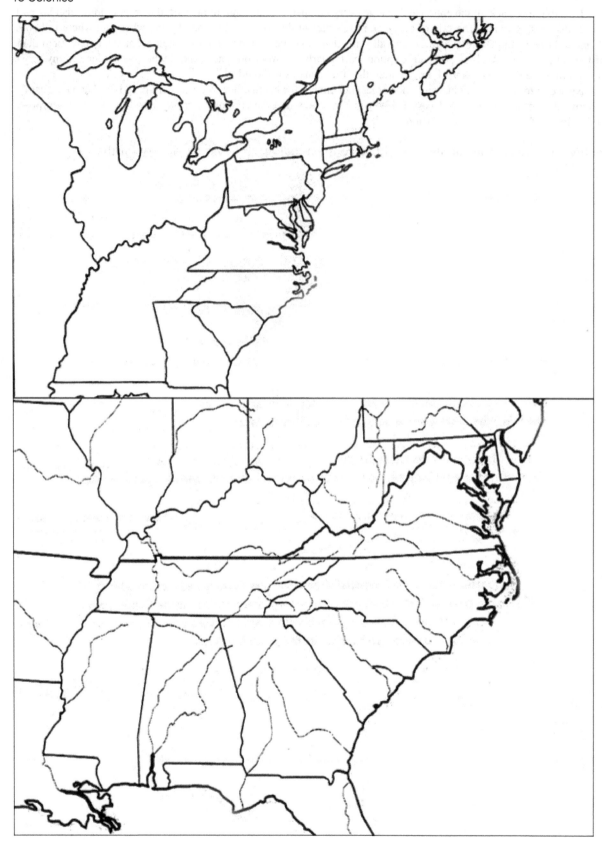

The Lower 48 States

MAP-1

Courtesy of Longman